THE CCL HANDBOOK OF COACHING

One of the most important and foundational skills for effective coaching is the ability to listen. Because we rely on listening so much in our everyday lives, we often take for granted our ability to use this skill. Much has been written in the counseling field about the science and art of listening. As CCL extends its presence into Asia, I find myself reconnecting with my own culture, one of the oldest in the world. In the Chinese language, the character for *listen* is one of the most intricate. I believe that understanding its construction and the meaning of its component parts, known as pictograms, powerfully conveys what is involved in listening, and it also reminds us, as coaches, of what we need to do as listeners.

The traditional version of the Chinese character for *listen* is composed of several pictograms:

- 耳 The symbol for *ear*—what you use to listen.
- 王 The symbol for *king*, because when you listen, you should pay attention as if the other person is the king.
- 十目 A pairing of the characters for *ten* and *eye*, to indicate that when you listen, you should pay careful attention, observe body language, and be especially observant—as if you had ten eyes.
- 一 The symbol for *one*, signifying that you should listen with undivided attention.
- 心 The symbol for *heart*, because you should listen not just with your ears and eyes but also with your heart.

-- *Sharon Ting*

THE CCL HANDBOOK OF COACHING

A Guide for the Leader Coach

Sharon Ting
Peter Scisco
Editors

Foreword by John Alexander

Published by Jossey-Bass
A Wiley Imprint
989 Market Street, San Francisco, CA 94103-1741 www.josseybass.com

Jossey-Bass books and products are available through most bookstores. To contact Jossey-Bass directly call our Customer Care Department within the U.S. at 800-956-7739, outside the U.S. at 317-572-3986, or fax 317-572-4002.

Jossey-Bass also publishes its books in a variety of electronic formats. Some content that appears in print may not be available in electronic books.

Library of Congress Cataloging-in-Publication Data

The CCL handbook of coaching : a guide for the leader coach / Sharon Ting, Peter Scisco, editors ; foreword by John Alexander.
p. cm.
"A joint publication of the Jossey-Bass business & management series and the Center for Creative Leadership"—
Includes bibliographical references and index.
ISBN-13: 978-0-7879-7684-2 (cloth)
ISBN-10: 0-7879-7684-9 (cloth)
1. Executive coaching. 2. Leadership—Study and teaching. I. Ting, Sharon, 1952– II. Scisco, Peter. III. Center for Creative Leadership.
HD30.4.C38 2006
658.4'092—dc22

2005036457

Printed in the United States of America
FIRST EDITION
HB Printing 10 9 8 7 6 5 4 3 2 1

A JOINT PUBLICATION OF
THE JOSSEY-BASS
BUSINESS & MANAGEMENT SERIES
AND
THE CENTER FOR CREATIVE LEADERSHIP

CONTENTS

CD-ROM: A LIBRARY OF RELATED CCL PUBLICATIONS

Building Resiliency: How to Thrive in Times of Change
Mary Lynn Pulley and Michael Wakefield

Choosing 360: A Guide to Evaluating Multi-Rater Feedback Instruments for Management Development
Ellen Van Velsor, Jean Brittain Leslie, and John W. Fleenor

Coaching for Action: A Report on Long-Term Advising in a Program Context
Victoria A. Guthrie

A Cross-National Comparison of Effective Leadership and Teamwork: Toward a Global Workforce
Jean Brittain Leslie and Ellen Van Velsor

Enhancing 360-degree Feedback for Senior Executives: How to Maximize the Benefits and Minimize the Risks
Robert E. Kaplan and Charles J. Palus

Evolving Leaders: A Model for Promoting Leadership Development in Programs
Charles J. Palus and Wilfred H. Drath

Executive Coaching: An Annotated Bibliography
Christina A. Douglas and William H. Morley

Forceful Leadership and Enabling Leadership: You Can Do Both
Robert E. Kaplan

Formal Mentoring Programs in Organizations: An Annotated Bibliography
Christina A. Douglas

Helping Leaders Take Effective Action: A Program Evaluation
Dianne P. Young and Nancy M. Dixon

Internalizing Strengths: An Overlooked Way of Overcoming Weaknesses in Managers
Robert E. Kaplan

Key Events and Lessons for Managers in a Diverse Workforce: A Report on Research and Findings
Christina A. Douglas

Learning From Life: Turning Life's Lessons Into Leadership Experience
Marian N. Ruderman and Patricia J. Ohlott

A Look at Derailment Today: North America and Europe
Jean Brittain Leslie and Ellen Van Velsor

Making Common Sense: Leadership as Meaning-Making in a Community of Practice
Wilfred H. Drath and Charles J. Palus

Management Development Through Job Experiences: An Annotated Bibliography
Cynthia D. McCauley and Stéphane Brutus

Managerial Effectiveness in a Global Context
Jean Brittain Leslie, Maxine Dalton, Christopher Ernst, and Jennifer Deal

Managing Across Cultures: A Learning Framework
Meena S. Wilson, Michael H. Hoppe, and Leonard R. Sayles

Perspectives on Dialogue: Making Talk Developmental for Individuals and Organizations
Nancy M. Dixon

Preparing for Development: Making the Most of Formal Leadership Programs
Jennifer Martineau and Ellie Johnson

Should 360-Degree Feedback Be Used Only for Developmental Purposes?
David W. Bracken, Maxine A. Dalton, Robert A. Jako,
Cynthia D. McCauley, and Victoria A. Pollman

Twenty-Two Ways to Develop Leadership in Staff Managers
Robert W. Eichinger and Michael M. Lombardo

Using an Art Technique to Facilitate Leadership Development
Cheryl De Ciantis

Using 360-Degree Feedback in Organizations: An Annotated Bibliography
John W. Fleenor and Jeffrey Michael Prince

Using Your Executive Coach
E. Wayne Hart and Karen Kirkland

FOREWORD

At the Center for Creative Leadership, coaching that focuses on leadership and personal development has long assumed a central role in our efforts to help individuals and organizations lead more effectively. Drawing on more than three decades of leadership training and research, the Center has developed a framework for coaching that is supported by five key elements: the relationship between the coach and the coachee; a well-tested model of leader development built on assessment, challenge, and support; and a commitment to long-term results. Having periodically coached senior executives and participants in CCL's leadership programs, I can personally attest to the power of this approach for stimulating positive change.

Our mission at the Center calls for us "to advance the understanding, practice, and development of leadership for the benefit of society worldwide." This handbook was fashioned in that spirit, gathering a comprehensive store of CCL's knowledge about leadership development coaching into a single volume. Our hope is that managers and executives in all sectors of society, many of whom are increasingly called on to coach colleagues, will find this book an indispensable resource for effecting change within their organizations and within themselves.

It is with much gratitude that I thank the editors and chapter authors who worked together to assemble this book. Coaching experiences are as varied as the leaders and coaches who take part in them, but this book reminds us of what all of these interactions might ideally have in common: coaches who are grounded in the very best practices available. Those practices are captured here, and they promise to nurture and challenge us as we seek to enhance our impact on leaders through excellence in coaching.

John R. Alexander
President
Center for Creative Leadership

ACKNOWLEDGMENTS

The knowledge and practice presented in this book have developed over time, through many different research and educational activities and through countless hours of coaching with managers and executives around the globe. We editors and all of the chapter authors would like to express how grateful we are for this entire knowledge community, as we are all learners and coaches together. We are privileged to be part of CCL's greater community and to have worked so closely with so many individuals and organizations in their quest to develop the best possible leadership capacity.

There are particular colleagues to whom we owe an extended measure of gratitude. They provided valuable input and feedback on various chapters. In many cases they were at the source of the knowledge development work that is articulated in this book.

Acknowledgments from Sharon Ting

First, I thank the many executives, managers, and organizational sponsors whose commitment to finding more and varied ways to facilitate leadership development within themselves, others, and their organizations is the raison d'être for this book. Our desire to work in partnership with them prompted us to examine our assumptions about the practice and deployment of coaching and to deepen our understanding of it. Their experiences and stories figure prominently in this book, and I consider them my coaching partners. The chapter on creating coaching cultures is a good example of the various coaching initiatives undertaken and the concepts developed by these organizations. Although no one organization has implemented all of the noted coaching practices and processes, each organization has been an innovator in some aspect of coaching. This knowledge has been acquired from working directly with these organizations and from presentations, conferences, and roundtable discussions. These companies include Millennium Pharmaceuticals, AstraZeneca Pharmaceuticals, Mass Mutual, Bayer, Xerox, Wachovia Securities, and Prudential Financial. Of special note are Sonoco Products and the Boston Consulting Group, with whom we have worked extensively to explore the use of coaching and coaching skills in a variety of settings. At times these efforts were huge successes, and at other times they were less so. Regardless, our work required all of us to let go of our expert status and become learners together. It's a process of partnership and cocreation where most answers to today's challenges lie in the future, not the past.

My heartfelt gratitude goes out to all of the authors in this book who drew on their own knowledge and experience and prevailed on their clients and colleagues to offer the best of their thinking. They cared enough to give time, energy, and passion to this book and treated me with kindness as they lived through my developmental learning as a first-time editor.

I also acknowledge the many colleagues who are not featured in this book but whose contributions behind the scenes were invaluable. I'd like to acknowledge Wayne Hart for his efforts to get this book underway and for his coauthoring with me the chapter on formal coaching in the second edition of CCL's *Handbook of Leadership Development.* That chapter was the first published description of CCL's coaching framework, and it helped generate our organization's interest in publishing a book dedicated to coaching.

Thanks also to Barbara Lemons for her confidence, support, and belief that this book would come to fruition even as we were living and learning in the moment what we were trying to give voice to in the book.

I thank Cindy McCauley for her ongoing guidance, conversations, and feedback on early drafts of this book's manuscript. Her urging to discuss ideas that were still emerging and her clear thinking and articulation helped shape this book. Her kindness in giving feedback and her encouragement to focus on contributing to the thinking in this field of coaching rather than writing the perfect book was motivating.

Special recognition goes to Ling Yuin Fong, who reminded me of my heritage and its deep connection to this work in the form of a single, simple Chinese character.

Thank you, Sara Nowlin, for your quiet and tireless administrative support of this project. Thank you, Marcia Horowitz, for your editorial guidance, wisdom, perseverance, and personal commitment to this project.

With the deepest appreciation, I thank my family. My father passed away during the writing of this book but was with me in spirit to the end. I thank him and my mother for their love and for being role models on taking risks and making change. Without their example, I wouldn't have had the courage to shift careers, be a coach, or write this book. Finally, I am indebted to my husband, Andre, and daughters, Arielle and Alexis, for generously and graciously giving up their time with me so that this book could be created. A large part of who I am as a coach evolved from my interactions with them and through their sometimes unsolicited but always revealing feedback on my coaching style. Thank you for encouraging and supporting my growth.

Acknowledgments from Peter Scisco

I join Sharon in honoring the effort of all the authors who contributed their time and ideas to this book. Writing isn't an easy task, especially when exploring complex issues and creating sense that hews to and supports a collective point of view. I am proud to have worked with all of them, and I am the better for it.

I thank my wife, who listened and sympathized and took me out for coffee during those times when I could not figure how best to help the authors reach their goal to make the ideas in this book engaging, understandable, and accessible to its readers. It's the editor's lot to discover and reveal shapes against an often inchoate sea of emerging ideas, tenable positions, and the imagined ideal. Thanks, Debbie, my island in the storm.

Authors' Acknowledgments

Marian Ruderman and Patty Ohlott thank Tzipi Radonsky, a CCL coaching partner; Alicia Rodriguez, an executive coach with Sophia Associates; and

Alyssa Freas of Executive Coaching Network for their consideration and conversation related to coaching women leaders.

Ancella Livers thanks Keith Caver for his contributions to coaching leaders of color. In addition, she is grateful to Sharon Ting, Syble Solomon, Will Lucas, Joyce Morley-Ball, Evelyn Morales, Gus Lee, Sam Manoogian, Colin Rustin, and Emily Page for their support while she wrote her chapter.

For their work on coaching across cultures, Lynne DeLay and Maxine Dalton thank Ann Houston Kelley and Fredrik Fogelberg of Nomadic Life in the Netherlands; and Christina Isolabella, a CCL coaching partner in Milan, Italy, for their time, contributions, and thoughtful review.

Ted Grubb and Sharon Ting thank their CCL colleagues David Campbell, Robert Ginnett, and Roger Conway for their helpful review, suggestions, and conversations about working with senior leaders in the Center's Leadership at the Peak program and Kerry Bunker for the dialogue and his insights while working together as a coaching team with senior executives in the Center's APEX program.

Kathy Kram and Sharon Ting also thank Kerry Bunker for collaborating, researching, and writing on this topic with them over the years, and they thank Andrea Sigetich, an executive coach and organizational consultant in Bend, Oregon, for her help with ideas behind coaching and emotional competency. Their thanks also go to Cary Cherniss and Daniel Goleman, cochairs, Consortium for Research on Emotional Intelligence, Rutgers University, and to Richard Boyatzis of Case Western Reserve University.

Charles Palus thanks Melinda Sinclair and Darlene Russell, faculty at the Adler School for Professional Coaching; and the organizers of the Research Symposium of the International Coach Federation, Francine Campone and Irene Stein, for their thoughtful review, enthusiasm, and support for artful coaching. David M. Horth and Sharon Ting, his colleagues at CCL, also deserve thanks for helping to define the relevance of creative sense making to coaching.

Mary Lynn Pulley thanks the following executive coaches for sharing their ideas and experiences: John Aldridge, aboutChange Solutions; Nancy Ashworth, Kaiser Permanente; Marilyn Blair, managing editor, ODNetwork Publications; Jeannie Coyle, president, Jeannie Coyle + Company; Chad Glang; Kathy Granger, vice president, Fort Hill Company; David Herdlinger, coach, Herdlinger Associates; Madeleine Holman, vice president, coaching services, Ken Blanchard Companies; Paige Marrs, Barrington Sky Consulting and

Coaching; Pamela McLean, Hudson Institute of Santa Barbara; Ginny Page; Bruce H. Reed, Results Oriented Consulting; Paula Stechschulte, School of Business, Fayetteville State University; Cynthia Morss Truitt; Cal Wick, founder and CEO, Fort Hill Company; Patricia M. Wiggenhorn, executive coach; Leni Wildflower; Brenda Wilkins.

Candice Frankovelgia and Jennifer Martineau thank their CCL colleagues Patricia O'Connor, for generously sharing her knowledge and experience in the field of action learning and leadership team coaching, and Ellen Van Velsor and Bill Drath, for their support and review of the manuscript. They also thank all of the transition coaches who worked with the Bryan Leadership Development Initiative, from whom they learned so much.

THE AUTHORS

Kerry A. Bunker is a senior enterprise associate at the Center for Creative Leadership. As comanager of the Awareness Program for Executive Excellence (APEX), he oversees and delivers an intensive assessment, feedback, and coaching experience designed to help senior-level executives enhance their effectiveness as leaders. Kerry also manages Leading Transitions, a family of custom interventions aimed at helping leaders respond to the challenges of ambiguity, change, transition, and downsizing. He is coauthor of *Leading with Authenticity in Times of Transition* and has published articles and chapters in numerous areas of management and psychology. He holds a doctorate in industrial and organizational psychology from the University of South Florida.

Maxine Dalton was a senior research scientist at the Center for Creative Leadership for fourteen years, serving in both research and educational activities. She designed, managed, and taught in a variety of programs for human resource professionals in the United States, Europe, and Southeast Asia. She has published on various aspects of leadership development, including 360-degree feedback, expatriate assignments, and global leadership. She is the lead author of *Success for the New Global Manager: How to Work Across Distance, Countries, and Cultures.* Her most recent research addresses effective leadership in the face of social identity conflict in the workplace. She received her doctorate in industrial and organizational psychology from the University of South Florida.

Lynne DeLay is the coaching practice leader for CCL Europe and designs, develops, and manages individualized coaching engagements throughout Europe and the Middle East. An executive coach and trainer, DeLay is comfortable in cross-cultural environments and specializes in helping organizations retain their workforce and assisting individuals to maximize their full potential. In addition to focusing on the individual's development and his or her issues within the context of the business, she brings to the executive coaching role multiple perspectives that come from her knowledge of management and work experience in North America and Europe in the public, private, and nonprofit sectors. She has served on the boards of several nonprofit organizations. She holds a doctorate in public administration from Nova University.

Wilfred Drath is a faculty member and a senior fellow at the Center for Creative Leadership. He has worked with managers on their development and has participated in leadership development design for the past two decades. His current research and educational work focus on the evolution of leadership and leadership development toward more inclusive and collective forms. He has written or collaborated on numerous CCL publications and journal articles on new frameworks for understanding and practicing leadership and leadership development. His book, *The Deep Blue Sea: Rethinking the Source of Leadership,* explores a relational-developmental framework for understanding leadership. He graduated from the University of Georgia and attended graduate school at the University of North Carolina at Chapel Hill.

Candice Frankovelgia is a coaching practice leader and a senior faculty member with the Center for Creative Leadership. In this role, she is a leadership development trainer, executive coach, and manager of adjunct faculty. She works frequently with senior executives and teams, including her work in CCL's Awareness Program for Executive Excellence (APEX), an intensive assessment, feedback, and coaching initiative for senior-level executives. Since 2000, she has designed and managed large-scale coaching interventions in global organizations. She directs a cadre of top-level executive coaches and has developed expertise in linking individual leadership development to organizational impact. Prior to joining CCL, she was in private practice as a clinical psychologist. She holds a doctorate in professional and applied clinical psychology from the Illinois School of Professional Psychology.

Ted Grubb is a senior enterprise associate at the Center for Creative Leadership. He is a faculty trainer in CCL's Leadership Development Program (LDP) and in the highly acclaimed Leadership at the Peak program, which serves senior C-level executives. He also designs and delivers custom programs. In addition to classroom training, Grubb continues to provide feedback and coaching to individual executives and their teams. He trains other executive coaches and consultants on a number of assessment instruments and in the use of effective coaching techniques. He codesigned CCL's Coaching for Development program and wrote many of the classroom and instructional materials for that course, as well as other training modules related to coaching and executive development. He holds a doctorate from the University of Massachusetts.

Kathy E. Kram is a professor in the department of organizational behavior at the Boston University School of Management. Her primary interests are in the areas of adult development, mentoring, diversity issues in executive development, leadership, and organizational change processes. In addition to her book *Mentoring at Work,* she has published in a wide range of professional journals, including *Harvard Business Review.* She is a founding member of the Center for Research on Emotional Intelligence in Organizations. During 2000–2001, as a visiting scholar at the Center for Creative Leadership, she worked on a study of executive coaching and its role in developing emotional competence in leaders. At the time of publication, she was serving a three-year term as a member of CCL's board of governors. She holds a doctorate from Yale University.

Ancella B. Livers is a group manager of open-enrollment programs at the Center for Creative Leadership. In this role she is the global manager of the Leadership Development Program (LDP). She also oversees the management of The African-American Leadership Program, The Women's Leadership Program, and the Coaching for Development program. She is the coauthor of *Leading in Black and White: Working Across the Racial Divide in Corporate America.* Prior to joining CCL, she was an assistant professor in the School of Journalism at West Virginia University. Earlier in her career, she appeared as a regular guest on the Baltimore public affairs television show, *Urban Scene.* She holds a doctorate in history from Carnegie Mellon University.

Jennifer Martineau is the director of the design and evaluation center at the Center for Creative Leadership. In her twelve years at CCL, she has focused on the evaluation of leadership development programs and initiatives, and the integration of the learning that results from evaluation into their improvement and into the leadership and leadership development systems within the sponsoring organizations. She has worked with an array of client organizations, including international for-profit and nonprofit institutions, school systems, and government agencies. She serves as internal evaluation coach to CCL faculty and staff, CCL clients, and other leadership development professionals. Her writing has appeared in book chapters, peer-reviewed journals, and practitioner-oriented publications. She has a doctorate in industrial and organizational psychology from Pennsylvania State University.

Sharon McDowell-Larsen is a senior associate at the Center for Creative Leadership. She trains the Fitness for Leadership module for CCL's Leadership at the Peak program and for custom initiatives. Her areas of interest include the relationship between leadership and fitness and the impact of exercise on reduction of risk factors for coronary heart disease. Prior to joining CCL, she worked as a research assistant for the U.S. Olympic Committee. In that capacity, she was involved in a number of research projects related to athletic performance. She is a member of the American College of Sports and a competitive triathlete, runner, and mountain biker. She holds a doctorate in exercise physiology from the University of Nebraska-Lincoln.

Patricia J. Ohlott is a former faculty member at the Center for Creative Leadership. Her current research interests include the career development of women managers and issues relating to the management of diversity and difference in organizations. She is coauthor of the book *Standing at the Crossroads: Next Steps for High-Achieving Women* and of the *Job Challenge Profile*, a CCL assessment instrument that she and her colleagues have used to study the developmental impact of job assignments. Ohlott has cowritten several CCL reports and has published articles in the *Academy of Management Journal*, *Personnel Psychology*, and other journals. She has a bachelor of arts degree in psychology from Yale University and has completed graduate coursework in business administration at Duke University.

Charles J. Palus is a senior faculty member at the Center for Creative Leadership. He conducts research on how groups of people make sense of complex challenges. He is project manager of the connected leadership practice, an emerging view of leadership as an inclusive and collective networked activity that occurs throughout organizations, and the inventor of Visual Explorer, a tool for facilitating dialogue amid diverse perspectives. He has published widely on topics related to adult development and shared meaning making and is the coauthor of *The Leader's Edge: Six Creative Competencies for Navigating Complex Challenges.* Prior to coming to CCL, he was a research engineer for E. I. Dupont de Nemours & Co. and a leadership instructor and program designer for the Hurricane Island Outward Bound School. He holds a doctorate in adult developmental psychology from Boston College.

Mary Lynn Pulley is the president of Linkages Workplace Consulting, based in Colorado Springs, Colorado. She provides executive coaching and leadership development to a variety of clients and serves as an adjunct trainer and coach at the Center for Creative Leadership. As a former enterprise associate at the Center, she served as the project manager for the Blended Learning Solutions project team. She is the author of *Losing Your Job, Reclaiming Your Soul: Stories of Resilience, Renewal, and Hope* and the coauthor of *Building Resiliency: How to Thrive in Times of Change.* A former instructor of the Fielding Institute and Vanderbilt University, she holds a doctorate in human and organizational development from Vanderbilt University.

Douglas Riddle leads the team of chief assessors in guiding the work of over three hundred adjunct professionals who provide coaching and feedback in the Center for Creative Leadership's programs worldwide. In addition, his group is responsible for establishing and maintaining the quality standards for the use of all assessment instruments involved in CCL's work. He has trained staff on all five campuses of the Center and served clients on four continents. He is licensed as a psychologist in California. His articles have appeared in a range of publications addressing issues of stress reduction, coaching, professional training, and change management. He holds doctorates in theology and psychology, and he serves as an adjunct faculty member in the graduate school of Human Behavior at Alliant International University.

Marian N. Ruderman is an R&D group director at the Center for Creative Leadership. Her research focuses on leadership across differences and the career development of women executives. She has written widely on these topics in popular magazines and professional journals. She is coauthor of the book *Standing at the Crossroads: Next Steps for High-Achieving Women* and coeditor of *Diversity in Work Teams: Research Paradigms for a Changing Workplace.* She is also a coauthor of CCL's feedback instrument, the *Job Challenge Profile.* Her published work has been cited widely in the press, and she speaks frequently to corporate and academic audiences about issues relating to the career development of women. She holds a doctorate in organizational psychology from the University of Michigan.

Peter Scisco is the manager of publication development at the Center for Creative Leadership. In this role he works with CCL faculty to create practical and authoritative publications that help leaders improve themselves and their organizations. He also coordinates the production of these publications as they are released through the CCL Press or through CCL's book publishing alliance with Jossey-Bass, a Wiley imprint. The author of more than two hundred magazine articles and the author and coauthor of four books published on a variety of topics in the trade and general press, he holds a master of arts degree in English from the University of Massachusetts.

Sharon Ting is the coaching practice leader and comanager for the Awareness Program for Executive Excellence (APEX), CCL's premier coaching experience for senior-level executives. She designs, develops, and manages a variety of coaching services as well as leadership development processes and programs for organizations. She has extensive international experience and personally coaches select senior executives. Prior to joining CCL, she was executive vice president of a public authority that designed and constructed health care facilities throughout New York State. She has coauthored a number of articles in professional and trade journals, including *Harvard Business Review.* She also sits on the board of trustees of the Rochester Institute of Technology in Rochester, New York. She holds a master of business administration degree from Wake Forest University.

Ellen Van Velsor is a senior fellow and R&D group director at the Center for Creative Leadership. She has expertise in the use and impact of feedback-intensive programs and 360-degree feedback, gender differences in leader development, how managers learn from experience, and the dynamics of executive derailment. She is coauthor of *Breaking the Glass Ceiling: Can Women Reach the Top of America's Largest Corporations?* and coeditor of *The Center for Creative Leadership Handbook of Leadership Development* (2nd edition). She serves on the editorial board of *Leadership Quarterly* and coedited a special double issue of the journal focused on leadership and diversity. Before joining CCL, she was a postdoctoral fellow in adult development at Duke University. She holds a doctorate in sociology from the University of Florida.

Michael Wakefield plays a variety of roles at the Center for Creative Leadership. He serves as the manager of trainer development and designs and delivers customized, client-specific programs. He also trains in several of CCL's open-enrollment programs, including the Leadership Development Program (LDP), Coaching for Development, and Building Resiliency: Leading in the Face of Change. Prior to joining CCL, Wakefield held a variety of training and counseling roles. He continues to apply his counseling and training background to enhance the effectiveness of leaders, managers, and employees. He is licensed as a professional counselor and certified as an addiction specialist. He holds a master of arts degree in psychology and is certified by the Society for Human Resource Management as a senior professional in human resources.

INTRODUCTION

The Center for Creative Leadership has been coaching leaders for over thirty years. We don't coach simply because it's our profession. We coach and teach others to coach because of our commitment to leadership development. We see coaching not only as an essential component of that learning process but also as an essential capability of good leaders and leadership.

We regard coaching as one way, but not the only way, to facilitate learning. As a process, it is highly compatible with CCL's mission to improve leadership for society and the world and with its philosophy of development. This philosophy contains these principles: (1) leadership can be learned, and experiences offer us opportunities to learn the lessons of leadership, and (2) understanding how others see us and our impact on them allows us to make choices on what and how to change and adapt.

This book, based on CCL's philosophy of leadership development and its rich experience in the practice of leadership coaching, summarizes our ideas and experiences with coaching. Over the years, CCL has built a coaching framework based on its knowledge and practice of leadership development that we believe underpins any good leadership coaching initiative:

- Relationship: The context within which the coaching occurs
- Assessment, challenge, and support: The core elements of CCL's leader development model
- Results: The direct and indirect outcomes of the coaching process

This framework shapes our working definition of the coaching relationship in which the coach and coachee collaborate to assess and understand the developmental task, challenge current constraints while exploring new possibilities, and ensure support and accountability for achieving goals and sustaining development (Ting & Hart, 2004).

CCL also recognizes, as do many of the organizations we work with, that experienced leaders are accountable for the development of individuals within their areas of responsibility and may also have organizational responsibility for development of leadership capacity. Consistent with CCL's long-standing principle (McCall, Lombardo, & Morrison, 1988) that development can occur during daily workday experiences, when coaching is incorporated into the leader's day-to-day staff-developing activities, it becomes a powerful tool that helps people access and use their lessons of experience.

We apply both the book's orientation to the leader coach and the use of CCL's developmental framework to coaching situations that reflect the expanse of environments, populations, and techniques that CCL professionals have encountered and researched. Covering these areas represents an expansion of what is known not only about leadership coaching in general but also about how the leader coach works within these areas. You will find, for example, chapters on coaching people of color and coaching women that provide specific information on their development needs plus suggestions on how the leader coach can address those needs and use the CCL framework to support that process.

Where We Are Now

CCL has integrated its coaching as a practice with other learning experiences and developmental processes. While we support the use of coaching as a stand-alone experience, and there are times when that may be the preferred development experience, our practice is consistent with our belief that a variety of learning experiences offers the greatest likelihood for success. In this spirit, we are moving our coaching services more into the organization's world rather than moving further down the path of bringing the leader from his world into ours. In addition, we are encouraging the use of a holistic approach, where coaching is fully integrated with a variety of developmental processes and is used on both an informal ongoing basis and strategically in a formal way.

This shift is reinforced by the growing expectation within organizations that their leaders be good coaches to other colleagues with whom they routinely interact. We see many companies that include coaching as a key leadership competency. Requests for programs and processes that help leaders and human resource (HR) professionals become better coaches to their direct reports, peers, and even bosses have become a growing part of our coaching work. This takes the form of classroom instruction and skills practice, shadow coaching where a professional coach works in tandem with a leader or peer coach, and ongoing workshops and individual coaching that offer special perspectives on coaching.

As a result, our work involving the practice of coaching now spans a much wider range. We offer stand-alone coaching work with top executives to mid-level executives that includes intensive assessment and development planning conducted in concert with internal HR processes. We have begun to establish practice norms for team coaching. We are involved with helping leaders, coaches, and HR professionals improve their coaching skills. We also integrate coaching with other learning experiences such as action learning projects and classroom-based learning.

What CCL Offers

This book builds on our long tradition, philosophy, and commitment to the belief that leaders are largely grown and not born. These are based on our thirty-five years of research, articulated through our publications, products, programs, and services and most succinctly captured in *The Center for Creative Leadership Handbook of Leadership Development* (McCauley & Van Velsor, 2004).

Thus far, our particular contribution in the arena of leadership coaching has been the integration of knowledge and research about the development process for leaders with the disciplines of psychology and the behavioral sciences, especially those involving behavioral and personality assessment and biographical perspectives. Although there are a fair number of popular publications about coaching in general, few focus specifically on the leader coach, how to effectively coach for the development needs of leaders who have unique characteristics or in particular contexts, and the broader role that leader coaches play in effecting organizational change through coaching.

We are taking this opportunity to build on traditional counseling practices by exploring and making accessible the use of less commonly known or applied constructs, approaches, and techniques. It also allows us to make explicit some of the principles that underlie techniques that are instinctively used or have become common practice among professional coaches. We believe that the more that leader coaches understand why certain approaches work, the better able they are to apply and adapt effective coaching skills in a variety of situations.

And we know that as the needs for leadership development have evolved, the role of coaching as perceived by leaders has grown. Executives, especially those with responsibility for developing leadership talent in their organizations, speak of it in terms of both the value of receiving coaching and the importance of coaching as a leadership competency. We noticed how client needs were constantly driving us to develop new practices, present the practice in ways that were more accessible to the leader coach, and consider new contexts in which to apply the practice.

We also know that the more we learn, our awareness of how much more there is to know grows. This book reflects a North American perspective, and coaching obviously takes on different significance and practices outside that perspective. We accept that the cultural perspectives in which our ideas are embedded constrain this book (as they do any other book). Some of what CCL has learned about leadership coaching is applicable to other cultures, and this book includes a chapter on cultural differences. Still, we acknowledge that there are arenas of leadership and leadership coaching that are as yet not well understood or articulated from that limited point of view.

What This Book Is Not

This book is not a primer on coaching. There are already books that discuss the basics of coaching applied in the work setting. They offer sensible how-to guidance and valuable coaching models and process steps. These books have made a substantial contribution in bringing communication techniques and concepts of behavioral change from the counseling and psychological fields into the managerial arena and making the skills accessible and less mysterious, such that managers could use and apply them in their workplace and supervisory interactions. We support and rely on those practices in our work and have chosen to take an additive approach.

We believe that the practice of coaching is evolving quickly, and we see value in documenting what we've learned through our experience with coaching for leadership development and also recording what we've learned through our work with clients about where we see leadership coaching heading.

This book is also not focused on the detailed steps in the coaching process. We believe that all coaches should have a specific structure and process that guides their actions and places boundaries around the coaching. For that discussion, we direct the reader to the second edition of *The Center for Creative Leadership Handbook of Leadership Development,* specifically, Chapter Four, "Formal Coaching" (Ting & Hart, 2004), directed to the external, professional coach. This book discusses the CCL coaching framework with a broader view of coaching, with the intention of generating wider thinking about how to expand the coaching engagement to other populations and other settings beyond the individual, about how to create more transparency and reach within the organization, and how at the same time to maintain appropriate levels of confidentiality.

We don't imply that this book is completely comprehensive in exploring the many facets of coaching for leadership development. There are other specialized areas of leadership knowledge inside and outside CCL that are not covered here. We acknowledge the breadth of that landscape and honor the far-reaching and insightful work in which colleagues in this field are engaged. And we hope that CCL's lens, while not taking in the complete panorama, does at least expand the view.

Who This Book Is For

This book is for leaders who practice coaching in their daily activities with the intent of developing other leaders and who are expected to take a broader perspective beyond their individual organizational unit for supporting the development of leadership bench strength. Our primary audience is the many leaders and bosses who are engaged in formal and informal ongoing coaching opportunities with their direct reports. (We discuss the nature of the role of the leader coach in Part One.) Such coaching takes place not just toward direct reports, but also laterally with peers and upward in the organization toward bosses (especially if the leader coach is part of a leadership team).

Secondarily, the book addresses the HR community: executives who have direct responsibility for making strategic choices about how and when to employ leadership coaching and the HR professionals and managers who are expected to function as partners to the businesses they serve. Regardless of the level, there is a growing demand for these individuals to take on explicit coaching relationships with select executives and managers in addition to their ongoing responsibilities to provide expert advice and counsel on personnel and HR matters.

Finally, the book can be of use to professional coaches who contract with individual executives or organizations to support leadership development efforts.

The challenges and opportunities for each type of coach influence the way and the arenas in which they can coach. None of these individuals coaches under ideal circumstances, but each relationship comes with its unique set of possibilities and limitations.

More important, there is a growing need for integrating, rather than compartmentalizing, the work of the various coaches. Increasingly, organizations are seeking to develop a practice of coaching, build communities of coaches, and integrate coaching with performance systems and development processes. In this book, we discuss this emerging need and how we see it evolving.

How This Book Is Organized

This book contains five parts. Part One lays the foundation by discussing CCL's assumptions about coaching and its framework for leadership coaching. This discussion expands on the CCL coaching framework presented in CCL's *Handbook of Leadership Development* (Ting & Hart, 2004). The expanded approach in this book shifts from the perspective of a professional coach to the leader coach's point of view. This shift does not change the underlying concepts for each element of CCL's coaching framework, but it has significant implications for what coaches consider in carrying out their work and what opportunities and limitations they face for putting the framework's ideas into practice.

In Part Two, the book looks at special populations that require leader coaches to possess special knowledge and perspectives about leader development and leadership in order to be more effective coaches. Specifically, it explores the context and some recommended practices for coaching leaders who are female, of color, or operating in a cross-cultural environment. We also look at the implications for coaching people who are at the very top of their organizations.

Many coaching publications place a heavy emphasis on coaching for the core competencies and skills that most leaders need and for the development issues that can be viewed as more universal than exceptional. This view doesn't account for the demographic shift that has changed the leader's profile in terms of gender, race, ethnicity, cultural roots, and other factors. It's certainly a fact that individuals outside the dominant white, male demographic profile will develop as leaders, even without coaches who have a deep understanding about gender, race, culture, or other influences. But the quality of their development experience and the possible outcomes for them and their organizations benefit from a more sophisticated understanding of what is unique about these leaders and where and how their leadership development experience may differ from white male leaders.

Part Three contains three chapters that organize ideas and practices pertaining to coaching for specialized needs or situations. Rather than looking at the needs of specific populations (as in Part Two), this part of the book focuses on specific leadership challenges that the leader coach can help others meet. The chapters describe mental and physical influences on performance that can emerge as coaching challenges: emotional competency, the turbulence of change and transition, and the role of fitness.

Part Four sheds light on coaching tools and techniques that may be less familiar to leader coaches. Much of coaching practice is an integration of a variety of therapeutic theories, counseling, and interviewing techniques and adult development constructs. The practice of coaching has many roots, primarily psychological and social theories, and aspects of that history and those philosophies have blended over time to inform its thinking and practice (Hudson, 1999). We believe that coaching works best when practiced in a nonprescriptive, self-discovering manner and when it relies heavily on the knowledge and skill of the people being coached to facilitate their learning. The coach serves as a catalyst in this process.

Part Four highlights some outcomes of that integration. Chapter Ten makes a connection between coaching and artistic techniques, a perspective that can enhance the coaching experience and stimulate the development of neglected leadership competencies. Chapter Eleven focuses on problem solving and skills development and discusses applying solution-focused therapeutic techniques to facilitate learning and behavior change. Chapter Twelve focuses on the internal stages of adult development and explains how constructive-developmental theories of human development can help coaches (and the people they coach) understand how certain behavioral goals seem immune to change. These are two important perspectives that can be particularly useful in leadership coaching. Despite their theoretical roots, they are accessible to leader coaches.

Part Five looks at forms of coaching that go beyond the typical one-to-one coaching relationship, occur on a larger scale, and involve organizational enactment and support. The ideas in this part include supplementing traditional face-to-face coaching with other modalities, such as the telephone and the Internet. They also cover coaching teams and collectives and examine initiatives designed to cascade coaching behaviors and mind-sets throughout organizations.

These expanded forms of coaching all contribute to creating the legacy of a coaching culture, the subject of Chapter Fifteen. The benefits of developing leader coach bench strength cannot be underestimated, and this chapter (combined with the discussion in Chapters Thirteen and Fourteen) emphasizes specific efforts that organizations can make to ensure permanency of their leaders' coaching. It also provides recommendations on how the organization can create a coaching community.

The book's Afterword anticipates future applications of coaching as a systemic intervention. Other chapters in the book address this issue in varying degrees, based on the nature of their content and the extent of experience and practice CCL has in those contexts. This final piece summarizes CCL's ideas about how different kinds of individual and collective interventions (those with some aspect of coaching attached) can be brought together in organizations to create a more holistic and broad-based approach to coaching for leadership development.

We have listed resources at the end of chapters in the Coach's Bookshelf section and in our references (pages 433–442). Our intent in creating those lists was to provide our readers with additional tools and techniques that they can integrate into their understanding and practice of coaching. The scope of the lists varies because in some instances not much research- or experience-based material is available that is sound, useful, and accessible.

How to Use This Book

We have three goals for this book. The first is to expand and deepen the understanding of what it takes to coach and develop leadership among special populations. The second is to expand the frameworks, methods, tools, and techniques available to coaches. The third is to anticipate the more systemic role that coaching could play in organizations, especially when practiced and championed by leaders.

One of the challenges in developing this book is our desire to not only speak to the specific needs of the leader coach but also to remain useful to coaching professionals (both consulting and HR). These diverse coaches occupy different places in relationship to the people they coach and the organization in which those people work, and so the book's chapters may hold varying degrees of appeal to each. We recommend that all coaches, regardless of their specific coaching role or position, read Part One because it sets out important assumptions and frameworks that underpin the book's ideas and approach. The structure of the subsequent chapters enables readers to dive in where they are in most need, to gain valuable knowledge about coaching practices that suit their specific circumstances.

For instance, a reader called to coach a foreign national in a multinational organization who is charged with leading a massive change initiative will find useful information in Chapters Five and Eight, and Chapters Three and Four if race and gender are issues at play. In this instance, by paying attention to matters of culture and climate, the coach can help the person being coached more accurately identify developmental needs and create a more informed coaching program. In addition to the circumstances illustrated in this example, readers can consider a number of additional points when using this book:

- Despite an overwhelming acceptance among organizations and individuals as a meaningful and productive pursuit, the practice of coaching is still evolving and has been largely built on the experience of coaches in the field. This book offers a wide range of specific practices and approaches that leader coaches can consider for application with a particular population or context. They do not represent the entire universe of possible approaches or even a select list of "perfect" approaches. However, the knowledge and practice captured in this book represent the cumulative experience of scores of coaches who have been engaged in leadership coaching for many years.

• CCL's five-part coaching framework is distilled from years of research that CCL has conducted into the process of leader development. In certain chapters, the application of the framework is explicit. In others, elements of the framework are more implicit than explicit, especially in discussions on how to coach.

• Some chapters have strong theoretical components, especially those dealing with less familiar coaching techniques. These chapters may appeal more to the professional coach interested in the intellectual underpinnings of our coaching practice; however, the ideas in these chapters are readily accessible to leader coaches, who can infer practical suggestions for applying them in their day-to-day coaching work.

• Some chapters focus more on special knowledge and information about the person being coached, such as the chapters dealing with unique populations. Readers can use these chapters to expand their appreciation for all of the elements that create the context for the people they coach and how that context influences not only their perspectives but also their behavior and their relation to coaching.

• Most of the chapters approach their content from the perspective of traditional, one-to-one coaching relationships. But the concepts in this book can be used effectively in other coaching settings and relationships.

• While not explicitly noted in every chapter, it is implicit in the nature of the leader coach's perspective that coaching be aligned with the organization's strategy and desired results.

Finally, we should explain our terminology. We use the word *coach* in this book to describe anyone who is formally or informally engaged in a coaching relationship with individuals and aspires to improve his or her leadership and in so doing improve the leadership capacity in an organizational context, and we use the word *coachee* for the person being coached (who to no less a degree aspires to improve his or her capacity to lead).

Conclusion

Coaching is first and foremost a way to facilitate learning. For leaders and managers at all levels and in all kinds of organizations, the most powerful lessons arise from experience. But it's not enough to just have the experience.

People need a way to process that experience: to reflect on it, place it in context, and create plans for acting on what they have learned. Coaching is an effective tool that can be used to help people learn from their experience. Midlevel and senior leaders occupy a unique position from which they can wield that tool with uncommon precision and effectiveness. They have the advantage of understanding the organizational context in which the people they coach work, and they have the lessons of their own experience to rely on when helping others harvest their own lessons.

When leader coaches engage more thoughtfully in coaching, they may recognize that they cannot expect changes from those they are coaching and remain unchanged themselves or expect the organization to remain untouched. Leader coaches often do not anticipate that revelation. But if they embrace that awareness, it provides for them the opportunity to draw lessons from the coaching process that may facilitate change within themselves and their organization (O'Neill, 2000). We encourage our readers to consider that systemic perspective on coaching. It not only provides a platform on which they can stand as champions of change, but it creates a cycle of learning and development to sustain the organization's effectiveness and success.

PART ONE

FOUNDATIONS OF COACHING

Leaders have enormous resources and skills, or they wouldn't be leaders. That's true even when they are involved in a developmental activity, such as when they receive coaching. A key role of a coach in that process, whether an internal human resource coach, a professional executive coach, or a leader coach drawn from the ranks of the organization, is to help those leaders gain clarity about themselves. That inevitably involves adding the perspectives of others to the coachee's own sense of self. The coach helps the leader see options, make choices among them, and garner support for his or her developing leadership capacity and reaching goals.

Basic coaching principles and skills include listening and questioning techniques, plus many other principles that well-known coaching authorities such as Robert Hargrove, Frederic Hudson, John Whitmore, and Mary Beth O'Neill have articulated in many ways. These principles commonly focus on the coachee's development and performance not as a problem to be solved but as a path toward growth and change.

Leader coaches beginning this book likely already use those techniques to help direct reports and others articulate aspirations, goals, abilities, and areas in need of development. Our goal is to encourage leaders to engage in more robust and complex forms of coaching, examine specific aspects of leadership coaching in greater depth, and help both leaders and others engaged in leadership coaching to consider incorporating these additional perspectives and techniques into their current coaching practice.

The two chapters in Part One orient readers to CCL's coaching philosophy and approach. They introduce a framework for coaching adapted from CCL's ideas about leadership development and enhanced with our experiences as coaches and as teachers of coaches. Our intent is to demystify certain aspects of coaching and help leaders see how they can access and apply this knowledge.

Three lessons form the heart of these chapters: (1) effective coaching often requires the coach to step beyond a purely behavioral approach; (2) with thoughtfulness and preparation, almost any leader committed to the process of coaching and the coachee can be effective at using a wide array of approaches; and (3) that it's possible for leader coaches to have deep and meaningful coaching conversations without stepping over the line into therapy. Leader coaches don't need clinical training to help the people they coach pursue change and develop their capacity to lead.

CHAPTER ONE

OUR VIEW OF COACHING FOR LEADERSHIP DEVELOPMENT

Sharon Ting

To understand CCL's view of coaching, it may be best to start with our intent: to help leaders understand themselves more fully so that they can draw on their strengths and use them more effectively and intentionally, improve identified development needs, and develop untested potential. Much of our coaching work involves helping managers gain clarity about their own motivations, aspirations, and commitment to change.

CCL coaches use approaches anchored in the behavioral sciences and defined by psychological and counseling practices. In addition, their coaching strategies draw on adult learning concepts—chiefly, that adults choose to learn when and what they want. It's no accident that coaching derives much of its practice from the field of psychology and human behavior. After all, psychological and counseling practices help people learn and change, just as coaching does—albeit in a different arena of their lives. This similarity makes it natural that coaching would draw on many of the best practices, skills, and techniques used in the counseling and therapeutic fields. Because of the evolutionary nature of our work in coaching, it is hard to point to one theory of development that forms the foundation of our work. It's fair to say that our approach to leadership coaching reinforces Hudson's perspective (1999) that coaching is informed by a variety of psychological and social theories and practices, including the work of many well-known theorists such as Jung, Adler, Erikson, Levinson, and Kegan.

Coaching from a base of psychological methodologies is not the same as practicing therapy, however, because the content and context are significantly different. CCL recognizes that there is concern, particularly among leader coaches, about this historical and practical connection. But we believe that their discomfort occurs when the use of skills common to both coaching and therapy are confused with content and outcomes.

These considerations have led us to think of coaching in particular ways and to loosely codify a set of ideas and systems that inform our practice. We start with six essential principles that are integral to our thought and practice, continue on to explore the important elements that define the depth of coaching work, discuss the sometimes too rigid distinction drawn between coaching for performance and development, and describe the role and differentiating skills of the leader coach.

It is important to keep in mind that the discussion of coaching here is foundational and historical. It reflects the conventional wisdom within CCL about leadership coaching and is linked to our history of one-to-one coaching with an external professional coach. Therefore, I do not highlight in this chapter practices that are more peripheral and supplemental but nonetheless highly effective because they've yet to be incorporated into the mainstream of our work. I see those as contributing to the future of leadership coaching practices, which you will read more about as the book unfolds.

The Principles of Leadership Coaching

Six principles guide our coaching. These rules of engagement ensure that our knowledge of leader development is applied across a wide variety of effective coaching styles and coachee needs. They are fundamental to CCL's beliefs about coaching and its practice, and they are significant to the coaching activities of the leader coach. Coaches may have to adapt the mechanics of implementing these principles to their context, but nonetheless the spirit of the principles remains foundational to effective coaching (Ting & Hart, 2004). We note for each principle the salient tension for or adaptation that may be required of the leader coach.

Principle 1: Create a Safe and Challenging Environment

It is the coach's responsibility to create a safe environment in which the coachee can take risks and learn. In the coaching process, the ability to live this principle depends on the coach's skill at balancing challenging and supporting behaviors. Regardless of what the coach believes may be true or right for the coachee, she should take care to ensure the coaching process does not damage the coachee's fundamental sense of self and worth. Creating a sense of safety is a real challenge for leader coaches, who often wear a second evaluative hat that may cause the coachee always to wonder if and how information he shares will be used outside the coaching discussion. At a minimum, it requires the leader coach to aspire to an open and a nonjudgmental attitude.

Principle 2: Work with the Coachee's Agenda

The learning experience is, first and foremost, for and about the individual leaders being coached. They are responsible for driving the process and directing their own learning. They decide which goals to work on and how to go about this work. The coach's role is to influence the agenda, not set it. This does not mean there cannot be alignment between the coachee's and the coach's or organization's goals. To the contrary, it is ideal when there is alignment. Sometimes the leader coach has a clear agenda, such as performance expectations, a specific action that is needed from the coachee, or a message that the organization needs the coach to deliver. In these cases, the leader coach would do well to evaluate if this requires her shifting into the managerial role to avoid the coachee's feeling manipulated or to avoid damaging the coaching relationship.

Principle 3: Facilitate and Collaborate

Although coaches typically possess considerable knowledge and expertise, they do not act like experts, making recommendations or giving answers. They do focus on the coachee's needs and avoid disclosing personal reactions, telling their own stories, or advocating their preferred theories and techniques. They should be highly selective about taking such directive actions and do so only to the extent that it is clearly relevant to the coachee's needs and agreed-on agenda and only when more facilitative methods will not work just as well. The coach is not there to lecture, opine, or pontificate. And although the coach may suggest options, the ultimate decision about what action to take rests with the coachee. This can be a difficult principle for leader coaches to adopt because they usually have a high investment in achieving the desired outcomes. If a leader coach takes a more directive approach, it should be as a last resort, and she should take some of the responsibility for outcomes.

Principle 4: Advocate Self-Awareness

Knowing one's strengths and development needs is a prerequisite to developing as a leader. By learning to better recognize their own behaviors and understand the impact they may have, coachees are better able to analyze or predict the outcomes of their interactions with others and take steps to achieve desired results.

Principle 5: Promote Sustainable Learning from Experience

Most individuals have the capacity to learn, grow, and change, given that they encounter the right set of experiences and are ready to learn. Reflecting on those experiences is a powerful method for identifying personal strengths and development needs, as well as opportunities and obstacles. We encourage coaches to help their coachees think about events from the perspective of what worked well and what did not and to use their findings to chart a course toward enhanced leader capabilities. A key element of this principle is helping the coachee learn how to move from awareness to action, to sustain that learning, and to create a developmental feedback loop to continually replicate the process.

Principle 6: Model What You Coach

It is the coach's responsibility to exhibit the leadership and emotional competencies (such as self-awareness, self-management, social awareness, and social skills) that the coachee is trying to develop (Goleman, 1998). It can be challenging for the coach to apply this principle because leader coaches themselves are likely to have relative strengths and weaknesses in these areas. Ideally, the leader coach has sufficient self-awareness to know if he has the capacity and skill to coach around a particular issue and if the coachee can be more effectively served by receiving coaching from another individual. Furthermore, in order to model effective, in-the-moment feedback, coaches may face the challenge of describing the negative impact that the coachee's behavior is having on them, an approach that often feels risky.

Levels and Depths of Coaching

In our years of working with leader and peer coaches, a recurring issue is their reluctance to fully engage with coachees when they are beginning to self-disclose more significant and sometimes personal information. When we ask why they pull back just when they are closest to facilitating movement in their coachees' thinking, underlying mental models, and self-perception, they often respond that they are afraid—afraid of going too far, of going too deep, of unlocking strong emotions that they feel ill equipped to handle. In short, they have a mental image of a rather tumultuous and out-of-control experience. We believe this reaction results from their discomfort with emotions and an often mistaken image of coaching as therapy in the workplace.

We offer two responses to these concerns. First, when things go bad, you can usually trace it back to poor practice on the part of the coach, not the practice of coaching. Second, coaches can guard against this possibility by thinking in advance about the appropriate ways they should be working with their coachee. A coach who believes there should be no boundaries around topics and depth of discussion is flirting with trouble. And those boundaries should be set by the nature of the relationship and agreement, not simply by what the coach is skilled at. Coaches can usefully characterize their work and articulate their philosophical approach to coaching by thinking about different levels of coaching.

Three levels of coaching that CCL has articulated are *behavioral, underlying drivers,* and *root causes* (see Figure 1.1). As we open this discussion, our intent is to provide guidelines that leader coaches can use to manage what they discuss with their coachees and to determine how deep the coaching conversations might go. Coaches can find reassurance in the fact that the coaching waters deepen gradually; moving from the behavioral level to root causes is not dropping suddenly from the platform to one hundred feet. We encourage leader coaches (and professionally licensed or clinically trained coaches) to

FIGURE 1.1. COACHING LEVELS.

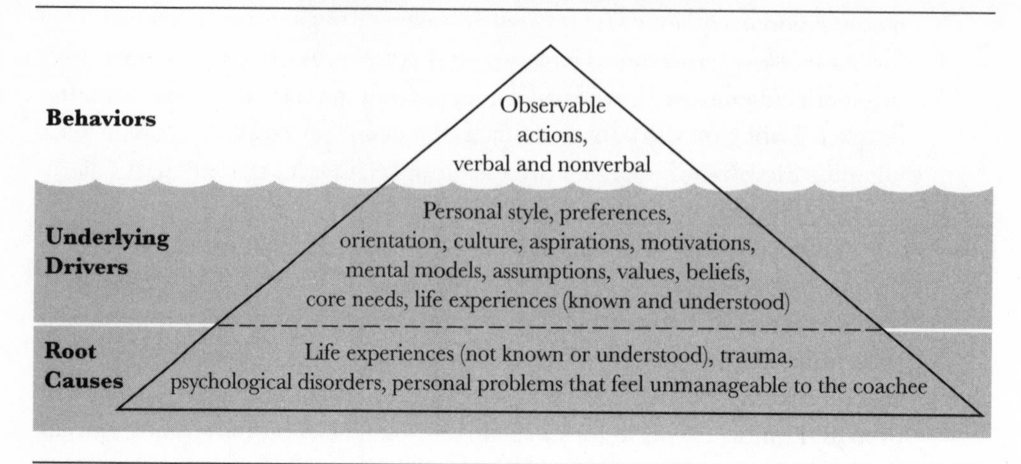

imagine that working at these levels is like moving from dry land into water. The farther out you go, the deeper and less clear the water is. You require different skills and confidence as you go deeper and, in terms of coaching, good judgment in knowing when the coachee's needs have surpassed your capabilities or role to address. The power of coaching often lies in the second level (underlying drivers), a very broad level that encompasses many rich perspectives.

Behavioral Level

Coaching at the behavioral level is certainly the most accessible and comfortable for the leader coach. This level addresses observable actions and behaviors, both verbal and nonverbal, that have an impact on others. You are coaching to what is visible and concrete. It relies on the assumptions that the coachee can understand, recognize, and has access to a range of desired behaviors and that the primary goals are to recognize the appropriate context in which to use them and to increase the frequency of their use. It also assumes that internal forces that may be preventing or limiting the coachee's using those skills are not so strong or so deeply entrenched that the coachee is unable to manage.

The approach to behavioral coaching assumes it is not necessary to understand causes or reasons for the behavior as long as the coachee understands that a different behavior is desired or viewed as more effective. The focus is on the desired behavioral change. With this approach, the coach and coachee focus on understanding what behaviors and skills are desired and relevant to organizational, business unit, or individual goals.

At this level, the coach makes sure that the coachee understands what those effective behaviors look like, identifies times and situations when the coachee is able to demonstrate them, and encourages repetition of skill. (See Chapter Eleven for a detailed discussion of techniques that are particularly useful at this level.)

While coaching at this level feels more familiar to leader coaches, that doesn't lessen the potential results that can be achieved by working at this level. The challenge is staying in the behavioral mode and focusing on future actions rather than rehashing the past and assessing intent. The power lies in the coach's effective use of questioning, probing, and diligence in staying with the process. Exhibit 1.1 provides an example of coaching practiced at this level.

Underlying Drivers

Underlying drivers lie at a deeper coaching level and comprise many elements that may be less visible than behaviors and in fact contribute to their existence. Behaviors are not random acts. Individuals choose how they want to behave. Sometimes those choices are conscious and deliberate; individuals likely understand what the impact will be.

EXHIBIT 1.1. COACHING AT THE BEHAVIORAL LEVEL.

Jon has recently ascended to vice president. After a series of weekly vice-president-level meetings, Jon and his boss, Marla, have a coaching conversation about how he is adapting to his new role. Marla notes that Jon employed a very take-charge style in the meetings and shares her belief that Jon would be more effective if he could adopt a more collaborative approach with his peers. Her specific behavioral feedback is that Jon talked first on every issue, used primarily declarative statements, and always insisted that action steps be taken even when consensus had not been reached.

Desirable collaborative behaviors at the vice-presidential level involve sharing meeting time, asking challenging questions that move the dialogue to a higher level, and building one's points on the ideas of others. Marla and Jon confirm the desired behaviors, discuss past situations where he exhibited those behaviors, and talk about ways Jon can reframe the meetings to support and stimulate his use of the desirable behaviors.

Sometimes, however, those behaviors are automatic. The individual is still making a choice, but it may not require conscious thought because it has become habit or unconscious from years of learning and associating certain behaviors with certain results. Furthermore, individuals may act in ways they know are not likely to have the desired effect, but nonetheless they are at a loss for making another choice and acting differently. In these cases, the less visible (even unconscious) cognitive or emotional processes that drive the less desired behaviors are so strong that even when individuals are motivated to change, they can't or their progress toward change is slow. Anyone who has ever tried to lose weight understands this dynamic.

Much of CCL's coaching practice has been built on examining and understanding underlying drivers as a way of appreciating how, in the coachee's understanding of and orientation to the world, the behavior makes logical sense. For that reason, CCL includes as part of its coaching discipline personality and work-style inventories. While we would not expect leader coaches to become trained in psychological instruments, we do believe through good questioning skills that relevant but less visible aspects about the coachee can surface and be factored into the change process. Some examples of underlying drivers are talents, preferences, orientations, traits, values, mental models, beliefs, needs, and life experiences.

Coaches can easily work in these arenas by taking time to understand what motivates their coachees, what natural skills and orientations they bring to the coaching process, and what experiences have shaped their view of themselves and the world that bear on their effectiveness. Coaches do not need to be licensed clinicians to have these conversations. Coachees are the experts on themselves. Effective coaches observe behaviors and are analytical and intuitive, asking thought-provoking questions to surface these underlying issues more readily. Leader coaches typically have a wealth of opportunities for behavioral observations. Their challenge is to interpret those observations from the perspective of what they reveal about the mental models and orientations of the coachee as well as what they mean for performance and leadership capabilities. Exhibit 1.2 provides an example of coaching practiced at this level.

Root Causes

Sometimes a coachee's behaviors are deeply connected to difficult life experiences, especially traumatic ones, or there is a familial history of psychological disorders, addiction, or chemical abuse. We would distinguish such deeply in-

EXHIBIT 1.2. COACHING AT THE UNDERLYING DRIVER LEVEL.

Andrew is coaching his direct report, Mona, about her behavior related to her expecting staff to routinely stay late or redo their work numerous times. He doesn't understand why it's so difficult for her to modify this behavior since it would reduce her long hours as well. What Andrew learns through informal discussions with Mona is that she has strong values related to doing her best, shaped by her personal and work experiences. Despite Mona's efforts to ease off on the degree of scrutiny to which she subjected her staff's work, she finds it nearly impossible to sustain a more empowering approach. The desired behaviors are competing with strong beliefs shaped by powerful experiences.

grained behaviors from those associated with underlying drivers by the degree of consciousness or ease with which the coachee's beliefs, mental models, and historical events can be revealed and discussed. Another differentiating factor is the extent to which the undesirable behaviors interfere with the coachee's productive functioning or the coachee feels incapable of managing those behaviors.

One behavioral indicator for the need to work at this level is that the coachee appears to be stuck. By *stuck* we don't mean the common experience when making change of overcoming the initial inertia or the natural tendency to revert or regress periodically to the old behavior during the process of shifting to a new behavior. The type of *stuck* we refer to tends to paralyze the coachee in a set of behaviors that are clearly having an adverse impact on work and possibly personal life, or even propelling him or her toward derailment.

Obviously coaches have conversations with their coachees about early life experiences that affect their current leadership style and skills. In fact, a biographical inventory is a useful assessment tool in coaching. Coaches can informally or formally introduce and use such an assessment to better understand the coachee's personal context. The difference between using such biographical assessment and delving into past life experiences is the coachee's ability to frame and make sense of those experiences. If coachees have such ability, then the experience falls within the realm of underlying drivers.

When working at the behavioral or underlying levels proves to be insufficient and the coachee feels the need to delve into past life experiences to relive and heal past wounds, then the leader coach (and professional coaches, for that matter) should consider referring the coachee to a clinical professional with whom the coachee would establish a therapeutic relationship. This relationship has different structure, goals, and boundaries from leadership coaching. Even if the coach has training in counseling or therapeutic practice, we do not recommend the coach engage in this type of work.

Most leader coaches are familiar with their organization's process for referral. Alternatively, the leader coach might encourage the coachee to seek professional services using his or her own resources and referral sources if the coachee chooses not to use internally offered services. Exhibit 1.3 is an example of coaching at the root causes level.

The Leader Coach: Orientation, Focus, and Skills

Individuals who are responsible for achieving organizational outcomes by directing others have likely exercised coaching skills to facilitate those results. If they did anything more than simply direct and evaluate their direct reports' work, such as asking them how they planned to approach a particular problem or what their career goals were, they were coaching their direct reports even if they were not aware of it or did not label it that way. If the proliferation of books, articles, and training about the subject is any guide, many managers and leaders are eager to learn how to coach better.

CCL's view of the leader coach recognizes that basic premise. Furthermore, we add three distinctions. First, leader coaches are intentional about their responsibility to coach their direct reports. They elicit desirable outcomes

EXHIBIT 1.3. COACHING AT THE LEVEL OF ROOT CAUSES.

Matthew is a young, charismatic, driven manager who is in his organization's high-potential group. One of his identified developmental areas is to become more consistent and predictable in his management style, a goal Matthew agrees with. His boss, Sherri, has been coaching him on the desired behaviors but is finding the process frustrating. What seems like a straightforward developmental issue that would improve as Matthew matured and received feedback and coaching appears more resistant to change. Despite their good coaching relationship and Matthew's articulated desire to improve, his behaviors have become even more volatile, swinging from almost manic periods of activity and engagement to periods of isolation and unpredictable bursts of anger. Sherri is beginning to feel she is at the limit of her capability to support Matthew's development through coaching on her own.

by increasing their direct reports' capacities and capabilities, and they provide ongoing feedback that enables continuous learning. Second, leader coaches focus their coaching on development as much as on performance and see those two paths as reinforcing and compatible. Third, leader coaches are a critical part of the context in which the people they coach operate, which may include a team, business unit, or larger organizational unit, and they cannot divorce themselves from that context. As a result, leader coaches need a heightened awareness about the issues that may emerge from the coaching process for and about themselves as leaders, the team and its dynamics and performance, and the organization's values and practices. They should have a systemic view of their coaching.

Leader Coaches Are Intentional

The process of developing leaders is no longer viewed as the sole responsibility of HR executives and professionals, with other leaders paying lip service. CCL often works with companies that include coaching and developing people as a core competency for individuals who are in leadership positions, which are typically managers and above. The Corporate Leadership Council is a membership based research organization that studies corporate HR issues. Its research supports CCL's view that coaching, developing, and giving feedback are critical skills of leadership, but its members also say that these skills are some of the lowest-rated skills among leaders. These same organizations see coaching and development as one of the most important means of ensuring competitive and effective talent management. Being purposeful about coaching is important for a number of reasons:

- Companies recognize and support the systematic development of coaching skills in their leaders from senior managers to very senior executives.
- The people who are the focus of the leader coach's efforts are more cognizant of the intent, which can increase the probability that they will engage more actively in their own development or at least be more aware of its importance.
- Organizations are better positioned to assess the skills and impact.
- The organizational environment may become more receptive to installing a systemic approach to coaching.
- The leader coaches are further legitimized for accessing coaching for themselves.

Leader coaches occupy unique seats that provide them valuable information that makes their coaching particularly relevant. They have more opportunity to observe and influence coachees' behaviors and development. They are also more likely to have information about the coachee that might anticipate future performance and therefore highlight current development needs and preparation. However, this can occur only if coaches are paying attention and are deliberate in considering their coachees in a holistic way. This means understanding their strengths and development needs and how they fit into the organization's needs, understanding their coachees' personal aspirations, and then overlaying these considerations with a present and future focus. This holistic view isn't possible if coaches take a narrow view and use coaching exclusively to address improvements to short-term business results.

Because their seats are often in the front row or in the middle of the action, leader coaches are especially challenged to not become too invested in their own points of view or lose coaching opportunities. This latter point is an essential aspect of being a leader coach. Opportunities to coach abound in the workplace; however, too often managers and leaders miss what we call the "coachable moment." These are the times when a business problem, organizational challenge, or interpersonal issue arises. What distinguishes the leader coach from the typical manager is how differently they respond. The leader coach seizes those coachable moments. Instead of giving the solution or offering to step into the fray, the intentional leader coach sees an opportunity for his coachee to learn and to achieve a positive outcome. The leader coach steps back and helps his coachee reframe the situation or surface more options for resolution.

That doesn't mean the leader coach won't step out of her coaching role, especially if her coachee seems stuck in his viewpoint or behavioral approach. Leader coaches have the ability at various times to play any of several development roles: feedback provider, sounding board, dialogue partner, accountant, role model, and others (McCauley & Douglas, 2004). A constant balancing act is required to know which role to emphasize and when. In addition, the leader coach has legitimate authority to help coachees access resources and developmental experiences to support their goals.

Leader Coaches Focus on Performance and Development

Coaching is a practice in which the development of common language, terminology, and meaning is evolving. One aspect that continues to engage practitioners and leaders in lively discussions is how coaching is applied in leadership development; in particular, what is the relationship between coaching for performance and coaching for development? Sometimes the terms are used interchangeably, but more often they are used to differentiate the focus of the coaching. We see the two forms as sitting in different places on a continuum of coaching rather than as polarities, and while our work is best understood as having a development focus, we believe the learning that occurs through coaching can benefit the coachee's performance and development. Calling out some of the differences adds to the perspectives of leader coaches who are more routinely engaged in performance coaching.

Witherspoon and White (1997) differentiate the two by emphasizing that coaching for performance generally relates to learning that focuses on a person's current job. It's geared toward helping people improve their effectiveness on the job, often over some span of time—several months to a year or more. For them, coaching for development focuses on their future. That can mean preparing for a career move, for example, or for advancement to higher levels in the organization.

A key distinction between the two is that developmental coaching has a focus on learning. That distinction helps to bridge the seeming gap between performance and development (Hunt & Weintraub, 2002). When there is a conscious learning focus, an intention to reflect and identify lessons for the purpose of being more effective in the future (whether that future is tomorrow or two years away), then development is occurring. So coaching for performance can be developmental when the learning that improves a coachee's ability to meet the current demands and goals of his current role is understood by the coachee as a step in a longer process of leadership development.

We encourage leader coaches to hold both a developmental and performance mind-set and offer the following supporting business analogy. Organizations pursue both a long-term strategy and short-term goals. The first is aspirational and usually involves the organization's developing new capacities and perspectives. The second are practical and immediate, relying on applying an established set of skills and behaviors to ensure the company's financial strength to pursue its long-term strategy. Both are needed for organizations to be successful. Leaders need to tend to both as well in themselves. They need to be equipped with the skills and attributes that ensure achievement of current expectations as well as anticipate the capabilities and attitudes needed for the next level of leadership demands.

Too often when an executive is unsuccessful at a particular job or derails completely, the warning signs were present but were missed, overlooked, or rationalized for various reasons (Bunker, Kram, & Ting, 2002). If a more holistic coaching approach that encompassed performance and development had been taken with such an individual, preventive measures might have avoided such a visible and costly failure. Such an approach might mean not using the individual's strengths to optimize short-term results but instead moving that individual into a role that will offer him the opportunity to employ and develop new skills that will benefit the organization's long-term objectives.

Leader coaches who are most often engaged in performance coaching can leverage their coaching by making the learning focus intentional and by making explicit the relationship of the current skills improvements to expanding the coachee's overall leadership capacity. The coach is readying the coachee for future leadership challenges. If the leader coach thinks strategically about his coachee's development, he will also seek to identify skills that may not present a current performance need for the coachee but will be needed in the future.

Leader Coaches Take a Systemic Perspective

Leader coaches look beyond parochial interests and short-term results to help develop the potential of all their direct reports. This requires the leader coach to take an organizational perspective and focus on leadership development (for sustaining and improving the pool of talented managers and leaders) as well as leader development (with its focus on the individual). It may mean facilitating the transition of high performers to another business unit in order to provide them new developmental experiences or constructing a special assignment so they can develop in their current position. It may also involve influencing people higher in the organization who can remove organizational impediments (such as barriers to lateral and cross-functional assignments) to developing greater leadership bench strength. It might even require leader coaches to work with an entire team if it becomes apparent that despite the effectiveness and skill of individual direct reports, their performance as a collective isn't meeting the organization's needs.

Leader coaches who are willing and able to see their coachee as part of a leadership system have less control over the relationship, which can create uncertainty. To operate with this perspective requires judgment and clear boundary management. The possibilities for learning are great at both an individual and organizational level. The potential for gain warrants the risk these leader coaches take in acknowledging they are not in complete control of the relationship.

Additional Leader Coach Skills

Leadership coaching happens informally and formally inside organizations all the time, and it often involves peers, internal HR professionals, and external coaching consultants. Leader coaches can access and learn to use the skills and approaches these other coaches employ. In fact, organizations can improve their leadership capacity by encouraging many coaching relationships. The skills described throughout this chapter and highlighted in the list below are not comprehensive, but are supplemental to basic coaching skills and essential to creating leader development capacity in organizations:

- Build awareness of and learn to challenge your own assumptions and biases. Assess the impact of those on the coaching relationship, and discipline yourself to initiate improvements.
- Recognize when factors hinder the development of a mutually meaningful coaching relationship, and acknowledge its limits or enlist someone else to coach.
- Clarify the mix of performance and developmental coaching that your coachee needs. In doing so, be keenly aware of what perspective you are taking: the coachee's, the organization's, or your own.
- Recognize and seek help when you need coaching yourself to better support your coachees or when you need coaching because you are too personally involved in the specific leader development issue that has surfaced for your coachee.
- Learn to monitor your self-imposed limitations on the coachee's developmental possibilities.
- Increase your ability to step outside the system and look at it from the perspective of being part of it and outside it at once. From that dual vantage point, assess the impact on your coachee's development.
- Learn when to move out of your coaching role and when to assume another role relative to the coachee. Make sure the coachee understands that you are making that shift and why.
- Help your coachees identify multiple responses to system constraints on their development.
- From the challenges your coachees face, generate positive leverage for change in them as individuals and in the organization as a whole.

Additional Leader Coach Considerations

As organizations explore the idea of coaching as an essential leadership competency, the task of developing and implementing that competency falls to the managers and leaders throughout organizations at all levels. As we discussed in the Introduction, this book is not a coaching primer. It's meant to broaden the leader coach's perspectives and skills so that she can help to develop others and contribute to the organization's sustained success and longevity. That said, there are come considerations general to coaching with which some leader coaches are not experienced. Those considerations include confidentiality, resistance, power and authority, role conflict, and organizational responsibility. Some initial grounding in these issues will enable the leader coach to carry out this important work more effectively.

Confidentiality

Confidentiality becomes a complex issue when applied to a leader coach context because leader coaches don't have the luxury of defining their relationship with coachees as private and personal. As we discussed earlier, leader coaches occupy a unique position from which they gain a view of the coachee that is more comprehensive than the one afforded an external coach. When it comes to confidentiality, it's important that leader coaches and their coachees discuss specific issues, such as: What types of information and discussions can and will remain absolutely confidential? What types of information cannot remain confidential because of organizational ethics, codes of conduct, and reporting requirements? What types of information may enjoy only limited confidentiality because of the leader coach's broader role in the organization? Leader coaches have to monitor constantly how confidential information affects their coaching. They must maintain their awareness about what information they have, how they obtained it, and whose confidence they obligated to ensure.

Resistance

When coachees don't accept feedback, don't agree to make changes, or agree to change but don't follow through, coaches can feel frustrated, impatient, annoyed, or disappointed. A leader coach may conclude that the coachee is not really committed to change or accepting of development needs. As a result, the leader coach might push harder, become more directive, withdraw energy, or give up. These are all reasonable feelings, thoughts, and reactions, especially if the leader coach regards resistance as unwillingness and defiance. However, we encourage leader coaches to see resistance in a more positive light. It can be a natural self-protection mechanism that some coachees use. After all, their way of reacting to leadership situations has evolved over time, and they have been rewarded for those practices. These tried-and-true behaviors form a natural protective covering that wards off not only negative external influences but also positive opportunities to change. When leader coaches encounter what they feel as resistance, they can benefit from stepping back and trying to better understand how the coachee's behaviors have enabled and supported her career thus far. With this perspective, the coach can then look for alternative approaches and tactics to engage the coachee.

Power and Authority

Good coaching relationships include openness, candor, trust, and dialogue. Leader coaches should be aware of how their coachees respond to power and authority and what impact that may have on the coachee's ability and willingness to engage openly in coaching. At the same time, the leader coach should examine her own views and responses to power and authority and how that might be affecting her expectations about the coaching relationship and about how the coachee should respond. By talking openly about this issue, the coach and the coachee may be able to avoid negative power dynamics from occurring, such as the overly compliant coachee who invests in his development goals primarily because his leader coach sees them as valuable. In such cases, the coachee is often responding to the implicit power and authority that resides in the leader coach's organizational role.

Role Conflict

Leader coaches encounter role conflict because of the multiple roles that they assume in organizations. At any one time they might be a business manager; a leader responsible for getting results; a manager responsible for enabling, evaluating, and developing; or an organizational citizen responsible for participating in and supporting broader organizational agendas. In each of these roles, the leader coach's relationship to the coachee shifts. These different roles can't be totally separated. Leader coaches need to understand these various roles, assess their ability to juggle their coaching role among them, and judge whether the circumstances have changed in such a way that it is advisable to alter the coaching relationship or its developmental content.

Organizational Responsibility

One of the benefits leader coaches enjoy is the ability to connect back to the organization in different ways. For example, because of an individual coaching relationship, issues may surface about organizational practices, and those practices may invite further examination or improvement. If coaching is defined as an individually focused activity, then what happens to this other learning? We encourage leader coaches to consider the extent to which they have an organizational responsibility to carry forward what they learn, both good and bad, about how the organization's values are enacted. This is not an easy task, but it's one of the unique platforms from which leader coaches can operate and effect positive change.

Conclusion

CCL has made a long-standing and unique contribution to the field of leadership coaching. This book melds its experience and practice into a coherent set of ideas and recommendations that can enhance coaching activities for the leader coach. Coaches can generalize from our six principles of coaching practice to serve their own work. Our evidence of experience endorses their practicality and utility.

The three levels of coaching introduced in this chapter reflect our observations of motivations and behaviors that consistently drive the need for coaching. As leader coaches wonder what exactly their roles are and what is expected of them in this seemingly complex world of coaching options, we hope they will find support in our descriptions of those levels. Leader coaches can coach effectively at different levels of engagement, and their work can benefit themselves as much as it benefits their coachees. The subsequent chapters in this book offer perspectives on the role and practice of the leader coach, as viewed from a particular context or with the help of a particular set of content. The ever changing and growing areas of coaching, such as that evidenced by organizational demand for leadership development systems, reinforces our eagerness to learn and adapt new ideas and practices and to develop new knowledge for leader coaches embarking on this journey.

Coach's Bookshelf

Bacon, T., & Spear, K. (2003). *Adaptive coaching: The art and practice of a client-centered approach to performance improvement.* Palo Alto, CA: Davies-Black.

Dotlich, D. L., & Cairo, P. C. (1999). *Action coaching: How to leverage individual performance for company success.* San Francisco: Jossey-Bass.

Fitzgerald, C., & Garvey Berger, J. (Eds.). (2002). *Executive coaching: Practices and perspectives.* Palo Alto, CA: Davies-Black.

Goldsmith, M., Lyons, L., & Freas, A. (Eds.). (2000). *Coaching for leadership: How the world's greatest coaches help leaders learn.* San Francisco: Jossey-Bass.

Hargrove, R. (2003). *Masterful coaching.* San Francisco: Jossey-Bass.

HBS Press. (2004). *Harvard business essentials: Coaching and mentoring.* Boston: Harvard Business School Press.

Hunt, J., & Weintraub, J. (2002). *The coaching manager.* Thousand Oaks, CA: Sage.

O'Neill, M. (2000). *Executive coaching with backbone and heart: A systems approach to engaging leaders with their challenges.* San Francisco: Jossey-Bass.

Whitmore, J. (2002). *Coaching for performance: Growing people, performance and purpose.* Yarmouth, ME: Nicholas Brealey Publishing.

CHAPTER TWO

A FRAMEWORK FOR LEADERSHIP DEVELOPMENT COACHING

Sharon Ting
Doug Riddle

In almost any human endeavor, a framework of ideas provides the structure for understanding and practice. It is no different in the field of leadership coaching. CCL's coaching framework, informed by research and buttressed by practical experience, is an integral part of its coaching practice. For individuals, such as leader coaches, who are not steeped in the discipline of coaching, the framework serves as a general guide. For professional coaches, we find the framework helps them correct their course when the coaching feels off-track. The chapters that follow apply CCL's coaching framework to a variety of situations: coaching different populations, coaching in different contexts, and coaching with emergent techniques, technologies, and practices.

Our coaching framework has three aspects, which are illustrated in Figure 2.1:

- Relationship—the context within which the coaching occurs
- Assessment, challenge, and support (ACS)—the core elements of CCL's leader development model
- Results—the visible outcomes, both direct and visible and those that are indirect, that coaching focuses on achieving

FIGURE 2.1. CCL'S COACHING FRAMEWORK.

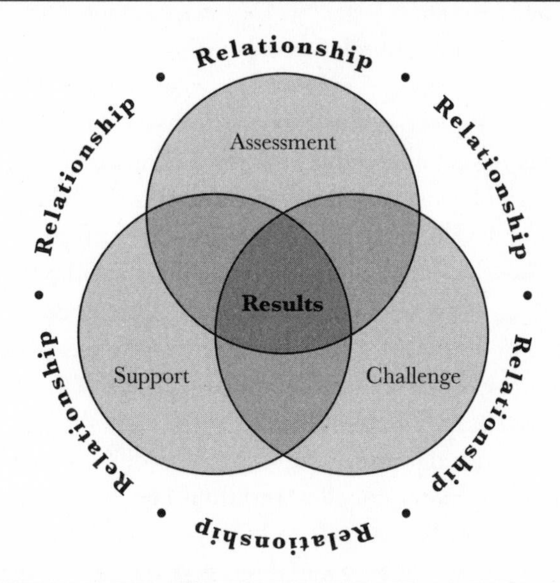

The three parts are synergistic. Relationship building, leader development, and results typically occur concurrently. Accordingly, each aspect informs and triggers new activity or perspectives in the others.

We discuss the framework here in general terms, with the understanding that it emerged initially in the context of a conventional one-to-one coaching relationship between a professional coach and a coachee. Since then, CCL and the organizations it works with have found the framework useful when applied across a range of coaching relationships, including those between managers and direct reports, among internal human resource professionals and their informal and formal relationships with managers and leaders, and between peers. By steering away from a prescriptive, sequential structure and embracing an approach that emphasizes the elements of effective coaching and development, CCL's coaching framework functions more as a compass than a road map.

Relationship

Many leaders can point to multiple individuals who played coaching roles at various times in their development. If you were to ask them to name some of the key elements that enabled them to be receptive to that coaching, chances are they would mention the quality of the relationship. They might characterize it as a confidential, private relationship. At its core, the coaching relationship is a strong personal connection between two individuals that typically occurs out of public view and whose workings may even appear mysterious to outsiders.

Coaching is fundamentally a process for facilitating learning and change, which is another way to describe development. What distinguishes coaching from other developmental experiences is the critical role that one person, the coach, plays in challenging and supporting another person, the coachee, to engage intentionally in the development process and in helping the coachee pull the important lessons from those experiences. That kind of intense, interpersonal work depends on the development of trust between the individuals involved in the coaching relationship.

That a trusting relationship is a precondition to effective coaching poses a challenge for leader coaches and their coachees, who usually don't have a choice about working together. When the evaluative aspect of their primary relationship is that of boss and direct report, that can have an inhibiting factor to the coaching relationship. Leader coaches may need to accept that not all of their coaching relationships with their direct reports will have the same degree of quality. While that may place some natural limitations on the level of personal closeness they may feel, it does not have to significantly diminish the effectiveness of the coaching. (For further discussion about trust, see Exhibit 2.1.)

Two other forms of leader coach relationships exist: laterally with peers and upward with superiors. Often these coaching relationships are informal and implicit. The inherent strength of these relationships lies in their consensual nature, because neither peers nor superiors have to accept coaching from a colleague. When peers or superiors allow themselves to be coached, usually a high degree of openness, readiness, and trust exists between them and their leader coach colleague because the peer or superior engages by choice.

Regardless of who the parties are in the coaching relationship, a close examination reveals three essential components: rapport, commitment, and collaboration.

Rapport

Rapport is the heart of the coaching relationship—the interpersonal connection that allows each party who is engaged in the process to say, "I feel I can work with this person. I feel he is willing and able to understand my point of

EXHIBIT 2.1. THE ROLE OF TRUST IN THE COACHING RELATIONSHIP.

Trust is a word used often in coaching, and yet it is more relative than absolute. In a coaching context, trust is often interpreted as the ability to hold all information as confidential. We caution readers from thinking of trust too simplistically. In a coaching relationship, especially one that affects people beyond the leader coach and the coachee, trust looks different behaviorally to each person. Developing ever-increasing trust is a desired goal that requires constant awareness and monitoring of the coach's behaviors and motivations that may bear on how his or her trustworthiness is perceived by others and an understanding and respect for what trust means to the person being coached.

Trust isn't highlighted as one of the three primary components of the coaching relationship because we believe it is the quality outcome that coaches strive to achieve in their relationships. Coachees should be able to trust their coaches, to feel they can rely on them and put confidence in them. In the absence of trust, little can be accomplished.

---

view." Coachees often describe their coaches as open, respectful, empathic, attentive, straightforward, trustworthy, and thought provoking. While the coach has primary responsibility for establishing the groundwork by exhibiting behaviors that have the impact described above, the coach cannot accomplish that alone. The coachee has to be open and willing to engage.

While rapport often reveals itself early in the coaching relationship (there is an ease, warmth, and genuine interest between the two individuals), the leader coach can develop this relationship aspect by working to understand and appreciate the coachee. Asking specific questions about the coachee's non-work interests, background, family, and views on the world is one way to develop rapport. Finding commonalities (similar musical interests or cheering for the same sports teams, for example) is another effective way to establish rapport. In the end, both parties need to agree that there is sufficient rapport between them before committing to a coaching relationship.

Commitment

Good intentions become new behaviors and attitudes when enabled through commitment. When commitment is present, both parties mutually pledge to follow a course of action to fulfill their responsibilities in the relationship, persevere through setbacks, and celebrate successes. They also understand and acknowledge where the limits and constraints are to each of their responsibilities. This commitment takes many forms, from small to significant. It ranges from being accessible, available, and respectful of scheduled time together to implementing respective agreed-on actions, to being open about uncomfortable emotions or dynamics in the relationship, to challenging each other in nonthreatening ways to improve outcomes.

For the leader coach, it may mean taking time to have a meaningful discussion about the goals the coachee is working on, providing developmental assignments within the person's primary work, or supporting the person in achieving his or her goals while on a learning curve. It can even mean taking risks—for example, delaying a promotion for that coachee, which might cause the individual to question whether he should exit the organization, to ensure the long-term effective development of that coachee. Commitment says the coachee is valued and valuable, and it can motivate the coachee to persevere through the performance dip that accompanies the learning curve.

Collaboration

Collaboration occurs when coach and coachee work together as equals, with mutual respect, exchanging thoughts and ideas for the purpose of generating new information, options, and solutions. They share a belief that each of them has had relevant experiences, holds important knowledge and perspectives, and brings essential expertise (the coachee about himself and his context and the coach about leadership development and behavioral change processes) that are needed to achieve the purpose of the coaching relationship.

Also, collaboration is the process through which much of the learning occurs. In its absence, coaching can take the form of lecturing, telling, teaching, persuading, advice giving, and even cheerleading. The danger of these alternative approaches is that they can engender resistance, create dependency, promote action without ongoing commitment, offer false reassurance, and, worse yet, reinforce ineffective behaviors. The give and take of dialogue, the two-way street of support and challenge—these qualities comprise the mind of collaborative relationship we recommend that coaches pursue with all those with whom they are involved.

The Coach's Role in the Relationship

Fully one-third of managers can identify other people from whom they have learned and describe how that learning occurred (Douglas, 2003; McCall & Hollenbeck, 2002; McCall, Lombardo, & Morrison, 1988). McCauley expanded on the concept and identified specific types of roles that people in relationships play for one another (McCauley & Douglas, 2004). Within the coaching relationship, the leader coach assumes different roles at different times. McCauley grouped these roles based on the components of the leader development framework of assessment, challenge, and support (discussed later in this chapter). Guthrie (1999) described some of these same roles in the context of CCL's coaching history (see Exhibit 2.2). Her descriptions can help guide the leader coach in becoming intentional about taking on a particular role at a particular time to help a coachee reach a particular goal.

Others in the Coaching Relationship

Although the coaching relationship envelops two central figures, others also have an influence on the relationship. Direct reports are mindful of the behavior of managers, and so any coaching relationship with one of their peers is bound to draw their attention. They may be tempted to make meaning out of the coaching relationship—perhaps surmising that a peer is not performing up to par or, conversely, that a peer who receives developmental coaching is on the fast track toward a leadership position. The leader coach should be aware of these undercurrents and balance coaching initiatives between development and performance issues.

Direct reports aren't the only others affected by coaching relationships. For example, in matrixed organizations, there are the leader coach's peers and other managers to consider. If a coach's direct report interacts with another manager or team, that coach needs to decide what to do with information received about the direct report's performance. Because coaching can make its greatest strides in an open, sharing environment, the leader coach should make that stance clear to other peers and managers with whom the coachee is in contact. This, of course, is an ideal state, and the realities of organizational culture and politics should be factored into decisions about level of transparency to others.

Beyond the work environment, the leader coach can be mindful of others who can also affect the coaching relationship—for example, the coachee's

EXHIBIT 2.2. COACHING ROLES IN CCL'S HISTORY.

Specific coaching roles were not immediately evident to CCL when it started coaching for development. But as CCL gained experience with using coaches, a number of specific roles emerged to replace earlier generalizations:

- Expert. The coach's expertise is different although not mutually exclusive from content expertise, which is generally subject related. It is appropriate for managers who are inexperienced in a role or whose job success potential would benefit from the perspective of someone who has been in a similar position.
- Reflective thinking partner. Coaches engage individuals in reflective thinking by probing assumptions, hypothesizing about outcomes, challenging, serving as a sounding board, and providing different perspectives. This role can be especially helpful to coachees as they review their mental models and understanding of the world.
- Feedback provider. In this role, the coach gives honest feedback about the coachee's actions. By citing examples and raising awareness in a tangible, focused manner, the coach helps the coachee wrestle with resolving skill deficiencies or developing strengths that the individual was not fully using.
- Feedback interpreter. The coach helps the coachee work through on-the-job challenges and helps this person address interpersonal issues and blocks in learning. The coach also helps the coachee strategize ways to remove blocks or confront them.
- Dialogue partner. Coachees sometimes expect their coach to have the answers—to tell them what to do, especially if they are struggling with a particularly difficult challenge. As a dialogue partner, the coach places the burden of learning and change on the coachee.
- Practice partner. In this role, the coach frequently serves as a way of enabling the coachee to role-play interactions or scenarios from different angles.
- Accountant. The coach holds the coachee responsible for plans and actions. In this role, the coach also recognizes the evolutionary nature of organizational life and provides some flexibility, which helps the coachee respond to the pace of change inherent in contemporary organizations.
- Positive reinforcer. The coach provides affirmation, praise, and encouragement when coachees attempt to make changes. The coach uses this role to express confidence in the coachee, modeling the behavior changes asked of the coachee.

EXHIBIT 2.2. COACHING ROLES IN CCL'S HISTORY, Cont'd.

- Counselor. The coach helps the coachee confront and deal with the emotional side of change and development, especially when that person is experiencing major shifts in role or responsibility in his organization. The coach provides support not as an advice giver but as a listener who can help the coachee develop appropriate strategies to deal with rapid and substantial change.
- Historian. Although not employed as often as the other coaching roles, the role of historian makes an important contribution to coachees' development by reminding them what they were thinking and doing two or three months before and how far they've come.
- Role model. By virtue of the coach's ongoing modeling of listening skills, openness, and willingness to engage in the learning process, the coachee learns ways to do that for others in the organization. The coach's interaction and modeling throughout the relationship are helpful in the coachee's attempt to interact more effectively with others.

family and the organization's customers or clients who interact with the coachee. Often the coach doesn't directly engage these other people. The coaching relationship occurs in a context of other relationships, and the leader coach should hold some awareness of all of them and how they might have an impact on or be affected by the coaching.

Assessment, Challenge, and Support

CCL's leader development model of assessment, challenge, and support (ACS) is at the core of its coaching framework and can be used to shape the dialogue and activities of any coaching event. We recognize that leader coaches can use the development model to help coachees clarify their motivation and develop goals to confront current performance concerns and future development needs.

The three elements serve dual purposes in the development process. First, they motivate people to focus their attention and efforts on learning, growth, and change. Second, they provide the raw material for learning: the information, observations, and reactions that lead to a more complex understanding of the world. To enhance the development of leaders, leader coaches need to help them find, create, and shape a wide range of learning experiences, each of which provides assessment, challenge, and support.

Assessment

The purpose of assessment is to get the fullest picture possible of current reality and future development opportunities for the coachee. The person, the performance, and the context define the assessment terrain. Through the assessment element of the framework, the coach and coachee work toward clarity by reconciling various perspectives. This is emphasized during the data-gathering phase of the coaching program and repeatedly surfaces throughout the coaching interactions as coach and coachee seek to learn from experiences. The coach's skills at interpreting, analyzing, intuiting, summarizing, projecting, and distilling assessment information, in collaboration with the coachee, are critical to leveraging the power of this element.

A critical point to take note of is that data come in many forms. In a coaching context, *data* does not necessarily mean hard, quantitative, objective information. Data are not always tangible. They can be what the coachee doesn't tell you or talk about. *Data* refers to anything that helps a coach understand a coachee and her situation with a sharper eye, ear, and heart.

Person. Assessing the person being coached means asking who that person is, what makes that person unique, what is important to that individual, how this person likes to operate and relate to others, what appear to be this person's mental models, what natural gifts and blind spots this individual possesses, what this person's aspirations are, and what motivates this person. Leader coaches often breeze by these questions or even ignore them because they so often concentrate on assessing behaviors and measuring outcomes as a path to improving a coachee's performance.

Consequently, the leader coach may neglect the personal aspects that are the source of many leadership challenges and may be key to unlocking a coachee's motivation to improve as a leader. Consider the story of Yvan, who is widely viewed as a high-potential candidate for a future seat on his organization's executive committee if he could overcome the perception of his being disorganized and questions about the seriousness of his thinking. Initially stung by the feedback, Yvan becomes defensive and argumentative. After further discussion, he acknowledges that he struggles with feeling constrained by routine. His attention is ignited by solving problems, and once he believes solutions are identified, he moves on to other issues. He considers that trait as personally empowering, but others experience his behaviors as making a splash and then abandoning them. Yvan's tendencies also manifest themselves in his lack of punctuality to meetings. His dislike for schedules and meetings results in two perceptions: that he is disorganized and that he is disrespectful of others' time. In Yvan's case, once he became more aware of the behavioral link between his innate drives and tendencies and perceptions of his effectiveness as a leader, he was able to make more selective and appropriate choices about how to manage those tendencies.

Sometimes life experiences define an individual's leadership model. Such is the case of Chih-Hung, a U.S.-based manager who grew up in China during the period of heavy policing and scrutiny of individuals' behaviors. These experiences taught him that to be open with his thoughts and feelings was dangerous to himself and others. It doesn't surprise those who know Chih-Hung and his personal history that as a leader, he is too self-contained, withholding his ideas and emotions. Years of learned behaviors adopted as protection are inseparable from who he is as a leader. But his first boss, who absolutely separated work and personal life, does not spend time understanding Chih-Hung. She misinterprets his behaviors as a lack of warmth and as competitiveness, and then compounds the misinterpretation by attributing his slow approach to change as resistance to feedback.

There are many ways to answer the question, "Who is this person?" but leader coaches occupy a powerful and unique position of having substantial and insightful information about the person they are coaching. They often don't realize or leverage this information because they haven't had the opportunity to reflect on what a coachee's behaviors say about the person. They tend to look at the behaviors from the perspective of performance: how well the person they are coaching has met the measures established for him or her by the organization. While assessing performance is critical, we can't emphasize enough the importance of understanding the coachee's unique qualities and the world as the coachee sees and understands himself or herself in it.

Performance. Performance is the most familiar aspect of assessment. Performance measures can be formal (annual performance appraisals or monthly or quarterly goals, for example) or informal (frequent reactions to how daily tasks are handled). Consider the following cases. Even before Amin engages in a full assessment of his leadership, he and his boss agree that his business performance highlights the need for improving his leadership. With a strong sales and marketing background, Amin lacks an appreciation for processes and details that is needed to turn the start-up business where he works into a solid, consistently profitable business. Amin could benefit from additional assessment, but coaching could and did begin as soon as that need was identified. In contrast, Reuben's performance was stellar, and his boss and superiors are blind to the toll it takes on his direct reports. In the absence of a more comprehensive assessment, the markedly different impact Reuben has on those above him in the organization versus those reporting to him might remain undisclosed and unaddressed.

But even in many organizations where performance measures are presumed to be well understood, often they are not because they are poorly communicated or received. Furthermore, the link between performance appraisals and compensation or promotion and relative comparisons to others can obscure any message the leader coach might give. For example, take Jeri's story. She doesn't understand the concerns being raised about her ability to get results through people and to create a developmental climate. Her performance appraisals are always above average; she receives commensurate bonuses. So where is the problem? Why isn't she viewed as ready for greater responsibility?

One answer lies in the fact that the language used in Jeri's performance appraisal document is vague and nonspecific. It also focuses on past performance, not on future development needs. The result is a gap between current feedback and future potential. Her boss acknowledges that although he talked to Jeri about potential areas of improvement, it seemed too harsh to commit those remarks to a formal document, and he worried that his feedback might jeopardize Jeri's standing relative to her peers.

To alleviate confusion like Jeri experiences, 360-degree feedback surveys are often administered as a supplement to existing performance data. If such surveys are administered as a confidential development tool, they can provide much clearer feedback about performance to coachees.

Data on performance and the impact of that performance can be a significant motivator to development when the measures are meaningful and relevant and the feedback is delivered in an effective manner. However, individuals receiving this kind of feedback have to be able to link those results to their behaviors, skills, and knowledge. Performance indicators are a key component to good assessment, but leader coaches should not rely exclusively on them. Although temptingly more visible and tangible, they often neglect the personal aspect of assessment or the context within which the coachee functions.

Context. Contextual factors greatly affect what leadership styles are tolerated and even thrive in organizations and which ones derail careers. Environmental factors, such as an unusual adverse economic environment or the emergence of new technology, and implicit organizational norms, such as "effort is appreciated but results are rewarded" or "don't challenge authority," can reinforce behaviors.

Despite the preponderance of research on the leadership behaviors that are viewed as universally positive, the actual assessment of effectiveness is often relative to organizational culture and norms. For example, a cost-conscious consumer goods manufacturing company hires a manager with a sales and marketing background with numerous start-ups. He runs into difficulties immediately as he launches a highly creative but expensive presentation at the annual industry trade show. He believes in investing to create visibility and marketplace image, a strategy that worked successfully in his previous companies. Yet he is surprised when his annual review, while excellent, contains feedback on perceptions that he is lavishly improvident. This manager is perplexed. His behaviors haven't changed, but his context has. The values and expectations at his new company are different than his previous ones.

Context also plays a key role in determining what the coachee may choose to develop and how she determines what form that development will take. Consider the case of a manager who has been successful with turnarounds. She has had three consecutive assignments to turn around struggling small businesses within the company. She has been successful in getting an assignment to run one of the company's core businesses that is large, has long-standing traditions, and has long-tenured employees. The manager's highly touted decisive, fast-paced, action-oriented leadership style is suddenly met with strong negative reactions, and word has already traveled to senior management that morale is down, which recently completed climate surveys will confirm. This manager is faced with a variety of development possibilities. Does she focus on learning how to adapt her style to leading in a stable environment? Does she work on her influencing skills to try and stimulate new thinking in the company's core business?

Context strongly influences coaching outcomes and constraints. Leader coaches and other coaches inside the organization (such as HR professionals) have access to rich and intimate data about the context, and that can create biases or self-limiting perspectives about the coachee and the possibilities. They also know what models of leadership and behaviors have succeeded within the organization and which have not. Imagine a manager who comes with a track record of revitalizing the operations of two business units at a previous company and is hired to inject a fresh approach. This manager has an entrepreneurial and maverick mind-set. This manager's boss and leader coach helped her sort through what seemed like a confusing message to her after she got feedback in her first six months with the firm that she was too self-reliant and independent. In essence, the company wanted her fresh entrepreneurial thinking around business solutions but enacted with greater involvement of others and through a more team- and consensus-oriented style. Creating results through teamwork was a key element of this company's leadership model.

Alternatively, coaches may be misguided if they misread or are unaware of important contextual information. Some of the more common contextual factors to consider are industry, company, and business unit culture, current climate and state, strategic vision, political dynamics, recent events, and trends. Therefore, an important part of the leader coach's responsibility is to be attuned to the nuances within the organization regarding the range of tolerated behaviors and leadership style and to help coachees make their own assessment, and then choices, around if and how they want to adapt their style as part of the coaching work.

Challenge

Challenges come in many forms and have one thing in common: they create disequilibrium, an imbalance between current skills and demands that call on people to move out of their comfort zones (McCauley & Van Velsor, 2004). In those moments when the coachee is no longer entrenched in his own reality, the opportunity for learning and change presents itself. The assessment process itself can create challenge by disrupting the coachee's self and other perceptions. Challenging experiences also result from the new and different behaviors or assignments that the coachee undertakes in the workplace. Often called action plans or development plans, these efforts are typically deliberate choices to practice different behaviors or develop new attitudes and perspectives. Because they are new, they tend to stretch the coachee's ability, which allows movement into new territory and new learning. Often the most difficult challenge for coaches and coachees is managing the internal and external obstacles that threaten good intent to change and achieve development goals.

Disequilibrium. Leader coaches can generate this state through their questioning skills or through their interaction and feedback to the coachee of their own experiences of their coachees' behaviors. The imbalance that results from a challenging situation is not always predictable or known in advance of the experience. To the extent that a coach is in a position to create the disequilibrium, it can be most helpful to the coachee if that is done with intention, purpose, and even forewarning. Two common and accessible forms for leader coaches are giving feedback based on direct observation or assessment surveys and providing assignments that require development of different skills or perspectives.

In that place of unease, individuals have the opportunity to learn either because they can't readily access old solutions or they know old methods are inadequate to meet the current challenge. The process of managing this imbalance can appear chaotic to the leader coach, who may even question whether the coachee understands as he attempts to right himself. It is natural for coachees to want to regain some sense of equanimity and stability. They may try a range of responses to achieve that, including denial and rationalization, before they land on an approach that feels more effective.

Leader coaches may face their own discomfort as they observe their coachee in these varying states as they try to make change. They may feel hopeful, impatient, exasperated, perplexed, or pessimistic. In any case, they will have to reflect on their role in that change process, how their thoughts and feelings are affecting the coachee, and what, if anything, they need to do differently.

Stretch. In addition to being intentional about creating disequilibrium, leader coaches can calibrate the degree of stretch that a coachee can handle based on the coach's assessment. This relates directly to the difficult goals described as one of the key challenges that create learning for leaders. Having the right amount of challenge or stretch contributes to learning. Too small a challenge defeats learning or minimizes growth; too much stretch, and coachees can become overwhelmed, defensive, discouraged, or burned out. Leader coaches can help by getting their coachees to set goals that are personally meaningful and achievable so they are more likely to sustain motivation through the behavioral troughs. Goals that are set in a vacuum may provide personal benefit and satisfaction and even leader development opportunities, but they don't leverage the potential organizational learning. Leader coaches should be aware of this aspect and use that knowledge to help the coachee determine what goals and what degree of stretch to aim for. The leader coach is uniquely positioned to:

- Ensure alignment between the coachee's goals and the organization's norms and business strategies
- Identify dissonance early, which might take a number of forms, including a disconnect between what the coachee agreed to work on and where she spends her time and energy, or unspoken tension between what the coachee wants to develop as compared to what the coach and the organization believes she needs to develop
- Test and prepare the organization's commitment to a possible performance dip, or learn early what the tolerance limit is for performance dips during the learning curve and be prepared to compensate or manage others' responses to that dip

Sometimes the coach and coachee determine that a significant relationship or condition exists that needs to be improved or developed if the coachee is to succeed. Typically the condition or person can be readily identified. One common example is found in the differences between the coachee and a peer team member. If the coachee is unable or feels ill equipped to improve that relationship with coaching support from the side, then the judicious leader coach might need to function as a coach facilitator in a three-way meeting to facilitate the learning for the coachee and potentially the other team member.

The leader coach has a natural responsibility and ideal opportunity to function in this capacity when coaching direct reports who may have conflicts or challenges in managing their relationships with one another or even direct reports who are having challenges with peers in other functional areas.

That said, the leader coach has to watch out for being overly invested in efficiently achieving the outcome for the organization that she intervenes too quickly and solves the problem for the coachee and his peer. The leader coach may see immediate results but not recognize that learning has really not occurred for the coachee. Often the perceived authority of the leader coach, even when he is in coaching mode, may be motivating the seemingly changed behavior or attitude when in reality the coachee has not altered his mind-set or perspective. If that happens, when a similar situation arises and the coachee's approach is unaltered, the leader coach may feel frustration because the coachee is not "getting it."

That leader coaches have a responsibility for achieving organizational outcomes cannot be denied. At times they will have to assume a very proactive coaching style that travels along a direct and instructional approach. But in their role as coaches, when they are at that point, they should pause to ask, "Is it time to move from facilitating to directing?" If the answer is yes, coaches should take time afterward to ask the coachee, "What did you learn from this?" Depending on the specific situation, more self-developmental questions could be appropriate: "What did you learn about yourself? What did you learn about your peer? What did you learn about how to manage and lead in these situations?"

Obstacles. Challenges are often presented as how to move from point A to point B and what needs to be done to get there. Those are the actions that move people forward. However, the learning and development that come from achieving a goal often come from working around or moving through the obstacles that block the path to the goal. Rarely does change look like a straight line. In coaching for leader development, forces acting against the change may be internal or external. A simple question often enables coachees to articulate their obstacles: "Six months from now, if you have not succeeded in achieving your goal, what will have been the reasons?" With patience and gentle but continued probing, most coachees can speak to the internal as well as external barriers to achieving their goals.

Internal Obstacles. Internal barriers can be subtle, and uncovering those requires patience and a healthy skepticism toward the obvious. Internal obstacles are the coachee's conscious and unconscious thoughts and feelings that hold him or her back from enacting desired, and verbalized, changes. These internal obstacles usually reside at the underlying driver level we discussed in the Introduction. Often the coachee's stated goal for behavioral change may actually conflict with another, although usually unstated, need. Some examples of common obstacles are:

- Rigidly held values or beliefs
- Discomfort with adopting a different style

- Self-limiting assumptions
- Low personal confidence
- Fear of a drop in performance

An example of such a situation is a manager who is technically superior but lacking in networking skills and has been passed over for a promotion. Despite agreement with the need to develop more relationships, the manager has not made much progress. He still eats lunch at his desk each day. His reasons are workload and time—in essence, blaming an external obstacle. The leader coach notices that when he does have lunch with others, he rarely talks and seems ill at ease. The leader coach speculates that something other than time is making it difficult for the manager to achieve his goal. Through further discussion, the manager discloses he is uncomfortable with chit-chat because it feels unauthentic, he has limited social skills, and he sometimes feels uninteresting to others.

An example of a self-limiting assumption obstacle is how a coachee's perceptions of and immersion in his or her own context may become an obstacle. Particularly if coachees have worked in their organizations a long time, they may have developed firm mental models about their organization or self that limit the possibilities they see for change. These may range from very negative beliefs that the organization won't support development or reward a more empowering leadership style to less negative but no more helpful mindsets that no change is needed or a very common thought pattern of, "If I make these changes, I will stop getting results." Knowing the difference between a self-limiting assumption and legitimately limiting organizational norms requires thoughtful consideration. Helping the coachee get a more accurate sense of organizational realities, opportunities, and pitfalls is an invaluable role for the coach to play. (A process coaches can use to help coachees surface and examine the competing commitments and unspoken assumptions that underlie and create the appearance of not wanting to change is described in Chapter Twelve.)

External Obstacles. The external obstacles may be easier to identify than internal ones, but they are no more responsive to efforts to change. Typically these are forces in the coachee's life such as time, business demands, and lack of support and resources or forces in the organization such as norms, culture, contradictory expectations, and even political dynamics. The leader coach can become a dialogue, as well as problem-solving, partner in finding ways that the coachee can use to manage those external factors and minimize their impact. The leader coach may need to be prepared to exercise authority or goodwill within the organization to remove or alleviate known organizational barriers. It could be as simple as asking for an exception to allow a coachee to attend a leadership activity that is typically reserved for other candidates or as complex as helping to arrange for a visible developmental assignment for the coachee.

External obstacles also include unintentional roadblocks that others and the organization may place in the coachee's way. There is a certain comfort in being able to predict and count on a certain set of behaviors or reactions from the coachee. It means everyone else can go on autopilot when in the presence of the coachee. They know what to expect and have likely developed their own set of coping skills. A potential obstacle for leader coaches to recognize is the collective and individual responses to their own sense of disequilibrium created by the coachee's shifts.

Another common obstacle is conflicting messages within the organization at different levels (you as boss, boss's superior, functional superiors) or among different groups (sales and human resources, for example). It is not uncommon for senior-level individuals to have differing views about the type of leadership that is needed. The coach role can be pivotal in helping the coachee marry her personal values around leadership with her beliefs about the strategic implications of the organization's leadership paradigms.

Seeking Options. One of the most difficult shifts for leaders to make as they engage in coaching is to not provide answers or solve the coachee's issues. The greatest gift they can give is to help the coachee consider ideas, approaches, strategies, behaviors, and other approaches and actions that he had not considered before or in the current context. Effective leaders solve problems and get results—fast. Effective coaches, in contrast, help coachees solve problems—often by slowing them down first. Effective leader coaches invite and sometimes prod their coachees to consider new approaches, often ones that run counter to their beliefs, mental models, or past experiences. They offer their own experiences not as solutions but as a way to trigger ideas from the coachee about what would work. As one coachee lamented about his very well-intentioned leader coach, "She clearly wanted to help me figure out some actionable steps to achieve my development goal. She offered as a solution an action that she had taken and worked for her. But then she stopped there. I was left with one actionable option and, frankly, not one that was workable for me. I am not wired to achieve the goal through that means. In the end, I was left with a clear challenge and no clear idea of what actions I would take to get there. I know she meant well, but the usefulness of her coaching was limited. And I know in six months she'll be angry that I haven't made more progress on my goals."

Leader coaches should pay particular attention to who is coming up with options (the coach or coachee) and make sure the options are actionable. One or two suggestions don't make an option; that's a decision. We encourage coaches to consider that a large part of the role they play in the challenge aspect of the framework is to press the coachee to explore options, draw them from her own experiences as much as possible, and seed and prompt the coachee's thinking as needed. The ease with which the coachee can engage in this process may reveal a lot about how well he and the coach have calibrated the level of stretch and anticipated obstacles. Ultimately it can serve as a feedback loop on the viability and appropriateness of the goals.

Support

Support is the third leg of the development stool. Without it, a well-crafted stool will fall; with it, you have stability and capacity to hold weight. How coachees perceive support for themselves is very individualized and comes in many forms, including other people, organizational and personal motivation, and tangible resources (McCauley & Van Velsor, 2004).

Our experiences from a coaching perspective align with that view of support. It's critical for leader coaches to heed the fact that individuals experience support in unique and personal ways. Our framework aligns with that fact by expanding the concept of assessment in a coaching context to include understanding the person. Coaches should be careful not to define support in universal terms and instead take the time to understand what their coachees view as support.

In general, however, coaches can offer support in four ways: maintaining motivation, accessing resources and strategies, celebrating small wins and managing setbacks, and creating a sustainable learning agenda.

Motivation. This support tactic often brings to mind either one of two contrasting approaches: cheerleader or tough love. Both are important in helping the coachee stay motivated. However, in the CCL coaching framework, *moti-*

vation refers to tapping into what really matters to the coachee and how working on the specific goals meets those needs. One of the most important roles a leader coach can play lies in helping the coachee clarify, articulate, and continuously reevaluate and reconfirm her motivations. In order to do that, the coach should explore and understand the coachee's core needs and values and how that translates into her work life. Having these types of conversations can be revealing and underscores why our framework is built on a trusting relationship. This is one of those areas where a leader coach may have to accept limits on his or her expectations for full sharing, especially if the coachee's motivations may not fully align with the organization's needs or aspirations for that individual.

It is not unusual for a coachee to lose momentum during the course of making the desired changes. The high excitement of new possibilities generated by insight discussions has worn off, life's daily demands overtake good intentions, and forces for the status quo remain stronger than forces for change. Before confronting or pushing the coachee, the coach might consider revisiting and reaffirming the source of motivation. Perhaps the goal never met a real need in the first place. Perhaps under the weight of everyone else's feedback, the coachee felt compelled to jump on the change bandwagon when in reality the goal was not meeting a core need or value of his. One way in which coaches support their coachees is to give them freedom to revisit their goals.

Asking the coachee directly if her original goals still feel meaningful and if she is motivated to achieve them can bear fruit. If she is self-aware, she might be able to articulate what her core needs are, how the goals align with those needs, and if a reexamination of the goals is in order. If she is unable to articulate those positions, then the leader coach can encourage the process with a prepared series of questions. For example, one aspiring and very well-liked leader was given feedback from her direct reports and peers that they felt she needed more balance between her personal and work life. Being a responsive leader, she included that as one of her top three goals. After six months, her coach noted that not much energy was going into that goal of balance. When asked directly, she acknowledged that she actually felt fine with the level of balance she had achieved. She realized that the issue seemed more important to others and she appreciated their concern. But she was satisfied with the balance she had created for herself, and she respected those varying needs for balance in the lives of her direct reports (and they concurred with that wholeheartedly). In fact, the perceived lack of balance was not reflected as hindering her performance or leadership effectiveness.

The moral of this story is that leader coaches should constantly monitor their own beliefs about what should matter to their coachees, be careful not to insinuate their own beliefs about what coachees should work on into their goals (in essence, don't lead the witness), help coachees stay clear about what matters to them (Is it a closely held value, or does it matter to them because it matters to others—which is a fine motivator but a different one?), and constantly check in on their motivation level relative to their goals. We said earlier that our framework is iterative, not linear. The coach and coachee are constantly reassessing, recalibrating challenges, and discerning the right forms of support. Each coaching discussion has elements of relationship, assessment, challenge, support, and results.

Resources and Strategies. Coaches often say that the toughest aspect of coaching is getting specific about the what, how, and who of implementing their development plan. We frequently hear leader coaches tell us that conversations become less focused and the goals seem to drift off into the distance. The coach can support the coachee in at least two ways with this part of the process—one structural and the other behavioral.

On the structural side, the coach can initiate a discussion of what other resources, besides their coaching, the coachees need to be successful. One approach, which links the assessment of the person with support, is to understand the approaches that the coachee tends to use when learning something new. Learning is enhanced with a wide rather than a narrow range of learning approaches (Dalton, 1998), and sometimes lack of success in learning a new task or behavior is related to nothing more insidious than employing too narrow a set of learning tactics (Bunker & Webb, 1992). The tactics identified were thinking, taking action, accessing others, and feeling (Dalton, 1999).

Leader coaches and coachees can use the following related questions to ensure a wide repertoire of tactics is used:

- What actions will I take and what behaviors will I experiment with, and in what situations?
- What might I read or reflect on on my own?
- Who else might be able to help me with this goal and serve in one of the developmental relationship roles?
- What are my internal emotions that may block my learning, what are most effective ways for me to manage, and what feelings can I access to support myself and support my achieving this goal?

On the behavioral side, the coach needs to be well armed with strategies and tactics when the coachee exhausts his options. Initial support comes from helping the coachee access his own pool of effective skills that can be applied differently or in more situations. For behaviors that are more resistant to change, the coach and coachee may need to look at other techniques and approaches. Engage the coachee in this process, and share the tools and resources generously because she knows what has worked in the past and can help guide her own learning.

Internal Resources. Most well-functioning individuals have tremendous internal resources and capabilities, many of which they don't consciously consider how to tap when tackling their development goals. Part of that results from the framing and the common assumptions we hold about the term *development goal.* If we are honest with ourselves, all too often we think of them as deficits, holes, or gaps in capabilities that need to be filled or taught from scratch. (Chapter Eleven discusses these issues in depth.) In the context of CCL's coaching framework, it's important for leader coaches to know that coachees have many of the internal resources they need to achieve their goals. They usually have demonstrated the desired behaviors in other contexts or exhibit elements of the desired behaviors but maybe not with the frequency desired. The coach's role in this aspect of support is to help the coachee become more conscious and intentional about using those skills. The coach might also help the coachee tap into internal resources that aren't behavioral but are nonetheless positive drivers for change, such as a desire to succeed, a personal way of managing the discomfort of learning something new, an optimistic outlook, and a sense of responsibility.

To some extent, internal resources are connected to motivation, but it's helpful to distinguish them in this way. Motivation in coaching relates to the underlying personal reasons to commit to change, and internal resources become the personal vehicle, comprising attributes and existing skills that will make that change journey a bit smoother. Internal resources become the complementary flip side to internal obstacles, which ask, "How might I stand in my own way?" A goal of the leader coach is to help the coachee reduce obstacles, tap those internal resources, and ask, "What in me will help to propel me forward?"

External Resources. The leader coach plays two key roles in this arena. First is to help the coachee understand what external resources are available and their value. Second is to act as a guide, sponsor, and sometimes broker in helping the coachee access the right resources. External resources can cover a wide range: services, programs, readings, new or special assignments, classes, networks, and others. What may be most valuable for coaches to consider here is their role in helping the coachee expand his or her understanding of external resources, what forms they can take, how to select, how to access, and how to make the best use of those resources. Too often developing leaders may have a more self-sufficient mind-set and not even think about the role of external resources, let alone know how to access them.

Wins and Setbacks. An essential role that coaches play for coachees is in helping them celebrate small wins and manage setbacks. Too often managers don't think to give positive feedback until the actual goal is achieved. Coaches also help coachees calibrate their own expectations for the speed of change based on the level of stretch they've undertaken. For example, reaching a goal of "reestablish trust with direct reports" will take much longer than "seek input from others before making decisions," which will take longer than "hold a weekly staff meeting and set priorities for the week." For longer-term goals, regular, genuine praise for small wins and encouragement when setbacks occur are important elements of support.

Professional coaches are trained to help the coachee see small gains and to use that as further motivation. Leader coaches can learn from their example. They are in an ideal position to offer support because they are more likely to see the behavior and can provide immediate positive or corrective feedback. However, they need to make more conscious effort in this regard. Since coaching isn't the leader's primary job, in the crush of daily organizational demands she may easily lose sight of opportunities to acknowledge progress. We also recommend that the coach reflect on the standard for achievement that she holds for herself and how that might bear on her expectation for her coachee. Finally, the leader coach may also be in the position to provide tangible rewards for progress and achievement.

Helping coachees manage setbacks is key to maintaining their motivation. The stress produced by challenges can block learning, becoming an obstacle in itself. Coaches can help coachees elicit the lessons from both positive and negative experiences. A coach's support can be like the cheering noise of onlookers is to a runner trying to finish a marathon.

As noted earlier, support is a highly individualized component of the coaching process. Coachees can have quite varying needs in that regard.

Coaches should ask their coachees what would be most helpful and then provide that. Coaches should resist the temptation to offer what they would want or to do more than they need. In the absence of coachees' ability to articulate what they need from a coach, understanding who a coachee is, especially his or her underlying motivators, can help determine the type of support that would be most useful.

Sustainable Learning Agenda. In addition to the learning involved with achieving development goals, the coachee has the opportunity to learn how to replicate the learning process in future development goals. This is the virtuous cycle of learning that we will discuss later as a key result of the coaching experience. Leader coaches have a high stake in helping the coachee reflect on the learning process and articulate an agenda that anticipates his or her long-term development plan and the general process to enact that plan.

Realistically, a leader coach will be coaching informally on a continuous basis and coaching in a focused, structured way selectively. The goal is not to foster dependency but to help coachees become self-sufficient learners. *Self-sufficient* in this context does not mean "to do on your own"; rather, we are talking about coachees who develop a learning mind-set and create an infrastructure that naturally draws or surfaces new learning opportunities for themselves as leaders. A large part of that infrastructure is the creation of a personal developmental network of relationships (Hall, 1996). This would likely include the leader coach as the boss, and therefore this is a key relationship in that developmental network. However, the prominence of the boss role as leader coach should recede or at least become one of many others that can offer different kinds of support for the coachee's development goals.

Consider the story of Hanna and Jorge. In learning how to be more diplomatic at meetings when she disagreed with the prevailing views, Hanna asked a peer, Jorge, to give her feedback and also to act as a role model. Jorge was excellent at managing himself when in a room full of people with disparate opinions and also at helping the group reach resolution. Through that process, Hanna and Jorge forged a relationship based on mutual respect and complementary skills that grew into a natural and mutually developmental relationship. Jorge realized Hanna had strengths around being decisive and taking action that he lacked and asked her to reciprocate. They became peer coaches to one another and a critical part of each other's ongoing learning process.

While the word *support* in a coaching relationship conjures up images of active and ongoing interaction by the leader coach, leader coaches at their best do more than help coachees acquire skills and experiences to be effective leaders. They foster the expansion of a coachee's capacity to learn and carry that ability into future roles.

Results

Results arise from the right balance of assessment, challenge, and support in the context of an effective relationship. Although results are an outcome and come at the end of our framework discussion, in reality the process of achieving successful results begins at the very early stages of the coaching relationship. Readers are cautioned about making too much of the sequential nature of our discussion in this chapter. Results should feature prominently in discussions early on in the coaching process, when the coach and coachee are agreeing to work together in a more deliberate and structured way. It's during these discussions that both parties should seek clarity regarding the value of being more intentional about their coaching relationship and the desired outcomes. Discussions about what each is hoping to achieve, for whose benefit, and to what end are just a few of the issues that help to ensure alignment about what success looks like and what tangible or intangible results they are hoping to achieve.

Another dimension of coaching that organizations are increasingly demanding is to explicitly align individual development goals and processes with "the business challenges in the total organizational context" and use an approach that is "organizationally tailored to the strategy, vision and values of the organization" (Freas, 2000, p. 28). In other words, organizations are asking, "What skills, attitudes, and behaviors do we need from our leaders to achieve our business strategy and goals?" Furthermore, they see coaching as enabling leaders to move from understanding to action, and especially putting into practice refined or newly developed skills and perspectives.

Results tend to focus on three areas: behavioral change, business performance improvement, and personal and professional development:

- Behavioral change: exhibiting more of, less of, new, or different behaviors as perceived by others in the organizational environment to achieve more effective leadership

- Business or performance improvement: although influenced by many factors in addition to coaching, the linkage of the behavioral and attitudinal changes to positive impact on the individual's immediate job performance and business outcomes
- Personal and professional development: identifying and engaging in long-term strategies and short-term tactics to enhance the individual's development as a leader, professional, and person, consistent with her values, vision, and goals and overall well-being

Measuring results is crucial because it tells coachees when they have achieved success and enables them to examine its impact. In the absence of that information, they may not realize when it is time to practice desired behaviors more, reevaluate tactics, try new approaches, celebrate success, or set new goals.

Most results can be measured by qualitative and quantitative means. Informal qualitative measurements involve the coachee's self-assessment (based on internal or more personal measures, such as the extent to which she feels more capable and competent on a certain leadership dimension). They may also include informal feedback from selected individuals. More formal qualitative measurements may involve reinterviewing respondents for feedback on the specific goals set or verbatim feedback on a written survey. Quantitative measures typically take the form of written assessment surveys.

As with effective assessments, using multiple means to review results offers a fuller view of the coachee's accomplishments. An overreliance on one or two sources of feedback or evaluation may result in new blind spots because the coachee has no alternative feedback loop to serve as a reality check or verify that perception. Also, a coachee who relies too much on highly contextual feedback runs the risk of adapting his leadership style to a particular situation or to a narrow audience.

For example, imagine a coachee who has received feedback that he needs to give more attention to and fully meet the needs of his work group. He does that but then begins to neglect his relationship with peers or becomes blind to others' perceptions that his group is not meeting the needs of internal customers. If he relies on only the personal feedback from his team without monitoring his effectiveness with other stakeholder groups, he may miss important signals that he has overcorrected or neglected other skills. At the other extreme, an overreliance on quantitative measurements of results may not fully capture what the coachee has learned or may cause the coachee to focus on too narrow an aspect of his development.

There is also a growing tendency for companies to want to measure leadership development in the same ways it measures business success and to demand tangible proof of a direct link to business results because quantitative measures are needed to justify the investment of development dollars. We caution companies from overstating the need for proof of causality with business results because many factors, in addition to leadership, contribute to business success (Martineau & Hannum, 2004).

Our caution notwithstanding, measuring results remains crucial. Organizations commonly expect coaching to deliver work-related behavioral changes. Other results may take longer to achieve and may be less visible. Perhaps most important, increased learning agility for the coachee is key to maximizing coaching initiatives. An increased ability to learn, the ability to direct that learning independently (including knowing how to perform self-assessment), the ability to employ a variety of learning tactics, and the capability of developing a sustainable learning agenda enables the coachee to find and embrace learning opportunities during times of change and to meet challenges with effective personal strategies and support systems. This is the result that promises a complete, ongoing cycle of leadership development.

Applying the Framework

Without a doubt, it's difficult for leaders to go beyond the daily supervisory and managerial duties that often define informal coaching. At the same time, improving ongoing performance and developing future capacity of others are key competencies of effective leaders. That is our experience, and it's what we hear from organizations around the globe. If leaders attempted to personally implement every aspect of the framework in its entirety and for each of their direct reports, it might well feel like another full-time job.

So how does a leader apply these concepts, and what value does the framework provide on a day-to-day basis? Our answer is that it fosters a coaching mind-set and an increased appreciation for the complexity of coaching. The framework looks simple and obvious. In fact, a leader examining one of his informal coaching relationships would readily see that the elements of relationship, assessment, challenge, support, and results are present. What might be less visible is how effectively they are executing these elements and whether they have adequately considered the specific and tangible practices that comprise each element as well as provided balanced attention on and emphasis of each element.

Leaders can use the discussion of the framework as a checklist and a way of self-reflecting on their own effectiveness as a coach by asking themselves how effectively they are applying the detailed elements of the framework to individual coachees. Are some aspects neglected, and if so, is that okay, or do these aspects deserve attention? Where attention is being given, might it be overdone or overwhelming to the individual, such as too much challenge?

Finally, leader coaches should remember that they do not have to personally provide each element of the framework for each coachee. They can use the framework to increase the coachee's understanding of development and the change process and to guide decisions about where, how, and from whom the coachee can fulfill her coaching needs.

Expanding Our Framework

CCL's work for nearly thirty years has focused mainly on leader development—the development of the individual leader. At the same time, CCL has evolved to recognize the larger landscape of leadership development—creating and maintaining leadership capacity in and among groups, teams, and organizations (McCauley & Van Velsor, 2004). Similarly, CCL's coaching practices have roots in leader development and the role of a one-to-one coaching relationship (typically between an external coaching professional and a single leader) in facilitating the growth of a single leader.

A large part of our interest in writing this book, in addition to sharing our views on the practice of leadership coaching, is to expand the views on who can do coaching, who can receive, for what purposes, and in what contexts. We have already discussed as a basic premise of this book our views about the essential role of midlevel to senior leaders as coaches. And in subsequent chapters we will discuss specific perspectives and practices that we believe should become part of the vocabulary and working knowledge about coaching special groups of leaders and for specific leadership challenges.

In Chapter Fifteen, we describe how and why certain types of leadership coaching require a systemic, developmental approach that supplements the rich practice of coaching individual leaders. Our understanding and practice related to this evolving view of coaching relate directly to our work with organizations that feel compelled to integrate learning experiences and the ongoing work of their leaders in order to create sustainable momentum in a turbulent world. From this work, we have developed an appreciation for the distinction between individual leader development and collective leadership development.

Leader coaches are embedded in the same organizational system in which their coachees operate. They are by definition part of a systemic coaching experience, even if their organization has not yet recognized, articulated, or implemented such a development strategy. CCL's coaching framework of relationship, assessment, challenge, support, and results provides managers with a means of practicing the kind of coaching we've found to be effective not only in developing individual leaders but in creating the coaching communities necessary for sustainability and renewal.

PART TWO

COACHING FOR SPECIAL POPULATIONS

Every leader is unique. But CCL's research and the work of many others reveal that certain leaders stand apart in their development needs. They face particular issues and challenges. CCL's coaching principles include the belief that in order to be effective, coaches working with leaders who possess special perspectives or experiences often need additional skills, experiences, and knowledge. Most of CCL's original and ongoing research and practice in this area focus on two groups: women and African American leaders. Further experience and practice has helped CCL develop knowledge about global leadership issues and the impact of culture and the development needs of senior leaders, who occupy unique positions in their organizations.

Until now, CCL hasn't formally described how the different leadership development needs of those groups affect what additional perspectives, knowledge, or skills are required of anyone coaching one of these leaders. Part Two covers the implications for leadership development and effective coaching strategies for working with the following leader populations: women leaders, leaders of color, leaders whose culture may differ from the predominant culture (or where there are a multitude of cultures represented), and senior leaders.

We are aware that others—even some of our readers—may not share our perspective that each of these groups warrants separate discussion. Questions and criticism could be directed at us from a number of vantage points, including, but not limited to, these:

- Why separate these groups rather than writing an all-encompassing chapter on working with coachees belonging to a group that is different from the organizational norm (in gender, culture, race, position, or some other defining factor) or different from the coach?
- Effective coaching skills are universal and should be adequate to address gender, race, and cultural issues.
- Why limit discussion to these particular groups and not include generational differences, sexual orientation, and even social class issues?
- The groups discussed in this section reflect a North American- or U.S.-centric perspective.

We recognize that CCL is an American organization with an international presence, and so it sees the world from that vantage point. We also accept that the increasing globalization of the world's economy compels CCL (and other organizations in the leadership development field) to understand how globalization affects the leadership development process and to accept that no matter how valiant our efforts, we nonetheless define many of those issues from where we come from and what we know. For example, the experience and challenge of being an African American leader may be uniquely American, but the issue of race exists in other cultures. What the specific racial issues are and how they manifest within the leadership development process are defined differently depending on the organization, country, culture, and other contexts.

Some organizations prefer to address such issues as race, gender, and culture in the broader context of differences rather than singling out specific types of differences. CCL's experience tells us that placing these issues into a single category of differences minimizes the importance of those specific differences and can foster a one-size-fits-all approach to managing what are essentially dissimilar differences. That approach can result in misassumptions or simple neglect in recognizing how a particular difference is important to a leader's development. Highlighting the subtleties and distinguishing characteristics of specific differences provides key lessons for leader coaches and other coaches. We don't cover every possible difference but discuss those that are most familiar to us and for which we have conducted research or engaged as coaching and learning opportunities. The resulting knowledge can sensitize coaches to the complexity of coaching leaders who have distinguishing characteristics.

CHAPTER THREE

COACHING WOMEN LEADERS

Marian N. Ruderman
Patricia J. Ohlott

Much of the language of leadership today reflects thousands of years of history. It is couched in masculine terms, and classical theories of leadership tend to favor traditional male experiences. Organizations, however, are bumping up against a new reality: women now hold half of the managerial jobs in the United States (U.S. Census Bureau, 2003). This increase in numbers is not unique to the United States; women managers are growing in numbers in many other countries of the world as well (Davidson & Burke, 2004; Powell & Graves, 2003).

With the huge increase in numbers of women in managerial roles and the barriers to access falling significantly, women leaders require development techniques that address their particular development needs. Coaching is one relatively powerful means of developing leaders.

In this chapter, we look at coaching issues as they apply to the leadership development of high-level women managers. A primary message in the chapter is that for coaching to be most effective, it is critical that coaches understand that organizations are not gender-neutral institutions. As we wrote in *Standing at the Crossroads* (Ruderman & Ohlott, 2002), "Conventional career wisdom based on the experience of married white men does not readily apply to women, and women's careers cannot be seen simply as exceptions to the male experience. Women managers and those who work with them need to know how to navigate in the new terrain, and their organizations should know how to develop women in a landscape that is more accepting of them" (p. 4). In this chapter, we point out the differences, describe the terrain, and offer recommendations for coaching in this context. Our intent is to provide as much information as we know on the characteristics of women managers so that leader coaches are informed about women's development needs and capacities.

The content for this chapter is based on a review of the literature on coaching managers, interviews with six seasoned executive coaches, and our own research on the development of high-achieving women. We start with the gendered context of organizations and the expectations society places on women. We then look at the nature of differences between men and women—what are they and what, if anything, that implies for coaching. The succeeding sections look at the leadership development needs of women (in what ways women seek to develop), consider these factors when applying the CCL coaching framework to coaching women leaders, address unanswered questions regarding the coaching of women, and discuss some caveats about the application of knowledge about women leaders to the coaching arena. We end with a summary that focuses on what we know about coaching female leaders.

Gendered Organizations: Expectations and Realities

A basic assumption of coaching is that it is important to understand the coachee's environment, in particular the leadership and organizational issues the coachee faces. Without this knowledge, a coach is handicapped in helping the coachee figure out reasonable goals and courses of action. In the case of women, this means understanding that organizations are not gender neutral (Acker, 1998; Connell, 1999). Having been created by and for men, modern organizations have systems, policies, norms, and structures that favor the male life experience. Behaviors and values regarded as the norm at work tend to favor traits and characteristics traditionally associated with maleness and undervalue traits and characteristics traditionally associated with femininity. Coaches should be aware of the many ways women leaders may encounter a gendered environment (see Exhibit 3.1).

One implication of a gendered environment has to do with the description of standards of success in male terms. In most organizations today, tra-

EXHIBIT 3.1. IMPLICATIONS OF A GENDERED ENVIRONMENT.

- Standards of success are measured in male terms.
- Women are excluded from informal networks.
- Wage and salary structures are different for work that is traditionally male or female.
- Different norms for male and female managers determine acceptability of behaviors.
- Different norms apply to the demonstration of vulnerability.
- Ongoing discrimination exists for women in managerial roles.

ditionally male work such as the creation and marketing of goods is highly valued. Measures of success in organizations tend to be captured in terms of dollars, percentage return on investment, units sold, and so on. Dominance, aggression, and competitiveness are highly valued. Traditionally female work such as maintaining relationships, developing others, creating community, and managing tension tends to be undervalued (Fletcher, 1999). Characteristics such as team consciousness, persuasiveness, and good communication skills are considered desirable, but many organizations don't reward them in the same way as they reward forcefulness and aggression. Recognition tends to go to team leaders, not to the individuals who developed team players, resolved conflict, or generated commitment. Fletcher (1999) argues that collaborative skills, historically associated with women, tend to get "disappeared" in organizations; they are not valued in organizational reward systems or power distributions. In the words of one of the coaches we interviewed, "Male organizational culture has kind of dissed female patterns of success." There has been some change in recent years with the emphasis on emotional intelligence and the introduction of skills relating to emotional competence into the managerial lexicon; however, a bias against valuing the stereotypical skills of women remains. Organizations tend to reward the individual rainmaker to a greater degree than they value those who settle disputes or collaborate well with others.

The significance for coaching is that women may be in situations in which their organizations overemphasize male standards of behavior and devalue traditional female standards. Coaches need to be aware of the problems implicit in the tendency to undervalue the relational work a woman leader may engage in. In helping women managers figure out what will be effective in their environment, it is important for leader coaches to understand the degree to which the organization has a gendered weighting of various skills and competencies.

Another outcome of the gendered environment is that women tend to be isolated and excluded from formal networks (Davidson & Burke, 2004). In most organizations, males hold the key positions of power and authority. In the United States, men hold 92.7 percent of line officer jobs (Catalyst, 2000). A natural result of this is that women have to struggle to be seen as relevant, capable, and visible. According to a recent Catalyst survey (2004), 46 percent of women managers name exclusion from informal networks as a barrier to career advancement in contrast to 18 percent of men. Furthermore, Mainiero's study of the development of political skills of female executives found that women have a lack of role models for being powerful and political in a business setting (Mainiero, 1994; Catalyst, 2004).

One executive coach we interviewed mentions that when this issue is a problem for a particular coachee, she recommends the executive consider group coaching or a networking format. Joining a network of women provides female role models and can provide a validating environment, a safe and supportive venue for trying out new behaviors and actions.

Another feature of the gendered environment is a wage and salary structure that perpetuates different pay for work that is traditionally male or female. According to a congressional study released in 2002 (U.S. General Accounting Office), the wage gap between male and female managers deepened between 1995 and 2000. In the ten industries that employ 71 percent of all female workers, male managers earn more than women managers. This situation is not unique to the United States. According to a survey of forty-one countries, the average woman manager is paid less than her male colleagues (Wirth, 2002). The point for coaches is that organizations differentially reward men and women. The reinforcements for good performance are not the same.

Another indication of a gendered environment is that there are different norms determining the acceptability of behaviors for male and female managers. For example, leadership tasks demand both forceful and enabling behaviors (Kaplan, 1996). However, social norms dictate that different forceful and enabling behaviors are suitable for men and women. Men have greater latitude with regard to forceful behaviors. They can show control in a variety of ways. Women are more limited and face a narrow band of behaviors that will be perceived as appropriate (Morrison, White, & Van Velsor, 1992). For example, consider the way force is shown when it is mixed with emotion. If a man pounds his fist to make a point, he is seen as powerful. If a woman does this, she is often seen as emotional or weak. There are different explanations of the same behaviors for men and women. Stereotypes limit the range of behaviors women can demonstrate. An executive coach we know has had male clients described as "tough as nails," and it is meant to be a positive comment. However, she has seen women with similar behaviors described as "a bitch in heels," a much more negative descriptor.

There are also different norms regarding the behavioral demonstration of strong emotion. A woman who loses composure can be seen as losing credibility. A man who loses composure may be seen as sensitive. The point is that society offers different evaluations for the same behavior depending on whether the actor is male or female.

Coaches should also be sensitive to the ongoing prejudice and discrimination women face in managerial roles. Although there has been considerable advancement in this regard, women managers still mention prejudice as an organizational barrier. A study by Catalyst found that 46 percent of women in their managerial sample see gender-based stereotypes holding them back, while only 5 percent of men feel a similar restriction (Catalyst, 2004). Many prejudices are passed on as prevalent stereotypes that imply that women are unsuited for senior management. Studies of stereotypes have found that when managers are asked to describe women in general, men in general, and successful managers, the descriptions of men in general and successful managers are markedly similar. Both men in general and managers are described as forceful, having leadership ability, aggressive, desirous of responsibility, and able to get the job done. Women in general are characterized as deficient in these qualities (Schein, 1973, 1975, 2002). Stereotypes can get in the way when leadership potential is evaluated or staffing assignments are made on the basis of merit or ability (Ruderman & Ohlott, 1990). Prejudice prevents supervisors and peers from seeing others as they really are. In the face of uncertainty, decision makers filling top positions are likely to select individuals with whom they feel more comfortable, and thus they choose same-gender candidates (Powell, 1999).

Leader coaches should be aware that this climate exists in many organizations. This is particularly important when it comes to evaluating data about the coachee provided by others. The coach needs to consider if the data are colored by bias.

These realities are important because they delineate the way an organizational environment can be different for women and men. To be effective, it is important that the coach understand where the coachee is coming from, her challenges, and her perspectives. Coaches should carefully appraise the way gender dynamics play out in the coachee's particular situation. In certain circumstances, it may be appropriate for the coach to say, "This is not your problem, but the problem of the organization." In this situation, the coach needs to consider how to address this important point with the organization. Leader coaches need to examine their own assumptions and strategize as to the best way for the coachee to handle the situation.

There is no clear road map for how to be a successful woman leader. This is good in that it allows multiple paths to effectiveness. The downside is that the signposts on the road to success display considerable ambiguity, which can keep capable women from bringing their talents fully to bear on organizational challenges.

Gender roles in the more private sphere of home life are in flux as well (Powell & Graves, 2003). Women are still expected to be primary caregivers, but men are starting to take on this responsibility in greater numbers. Women receive competing messages from society: it's okay to become a manager; however, don't forget to take care of the sick, the elderly, and the children. These competing expectations make for a certain craziness in the environment that women leaders must deal with.

Organizations and society create complexities for women leaders that they do not create for men. Organizational and social dynamics are just as likely to arise as a result of stereotypes, misperceptions, prejudice, and discrimination as from any real differences in skills, behaviors, thoughts, and feelings between women and men. To be effective, a leader coach may need to ask a lot of questions about what the female coachee sees going on not only in her organization but also in her life and what the impact of working and living in those environments is (see Exhibit 3.2 for examples of these kinds of questions).

Gender Differences That May Affect Coaching

Other than the obvious biological and physical differences, are there other gender differences a coach should be aware of when coaching a woman leader? Knowledge of potential gender differences can help coaches decide whether to consider altering their coaching behaviors dependent on the gender of their

EXHIBIT 3.2. QUESTIONING GENDERED ENVIRONMENTS AND EXPECTATIONS.

- Generally, how are women treated in this organization?
- What are the obstacles women face in advancing in this organization?
- If you could create the perfect job environment, what would it be like?
- What is the reward structure in your organization?
- Do other women in the organization receive feedback similar to yours?
- Have you ever received this feedback before?
- Has anyone outside this organization given you this type of feedback?
- Is diversity valued in norms and rules, and are there consequences if it is not?
- What does the organizational chart look like? Who answers to whom, and who makes the decisions? What are the possibilities for professional advancement? (Talk about recruitment and hiring practices.)
- How do people feel a part of this organization? Are these feelings attended to and communicated? Do people who are "different" feel included or excluded?
- What are the roles you play, at home and at work? What are the expectations of you in these different roles? How do these expectations interact? Do they conflict in any way?
- What are your career goals? How supportive is your organization of them?

coachees. It can also help coaches better understand the issues that women managers raise, as well as identify appropriate strategies for addressing them.

Studies showing differences between men and women abound in both the popular and scientific press, but there is little to no research that directly examines the relationships between gender and executive coaching. The media tend to ignore the more common research that often shows no real gender distinctions and instead play up any minor differences that may be found. However, other domains of study suggest factors coaches may want to be aware of in their work with women leaders.

Biological and Neurological Differences

At a physiological level, biological and neurological differences between men and women have been identified. How these differences play out in terms of behavior is arguable, as behavior is also significantly influenced by social norms and expectations, upbringing, and situational context. The major cognitive gender differences have been declining significantly over the past several decades, including the traditional differences of superior male spatial ability (Linn & Hyde, 1989; Voyer, Voyer, & Bryden, 1995). Neurological studies have documented that men's and women's brains differ in the composition of their cerebral cortex, the part of the brain that is responsible for voluntary movements, perceptions of sensory input, and complex functions such as language, reasoning, memory, and learning. While men have a greater number of neurons in their cerebral cortex, women tend to have more neuropil, the tissue that fills the space between nerve cells and contains nerve cell processes that enable neurons to communicate with other nerve cells (de Courten-Myers, 1999). Neither gender variation is superior to the other; however, they may cause differences in how the brain functions. At this point, researchers do not completely understand how the structural differences influence brain function. It's possible that male and female brains work at a similar capacity but simply process information differently. For coaches, what is important is to recognize that not everyone processes information the same way. For example, some coachees prefer to see information presented visually in graphs and charts, and others prefer to read comments or to hear the feedback verbally before beginning to make sense of it. One of the coaches interviewed for this chapter observes that male coachees tend to compartmentalize the different roles in their lives and struggle to integrate the different pieces in order to grow. Female coachees handle the integrative work more easily, but it's more difficult for them to prioritize and set boundaries, and they risk becoming overwhelmed by the complexity of their lives.

A landmark study by Shelley Taylor and colleagues at UCLA suggests that women respond to stress with a cascade of brain chemicals that causes them to make and maintain friendships with other women (Taylor, 2002; Taylor et al., 2000). Prior to the publication of these findings, scientists generally believed that stress in people triggered a hormonal response that prepared the body to either stand and fight or flee as fast as possible. The UCLA research suggests that women under stress have a larger behavioral repertoire that is far broader than "fight or flight." Interestingly, when the hormone oxytocin is released as part of the stress response in a woman, it buffers the fight-or-flight response and encourages her to tend children and gather with other women instead. Engaging in this "tend-or-befriend" behavior actually stimulates the release of more oxytocin, which further counters stress and produces a calming effect. Men do not experience this same calming response because men produce testosterone in high levels when they're under stress, and testosterone seems to reduce the effects of oxytocin, while estrogen seems to enhance them.

It is likely that since women tend to respond to stressful situations by seeking social contact, many women will bring discussions of stressful events and situations into the coaching relationship. An awareness of the fact that women may respond differently to stress than men do may aid the coach in helping the woman articulate some creative strategies for dealing with the stress. Furthermore, the fact that women under stress turn to their relationships for comfort and support reinforces the idea that coaching may be a particularly appropriate developmental technique for women. One coach we spoke with notes that although we have worked hard to open up gender roles and opportunities for our daughters, powerful social pressures still encourage girls to ask for help, while boys continue to be rewarded for figuring things out on their own. Thus, many women have "a long experience of finding that other people can be useful as a sounding board, an opportunity to talk out what they're thinking, to get another point of view, so they have experience of that as a useful approach to self-development," suggesting that women may be more attuned to the potential benefits of a coaching relationship (personal communication, 2004). It is important for the coach to work with the coachee to find the most effective ways of seeking help in her organization. In an organization with a predominantly masculine, individual-achievement-oriented culture, seeking help may be viewed as a sign of weakness. In her study of how engineers used relational practices to enhance their own achievement, psychologist Joyce Fletcher (1999) describes an extremely effective practice of "relational asking," or asking for help in a way that calls for responsiveness in others and makes it likely a woman will get the help she needs. Rather than asking for help in an exploitive way, the coachee should make it clear how the other's expertise will add value not only to herself but perhaps also to others in her work group and even to the larger organization.

Psychological Differences

In the athletic arena, Holbrook and Barr (1997) argue that while coaching females is not significantly different from coaching males, important gender differences occur in some psychological domains that may affect the coaching relationship. They found differences in the manner in which women respond to positive feedback and noted that females seemed to value personal improvement over winning more than males do and regard team unity as a stronger motivating factor than males do. It's important to note that these differences had no relationship to the female athletes' skill levels, desire and willingness to work, capacity to learn, and mental toughness.

A 1997 report on sport and physical activity in girls' lives by the President's Council on Physical Fitness and Sports (cited in Stewart, n.d.) also concluded that there are more similarities between the genders than differences. However, the report identified specific differences, of which coaches should be mindful. It concluded that females in general are more internally motivated by self-improvement and goals related to team success and appear more motivated by an external environment that is cooperative, caring, sharing, and team oriented. It is not that female athletes want to win any less than male athletes do, but females may approach competition differently from male athletes. The report elaborates that in some competitive circumstances, female athletes place greater emphasis on fair play than do males. Furthermore, females have a tendency to blame themselves first for the poor performance when their team loses. Under similar circumstances, males appear to be more self- or ego-oriented and tend to be more "win at any cost" in their approach to sport. Males are more likely to break rules to achieve their goals and blame others (the referee, the weather, the coach) when they fail. The causes for the psychological differences are unknown. They could be gender related, but could also be influenced by cultural or social norms and expectations (Gill, 1994).

Understanding potential psychological differences by gender makes us aware that males and females may react to the same organizational event or situation differently and thus can help the coach better understand the issues the woman is raising about things going on in her organization.

Communication Differences

Numerous articles and books such as *You Just Don't Understand* (Tannen, 1990), *Women and Men Speaking* (Kramerae, 1981), *Women, Men, and Language* (Coates, 2004), *He Says, She Says* (Glass, 1993), and *Men Are from Mars, Women Are from Venus* (Gray, 1992) suggest that differences in communication preferences and styles can create conflict between the sexes socially, professionally, and intimately. Yet success in organizations depends in large part on a willingness and ability to understand and be understood. A complete discussion of potential differences in communication is beyond the scope of this chapter, so we will highlight aspects that may be most relevant to coaching (most of the research mentioned below is reviewed in greater detail in the books cited).

One of the basic communication differences between men and women is their reason for conversing and what they actually talk about. Jennifer Coates (2004) studied men-only and women-only discussion groups and found that when women talk to each other, they reveal a lot about their private lives. They also stick to one topic for a long time, let all speakers finish their sentences, and try to have everyone participate. Men rarely talked about their personal relationships and feelings but rather seemed to be in competition to prove themselves better informed on a variety of topics. Time after time, research has shown that in meetings, conferences, mixed-gender groups, and other public gatherings, men gain the floor more often and keep the floor for longer periods of time, regardless of their status in the organization. Men are more likely than women to interrupt the speaking of other people, and they are more likely to interrupt women than they are to interrupt other men. In turn, women are less likely to resist the interruption than are men.

In contrast, women strive to build connections and intimacy through their communications, and they seem to perform best in informal, collaborative ventures, where people jointly build ideas, operate on the same wavelengths, and have significant conversational overlaps. Their relational style of communication may put them at a disadvantage in the business world. It has been suggested that women tend to use a less assertive style of speech, using tag questions ("I really like this idea, don't you?"), disclaimers ("I may be wrong, but . . ."), and question statements ("Won't you create that report?") and even tending to change the inflection of their voices so that statements sound like questions even if they are not. Research has not confirmed that women and men differ in the frequency of their use of these forms. It's worth noting, however, that people perceive those who use such a deferential language style as having more personal warmth but less power. Differences in communication skills between men and women are common; they often cause men to think women are weak, indecisive, and uninformed and women to think men are not paying attention to what they are saying.

There is enormous diversity in communication style and practices within each gender group. Most women and many men have at their disposal a variety of conversational and speech skills, any one of which they may draw on, depending on the situation, their purposes, the roles they are playing, and the context. Furthermore, as with the other differences we have discussed, Canary and Hause's review (1993) of sex differences in communication found that the differences were generally quite small. However, a coach may want to explore with her female coachees the extent to which they fall into some of these traps and how they may need to adjust their communication styles.

An understanding of the physiological and psychological capacities of women and how they differ from men is essential to understand for effective coaching. To put that understanding into practice, leader coaches also need to know what the actual development needs of women are.

Development Needs of Women Leaders

To better understand the developmental issues confronting high-achieving women managers, CCL conducted a longitudinal study of sixty-one women leaders from nonprofit, government, and Fortune 500 organizations in the United States. These women were participants in CCL's The Women's Leadership Program, a five-day intensive development program. One key component of the program is an extended session with a coach in which women review their assessment data and work on career planning, goal setting, and development. The women in the study came from a variety of functional and organizational backgrounds and were at different stages in their careers; they ranged in age from twenty-six to fifty-eight, with the average being forty. Seventy-one percent were married or involved in a committed relationship, and half had children under the age of eighteen. (For a full report of the research, see Ruderman & Ohlott, 2002.)

We interviewed each of the women three times: shortly after they completed the program, six months later, and one year after the program. In each session, we asked them to talk about work or life issues with which they were currently struggling and to tell us how they were responding, what kind of progress they were making on their goals, obstacles they were encountering, and what strategies, if any, seemed to be working for them. To gain additional perspective, the women's career coaches were also interviewed.

From our analyses of the women's rich stories, we identified five prominent themes that guide the personal choices and trade-offs that women in leadership roles typically confront: authenticity, connection, controlling their own destiny, wholeness, and self-clarity. They also reflect issues that are likely to come up at some point during a coaching relationship with a woman and can help the leader coach understand the dilemmas a woman is grappling with at different points in her life (see Exhibit 3.3).

Authenticity

The first of the five themes looks at the degree to which daily actions and behaviors are in concert with deeply held values and beliefs. A woman who is authentic has a good understanding of her priorities and emotions. Authenticity is important to development because adults learn best when they feel they can be authentic in that setting. It is difficult to grow as a leader if you feel you must hide your true values, styles, and preferences. Women managers in our study lamented that it was difficult to develop their own style in an organization that prescribes a particular style of leadership. Some women who worked for organizations with an authoritarian, command-and-control style of leadership found it particularly difficult if their personal nature was more collaborative. Many organizations measure effectiveness by individual achievements. These organizations undervalue a collaborative relational style, making women who engage in these behaviors feel as if they are behaving counter to standard practice. Women who regard this as their primary leadership style have a hard time feeling both effective and authentic in traditional organizations.

Connection

In a general way, *connection* refers to the need to be close to other human beings: family, friends, community, and coworkers. Connection is important to the development of women leaders. In fact, several psychologists argue that

EXHIBIT 3.3. DEVELOPMENTAL THEMES FOR WOMEN.

- Authenticity: Having alignment between inner values and daily behaviors
- Connection: The need to be close to other human beings
- Agency: Being an active agent in your own destiny
- Wholeness: The desire to unite and integrate different life roles
- Self-clarity: Understanding one's own motives, behaviors, and values

an inner sense of connection is the central organizing force in women's development (Jordan, Kaplan, Miller, Stiver, & Surrey, 1991; Miller & Stiver, 1997). Many of the women in CCL's study did not have the close relationships they desired and sought to develop greater intimacy in their personal lives. Women continue to be isolated in their organizations and simply want to belong to a community of women with whom they can share experiences about similar challenges.

For some women, it may be particularly complex to sort out the source of their isolation. The task of the coach is to help the woman figure out how much of her lack of connection is due to the fact that she may be the only woman at her level or excluded from male networks and how much of her isolation has become self-imposed as she distances herself from others, perhaps because of her increasing focus on her career and her drive to be successful and effective. Once the sources of isolation are understood, appropriate strategies for dealing with the problem can be identified.

This lack of connection for women is particularly striking in the light of the research on stress discussed earlier (Taylor, 2002; Taylor et al., 2000). Recall that this research showed that during times of stress, women coped by exhibiting "tend-or-befriend" behaviors. Women who lacked these close connections were at a significant disadvantage in times of stress. Gae Walters (2002) suggests that leaders become isolated in two ways: through externally created conditions and through self-imposed ones.

Agency

The third theme is the desire to control one's own destiny. This is one of the strongest needs of high-achieving women. Psychologists refer to this quality of acting assertively on one's own behalf as *agency* (Bakan, 1966). Traditional psychological models say that agency and connection are fundamental human drives. Historically, agency has been associated with the qualities traditionally considered masculine, while connection has been associated with the qualities considered feminine. Leadership positions require both. For some women, their need to develop agency became apparent when they were stuck in a difficult situation and needed to take a risk or some other decisive action to resolve it. For others, it became an issue when they needed to negotiate in a political climate or act as an authority during challenging organizational times. Sometimes a woman employing the behaviors of agency (assertiveness, self-promotion, or questioning practices that do not meet needs) is seen as inappropriately aggressive. A man using the same behaviors, however, is seen as powerful. It can be a challenge to develop effective behaviors of agency when others in the organization do not view the behaviors in the light in which they were intended.

Wholeness

The fourth theme influencing the development of women leaders is that of wholeness, the desire to feel complete and integrated as a full human being. According to Still (1993), integrating various life roles is a driving force in the behavior of many high-achieving women. The insensitivity of organizational life to caregiving needs makes this hard to achieve. Women strive to address the needs of multiple life roles to fulfill the desires of their personal and professional lives. Most organizations, however, are built on a male model from the 1950s that is based on the norm that the ideal worker gives work a higher priority than all other aspects of life. This prevailing norm makes it difficult for women professionals to address their other life needs.

Despite the many ways organizations deter women from having a whole life, wholeness is beneficial for both the organization and its individual employees. It has been demonstrated that there is a relationship between multiple roles and managerial performance such that as commitment to nonwork roles increases, so does effectiveness in the managerial role (Ohlott, Graves, & Ruderman, 2004; Ruderman, Ohlott, Panzer, & King, 2002). Furthermore, this is not the only positive outcome associated with a whole life. These same studies also found that commitment to multiple roles was associated with psychological well-being in terms of life satisfaction and self-acceptance. Litwin and Michael (2001) note that women have a more holistic perspective, so coaching women tends to be more inclusive of whole life issues.

Self-Clarity

The fifth and final development need is the desire for self-clarity. The women leaders in our study expressed a need to understand themselves within the context of the world in which they operate. They wanted to know more than just how others see their strengths and weaknesses; they wanted to see themselves in the context of the many ways organizations treat men and women differently.

They struggled to understand how stereotypes and perceptions of women influenced how these colleagues saw them.

The desire for self-understanding is important for both women and men. Self-clarity allows women to grow by enabling them to recognize their values so as to live authentically, improve their ability to connect with others, enable their own agency, and allow them to make choices that produce feelings of wholeness.

Many women reported that it was difficult to develop self-clarity in an organization with a climate that is hostile toward women. Such an environment makes it hard for a person to get an accurate picture of how others see her because she will doubt the validity of her feedback. For example, if she receives negative feedback, she has to determine if the feedback is an honest reflection of her performance or if it is colored by the giver's issues with women. Without trustworthy feedback, it is difficult to plan or to understand how to be more effective.

Applying Developmental Themes to Coaching

These five development needs are extremely important to women leaders. The types of needs are similar to those elaborated in theories of development based on studies of male executives over the years. However, they differ in how they are expressed. Women do not progress through them in a linear fashion; different themes will be salient at different points in one's life dependent on, among other things, career and family stage and structure. We believe that an understanding of these development needs can provide coaches with a means for exploring the developmental issues and goals of the women with whom they work.

A coach can use this understanding to open up the discussion concerning issues the woman currently struggles with, to help articulate goals, and to identify strategies toward realizing those goals. The coachee can use an understanding of these issues to articulate the issues that seem most relevant and pressing to her. Together the coach and coachee can generate goals and strategies to achieve greater effectiveness and satisfaction in these areas. Nancy Adler (2002) suggests that the privacy and supportive advocacy of the coaching session allow a woman to acknowledge that she is uncertain or just doesn't know. In her view, the coaching dialogue "can foster a depth of questioning" that encourages women to explore alternatives "that reach beyond the accepted 'wisdom' of successful men who have worked worldwide with other men"

(p. 367). We hope that sharing the wisdom of these successful women will support both the coach and coachee in their dialogue.

Women Leaders and the CCL Coaching Framework

Although both women and men benefit from coaches who apply the fundamentals of coaching effectively, there are several nuances to take into account when applying CCL's coaching framework to the development of women leaders. The relationship, use of assessment, challenge, and support, and results may unfold differently for women than for men. Each of these aspects of the coaching process works to trigger new outlooks or actions on the part of the coachee.

Relationship

Relationships are central to a good coaching experience. The rapport between coach and coachee, a collaborative stance, and commitment combine to facilitate leader development (Ting & Hart, 2004). Coaches use the safe and supportive relationship they cocreate with their coachees to establish an environment for growth and learning. When considering gender in the context of a coaching relationship, there are two key points to be mindful of: (1) coaching may be a particularly useful method for facilitating the development of women (Litwin & Michael, 2001), and (2) sexual tension between a male coach and female coachee can get in the way of forming an effective coaching alliance.

Research on girls and women suggests that coaching may be a particularly appropriate methodology of leadership development for women leaders. Relationships are often a catalyst for growth for women. Consider the several similarities between the principles of coaching and the tenants of relational theory, an approach to understanding the growth, development, and effectiveness of women. Jean Baker Miller (1976, 1986) and Carol Gilligan (1982) developed relational theory, arguing that the central mode of growth for girls and women is through connection with others. In other words, safe and authentic relationships are key to growth for females. According to relational theory (Miller & Stiver, 1997), development in women is fostered by mutual empathy and empowerment. This suggests that coaching may be especially well suited for the development of women.

Mutual empathy means that both parties are engaged together in sharing their thoughts and feelings. Being understood and understanding others creates a flow of ideas and movement toward growth. A good coach demonstrates mutual empathy by being fully engaged in the shared experience. What's especially meaningful for leader coaches is that they and their coachees can be at different levels in the organization and still be mutually engaged. Both parties don't have to draw the same outcomes from the relationship. Power differentials don't preclude mutual engagement. But that's not to say they don't exist. The implication for coaches is that it is important to be aware of the power differentials between themselves and their coachee. In order to be mutually empowering, it is important to be attentive to the dynamics of power. Coaches should be conscious of working with coachees jointly and not directing or ordering them.

A second factor to take into account when considering the coaching relationship has to do with sexual tension that may enter in the relationship when the coach is male and the coachee is female. While rapport remains an essential ingredient for developing a trusting relationship, rapport between individuals of different genders carries different implications. Although we came across no literature discussing this issue, interviews with some of our coaches suggested that it is something to be mindful of. Psychotherapists discuss techniques for dealing with the seductive patient (Klopfer, 1974).

Although coaching relationships don't approach the intimacy of psychotherapeutic ones, it is likely that sexual dynamics can still have an impact. Coaches (both male and female) need to be conscious of the unspoken sexual dynamics. For example, consider body language in sexual terms. Coaching is a professional arrangement, so it is important to take care not to lapse into body language that might appear seductive to the coachee. One female coach told us that she observed a male coach stretching out in front of a female client in a seductive way. A male coach told us that when he is coaching a woman, he is conscious of how he sits and the jokes he makes. He makes sure that he does not sit between the coachee and the door. He avoids humor that could be misconstrued in a sexual way. He does whatever he can to show the coachee that he is safe. Another coach told us that it is important to be mindful of where to meet the coachee, particularly if it is a dinner meeting. It's important to clarify the boundaries of the coaching relationship at the start to reduce the ambiguity that can enter into a male-female coaching relationship.

Another point, and this is relevant in the case when a man is coaching a woman, is to be mindful of the gender expectations for men in our society. Men are expected to play the dominant role, to be in charge. This doesn't work well in a coaching relationship. A male coach may need to work to get past expectations of the female coachee that he take charge and give her advice as to how to fix the problem. Thus, coaches, particularly male coaches, may need to be mindful of and vigilant about honoring the principle of working to the coachee's agenda and taking a collaborative approach in the relationship. One male coach told us that he is very purposeful in explaining the egalitarian nature of coaching early in this relationship. Again, we see that careful discussion and continuous review of those conditions help to set up useful boundaries for cross-gender coaching.

Assessment, Challenge, and Support

The principles of assessment, challenge, and support sit at the core of CCL's individual leader development processes. When it comes to coaching, they constitute the primary methods by which coaches facilitate development. The principles of assessment, challenge, and support work well for both men and women. Nonetheless, there are some nuances in the application of these principles that coaches should keep in mind.

Assessment. There are two primary factors to be mindful of in the assessment of women leaders. The first has to do with the selection of the instruments themselves and the second with the dynamics associated with ratings on a 360-degree evaluation.

When selecting instruments to use with women (or with any other defined population, for that matter), there are three key considerations. The first has to do with the appropriateness of the assessment content. If the assessment is to be used with women, it is critical that the instrument rest on a model that applies to women as well as to men. A competency instrument or personality inventory designed with a male-only sample is gender biased. A second factor is the validity of the instrumentation. If the instrument has not been validated on a sample including a large number of women, it is not prudent to use it. The last consideration has to do with the norms for the instrument. Many assessment devices provide scores in relationship to a normative base. This helps the recipient understand how she is doing compared to others, which adds to the power of the feedback. Clearly it is important for an instrument to use a normative group that is appropriate for the individuals being assessed. Women may be interested in getting feedback on how they compare to women as well as to male managers. Many assessment instruments, but not all, provide these data. Coaches need to be equipped to answer these questions about how women score on the instruments used.

Rating dynamics can emerge as an issue in the assessment phase of coaching. Evaluations using 360-degree feedback are quite commonplace. These involve an individual being rated by her subordinates, peers, and superiors as well as doing a self-assessment. For feedback to have the desired effects, the recipient must believe that the data are credible, important, and useful (Dalton & Hollenbeck, 1996). Feedback that the coachee sees as accurate and honest can be a catalyst for change; feedback that the coachee sees as biased can be dismissed.

The expected response when managers receive positive feedback is that they see it as indicating an area of strength. The expected response for negative feedback is that managers see it as signaling a need for change. There is, however, the potential for this process to go awry should recipients believe negative feedback is shaped by prejudice and bias (Cox, 1993). Women managers face the complexity of figuring out whether prejudice or discrimination has influenced their feedback. Managers are not able to learn from discrepancies between self-views and the views of others if they believe prejudice is involved. Coaches of women need to be sensitive to this point and help women coachees grapple with figuring out if the data are a realistic assessment. It may be easy for clients to reject negative data as biased. The coach needs to help the coachee get past this way of avoiding the data and assist the client in finding the message in the feedback. Questions that reflect an understanding of the client's perspective but challenge the assumption that negative feedback is solely due to bias are helpful.

If the coach collects data face-to-face through interviews, it is essential that the coach work to clarify responses as much as possible so as to overcome any possible biases or the perception of bias. Good interviewing practices such as asking for examples are a must. Also, using his or her own observations as a coach is an important way to examine observations from the data. The key point is that the coach uses the data from others to help the client identify significant issues. One of the challenges for the leader coach who chooses to personally engage in a robust assessment process that includes interviews is eliciting honest feedback. Probing further in the interview for subtle bias might cause the respondent to become wary or closed. Yet not seeking further clarification can render the data less useful to the coachee. One option for leader coaches to consider is using written responses that are kept anonymous. Although this does not fully overcome the concern stated, it might allow more freedom and spontaneity of response. One client whose senior executives engaged in this level of coaching found that written responses provided a good compromise to the potential chilling effect that their direct interviewing might have on the process.

Not only is it important to look at the ratings of others in terms of gender, it is also important to consider the self-ratings from the perspective of gender. Women have a reputation for being more adept at self-criticism than men are. Research evidence backs this up: women tend to rate themselves less positively than do men (Fletcher, 1999). Women are less susceptible to the tendency to rate themselves with leniency. This means that women tend to have higher agreement with the ratings of others than men do (Alimo-Metcalfe, 1998; London & Wohlers, 1991). In other words, the self-ratings of women are more congruent with the ratings from others than are the self-ratings of men.

The other two elements of assessment, the person and context, have been touched on throughout this chapter in discussing the importance of understanding the female leader's perspective, experiences, and perceptions about the organizational orientation toward gender. Values, aspirations, and beliefs underlie the essence of any individual. Those issues are embedded in developmental themes and may become magnified for female leaders. Each female coachee has her unique needs. However, the developmental themes outlined in this chapter can serve as a useful guide to understanding more fully the person who is a coachee.

Challenge. A key role of the coach is to challenge the coachee to better understand her situation and what is keeping her from reaching her goals. There is no direct research addressing whether there are different approaches for challenging female versus male leaders in a coaching relationship. Challenges can be generated in any number of ways. The key factor relating to challenge that coaches of women need to keep in mind is that women experience organizational life differently than men do. Organizational realities create a different environment for women. These realities can create obstacles for women that men don't experience—for example, isolation, having to fit into a man's world, or the difficulty of integrating work with the rest of life. The key point for the coach is to take these into account when challenging the coachee to figure out what is holding her back. There may be some issues that a woman cannot realistically address because they stem so strongly from the environment. These are issues that a coach may want to consider bringing up with the organization at large.

Support. Support can be of particular importance to women coachees. At the uppermost levels of organizations, women are more isolated than men and naturally get less support. Women are less embedded in the key organizational networks and may have less access to peer support due to their relative isolation. Consider the example of a top woman executive in a key meeting in which she is the only woman attending with eight men. In the men's room during a break, the men continue a conversation about an important issue. Our woman executive is left out. When the meeting formally continues, she has to ask for an agreement that these sorts of issues be brought back into the room where the discussion is being held and not discussed in the men's room. This example illustrates some of the isolation that women still experience in organizations. Obviously men need support too, but to the extent women may be left out of some exchanges, it becomes even more important that they get support through the coaching relationship.

Many coaches supplement the support they offer with the recommendation that women get involved in some type of networking group. Networks may be industry specific, regional, or organization specific. They function as a mechanism for helping women get both informational and emotional support. One way to provide coaching support is to help coachees access resources such as networks within and outside the organization.

Results

Measuring progress is important for both the coach and coachee, regardless of gender. Coaches are committed to helping the people they coach set goals and assess progress against those goals. One of the keys in understanding progress is to consider the coachee's view of success. In general terms, men and women view success differently (Sturges, 1999). Men have a tendency to define success in terms of quantifiable outcomes: money, status, and possessions. Women, in contrast, use more subjective indicators (how life is generally going). In addition, men tailor their definition of success to the workplace, and women tend to have a more holistic orientation.

Coaches of women (and men) need to be clear up front as to what constitutes success. It is important that women clients measure results in accordance with their own values and priorities. Coaches may very well discover that of the four yardsticks for results that our framework offers—behavioral, performance, business, and personal growth—the last may hold the most meaning for many female leaders.

Unanswered Questions

This discussion of coaching the female executive raises a number of important questions. One has to do with whether executive coaching is an effective leadership development technique for women. Relational theory (Miller, 1986; Miller & Stiver, 1997) suggests that coaching, with its emphasis on a safe, empowering, collaborative relationship, would be a particularly useful leadership development technique. However, the fact remains that there has been little research on the efficacy of coaching for women—or men for that matter (Kampa & White, 2002; Kampa-Kokesch & Anderson, 2001; Wasylyshyn, 2003). The studies that do exist suggest that coaching shows some promising outcomes, but it is premature to draw definite conclusions about the use of coaching for women. Nonetheless, coaching is growing in popularity as a tool for development for the managerial and executive ranks. At the Center for Creative Leadership, our own data suggest that 46 percent of the new coaching contracts we developed in a recent one-year period were for women coachees.

Given the growth of executive coaching as a developmental technique, an important question is whether it makes a difference if a woman's coach is male or female. There is little research on this question. Hall, Otazo, and Hollenbeck (1999) argue that gender in general doesn't make a difference if the coach is qualified. Gegner (1997) found weak associations between gender and outcomes of a coaching relationship. All six of the seasoned coaches interviewed for this chapter said that the key point is that the coach is able to develop a strong connection with the coachee; this can happen regardless of gender. Coaches and coachees relate in terms of common styles and interests. Although some women coaches may connect with coachees around gender, this is one of many attributes they may use in establishing a relationship. The coaches interviewed stressed that being seen as helpful, empathetic, and trustworthy trumps gender as a basis for a good coach-coachee pairing. Strong coaching bonds can be developed between both male-female and female-female pairings.

This chapter explores some potential issues for coaches to be aware of when working with a woman leader and has highlighted some potential differences in coaching a woman versus coaching a man. However, leader coaches should be mindful that the knowledge about this subject has its limits. For example, many (if not most) of the psychological and physiological gender differences we discuss are relatively small. Furthermore, in most cases, the variation among women is greater than the variation between men and women. Women do not comprise a homogeneous group, so leader coaches should exercise caution in making assumptions or inferences about any individual woman's beliefs and values, situation, experience, or motivation. In addition, most of our information and data are based on studies of white, American women, and we suspect that adding race or nationality to the mix would introduce different issues. Thus, it is important for the coach to keep in mind that people have multiple identities, recognizing that gender may be only one identity of many and that it may not even be the most salient identity to any given woman at any particular time. The ways that race and gender or gender and ethnicity interact are issues a coach needs to explore with coachees on an individual basis. Finally, the process of gendering organizations changes over time. What appears to be gendered for one generation may not be for the next. In other words, the context keeps changing, so leader coaches need to keep reevaluating and revising their knowledge and how they apply it.

What We Know for Sure

As we conclude, several points bear emphasis. Although a definitive study of coaching the female leader has not been conducted, our review of existing knowledge based on the literature and the tacit knowledge of seasoned coaches yields some suggestions.

Women and men experience organizational environments differently. There is ample evidence that the two genders encounter different challenges and obstacles. Although organizational realities are changing, traditional organizational environments still give advantages to men. The implication is that coaches need to understand and help the women they coach understand if gender dynamics play a role in their experience of the organization.

Actual documented differences between men and women are few and far between. There are neurological differences suggesting that men and women may appreciate different tactics for understanding data and some biochemical differences suggesting that men and women use different strategies in responding to stress. Psychologically, women are more motivated by self-improvement and goals related to team success. Differences in communication styles may cause women to be misunderstood or underestimated in organizations.

The development needs of high-achieving women can be described in five themes: authenticity, connection, agency, wholeness, and self-clarity. These themes can be helpful to coaches in opening up discussion around issues the client struggles with and can help the client articulate goals and identify action strategies.

CCL's coaching framework is relevant to women, and coaching appears to be a particularly appropriate leadership development technique because it uses a relationship to foster growth. When applying the assessment part of the coaching model, it is important to take into account that prejudice against women and stereotypes add some ambiguity to the interpretation of assessment data. The challenge and support aspects of the model apply in a way very similar to men, the only caveat being that women may be experiencing extra challenges from the environment, on top of the challenges introduced by coaching, that men do not. There is also some evidence that men and women define success differently, and that may influence the goal-setting process and monitoring of results.

The coaching field has not adequately looked at the question as to whether coaching is an effective leadership development technique for women. Nor has it empirically examined whether the gender of the coach has an impact on the coaching experience. From the information we gathered in our own research, through our interviews with coaches, and from other of relevant studies, the guidelines summarized in Exhibit 3.4 point to an effective coaching strategy.

Although we have identified several possible gender differences that may influence coaching, bear in mind that the variations among women are greater than the differences between the sexes. Treat anyone you might coach as an individual. Do not assume a female coachee has "women's issues." Beware of your own expectations and stereotypes of women.

EXHIBIT 3.4. A SUMMARY OF GUIDELINES FOR COACHING WOMEN LEADERS.

- Men and women may react to the same organizational event or situation differently. Organizational environments are gendered. Coaches need to understand both real and stereotypical gender differences, and they need to integrate that knowledge with their understanding of the organizational context to help the coachee understand her situation and so she can develop more effective behaviors and coping strategies.
- Leader coaches who examine and understand the patterns that underlie the dilemmas and choices that women make in their lives can be effective in developing leadership capacity.
- Coaches can help the female coachee figure out how a lack of connection is linked to her being the only woman at her level, to being excluded from male networks, and how much is self-imposed as she distances herself from others, perhaps because of her focus on career and her drive to be successful.
- Be aware of the power differential between yourself and your coachee. The leader coach should work with the coachee, not direct or order her.
- If you're a male leader coach working with a female coachee, be especially mindful of the gender expectations for men in our society.
- Assessment instruments should rest on a model that applies to women as well as men. They should also have been validated on a sample that includes a large number of women and make comparisons that are appropriate for the individuals being assessed.
- Coaches of women need to be sensitive to the fact that women managers face a hurdle of figuring out whether prejudice or discrimination has influenced the feedback they receive.

Coach's Bookshelf

Catalyst, Inc., http://www.catalystwomen.org/.

Families and Work Institute, http://www.familiesandwork.org/.

Gray, J. (2004). *Men are from Mars, women are from Venus: The classic guide to understanding the opposite sex.* New York: Perennial.

Kolb, D. M., Williams, J., & Frohlinger, C. (2004). *Her place at the table: A woman's guide to negotiating five key challenges to leadership success.* San Francisco: Jossey-Bass.

Patterson, V. (2003). Breaking the glass ceiling: What's holding women back? *CareerJournal.com/Wall Street Journal,* Nov. 11, 2003. Retrieved September 28, 2004, from http://careercenter.nd.edu/article.php?articleid=493&&cwebmenu=alumni.

Perrault, M. R., & Irwin, J. K. (1996). *Gender differences at work: Are men and women really that different? Research report.* Agora Hills, CA: Advanced Teamware.

Ruderman, M. N., & Ohlott, P. J. (2003, Winter). What women leaders want. *Leader to Leader, 31,* 41–47.

Simmons College Center for Gender in Organizations, http://www.simmons.edu/gsm/cgo/.

Sloan Work and Family Research Network, http://ecsvl532.bc.edu/.

CHAPTER FOUR

COACHING LEADERS OF COLOR

Ancella B. Livers

The newspapers rolled off the giant press as if they were cards being spread across the table by the local card shark. Each paper covered the bottom two-thirds of the next, neatly folded, each headline shrilly portraying that day's news again and again. It was the color picture at the top half of the paper that drew the press operator's attention. Color on the front page was a recent development for this daily newspaper. While the image was easy enough to make out—a tree in a park with a child on a swing—the reds, blues, and yellows used to create the color palette were not in sync. Consequently, instead of a brown tree trunk, the tree and child seemed to be blurred multicolored images of themselves. The nuances of the photo were lost as the press pushed to service a new reality (the public's appetite for and expectation of color photos) through a process designed for fast black and white printing. It would take the press operator's growing understanding of color printing and the fine yet important distinctions needed when handling it to enable the newspaper to make color pictures a regular part of its daily presentation.

The situation of people of color in organizational life shares some similarity with this newspaper's early experience with color pictures. Although the experiences of people of color are akin to those of their white colleagues, there are some distinctions that throw their experiences slightly out of focus, blurring their chances of being seen for who they really are and what they really can do—throwing them out of sync like the colors in that newspaper's front-page photo. This is especially observable when illuminated by an environmental condition within organizations called miasma. *Miasma* is defined as the extra burdens and potentially negative consequences that pollute the corporate environment in which people of color perceive and are perceived. It is an extra layer of challenge for the person of color and can be a major obstacle (Livers & Caver, 2003).

This chapter deals with the issues and problems faced by people of color in the North American workplace, particularly in the United States. While the chapter looks at a largely U.S. phenomenon, it has larger implications in that it deals with the kinds of issues often faced by nondominant groups who are working and living in a dominant group context. In such contexts, issues of differential power, status, and experience are often at play. Although these matters may look behaviorally different in other cultures or through the lens of other differences, questions or topics around bias, respect, trust, and perspective may provide an unspoken undercurrent or spoken need to be managed, addressed, mitigated, or acknowledged in a coaching relationship, regardless of the circumstance.

Such intrusive obstacles drain productivity. With more and more people of color entering the workplace, leaders and organizations cannot risk the consequences of a substantial portion of their employees being sidelined because of lack of understanding of their capabilities and their perspectives. Very often it is in the intimate setting of a coaching relationship that these issues get worked out. Leader coaches (professional and internal HR coaches as well) find themselves experiencing new challenges and rewards as people of color comprise an increasing percentage of their coachees.

In this chapter, people of color are defined as African American, Hispanic, and Asian (both Asian American and Asians working in the United States). This chapter refers to their general experiences as a group that has not received equitable treatment in the workplace. Although many people who are not of color now assume that the workplace is mostly color-blind, a recent report strongly disputes that notion: "For many workers—particularly African American workers—an equitable workplace has proved elusive" (Dixon, Storen, & Van Horn, 2002, p. 1). This report goes on to say, "Almost forty years since the passage of the Civil Rights Act of 1964 that mandated legal equality for minorities, race remains a major barrier among Americans in the workplace, both in how people perceive and experience discrimination and what they want done about it" (p. 1).

Obviously those who call themselves people of color will have identity issues that transcend their membership in the wider group. African Americans daily confront the legacy of slavery and discrimination. Hispanics and Asians also face discrimination, along with cultural and language differences that are different from each other but can create particular barriers for each. There are tensions between and among these groups as they compete with one another for economic and social space. The one thing that unites them is that they have been judged, perceived, and treated according to race and skin color.

This chapter explores the impact of race and culture on those who coach people of color and on the coachees themselves. The intent is to take into account the fact that before leader coaches can effectively coach African American managers, Hispanic managers, or Asian managers, they must be aware of the environment and the special challenges that managers of color face. Concepts like trust and responsibility have different meanings and implications for people of color. The effects of miasma are ever present. A baseline understanding of these notions is key. Armed with this information, the leader coach should be prepared to build an effective coaching relationship that recognizes how discriminatory issues affect development and performance.

Starting with demographic information about the explosive growth of people of color in management positions, this chapter continues by explaining the concept of miasma and some of the issues associated with it that have special significance for coaches. The chapter looks at the impact that race may have on the coaching process (Livers & Caver, 2003, p. 4). Furthermore, it explores some of the issues people of color may bring to the workplace and some strategies coaches can use to make the coaching relationship deeper, more effective, and results driven. It also discusses the implications of adapting CCL's coaching framework to people of color. Finally, it ends with some statements to keep in mind about the mind-set of the coach who coaches people of color.

Much of the material gathered in this chapter comes from several interviews that my colleague Keith Caver and I have done with other coaches, both white and people of color. Their views and direct quotes are interwoven throughout the chapter. The expertise of these executive coaches is used to tease out skills and strategies leader coaches can use when working with people of color. The names of these coaches are not revealed, but their identities according to racial or cultural group are provided.

The Changing Workplace

For several years, the percentage of leaders of color in the workplace has been increasing. Mitra Toossi projects the following changes for the years 2000 to 2050: "The share of white non-Hispanics is anticipated to decrease from 73 percent in 2000 to 53 percent in 2050. Over the same period, Hispanics are expected to more than double their share from 11 percent in 2000 to 24 percent of the labor force in 2050. Blacks also are expected to increase their share, from 12 percent in 2000 to 14 percent in 2050. Asians, the fastest-growing group in the labor force, are projected to increase their share from 5 percent to 11 percent between 2000 and 2050" (2002, p. 16).

These are figures for the entire labor force, but the figures are also expected to rise proportionately for those people of color engaged in managerial positions (Table 4.1). For African Americans alone, the 2000 census reported that 17.7 percent of black men and 25.2 percent of black women were employed in managerial or professional roles. A significant rise in these numbers is reflected in Department of Labor statistics, which report that in 2004, 21.7 percent of black men and 30.6 percent of black women were employed in management, professional, and related occupations (U.S. Department of Labor, 2005, p. 208). Add to that the increasing numbers of Hispanics and Asians pouring out of America's universities and professional schools, who are now entering the workplace in record numbers. The Department of Labor statistics for 2004 show that of all employed Asians, 46.3 percent of men and 43.8 percent of women occupy professional positions. For those of Hispanic

TABLE 4.1. PEOPLE OF COLOR IN MANAGEMENT, PROFESSIONAL, AND RELATED OCCUPATIONS, 2004.

	Percentage in Professional Jobs	
Total in Workforce	**Men**	**Women**
Hispanic or Latino: 17,372,000	14	22.4
Black: 14,739,000	21.7	30.6
Asian: 5,756,000	46.3	43.8

Source: U.S. Department of Labor (2005).

or Latino ethnicity, 14 percent of men and 22.4 percent of women hold professional positions (U.S. Department of Labor, 2005, p. 209).

Added to the growing proportion of professional workforce represented by people of color and the associated coaching challenges for leaders to develop their potential is the challenge of helping them develop into leadership and executive roles. With a traditional workplace of primarily white managers who have shared a common culture of how to act, how to lead, and how a business should be run, these new leaders may present themselves and be seen as "nontraditionals," bringing differing cultural and racial perspectives. Their presence, their numbers, and their influence are bound to challenge longstanding norms, causing some reflection in the organization about how misunderstanding can be handled and how conflict can be understood and dealt with. Diversity professionals try to parse out the issues and develop programs that at least can get at the fundamental points of friction. But where matters become significant for those of color is through the many relationships they will have over the course of their career. One of those, the coaching relationship, can play a critical role in that individual's development as a leader. The coach and the coachee first have to cut through the thick fog of misunderstanding, misperceptions, distortions, and degraded communication that often accompany the career of a person of color. It's a kind of miasma, and before any coaching relationship gets to basic performance issues, an understanding of its dynamics and consequences is essential (Livers & Caver, 2003).

Miasma: A Thick Fog

"Maybe it will happen today and maybe it won't," a black manager might muse, referring to the possibility of misunderstanding that is always lurking. She is familiar, as are all other people of color (indeed, all people who are different from the traditional norm), with the phenomenon of miasma in the workplace. Miasma operates like a low-lying cloud that surrounds those who have to bear extra burdens and exert extra energy in ways that are not related to the work itself. It is responded to with wariness, self-defensiveness, and an expenditure of time and energy that is counterproductive.

When people of color work with others or organizations that have low tolerance for individual or cultural difference, the resulting miasma becomes denser and more difficult to maneuver. Increased miasma can lead to degradation of communication, interpersonal interactions, and work performance as individuals become more guarded and less participatory in the organization. Conversely, in organizations with a higher degree of acceptance for the differences of others, the miasma is less dense and more easily managed. In these instances, people of color benefit from enhanced recognition and the valuing of their unique contributions. This inverse relationship can be seen in Figure 4.1.

Miasma is seen most often when there is introduction of difference into a situation and there is a response to that difference. Of course, the salient points will differ for blacks, Hispanics, and Asians, but the impact of the consequences on their group will be similar. For instance, if the issue of cultural identity for any particular individual of color is introduced into a workplace situation, it can become a flash point that can create an environment for misunderstanding and distortion for his or her entire cultural or racial group.

The implications for coaches are many. Miasma is not simply an extra hurdle to confront before getting on to the workplace and leadership issues that all managers face. Rather, it is a reality that can distort the manner in which organizations or individuals perceive and judge the skills and capabilities of people of color as they interact in the workplace and engage in leadership issues.

FIGURE 4.1. THE DIFFERENCE FACTOR.

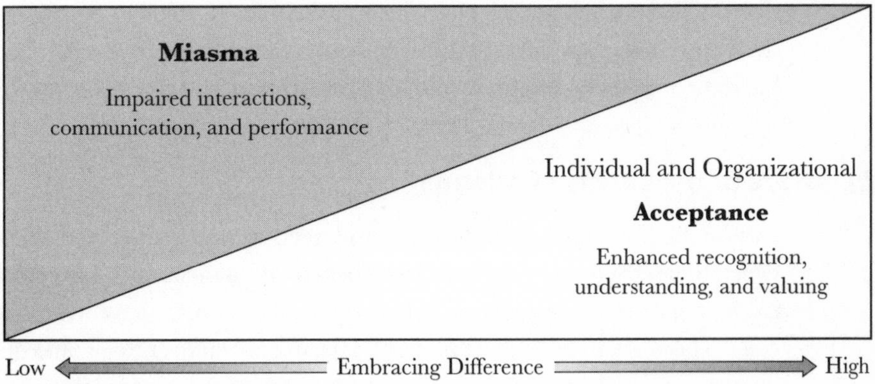

Source: Livers & Caver (2003, p. 18).

Coaching Through the Fog

Certain aspects of the coaching interaction take on more emphasis with people of color because the coach must deal not only with everyday workplace issues but also with the toxic effects of miasma. Coaching through the fog, understanding and breaking down the miasmic aura, requires that coaches pay particular attention to the following essential factors when coaching people of color:

- Build rapport.
- Be aware of the effects of miasma.
- Recognize and acknowledge bias.
- Be careful of overempathizing.
- Be careful of racial stereotypes.
- Don't overassume similarities.

Build Rapport

Building a strong rapport is a critical step for coaches and managers if they want to have effective relationships with their coachees. Although this is important for all managers, relationship building is probably the single most important step a coach can take when working with people of color. This step is critical because the experiences and history of people of color may lead them to be wary of or distrust their coach as well as their organization. If coaches do not get to understand these experiences and viewpoints through a process of relationship building, it is likely that their coaching intervention will be unsuccessful.

Be Aware of the Effects of Miasma

Although most coaches understand the need to be sensitive to the context in which their coachees work, coaches of people of color must be particularly open to considering their coachees' organizational circumstances. Many people of color who work in an environment of miasma are subject to an atmosphere informed by stereotype and bias that create misperceptions and distortions.

Coaches interviewed for this chapter provide valuable perspectives on the effects of miasma. A white coach, commenting on the challenges of miasma for people of color, said, "The question arises, Can people of color exercise the same behaviors as do their white counterparts without having their behaviors be misconstrued? Often minorities have a narrower band of acceptable behavior." This environment affects how both the coaches and coachees perceive each other personally and each other's and their own job competence and readiness. An Asian American coach said that corporate culture is a highly pressured environment where executives lack focus. Furthermore, said this coach, the psychic cost from "pressure, insecurity, trust, and the absence of harmony is high. It is in this already difficult environment that managers of color must navigate not only organizational but racial and cultural currents." Managers who see themselves as "irretrievably different," the coach continued, "have both advantages of heartiness and resilience. On the other hand, there is an emotional vulnerability." As a consequence, coaches of color as well as white coaches have to make certain they understand all of the forces that are weighing on their coachees. They also have to be careful that their own racial baggage does not unduly influence the coaching session. Each group—white coaches, coaches who are the same race as their coachees, and coaches who are of color but of another race or ethnicity than their coachees—has to beware of specific yet different pitfalls.

For white coaches, the impact of miasma on coaching can be particularly pernicious. While miasma is often very real to people of color, it just as often goes unnoticed by their white colleagues. Indeed, the Work Trends study, *A Workplace Divided: How Americans View Discrimination and Race on the Job* (2002), reports that race is the "most significant determinant in how people perceive and experience discrimination in the workplace" (p. 1). Furthermore, the study says that nonwhite workers, particularly those who are well educated and earn more than forty thousand dollars a year, are far more likely than white workers to say that they or someone they know at work has experienced unfair treatment.

A white coach interviewed for this chapter says that when he is trying to determine whether his coachee is dealing with an issue of poor performance or bias, he asks himself, "Would someone who is not a person of color be treated the same way?" The question signals a willingness to acknowledge that coaches must push beyond their own understanding to help guide others through experiences that may be uncomfortable for the coach to accept. White coaches who do not perceive inequitable treatment or are unwilling to investigate if it exists may miss a key element in their coachees' experiences and thus set a coaching direction that misses the mark. In addition, white coaches who are reluctant to explore their coachees' perception of their environment may irreparably harm their coaching relationship.

Recognize and Acknowledge Bias

While coaches must push their coachees to challenge their own worldview in order to help them change their behaviors, white coaches run a severe risk if they seem to deny the existence of biased behavior in organizational life. This is because people of color may view white coaches as biased if they act as if prejudice does not exist. In addition, white coaches need to recognize that what they see as appropriate skepticism of their coachees' perceptions, those individuals may understand very differently and quite negatively. Although this does not mean that white coaches cannot or should not confront their coachees' assumptions of racism if they believe the assumption is unwarranted, it does mean white coaches first need to challenge their own reasons for being skeptical about a coachee's claim of bias. They also need to find ways to let the coachee know that they are as open to recognizing bias as they are open to exploring other workplace obstacles.

Be Careful of Overempathizing

Coaches who are the same race as their coachees have to be careful of their potential loss of objectivity and their willingness to overempathize with the people they are coaching. Because they may have had very similar experiences to those of their coachees or they assume they have had similar experiences, these coaches may have to guard against their own feelings of hurt, anger, or even desire to help. "You have to be able to see things taking place," says one African American coach who often coaches other African Americans. "You can't be so caught up that you can't be effective." Another African American coach agrees: "The issue of self-management as a coach is critical. I have to be careful not to overempathize. I must always ask the tough questions."

A benefit to being a coach who is the same race or culture as the coachee is that such coaches have more leeway to challenge the coachee's perceptions or behaviors around such sensitive areas as race or culture. An Asian American coach said that when she is coaching someone of the same race, she might be "more direct and forthright" about bringing up these kinds of issues. An African American coach interviewed for this chapter agrees, saying that particularly when he is dealing with other African Americans, race "can ease the process of acceptance."

Be Careful of Racial Stereotypes

Coaches of color but of another race have to be careful not to believe racial stereotypes they may have heard about the group of the person they are coaching. Although they also may be victims of others' stereotypical thinking, these coaches may still harbor conscious or unconscious biases about their coachee. Being of color themselves may even complicate matters; these coaches may be lulled into a false sense of security because they are erroneously certain about their own open attitudes and consequently unwilling to acknowledge the biases they hold.

Don't Overassume Similarities

Another danger for leader coaches is their relying too heavily on their similarity with their coachee because they are both people of color. "I know people of color have common understandings, and we know each of the experiences are different," says one Asian American coach. "Just because I'm a person of color, I may not understand your experience." A Latina coach agrees: "I can't say I have the same degree of experience, but perhaps I'm halfway there." She added that she brings up their differences when she is dealing with coachees of another race "in such a way as to not overassume." Coaches of color who do overassume similarity with their coachees may risk their coachees' seeing them as inauthentic and unworthy of an open, honest dialogue.

However, while overassuming similarity can be problematic, coaches or managers of color but of a different race or ethnicity from their coachee often do have an important foundation on which to build. An Asian American coach says, "Other ethnic minorities share similar challenges that white coaches may not see." This affinity, he said, creates respect for different backgrounds and fosters connections. "It enhances trust and enables us to get to the real stuff." Another Asian American woman interviewed for this chapter says that as a person of color, she believes people can have some common understandings of what it is like to be different. But having said this, she clarifies: "Just because I'm a person of color, I may not understand your experience, but I may have more insights than the mainstream." It is this balance of understanding and willingness to seek further clarification that can help coaches and coachees of color but of different races or ethnicities to create strong, effective coaching relationships.

Trust and the Challenge of Responsibility

Two factors play a large role in workplace dynamics for people of color: trust and responsibility. It would be no exaggeration to say that these issues confront people of color far more often than they confront their white colleagues.

Trust

Trust is probably the single most important dynamic that affects people of color and their environment. The impact of the miasmic experience of people of color is a broad one that can have significant implications for coaches and coachees in terms of the issues they face. People of color have somewhat different workplace encounters, opportunities, and challenges than their white colleagues do. While these differences are often subtle and nuanced—people of color often get less challenging assignments, less visibility, less support—they can have a significant effect on the way people of color perceive and approach their workplace.

Trust is one of the most critical casualties to these covert and sometime overt tensions. Many people of color believe it is unwise to trust whites and may be skeptical of people of color of other races. An African American coach interviewed for this chapter says that because many of his clients "have a paranoia about trusting white people," he finds that it is important to help them determine if their feelings are based on their assumptions or on something that has actually happened. "I think it's important to talk about their reluctance [to trust] and bring out the experience of race."

Because the coaching relationship can be quite intimate, it can plunge coaches into the complex world of racial politics. In that space, little may be articulated, but much is judged. How individuals portray themselves determines how much candor will emerge. Consequently, the relationship aspect of the coaching framework takes on added significance as leader coaches strive to create an authentic venue for change.

An Asian American woman coach says the degree to which she is able to raise sensitive issues with her coachees of color is predicated on the level of trust she is able to achieve. A white coach says she always tries to create a solid relationship with her coachees. However, when she is working with people of color, "the difference is that it's much more important to establish that rapport with people who have something different—people of color, nationality, or physical disability, for example. I think they come in expecting to be judged, and I need to let them know that this is a safe place."

Although coachees may find it more difficult to trust coaches of color who are not of the same race or ethnicity as themselves than they would a coach of the same racial or ethnic group, they are also more likely to give those coaches an early benefit of the doubt. One coach wonders if she isn't given some level of trust because she is a coach of color and her coachees believe she can comfortably explore the kinds of issues they face. An Asian American, she says when she is coaching a person of color, she hopes "they say, 'perhaps this person understands more of where I come from than I might have assumed.'"

Responsibility

Often, because the workplace or society in general has been nonaccepting of them, people of color have found it necessary to care for or be responsible for each other's welfare or guidance. This phenomenon, for example, occurs with a high degree of frequency for African Americans. In fact, 95 percent of African Americans in one study we performed said they felt responsible for other African Americans at work (Livers & Caver, 2003).

People of color may bring the issue of responsibility to the coaching relationship. They will recount the burden that the organization may be placing on them to act as role models for others of their racial group or culture in the workplace. People of color may be asked to take on formal and informal activities that benefit others in their group, but it is often at the expense of their time and energy. But they are reluctant to say no, given their sense of responsibility to both their own group and the organization, and history has often suggested to them that what others in their group do and how they perform reflect on them. Indeed, people of color often think that their mistakes are generalized to others of their group in the organization. They are often collectively invested in the performance of others of their group and can be hyperaware of new hirings of group members and their subsequent performance. This places a weighty set of expectations on the person of color that is extraneous to his or her work responsibilities.

Sometimes the fallout from elevated expectations can come from unexpected quarters. Consider the story of a particular African American administrative nurse. Because she was the first black woman to hold that job, other African Americans felt invested in her success as well as her actions. The nurse just wanted to do her job, but found herself expending a great deal of energy handling the expectations of other black employees. This caused tensions between the nurse and the other African Americans, who might otherwise have been a support base for her (Livers & Caver, 2003).

The important idea for coaches to keep in mind is that for people of color, there is often a parallel support structure that may work in tandem with the coaching relationship or may affect it in negative ways. While all groups may have internal politics and support structures, those of people of color may take on added importance because they are often unrecognized and therefore their influence is unaccounted for. A person of color may be receiving formal or informal mentoring from another person of color that will likely take into account the racial and cultural environment and the effects of miasma. Often such advice is sought because the coachee may believe the coach is ill equipped to understand or advise on an organization's racial politics. Yet mentoring from someone in their own group can give coachees validation and a perspective that the coach lacks. While many coachees may seek advice outside the coaching environment, leader coaches, particularly those who are white, should be aware that coachees of color may be heavily weighting the counsel of others of color whom they may see as credible because of perceived common understandings.

Coaching Needs for Leaders of Color

Although coachees of color have many of the same needs and concerns as their white counterparts, coaches interviewed for this chapter identify other recurrent themes often faced by this group:

- Problems with relationships
- Aversion to risk
- Lack of self-esteem

Problems with Relationships

People of color may have challenges with creating bonds with people at work. "Something that comes up fairly regularly," says one African American coach, "is building relationships. They want to be able to influence people and build capacity." He adds, though, that many of his coachees are reluctant to build personal connections, particularly across racial lines. Another African American coach says that many of the people whom she has coached are more trusting of affiliations outside work than in. This trust is often because the coachee feels these out-of-work connections are safer and more authentic than the ones they have at work. Within the workplace, she has found most relationship problems center on the boss. "Their belief is that the boss is not as respectful as they should be—that they don't recognize things that are positive," she says of her coachees.

An Asian American coach says that bridging the differences in experiences between colleagues can be a challenge for coachees of color. Senior managers, in particular, may have trouble with relationships because they don't know how to fit in. Sometimes senior leaders behave as if they are no longer different. This seeming assimilation can cause a rift between them and others of color, particularly those of their own race. Because they are senior leaders, "they can feel an increasing separation (relationally) from their peers," he says. While this distance between former peers is one of the difficulties most leaders face, it can be particularly difficult for leaders of color, who may also feel isolated from their white peers and thus completely unsupported in the organization. Because of the difficulties that people of color can feel related to support, the encouragement and assistance managers and coaches show them in a coaching relationship may take on added importance.

Aversion to Risk

An African American coach says it is often difficult for people of color to take chances. In the people-of-color community, she says, "We're often not given permission to take risks." She says many people of color are simply concerned about getting a steady paycheck and consequently are less likely than their white counterparts to challenge their organization. This coach suggests that this behavior may come from some people of color having a survival mentality. Work for many of them is something done for security and to pay bills. It is not necessarily a place where one can or should expect pleasure or growth. A white female coach has seen echoes of this mind-set in her coaching practice. "If somebody is the first to get education [in their family], they are pushed to go in what they'll make money in or what they're good at," she said. "They may be good in math and science, but that may not be where their passion is. It is not where they would go if they had a choice." Since many people of color are the first or one of the few in their families to have professional white-collar jobs, the job itself, and the risks associated with losing it, may take on different or additional meaning than it does for white colleagues.

People of color often have a heightened sense of responsibility to others of their race or ethnicity. Many African Americans in particular feel a keen sense of what their professional jobs mean for their family and extended community (Livers & Caver, 2003).

A study from Lore International Institute (2001) also reveals that people of color tend to be more risk averse. The paper published from that study states that because people of color are often held to a higher standard than the mainstream population, their mistakes are greatly magnified and they are more likely to derail; consequently, they tend to strive for perfectionism. But "perfectionism makes people risk averse," the study says. "They disregard the important intuitions and subtle internal cues that are often our best sources of insight" (p. 3). An African American coach agrees, saying many of the people he coaches are always dealing with the stress of having to prove themselves: "They have an unbelievable commitment to do a good job in the face of obstacles."

Lack of Self-Esteem

Because people of color are often not fully recognized or supported in their workplaces, they may not see themselves as valuable contributors. An African American coach, in discussing the lack of self-esteem many people of color feel, says it often prohibits them from being able to envision successes for themselves. Many Latinos, for example, "see themselves at the bottom of the barrel," she says. "They don't see themselves as being able to break through as far as the workforce goes." In fact, this coach feels that Latinos and African Americans share views in this area. She says that their "mind-sets of how they see themselves in the larger society inhibits them from seeing themselves in bigger, grander roles." A Latina coach says that one of the first things a coach has to do when dealing with people of color is to make sure they have overcome any early messages they've gotten about people of color being "less than." She says coachees "have to have a lot of confidence to let go and work through others." Although coachees can be great individual performers, she says, "letting go to trust can be a tricky shift."

An Asian American coach interviewed for this chapter says midlevel managers are often dealing with a double-edged sword: "On one level, they may think they're only there because of their color. On the other hand, they may feel they are being overlooked for more senior roles because of their color." The effect of managers' uncertainty about the impact of race on their current position and future prospects can be significant because it can slowly erode their belief in their own ability. A white coach notes, "Success is contaminated both personally and professionally." Managers often have to ask themselves whether they were promoted because of their competence or their color, he explains. Matters are further complicated because many people are uncomfortable with discussing race; consequently, though managers may wonder if race has played a part in their career movement (or lack of movement), they often have no one with whom they can discuss it. This lack of information may lead managers to think the worst of either themselves or the organization. Neither viewpoint is an ingredient for organizational success.

Strategies for Coaching Leaders of Color

In dealing with the unique perspectives people of color bring to the coaching sessions, the coaches interviewed suggested that coaches and managers need to have a number of strategies to help them be successful. While these techniques are important regardless of whether the coach is a person of color, how these strategies are employed often depends on the coach's race (see Exhibit 4.1).

Inspire Trust

Building trust is without question a cornerstone of any coaching relationship. For people of color, the issue of trust is paramount, particularly if the coach hopes to have any chances of engaging the coachee on a personal level. A white coach notes that race magnifies the issue of trust in the coaching relationship. It is the foundation of any other strategy the coach may use. One African American coach observes that confidentiality is an essential part of

EXHIBIT 4.1. COACHING STRATEGIES FOR LEADERS OF COLOR.

- Inspire trust.
- Find similarities.
- Appreciate the social context.
- Understand the organizational context.
- Name the difference.
- Challenge the coachee.

trust, not just for its own sake but because of its impact on building or destroying the trust in a relationship. All of the other strategies that coaches talk about related to coaching people of color flow from and are supported by trust. To a great extent, successful coaching outcomes are determined by the presence or absence of trust in the coaching relationship. At the same time, the other strategies discussed in the following sections can advance the coaching relationship because they can deepen the trust between the leader coach and coachee.

Find Similarities

Finding common experiences or other similarities can lay the groundwork for the coaching relationship. "I try to find some basis we can connect on," says a white coach. An Asian American coach, who is married to an African American, also thinks it's important to find common ground: "One of the things I do when I'm working with an African American, is I let them know my children are biracial." The information often helps to ease the difference between her and her coachee. By finding places where they are similar, leader coaches can reduce the distance between themselves and their coachees. For whites, in particular, the distance is often more than just that felt by two individuals who are barely acquainted; it is complicated by the pervasive sense of otherness one or both may feel toward each other. Finding similarities (children, pets, hobbies, locations, schools, or work experiences are just a few connection points) can be an early step for the coach and coachees toward becoming more comfortable with each other.

Appreciate the Social Context

Many coaches say that understanding the social context in which the coachee is operating is an important strategy in learning what coachees need and how they perceive the world. An Asian American coach says that she has a heightened awareness about the need to listen to her coachees and to get them to tell her as much about their past context and life as possible. One reason that listening to context is important, she says, is that it allows her to determine if any assumptions she has made about her coachees' lives are inaccurate.

For people of color, socioeconomic and political context often impinges on their lives in ways that it does not for their white colleagues. In one coaching session, an Asian American coach says, the coachee talked about growing up in a deeply segregated United States. Another coachee discussed his life in Korea and what it meant to grow up there. "They don't say this is the context explicitly and say this is my life and this is how it has impacted me," she says. "You know by the way they speak about it. You wonder how it plays out [at work]. I don't think they think about it in a conscious way. As you go forward coaching them, you find it in the air." Recognizing and understanding a coachee's socioeconomic and political context can add texture and depth to comprehending the coachee and his or her experience.

A white coach notes that age is one of the places where the socioeconomic and political understanding may affect people's viewpoints. A person of color who is fifty or older and who may have experienced extreme, overt discrimination growing up and in the workplace is likely to have a very different perspective from a person of color who is in his or her twenties. Beyond age, this coach also looks to see what field the coachee is in and how many other people of their race or ethnic background are in the same field. "If there are a lot of people in that position," she said, "that's very different from someone who is in a field in which they're the only one for miles around." A person who is "the only" or one of "the few" in a position or at a given level may have many fewer support systems than others in the same position. In addition, that person may have more questions about his or her upward mobility since there are few role models to point to who have moved into the higher ranks of the organization.

A Latina coach says she asks coachees to discuss what it was like for them growing up in terms of educational attainment—whether, for example, they were the first in their family to go to college. She also says when she's coaching

Latinos, she discusses how they perceive power and authority because many Latinos are ambivalent in their view of power because of how it may have been used or abused in their countries of origin.

Understand the Organizational Context

Understanding the organizational context in which the coachee must work is important to the leader coaches helping the coachee navigate the workplace effectively. For example, it is important for the coach to understand how the organization measures success, what characteristics make up the organization's values and culture, what constitute the major environmental tensions, and who are the significant players in the coachee's work life. These and other issues can seep into and affect the coaching relationship, and they determine to a great extent what the coachee needs to do to be successful. "If the organization presents an unsafe environment," a Latina coach says, "the coaching relationship will be stalled, often leading to lack of follow-through and fear [on the part of the coachees]." An African American coach also notes that the organization plays a critical role in setting up the coaching environment. For example, the organization can subtly suggest that coaching is a gift that is important for development or that it is a punishment for those who need to be fixed. If the latter notion prevails, coachees are less likely to take part in coaching voluntarily and are generally less likely to enter into the experience positively. Given that many people of color are already unclear about their organizational status, getting mixed messages about the reason for coaching can greatly affect the success of the endeavor.

Managers who coach their direct reports may have an additional obstacle within the organizational context. Leader coaches have to be particularly careful not to assume they already know the workplace context in which their coachees operate. Because they are likely to be at different levels in the organization, their contexts are likely to be different. Also, if the coachee is a person of color, his or her sense of the workplace may be different from that of the leader coach. A white coach says, "Some organizations are relatively colorblind; some are color sensitive." The coach's comment suggests that the leadership in some organizations thinks racialized thinking does not affect their behaviors or influence their policies, when in fact it does. How people experience the organization on this dimension may be different depending on whether they are people of color. For example, coachees of color may be less likely to see their organizations as being color-blind because they often feel they have fallen prey to biased or noninclusive systems. Leader coaches may have to be willing to challenge their own notion of the organization's color-blind status.

A coach may also overlay a coachee's social and organizational contexts to get a fuller view of the coachee's situation, or at least their understanding of it. Such a technique might be particularly important for coaches who are trying to ferret out the subtle nuances that are influencing their coachee's behaviors and attitudes.

Name the Difference

One of the most successful strategies coaches use when working with people of color is probably one of the most underused: naming the difference or giving permission for it to be discussed. A white coach says she will tell her coachees that some of their responses are similar to those of other people of that race or ethnicity. When she does this, she says, the response to her acknowledging their difference is almost palpable: "It's wonderful. It's like you can hear them breathe a sigh of relief. They're so used to being masked or on edge that they don't think about it. They don't talk about it. They just do it." Once the issue of difference is brought up, she says, "They feel like it's much safer, even if it was safe before. They share really interesting stories." She says coachees shift from telling analytical stories to telling more revelatory personal stories about others and themselves. A Latina coach agrees: "By bringing it up, it creates a greater degree of intimacy. Some can and do choose to stay away from it, but if you can relate by personal experience, it creates a much greater sense of intimacy."

While bringing up race can and often does create increased understanding in a coaching relationship, bringing up race or ethnicity awkwardly can enlarge the very distance the leader coach is trying to shrink. White leader coaches in particular have to be careful about how they broach the topic. They have to be comfortable in their relationship with the coachee and comfortable with issues around difference. When they mention race, leader coaches need to have an open, nondefensive, nonjudgmental attitude around the subject. This does not mean the coach must agree with everything the coachee says, but it does mean the leader coach must be willing to explore his or her own attitudes on these subjects while asking coachees to explore theirs. Most important, leader coaches have to have a strong bidirectional trusting relationship with their coachee if a conversation around difference is going to be valuable. If the coachee does not feel safe, the conversation is unlikely to be authentic or fruitful.

Challenge the Coachee

Many people of color do not receive good developmental feedback in the workplace. Whether the cause is due to actual racism, inability to hear feedback they've received, or the manager's fear of being called racist if he or she does give feedback, people of color often are not challenged in the same way as their white colleagues. "Most executives of color may not get the same kind or quality of feedback," says a white coach. "They may get praise but not the real developmental feedback they need to grow." Although it is not the leader coach's job to do performance appraisals, helping coachees expand their views is. This may require the coach to challenge and push their coachees. "We have to challenge people of color to think outside the box," says an African American coach. "We have to give them permission to take risks and think in new ways." Often this feedback is a way to help people of color "deal with their gremlins," says another African American coach. Yet another black coach says that coaches need to help coachees "address the perceptions and assumptions that they make that may or may not be true or accurate." It may be difficult and inappropriate to challenge the coachee before a trusting relationship has been created. After such a foundation has been built, however, challenging the coachee may be one of the most important functions that a leader coach can offer.

A Coaching Framework for Coaching Leaders of Color

Every coaching interaction has an operational framework that enhances its effectiveness. CCL's coaching framework—relationship, assessment, challenge, support, and results—has special meaning when applied to coaching people of color because difference is a significant factor for the coach to consider. Overall, leader coaches should carry a heightened sensitivity to the importance and way in which each component is applied. At the same time, the leader coach doesn't need to become self-conscious or overly cautious, although those feelings are understandable in early stages of the coaching relationship. The factors this chapter has discussed up to this point distinguish the developmental process for leaders of color, and so leader coaches would be well advised to familiarize themselves with and internalize CCL's framework in that context to determine how they might use it to achieve positive coaching outcomes.

Relationship

Rapport is at the heart of a good coaching relationship. This state is achieved when the coach and coachee connect, understand each other's perspectives, and appreciate each other as people. This is even truer when coaching people of color. The other two components, commitment and collaboration, that along with rapport help to build trust—the goal of building a relationship—are also important and may need to be applied differently given this unique context (Ting & Hart, 2004).

Given this chapter's attention to the nature of trust in the context of coaching leaders of color, the leader coach needs to accept that she or he may have to be proactive in initiating the relationship. This could mean the coach has to exhibit commitment multiple times and in multiple ways before the coachee begins to trust in the coach's intent and desire to be in a meaningful and developmental coaching relationship. This behavior may run counter to the leader coach's belief and experience that individuals need to take responsibility for and create their own networks of support. It also may feel even more time-consuming than the normal challenge of making time to coach. But the coach who wants the coaching to make a difference in the coachee's development as a leader may need to offer a heightened level of commitment. The reciprocal nature of commitment goes a long way toward creating an effective coaching relationship (Ting & Hart, 2004).

Collaboration becomes critically important in a coaching relationship between a coach and coachee of different colors. This is true not only because every good coaching relationship puts the coachee in the driver's seat, with the coach serving as a guide and sounding board, but because if the coach and coachee have had different life experiences, the coach will need to rely even more on drawing out the coachee's perspective and understanding of herself in the current context. This process of sincere collaboration helps to build trust. If the leader coach makes assumptions about the coachee's aspirations, self-assessment, and professional and personal goals, those assumptions are likely to be inaccurate and, worse yet, may confirm a coachee's concerns of being misunderstood, creating distance in the relationship.

The leader coach also has to perceive the relationship-building skills of the coachee. For people of color, building relationships is crucial because when people get to know them, it enhances their validity beyond just their race or culture. Consequently, people of color need to be willing to bridge gaps, take the initiative, and exert energy in order to create relationships. They should not be so concerned or prepared for disappointment that they inhibit their own prospects for success.

Assessment

Coaches interviewed for this chapter claimed that one of the biggest problems with either formal feedback or informal observation is the fairness of the assessment measures used and the value placed on them. If those receiving feedback perceive it as being shaped by bias and prejudice, the process of assessment is subverted (Livers & Caver, 2003). The person receiving the feedback has a difficult time learning from discrepancies between self-views and views of others. This phenomenon is something that has to be carefully controlled in the coaching relationship. It is virtually impossible to develop an assessment that is completely bias free because the values and underlying beliefs, as well as the measures for leadership effectiveness, are set by the prevailing social or organizational context.

However, because people are often working hard to be unbiased or afraid that their concerns about people of color will be misunderstood, coaches who interview colleagues on the behaviors and skills of people of color sometimes receive watered-down feedback. In using interviews to gather information to conduct robust and contextual assessments, it's common for respondents to acknowledge they are uncomfortable offering feedback and say that they sometimes hold back in an effort not to offend or have their feedback misinterpreted or overinterpreted. Their intent to not cause undue harm is laudable, but it may also shield the coachee from valuable information about the impact he or she has on others.

Another aspect of assessment that may challenge the leader coach is helping the coachee determine which feedback and data are relevant to his or her defining and developing more effective leadership behavior. Most coaches need skill and judgment to perform this task, and it becomes an especially complex process when the leader coach is trying to help a coachee decide how (if at all) the feedback is laced with subtle but nonetheless real racial assumptions or biases.

Another challenge arises because people of color often endure more intense scrutiny than do their white colleagues. While this is not always a conscious behavior, it can still be disruptive. Managers or colleagues may unconsciously assume that a person of color is not capable and may be on the lookout for mistakes. Other managers or colleagues may want to see people of color fail and so are alert for behaviors that will confirm their own beliefs or suspicions. In either case, observers may be hyperaware or hypercritical of the actions of people of color.

Overassessment is another area in which leader coaches should exercise caution. An excessive collection and review of data prior to a promotion or closer supervision when given a developmental assignment adds significant challenge. People of color may feel a need to exceed expectations and manage perceptions that are often not flattering or even consistent with their own perspective and values.

Exploring and assessing the person or the context presents its own challenges to the leader coach, especially if the type of relationship that would allow an in-depth understanding of these two critical aspects of assessment is not yet formed between coachee and coach. The leader coach may be inclined to avoid or move on after just a few attempts to learn more about these two aspects. But most coaching relationships, and particularly those where the coach and coachee have differences, succeed when the coachee feels understood (which is different from agreeing with the coachee's perceptions) and then is supported in finding new or different ways to respond to developmental challenges.

Challenge

The rewards of challenging assignments include developing new skills, getting out of the comfort zone, and mastering new knowledge. Managers learn to motivate others, shoulder responsibility, confront problem employees, and find new ways of thinking about problems, among others. These are all standard developmental activities for any manager willing to take the risks, but the leader coach has to be aware that there is another layer of challenge for the person of color. Parallel with the discomfort of stepping out of familiar managerial roles is the additional discomfort of wondering how one's race will affect the process. Creating disequilibrium may be an entirely different experience for a person of color.

Consider the story of Juan, a Hispanic manager in a large insurance company, who has been asked to lead a technical group that will create a new database for another department. Juan is familiar with the activities of that department but has not worked within it. He does, however, have the technical expertise, having had ten years of experience as an information technology manager before he came to the insurance company, and his bosses would like to see him stretch his capabilities. Still, Juan perceives some resentment around him from people within the department who think that they are more qualified to take on this assignment. In such a circumstance, Juan may wonder if others believe he is being favored because he is a minority. Is he putting too much stock in what he thinks he perceives? Perhaps the tension he feels has more to do with his being an outsider to the department and the organization than with race.

It's worth noting that in this case, regardless of the real reasons for the tension, Juan is facing more than the challenge of a stretch assignment. He is also having to face and deal with resentment from others in the department and the question of whether the resentment is related to race or ethnicity. A leader coach could help Juan with those challenges.

Leader coaches soon realize that what may seem to be a standard management issue with others can be a tangled web for people of color. As one African American manager says about being a person of color, "Everything I do will be different. Even if I do the same things that everybody else does, it will be viewed as different because I am different" (Livers & Caver, 2003, p. 25). Determining the right amount of stretch for a coachee, where to stretch, understanding the potentially unique obstacles, and exploring feasible options can move the leader coach into his own form of disequilibrium and discomfort, one that if the coach isn't honest in acknowledging and willing to embrace can easily result in minimization or reversion to safer (and possibly less effective) coaching areas.

Support

The workplace is not color-blind, but people often assume it is. This creates an organizational environment that does not offer official or formal support to people of color because it is not perceived as a need. A study from the University of Connecticut supports this contention: "Many Americans do not believe that they or their colleagues are the victims of unfair treatment" (Dixon, et al., 2002, p. 1). Thus, people of color often rely on informal networks for support.

Often this support is less about career needs than personal ones. People with similar cultural and ethnic backgrounds often tend to congregate and share their experiences through their respective cultural lenses. Consequently, cafeteria tables and other informal gathering places are often populated by groups predominantly made up of one or another racial, ethnic, cultural, or gender group. For people who are in the numerical minority, such socializing, where they can be validated and culturally comfortable, may take on importance as a coping and support mechanism.

Organizational reward systems can be important support mechanisms because they offer recognition for people of color who are often overlooked within organizations. Recognition for doing a job well, educational achievements, or acquisition of new skills can be proffered through feedback, formal announcements, celebrations, salary increases, and promotions. Recognition helps establish credibility and reinforce capabilities.

An aspect of support for people of color is that if the challenges that they have confronted are particularly demanding, the support has to be even more robust in helping these individuals find a center of balance. Coaches have to assess how to offer support that both enhances the rewards of the challenging experiences and mitigates its discomfort. In addition to helping the coachee stay aware of his or her professional goals, put setbacks into perspective, and find the proper resources to succeed, the coach has to take into account the effects of miasma and the distortions to the manager's growth that it may cause.

Creating a personal learning agenda and a self-sustaining developmental system is perhaps the ultimate form of support because the coach is consciously reducing the importance of her role in the coachee's development. Having multiple relationships that provide support in different ways is often one of the distinguishing features of a coachee's success (McCauley & Douglas, 2004).

If a leader coach and coachee are successful and the coachee requires less ongoing coaching support, one possible option is for the relationship to transform itself into a different type of relationship, perhaps that of a mentor.

Results

The common results of coaching—behavioral, performance, business, or personal—all benefit coachees of color. Aside from those outcomes, an overarching result may be to help the coachee manage the miasma of his or her environment. This does not mean that the miasma fog dissipates completely, but the coachee may learn to find a clearer path through it and perhaps feel less of a burden during that journey.

An effective coaching relationship generates learning for both parties but does require the coach to maintain his openness and not shy away from his own discomfort. And it may require some risk taking on the part of the coach to challenge the coachee as well as the organization at pivotal moments. Indeed, one significant result that can evolve from this form of coaching relationship, especially where the coach is of a different color, is the learning for the coach and the organization.

The Coaching Challenge and Mind-Set

Leader coaches have challenging work ahead if they choose to coach leaders of color. If you have made that choice, be prepared to look inward, challenge your assumptions, look honestly at organizational barriers, and appraise your supportive role in the coachee's development. At the same time, you will have to manage the boundaries of the coaching relationship and maintain the coaching principle that places the coachee's well-being first and respects the coachee's agenda. The leader coach walks a difficult path among acknowledging the impact of the coachee's color on his or her development, honestly assessing the organizational stance toward leaders of color, acting at times as an advocate for change, and conveying the organization's expectations. Juggling these considerations can create uncertainty, internal conflict, and stress for the coach. Applying the coaching framework and process requires careful deliberation because there are so many variables for people of color. For instance, during assessment, how might you determine what, if any, of the feedback contains subtle bias? When challenging your coachees, how will the two of you define reasonable goals, and what obstacles are created by your coachee and which ones are externally imposed? When offering your support as a coach, when and how do you play the role of advocate?

Strategies you can use as a coach to manage the complexity inherent in these coaching relationships include reflection and self-coaching. You may also find it helpful to seek peer coaching from colleagues who share your commitment. For example, you might seek out a peer who shares your coachee's race or life experiences and use that peer as a sounding board or learning resource.

An outlook geared toward building trust and understanding, particularly when coaching people of color, is one of the single greatest assets a leader coach can possess. As a leader coach, if you can orient yourself toward the outlook expressed in the following suggestions and diligently practice that outlook, your work with people of color can bring mutual benefit:

- *Keep mutual respect paramount.* Often unconscious assumptions drive coaches' thinking as they deal with coachees of color. These assumptions about what is normal or appropriate can lead people to dismiss another's viewpoint or concerns. In order to be an effective coach, consciously respect your coachee's concerns, viewpoints, perspectives, and customs. As a part of this respectful relationship, you may have to support ways of understanding that are new to you, and you will have to appropriately challenge ideas that inhibit your coachee's effectiveness.
- *Don't assume your experience is your coachee's experience.* It is often the nature of people to assume that their experiences, in a very general way, mirror the experiences of others. Such an assumption is particularly seductive when coaches are working with someone with whom they seem to share economic and educational levels. Yet such a belief may be completely erroneous. Even if coachees do have a similar socioeconomic background, their experiences growing up and in the workplace may still be markedly different.
- *Challenge those assumptions about your coachee you most want to protect.* Because many assumptions about difference are unconscious, people are often unaware of their own biases. One way to become attuned to unconscious areas is to note and then challenge thoughts that you most want to protect. These are often areas where coaches or others become almost instantly and unthinkingly dogmatic or categorical. Such a reaction should signal coaches to reassess their reaction and determine if their feelings and emotions are factually based.
- *Understand that differences among people really do matter, as do their similarities.* Many coaches believe it is important to focus on how their coachees are similar to their more mainstream colleagues. Indeed, it can be an article of faith for some to suggest that differences don't really matter. However, many people of color would argue that differences do matter if you are the one who is different. It is their differences, they might say, rather than their similarities, that are causing them difficulties. As a leader coach, work to balance your understanding and appreciation for your coachee's similarities and differences.

• *Be willing to broaden your outlook.* For coaches to be successful with people of color, they must be willing to broaden their viewpoints and stretch beyond their personal experiences. The key is for the leader coach to be willing to grow and learn while helping coachees do the same.

• *Be willing to wrestle with complexity and nuance.* Diversity issues are often simplified into issues of right and wrong, black and white. Yet to be effective, coaches must be prepared to wrestle with complicated issues, feelings, and experience. They have to recognize that there are internal racial politics as well as those between dominant and nondominant groups. They must understand that issues of diversity are inextricably bound with issues of identity, humanity, fear, and status and so are inherently complicated. To be a successful leader coach requires pushing beyond simplistic understandings of diversity.

• *Expect to be surprised at the diversity within diversity.* Most of all, coaches should recognize that people of color are as diverse as any other groups of people. Thus, coaches have to expect that their coachees will have wide-ranging experiences. Although this idea may seem obvious, portrayals of people of color are often limited to very narrow roles. Coaches may have accepted as true more of these portrayals than they recognize. Consequently, they may not expect to work with people of color who have come from privileged circumstances or have had other experiences that seem outside the norm. Failing to recognize that there is diversity within diversity can create a barrier between coach and coachee if the coachee believes he or she is being made to conform to the coach's mental view.

Conclusion

Coaching people of color is similar to any other coaching experience in that it calls on honesty, authenticity, and relationship building. What is different, however, is how the experiences of the coach and coachee intermingle and are influenced by their personal views (along with the larger national and organizational discussions) about race and ethnicity. Because of the socioeconomic and political context in which the coaching relationship exists, what one says, who says it, and how it is said become more crucial than in many other relationships.

How a leader coach depends on CCL's coaching framework in this context may shift as the relationship becomes key to understanding not only the coachee but his or her experience. It is only within that understanding that a leader coach can accurately gauge the extent and type of assessment and challenge that the coachee is receiving and the kind of support he or she needs to gain successful results.

Coach's Bookshelf

Bates, A. L., & Klein, K. J. (2004). Multilevel analysis of the impact of surface-and-deep-level diversity and identification on mentoring. In K. M. Weaver (Ed.), *Academy of Management Proceedings.* New Orleans: Academy of Management.

Bell, E., & Nkomo, S. (2001). *Our separate ways: Black and white women and the struggle for professional identity.* Boston: Harvard Business School Press.

Castro, A. (2003). Effective leadership of Latino employees. *Club Management, 82*(2), 36–41.

Caver, K., & Livers, A. (2002). Dear white boss. *Harvard Business Review, 80*(11), 76–81.

Hyun, J. (2005). *Breaking the bamboo ceiling: Career strategies for Asians.* New York: HarperBusiness.

Kilian, C. M., Hukai, D., & McCarty, E. C. (2005). Building diversity in the pipeline to corporate leadership. *Journal of Management Development, 24*(2), 155–168.

Thomas, D. A. (2001). The truth about mentoring minorities: Race matters. *Harvard Business Review, 79*(4), 98–107.

Thomas, D., & Gabarro, J. (1999). *Breaking through: The making of minority executives in corporate America.* Boston: Harvard Business School Press.

CHAPTER FIVE

COACHING ACROSS CULTURES

Lynne DeLay
Maxine Dalton

Ralph is an American expatriate who has been in Belgium about a year and a half. In the United States, he had been successful in his position, but in his new role as regional head of the key businesses in Europe, he is not performing as the company wants. Despite Ralph's long hours, Sarah, his boss, is afraid she has made a mistake promoting Ralph into this position. His four direct reports, who are German, Italian, Belgian, and French, are complaining that his leadership is weak and he does not understand how business is done in Europe.

In a recent meeting, Ralph's coworkers confirmed Sarah's belief that all is not going well. However, Sarah wants to give Ralph a chance to improve and thinks that she might be the best one to coach Ralph because she once held his position. As a British citizen who has lived in Belgium for over ten years, she also shares with Ralph the expatriate experience. Her goal is to help Ralph become more effective as the head of the organization's four major businesses in Europe. Growth in these businesses is critical to its European strategy.

Sarah seeks the advice of the organization's HR professionals for basic guidelines on how to proceed. It's the first step in her proposing to Ralph that they engage in regular, structured discussions about his new job and assess how he is acclimating to his new position.

This example is not unusual: expatriate managers who are successful in their country of origin are often promoted to larger roles that involve managing individuals from many different cultures. Sarah now finds herself in a situation where she and her coachee, Ralph, must confront the challenge of understanding the multiple perspectives of peers, direct reports, and bosses (in this example, Belgian, Italian, German, French, and American). The ultimate goal is improving Ralph's effectiveness as a leader to managers who may have different ideas of what leadership effectiveness looks like. In short, Sarah must not only coach across two different cultures (hers and Ralph's) but also help Ralph develop his leadership effectiveness across the different cultures he encounters as an international manager.

Why Cross-Cultural Coaching Matters

The need for leadership coaching of executives in multinational organizations has grown significantly because of globalization. Multinational companies routinely reach across national boundaries for employees, and it is not unusual for leaders to work with peers and manage direct reports who are of different cultures or are expatriates themselves.

The stakes are high. The shifting socioeconomic environments that arise from globalization make performance improvements essential to long-term growth and survival. Organizations recognize that coaching, as a leadership development technique, is an effective way to address performance issues among people of many cultures and nationalities. They also acknowledge the critical role it plays in developing leaders. Developmental coaching can address the unique needs of each person and situation more effectively than standardized group programs can. Some multinationals invest in leadership development programs with ongoing coaching components for their managers who live around the globe. These same companies often expect their leaders to coach and develop the managers who are their direct reports. The burden of finding effective means to cross barriers and jump international borders falls on the leader coach.

This chapter explores the issues that are important to consider when coaching across cultural barriers and offers approaches and practices for effectively coaching cross-culturally. As companies globalize and more expatriates lead international groups in countries that perhaps none of the employees call home, leader coaches face a growing need to understand the cultural dilemmas that appear in two situations that occur with increasing frequency:

- The coachee has problems managing effectively, and some of the issues may be related to culture.
- The coach is of a different nationality from the coachee and the coachee's coworkers.

In the case of the first situation, organizations spend quite a bit of time and effort to mitigate distress that can dominate the work life of expatriate or global managers so that they can attend to important everyday business challenges. Research into the work of global managers and experience in working with them reveals that the distorted communication and insensitivity that can accompany management across cultural barriers can cause divisiveness and poor performance—outcomes that any organization wants to avoid (see Dalton, Ernst, Deal, & Leslie, 2002, for more information on global managers).

Coaches play an essential role in alleviating the distress of the manager caught in the crosshairs of negotiating multiple cultural perspectives. But coaches have their own dilemmas when the interaction takes place across cultures or national boundaries.

In order to illuminate the challenges for the coach, the environment for the coachee, and the context in which they operate, we examine the cultural implications implicit in any cross-cultural coaching relationship and use CCL's coaching framework as a lens through which cross-cultural coaching can be compared, examined, and assessed. Our goal is to give leader coaches information and practical approaches that will equip them to identify and begin to address cross-cultural issues in their coaching situations. In applying CCL's coaching framework, we compare what may be similar to coaching individuals from the same culture and what may be different when coaching individuals from another culture.

The first section of the chapter defines culture. We look at how culture, in a general sense, affects the coach and coachee and explore the coach's own attitudes toward cultural differences. We review three critical mind-sets that are subtly influenced by culture and are essential for leader coaches to understand to bring about positive outcomes for the coachee and themselves: the coachee's understanding of leadership, the coachee's beliefs about the development process, and the coachee's openness to coaching. We then highlight some cultural assumptions that underpin CCL's coaching framework and examine how the framework and its individual components apply to and can facilitate an effective cross-cultural coaching relationship when the coach and coachee do not share a common nationality. We conclude by offering some important practices for leader coaches working across cultures and some ideas about perspectives and orientations.

Culture: Its Elements and Cautions

That an individual's behavior depends in part on cultural context is an obvious but critical observation. The basic concepts of culture we introduce here have stood the test of time. We think it's important to separate the notions of culture from other principles and techniques that a coach may bring to the process.

What Culture Is and Its Implications for Coaching

Culture is a term for describing how common experiences—history, physical climate, environment, language, and religion—shape the members of a society such that they develop common assumptions, values, and beliefs about core issues. These issues include the individual in relationship to the group (for example, family, tribe, religion, workplace); expectations about how power, responsibility, and status should be acquired and shared; the relationship of human beings to time, uncertainty, and the natural and social world; the role of work in relationship to the whole of life; and who should fulfill the roles of authority and caretaking within a community. Williams (1970) defines cultural values as socially shared, abstract ideas about what is good, right, and desirable in a society or other bounded cultural group.

Culture and the Individual Coachee. The concept of culture does not imply that all individuals in a region, society, or country hold identical attitudes, beliefs, and so forth. Cultural values do not define what an individual might expect or believe; rather, they reflect the unspoken normative climate of a place. Individuals may act in accord with, different from, or in opposition to the dominant values of their home culture without being able to articulate what is influencing their expectations or behavior.

Just as fish are unaware of the water they swim in, individuals are often unaware of the subtle influence that their culture has on their behavior. Some people even deny that there is such a thing as culture. For some, the notion that their deeply held values are relative among the values and beliefs that others hold is too threatening. These people hold to a world of absolutes—right and wrong, black and white. Others reject the idea of cultural influences on behavior because they confuse the notion of cultural prototypes with socially undesirable attitudes and behaviors such as stereotyping and prejudice.

A cultural prototype is simply a probability statement: people with shared experiences are likely to have certain beliefs, customs, and values in common. It represents a useful mental map, a temporary hypothesis. In contrast, a stereotype presumes that the cultural prototype always explains all of an individual's behavior—lived experience notwithstanding. It is an unwavering belief. Prejudice is a judgment of others as less valuable and treating them as less valuable based on a stereotypical (and incorrect) view. Leader coaches (all coaches, for that matter) must have knowledge of basic cultural prototypes to help them understand their own behavior and the behavior of those they are coaching. It is one tool in the cross-cultural coach's toolbox.

Culture and the Coach. An effective leader coach works from a base of self-knowledge so as not to unconsciously impose personal beliefs, expectations, and values onto the coachee. This self-knowledge takes on a new dimension for the coach working cross-culturally. Even the best-intentioned and most experienced coaches will be surprised and embarrassed on occasion when they are caught in an unexpressed and unrealized cultural assumption.

Say the leader coach comes from a culture in which individual career achievement is important—a live-to-work culture. On the other side, the coachee comes from a culture in which work is just one aspect or facet of the whole of life—a work-to-live culture. Given these perspectives, the coach may see a successful manager as one who is entrepreneurial and takes risks. But the coachee may define a successful manager as one who can master the bureaucracy and work the system. From the leader coach's point of view, a successful manager is one who delegates the details. The coachee sees it differently: the successful manager is the one who has the greatest amount of detailed knowledge about a given project or task. Without a working knowledge of culture, a leader coach risks misunderstanding the coachee's needs, goals, and aspirations.

John, a manager, is assigned to coach Amass, a Saudi Arabian expatriate who is on temporary assignment in America at the organization's headquarters. When John asks Amass what he wants next in terms of his own career progression, Amass responds,

"That is not for me to say. That is for my boss back in Saudi Arabia to say." John changes tack and asks him what he hopes to accomplish on his current assignment in terms of his development. Amass responds, "Ask my boss." John, influenced by his growing up in the individualistic and career-oriented United States, has an unspoken belief that a person should take responsibility for his or her own career. He sees his coaching responsibility as helping Amass have a successful developmental experience, to coach him to define his goals and figure out how to use his current assignment to help him achieve them. The responses Amass gives clearly suggest that he does not share John's cultural assumptions.

This kind of cultural dissonance is a learning opportunity for the leader coach and for the coachee. It reminds us that culture matters. And it also reminds us that the coaching process revolves around the coachee's agenda, not around the coach's agenda.

Broad cultural issues influence individual behavior, but organizational culture is also a powerful influence. In fact, national culture, corporate culture, industry culture, and the core profession of the organization interact in complex ways that are beyond the scope of this chapter. Still, a few words about this subject are worthwhile.

Many forces shape organizational culture, such as the company's mission, the influence of the founders, and the cultures of the home and host countries. Organizational culture can strengthen, complement, or clash with national culture. Since global organizations derive many of their values from their home culture, tension is most evident between headquarters and host country operations.

For the leader coach, this means that accounting for how national culture influences a coachee's behavior is not enough. The coach needs to understand the interaction of home country and host country values within the organization and help the coachee deal with this complexity. Leader coaches are in a strong position to do this, as they have shown through their own success that they have learned to navigate and work in this environment.

To gain such understanding and become more effective in coaching across cultures, it's helpful if the leader coach develops a working knowledge of at least one of the cultural frameworks that scholars have developed. These frameworks or prototypes provide a handy mental map for a coach to refer to in order to diagnose or understand what may be happening in an encounter. We provide two such cultural frameworks in Exhibits 5.1 and 5.2.

EXHIBIT 5.1. SHALOM SCHWARTZ'S CULTURAL FRAMEWORK.

Shalom Schwartz has been working on concepts of individual values and cultural values for more than fifteen years. He sees cultural values as a response to three societal issues:

1. The relations between the individual and the group
2. The need to assure responsible social behavior
3. The role of humankind in the natural and social world

In addition, he describes three bipolar dimensions that reflect cultural solutions to these three basic issues:

1. Embeddedness versus Autonomy (maintenance of the existing social order)—emphasis on maintenance of the status quo, propriety, and restraint of actions or inclinations that might disrupt the solidarity of the group or the traditional order versus a culture in which the person is viewed as an autonomous, bounded entity who finds meaning in his or her own uniqueness . . . and is encouraged to do so. Autonomy has two components: Intellectual Autonomy and Affective Autonomy.
2. Hierarchy versus Egalitarianism (how responsibility is understood)—emphasis on the legitimacy of hierarchical allocation of fixed roles and resources versus emphasis on transcendence of selfish interest in favor of voluntary commitment to promoting the welfare of others.
3. Mastery versus Harmony (the relationship of humankind to the natural and social world)—emphasis on fitting harmoniously into the environment versus getting ahead through active self-assertion, through changing and mastering the natural and social environment.

Source: Schwartz (1999, pp. 33–34). Used with permission.

EXHIBIT 5.2. GEERT HOFSTEDE'S CULTURAL FRAMEWORK.

Geert Hofstede is best known for his groundbreaking work on culture that first appeared in 1980. He addresses five questions that human beings must wrestle with at the societal level:

1. How do members of a society cope with social inequality?
2. What is the relationship between the individual and the group?
3. What social and emotional roles between men and women are based on their biological differences?
4. What is the cultural template for dealing with uncertainty?
5. How do members of the society think of and deal with the passage of time?

The answers fall in a range that can be defined by its end points:

1. Power distance (high/low)—Power distance describes the degree of inequality that is perceived to be tolerated and appropriate between people of high and low status, or high and low achieved or ascribed authority.
2. Individualism/collectivism—Individualism pertains to societies in which the ties between individuals are loose: everyone is expected to look after himself or herself and his or her immediate family. As its bipolar opposite, collectivism describes societies in which people from birth onwards are integrated into strong, cohesive in-groups, which throughout people's lifetime continue to protect them in exchange for unquestioning loyalty.
3. Masculinity/femininity—This dimension describes the distinction between a culture that values competition and assertiveness versus service and altruism.
4. Uncertainty avoidance (high/low)—Uncertainty avoidance describes the degree to which the majority of people in a country prefer rules and explicitly structured activities to deal with unclear or unpredictable situations.
5. Long-term/short-term orientation—Long-term stands for an emphasis on virtues oriented toward the future, in particular, perseverance and thrift. Short-term emphasizes virtues related to the past and present, such as respect for tradition, preservations of "face," and fulfilling of social obligations.

Source: Hofstede (2001).

How Culture Affects Leadership Development

Just as culture affects the concept of coaching in general, so it affects the way individuals understand leaders to develop. It's essential for leader coaches working across cultures and coachees to discuss their models of leadership and beliefs about development. It's also useful to explore their views on coaching's role and value in helping people to develop as leaders.

Universal Models of Leadership

Because there is no single, universally accepted model of leadership, CCL uses a model that is based on the functions the leader fulfills rather than on the leader's traits, skills, or abilities. In this view, a leader sets the direction of the organization, gains the commitment of stakeholders to move in that direction, and maintains the alignment necessary for success and high performance. It's a workable definition, but it begs the question of what traits, skills, and abilities a manager in a given country needs to be able to fulfill these functions effectively. (For more information about desired leadership traits in different countries, see Exhibit 5.3.)

Without a universal model of leadership, different cultures are free to define what it takes to be a successful leader. Leader coaches should not assume that their coachees define good leadership in the same way they do. The coachee may believe that an effective leader is a strong authority figure, somewhat dictatorial, who pays attention to details and has at his fingertips the an-

EXHIBIT 5.3. PROJECT GLOBE.

This extensive, multicountry study was designed to identify traits universally valued in leaders. The researchers assigned to the project have identified five more or less positive traits and one more or less negative trait. However, when they compare these traits at the cultural level across ten country clusters, they report cultural-level variation in the relative importance of these traits between cultures. For example, Being Team Oriented is rated highest of all the leadership traits in the country cluster of Latin America, rated moderately in Nordic Europe, and rated lowest in the Middle East.

Source: Dorfman, Hanges, & Brodbeck (2004).

swers to most questions that a direct report might raise about the work (as is the case in France). A leader coach grounded in the culture of the Netherlands might believe that an effective leader is more egalitarian and team oriented, a person who camouflages power rather than flouts it (Mole, 2003).

If effective leadership practices look different from culture to culture and can even be quite foreign to any specific leader coach, how does a coach evaluate if a new behavior or approach that a coachee is considering will be effective? One way to address that dilemma is to build multiple "check-ins" into the coaching process. For example, the coach can assign the coachee the task of getting feedback from key stakeholders in the organization about how a new behavior is working or conduct a number of short interviews with key stakeholders. Another important check-in would be with the coachee, to get his or her perspectives regarding progress.

Just because different models of leadership exist across cultures doesn't mean that each coachee can use difference as a crutch for ineffective behaviors. But a key responsibility for the leader coach is to remain sensitive to cultural difference as a factor in the coachee's leadership style and to help the coachee articulate those assumptions, clarify the organizational expectations for leadership, and then help the coachee align the two. These additional windows into the coaching process are useful when both coach and coachee are in the same culture; they become invaluable when big cultural differences exist. A coach working across cultures might think more in terms of tentative or working hypotheses, not conclusions. Leader coaches must be open and flexible to changing their ideas and opinions as more information becomes available and be willing to challenge and even transcend their own frames of reference.

Beliefs About Development

As the coach begins to discern the coachee's personal models of leadership, the next set of assumptions and beliefs that the coach will want to understand is the coachee's views on development, especially as it applies to herself or himself. Some managers believe that leadership capabilities are largely innate and that the development process has limitations. Although this is no longer a prevalent view, even people who believe in development may have a prescribed perspective on what that looks like, and their view may or may not incorporate a coaching relationship. These issues are not unique to the leadership development process in a cross-cultural setting, but they do affect how a coachee might express interest in or accept coaching.

For instance, U.S. organizations generally support continuous learning—to the point that some large organizations have created internal "universities" or training centers. American culture favors structured learning that is codified and often linked to specific stages of career development and job responsibilities, and it supports the idea of an educational system that is open to all. Other cultures tend to see learning as something attained on the completion of a particular degree or certificate. In such cultures, individuals might expect an organization to operate paternalistically, selecting career moves by reviewing an individual's level of degree obtained and the reputation of the university from where it was obtained as the primary indicator of career progression. In these cultures, there is more of a tendency to accept one's position in society—accepting even a selective access to advanced education.

Orientation to and Appeal of Coaching

It is not by accident that coaching has proliferated to such a great degree in the United States. The American culture leans heavily toward a mastery orientation (refer to Exhibit 5.1), which is consistent with the use of coaching for development and with coaching's roots in counseling and psychological processes.

Coaches should not assume that this level of acceptance carries around the globe. CCL's perspective on coaching—that it is a relationship between individuals in which they collaborate to understand the coachee's development needs, challenge current constraints, explore new possibilities, ensure accountability and support for reaching goals, and sustain development—is possibly culturally offensive. Some individuals in certain cultures (those Hofstede refers to as high-power-distance cultures, for example) may not accept that a leader can function in this enabling way with a direct report. Even in the United States, this view of leader as coach is evolving.

Other assumptions within coaching (for example, like the process CCL adheres to) can run counter to cultural values outside the United States. For instance, there is a strong expectation that the coach will keep confidences shared by the coachee. This is an individualistic perspective that places the individual's need above the organization. Not all cultures share this view, and some might even see such a perspective as overly focused on the self.

Crossing Cultures with CCL's Coaching Framework

Culture exerts an enormous influence on the way people understand coaching and development. In this section, we address how CCL's coaching framework plays out when embedded in a cross-cultural setting. But before we discuss the applications of the framework, it is useful to explore some general underlying principles that reflect U.S. cultural assumptions (because, obviously, those cultural assumptions can affect parts of CCL's coaching perspective). Armed with an understanding of the cultural viewpoint embedded in CCL's framework, the leader coach can make more conscious choices about if, when, and how to adapt its guidelines.

Cultural Assumptions in CCL's Coaching Framework

When coaching cross-culturally, leader coaches must be aware of the cultural assumptions that are embedded in everything from "the way we do things around here" to models that others and themselves use to explain the world. It's simply not possible to create a model or framework that is free of cultural assumptions. The ideas used to construct a framework contain within them a set of subtle cultural assumptions. The CCL coaching framework was developed in the United States, and therefore it is a product of many American cultural assumptions.

Michael Hoppe (2004) notes that studies of culture have typically described the U.S. culture as "individualistic, egalitarian, performance driven, comfortable with change, and action-oriented" (p. 135). These mainstream beliefs underpin CCL's philosophy about and approach to leader development and its views on the role and value of coaching. Specifically, while CCL acknowledges that inborn traits may play a large role in someone's orientation to leadership, it chooses to focus on what the coachee can influence and learn; hence, its fundamental belief is that much of leadership can be developed. This reflects an egalitarian and mastery orientation that spotlights a specific belief about the development process and its role in leadership. This critical set of assumptions should be discussed early on between the coach and coachee so they understand the degree of alignment that exists between them.

A number of other explicit and implicit principles guiding CCL's coaching practice would benefit from coaches' and coachees' reflecting on how readily they translate across cultures. The leader coach can make this determination in conjunction with the coachee, and neither should dismiss too quickly a concept that feels counter to a cultural assumption or attribute too quickly to cultural differences what may be their own personal discomfort with a specific coaching practice. Sometimes transcending not only personal models but also cultural models is needed in order to gain new insights and strategies.

Following are some of these coaching principles that would benefit from the reflection described:

- *Coaching focuses on the individual.* CCL views this only as a starting point; its perspective on coaching is shifting toward an emphasis on collective performance and the individual's impact on the collective.
- *Collecting, quantifying, and feeding back behavioral data from a variety of sources is a valuable and meaningful way of explaining a leader's effectiveness.* This concept comprises a mix of egalitarianism (the views of others, regardless of their level in a hierarchy, should be valued) and quantification (something as organic and intangible as human behavior and interactions can be codified and quantified in a useful way).
- *Individuals can grow and change and control their own behaviors.* This principle has a strong mastery and egalitarian perspective. There is a clear cultural underpinning to this concept given the social, political, and historical origins and development of the United States. Due to the current global environment, replete with a ubiquitous media and communications, much of the U.S. philosophy regarding individual freedom and autonomy has influenced other societies.
- *The coach offers a safe environment for learning and takes a guiding rather than controlling role in that learning process.* This principle mixes an egalitarian and mastery perspective. The notion that a coachee is not totally dependent on the collective and her boss to determine her path within the organization and that the coach does not necessarily play just an advising role may be more thought provoking than this principle assumes. It's worth noting, however, that around the globe, there often are different words and concepts that reflect parallel ideas. For instance, the concepts of self-discovery and being "comfortable in your skin" are used frequently by U.S. coaches and are similar to ideas expressed somewhat differently by other cultures. Leader coaches should not assume that if the language they are using is not understood, then the concept

they are explaining is not understood. Those who are coaching cross-culturally should ask for clarification. They may discover that they have much in common with their coachees but use different words to characterize a particular experience or process.

This principle also embodies an assumption of increased self-disclosure in the coaching relationship, which may raise eyebrows. Even in the United States, the notion of the coachee's sharing personal aspirations and struggles with a boss or peer acting as a leader coach may generate questions about the role of leader coach and about perceived or real power imbalance when the coachee is a direct report.

Cross-Cultural Application of CCL's Coaching Framework

In this section, we explore how the CCL framework (relationship, assessment, challenge, support, and results) applies to the practice of coaching across cultures. We look at where and how coaches can apply the framework in a similar manner to how it can be used in the United States or in other countries characterized as autonomous, moderately egalitarian, and high on the dimension of mastery (see Exhibit 5.2).

Relationship

Most individuals in most cultures will accept that good rapport and a positive relationship are necessary for effective coaching. For coaching to have impact, the coachee should perceive this relationship as open, honest, trusting, respectful, and reciprocal. It should be a relationship in which the coachee is willing to be vulnerable and knows that the coach will not make judgments. These qualities are important characteristics for developing trust in a coaching context, and trust is viewed almost universally as a pivotal element of coaching.

However, the meaning that each culture attaches to the concept of relationship and the expectations for how one "in relationship" behaves does vary. Rather than try to learn the range of individual meanings that might be attached to the word depending on the culture in which it is used, it's more fruitful if leader coaches become aware of the dimensions or qualities needed to establish a relationship when working across cultures. While not inclusive, the following dimensions and factors affect relationship at the heart of coaching.

Time, Type, and Frequency of Contact. Non-U.S. coachees we have interviewed often comment that when a coaching session does not go as well as they would have hoped, it is because they had insufficient time to build a comfortable relationship with the coach before tackling a developmental assignment. The more relationship oriented the culture is, the longer it takes to build rapport and a personal relationship. It also critically affects the degree of comfort that a coachee feels toward the coach. High-relationship cultures prefer developing relationships face-to-face, and coachees from these cultures often assume that coaching will take place that way. Contemporary global managers in almost all cultures daily interact with people they have not met through telephone and e-mail, but when it comes to formal coaching, the use of telephone or e-mail for developmental dialogue is not well accepted outside the United States and the United Kingdom, and particularly in Europe and Asia.

Experience, Credentials, and Credibility. A broadly defined concept of partnership is generally acceptable across Western cultures, but outside that point of reference, the concept looks different. In the United States, for example, the term carries an egalitarian connotation. In hierarchical cultures, a leader coach may be able to use the word but not without accepting the nuances that make it culturally consistent. For leader coaches, this is a particular challenge even in the United States, because the leader coach often occupies a hierarchical position that is not equal to the coachee. The issues of hierarchy and power challenge and may limit all leader coaches, regardless of culture. An effective coaching relationship features collaboration and work between equals, at least in the exchange of ideas, thoughts, and feelings.

In some cultures, partnership may not be seen as between two equals. The coachee might expect the coach to be more of an expert, more directive, or older than the coachee. It becomes a matter of credibility, especially in cultures that respect age (as do many of the Asian cultures) and in those cultures that venerate the relationship of master and student. When the coach and coachee come from different cultures, establishing credibility in the context of the coachee's national culture and life experiences is a key element in the development of trust. It's not unusual in organizations today for leaders to be younger than their direct reports. A coach who fails to reflect an understanding of these basics may be unable to establish sufficient trust and credibility. The leader coach has to work to demonstrate that he or she understands the coachee's world and the coachee's place in it.

Reciprocity and Boundary Management. Some cultures are more relationship oriented than others. This difference, probably the biggest one between the United States and Europe and Asia, is a common source of misunderstanding, frustration, and even hurt feelings to non-U.S. individuals—whether they are coachees or coworkers. A European coachee interviewed for this chapter expressed significant disappointment when her U.S. manager returned home after four years of their working together and stopped all communication. The coachee was hurt and confused. "I don't understand," she said. "I thought we were friends." In task-oriented or mastery cultures, relationships are often instrumental, a perspective that people in relationship-oriented cultures often see as superficial. Complicating this picture, some leader coaches may see the fostering of a deeper, more personal relationship as possibly creating perceptions of favoritism or leading to difficulties if the coach has to move into a boss role and address a coachee's serious performance issues. This tension exists regardless of culture and may be exacerbated by culture.

Assessment

The purpose of the assessment component in the CCL coaching framework is to get an accurate picture of the coachee. It is critical to have an accurate picture of where the coachee is in order to decide where the coachee needs to go. Assessment includes understanding the coachee's performance and how others perceive that person's leadership capability; however, in a coaching context, assessment is fundamentally about understanding who the coachee is and what context he or she operates in.

Organizations spend a lot of time assessing their managers' performance with quantifiable measures because they are tangible and create a sense of certainty. This approach presupposes a Western preference for the rational, objective, and quantitative approach to assessment of behavior and performance. It's a dubious strategy when working across cultures because not all cultures place great value on measuring human behavior and because the validity of the measurements is typically based on the country of origin. For some cultures, this approach may seem foreign, and coachees may require a great deal of explanation regarding its value.

Person. This aspect of assessment is similar to relationship; as a leader coach, you can rarely go off track if you take time to understand the unique dimensions of your coachee as a person. How a leader coach might go about learning more about a coachee as a person beyond his or her worker persona can vary greatly across cultures. Pay attention to the pace at which your coachee is comfortable disclosing information because that pace is uniquely personal and can be culture dependent.

Professional coaches often use personality assessment tools, but leader coaches should avoid depending on such measures, especially when working across cultures. Few leader coaches are certified to discuss such data, and not using these does not diminish their effectiveness as a coach. The person most expert on the coachee is the coachee. No instrument can override that fact. Granted, such a view reflects CCL's coaching perspective as the product of an individualistic culture; however, respect for the individual is paramount in CCL's view of coaching, even if the coaching work occurs in an environment that values the collective more highly than the individual. You can learn as much and more about your coachees by asking questions, listening to what they say as important, and observing their behaviors.

Context. In addition to being influenced by their culture, people operate with different beliefs and expectations using mental models that are shaped by the educational system, the political system, and the religious system of their country. In the CCL view of assessment for development, one role of the coach is to understand the coachee's mental models—the underlying beliefs that may drive behavior. This is especially true for the coach who works across cultures. There are three key areas for the leader coach to keep in mind when working cross-culturally:

1. The coachee's educational level and educational system, specifically:

    What is the highest educational level the coachee has obtained, and is this advanced education pragmatic or philosophical?

    In what country or countries was the coachee educated if different from the country of birth and in what subjects? What is the role of teacher, facilitator of learning, or expert?

    What is rewarded in the educational system that the coachee has been educated in (for example, rote learning and reliance on the teacher-expert or challenging the professor's ideas and student initiative)?

What impact does the educational system have on the composition and value system of the corporate elite (for example, the influence of the *grande écoles* in France and doctorates in Germany)?

2. Religion

   What is the dominant religion of the country regardless of whether the coachee practices it?

   How does religion affect business and society in the coachee's country of origin?

3. Political and economic system. See Exhibit 5.4 for an illustrative story.

Performance. The first challenge coaches face when using data and analyzing feedback while working across cultures comes from the assessment instruments themselves. Few of them exist in languages other than the language they were created in. Even fewer have been validated outside their country of origin. Instrument publishers that attempt to provide country-based normative samples for comparison purposes often have very small country samples. This leads to no additional information at best and misinformation at worst.

EXHIBIT 5.4. THE CONTEXT OF POLITICS AND ECONOMICS.

Maria, in her role as HR manager, found herself coaching one of the managers in her organization working for a division set up in a former communist country. The manager wanted some guidance in dealing with a performance problem from one of his direct reports. Maria, who was new in her role in this affiliate, explained the "proper way" to deal with employee performance problems: discussing the issue with the direct report, documenting if performance did not improve, and so forth. She noted that while her coachee appeared eager to learn, he didn't seem to fully grasp the concept. He kept asking, "And then what do you do?" Maria, a little perplexed, finally said, "If things don't improve, you fire him." The manager became silent for a few moments, and Maria wondered if she had said something wrong. After a few moments, he responded, "But we don't fire people." Maria learned from this coaching experience that she needed to be more aware of her assumptions, which were built into the Western employee practices she took for granted. She realized that she needed to spend time getting a better understanding of the context her coachee was working in.

Given these problems, your coachee might be skeptical and may not accept the results of assessment instruments as accurate. (The results may very well not be accurate or meaningful.) It makes the job more difficult because the leader coach doesn't know when to agree with the coachee and when and on what basis to challenge his or her position. The obvious solution is for the coach to understand thoroughly the limits of each assessment instrument and to avoid the use of those that are not appropriate for use in places outside the country of origin. But realistically, that presents a difficult challenge to most leader coaches. One workable solution for the leader coach is to rely on knowledgeable HR professionals to select assessment tools based on the specific context in which he or she will be coaching. Nevertheless, it is still important to understand the limitations of the selected instruments.

In a cross-cultural environment, confidential interviews offer the best opportunity to provide assessment in context. These are more time-consuming than instruments to complete, and they require a climate where respondents believe their responses are anonymous and confidential. However, they provide the rich and nuanced information that a leader coach working across cultures may need to be most effective.

Challenge

Generally CCL's concept of challenge—moving out of the comfort zone for the purpose of changing the status quo—is understood in organizations that operate in a global or international context. Challenge encompasses stretch goals, removing obstacles to development, and creating robust action plans that allow coachees to increase their effectiveness as leaders. Much of the English-speaking world aligns toward the mastery side of Schwartz's mastery-harmony continuum (see Exhibit 5.1); there is general cultural alignment with the challenge concept in Canada, Australia, the United Kingdom, and New Zealand. However, in western and eastern European countries that fall closer to the harmony side of the line, leader coaches may have to provide more explanation about how challenge can be developmental. The strongest objection to this view of challenge is likely to come from cultures that reject Western beliefs on their face.

One example is the Islamic culture, although it is not the only one. In the Islamic culture, beliefs such as "the future is in Allah's hands" predominate in the attitudes and beliefs of people in the Middle East. A leader coach cannot operate effectively in the Middle East without a basic understanding of Islam, which not only governs beliefs around time and the future but also influences the general behavior and code of conduct in most business matters. For a Muslim who accepts that Allah alone controls the future, an attempt by a coach to determine what might happen in the future (perhaps even to the degree of scheduling the next coaching session) can be perceived as presumptuous or even bordering on blasphemous. If meeting times are scheduled, they may not be adhered to, and an apology might not be made for missing the allotted time. Western ideas of time and time-keeping seem unrealistic to a Muslim. Islamic beliefs include the idea that only God controls the future, yesterday is over, and therefore neither is relevant now and can't be altered (Williams, 1998). Although a leader coach might intellectually understand this difference, it could increase the coach's difficulty in seeing that a coachee's lack of progress might be a natural result of Islamic beliefs, particularly when the culture in some Muslim countries includes a reluctance to say no.

Support

Culturally the concept of support in CCL's coaching framework, with its emphasis on creating safety for taking risks, experimenting, and making mistakes as one learns, is also generally understood with little resistance from coachees and organizations, at least in the Western world. Leader coaches play a powerful role in helping coachees confirm commitment, maintain motivation, monitor progress, and identify and secure resources. Still, even in the United States, what support looks like and means to each coachee is unique. To provide effective support, leader coaches must inquire about and explore what would be most meaningful and valuable to the coachee. Using those tactics, they are unlikely to disappoint their coachees when applying support in a cross-cultural setting. They may need to assume more of an adviser role for coachees who are less used to a self-sufficient, autonomous perspective that is intended to give them control over their development.

Leader coaches should know, however, that when working across cultures, corporate sponsors may say they understand and even endorse the support concept, but in organizational and national cultures that value independence and self-reliance, there is a tendency not to make a commitment to making support a reality. In other words, coaches and coachees can often be left to their own devices when securing support. Organizations in this kind of culture sometimes invest in a development program with solid assessment and feedback but do not invest in the continued follow-up or coaching that is necessary to ensure the transfer of learning back into the workplace. Furthermore, they may not provide the support necessary to maintain motivation and behavior change over the longer term. Individuals in such cultures may underestimate their need for follow-up sessions and the length of time they need to solidify real change in their behavior.

Results

Every culture values results, but what those results look like can vary dramatically and be culturally specific. Individualistic cultures, such as that in the United States, focus on individual results and may link those results to the organization's performance. In collectivist cultures, the whole idea of results takes on more of a group flavor. For example, in some Asian cultures, cross-cultural leader coaches may find themselves having to guide coachees toward results that benefit the group as a whole.

When coaching across cultures, leader coaches should seek specific direction about what results look like in terms of behaviors, since it is not uncommon for different stakeholders to have different ideas. Goal phrases like "be more effective," for example, may be a good starting point, but each key stakeholder may have radically different ideas of what being effective looks like.

Suggestions for Coaching Across Cultures

By this point, leader coaches reading this chapter may be wondering how they can become skilled enough to handle this added complexity. Coaching is a difficult enough skill to acquire, on top of the primary responsibilities to get results, manage resources, influence others, and innovate. Adapting their mindset to the cross-cultural environment and being aware of general principles for cross-cultural practice are the two primary areas in which leader coaches can acquire and develop skills necessary to coach across cultures.

Preparing to Coach Cross-Culturally

Coaches who work cross-culturally, in addition to having strong self-awareness, must come to know themselves in a different way—to understand their own response to culture. Leader coaches with this kind of coaching assignment would benefit from an assessment of their attitudes toward people from other cultures. One assessment tool that might help is the Intercultural Development Inventory (Bennett & Hammer, 2000). This inventory provides a reliable and valid measure of one's place within Bennett's Developmental Model of Cultural Sensitivity. He proposes that comfort and effectiveness with culturally different others can be represented as sequential life stages. Each of Bennett's stages expresses certain kinds of attitudes and behaviors related to cultural differences. He proposes that as individuals come into contact with people from different cultures, they move through a series of stages, beginning with denial and ending with integration (for a full picture, see Exhibit 5.5).

EXHIBIT 5.5. BENNETT'S DEVELOPMENTAL MODEL OF INTERCULTURAL SENSITIVITY.

Ethnocentrism: One's own culture is experienced as central to reality.

Denial: One's own culture is experienced as the only real one. Other cultures are avoided by maintaining psychological or physical distance.

Defense: One's own culture is experienced as the only good one. People at this stage are threatened by cultural differences and tend to be highly critical of other cultures.

Minimization: One's own cultural views are experienced as universal. These absolutes obscure deep cultural differences, and other cultures may be trivialized or minimized. People at this stage expect similarities and will correct others' behavior to match their own expectations.

Ethnorelativism: One's own culture is experienced in the context of other cultures.

Acceptance: One's own culture is experienced as just one of a number of equally complex worldviews. Acceptance does not mean agreement. People at this stage are curious about and respectful toward cultural difference.

Adaptation: The experience of another culture yields perception and behavior appropriate to that culture. One's worldview is expanded to include constructs from other worldviews. People may change their behavior to communicate more effectively in another culture.

Integration: One's own experience of self is expanded to include the movement in and out of different cultural worldviews.

Source: Bennett (1993).

To illustrate, let's return to the story of Sarah and Ralph that opened this chapter. Sarah is aware that she experiences her British culture in the context of other cultures. For her, other cultures and their ways of doing things are equally valid. She learned this through experience by working previously in a French firm and from working with her current American employer. Being aware of the key differences among cultures, she adapts her approach and behavior so that they are appropriate for the culture in which she is working. In Bennett's model, she is in the ethnorelativistic stage, somewhere between adaptation and integration.

Because this is his first assignment outside the United States and his organization gave him no cultural orientation to prepare, Ralph experiences his culture as being the central one. His responses to differences are on occasion defensive, and he feels increasingly frustrated when his direct reports do not react to him in the manner that he has grown accustomed to in the United States. He experiences what they want from him as conflicting with organizational directives, and he expresses his frustration in unproductive ways. The situation is exacerbated by the fact that Ralph feels that since they are all working for the same U.S.-based company, others should adjust to the American style of working. Ralph is in what Bennett describes as the ethnocentric stage of development, in defense.

There are two ways a leader coach can use such a cultural assessment. The first is for self-assessment and greater self-awareness within the context of cross-cultural coaching. The second is to use the assessment with a coachee who may be experiencing frustration or unproductive responses to other cultures.

For the coach, such an assessment leads to three benefits: (1) greater self-awareness of his or her own strategies for dealing with differences, which helps the coach know where and how to work comfortably with someone from another culture and where he or she might have to modify a coaching approach; (2) a framework and language with which to understand and discuss responses to differences; and (3) help in guiding the coachee toward more effective strategies in dealing with cultural differences.

This kind of assessment benefits the coachee. It provides greater self-awareness as to where the coachee might be in his or her cross-cultural development. It also helps create a common language between coach and coachee to discuss differences and development.

Knowing their own response to culture is only one variable for leader coaches in cross-cultural coaching work. To be effective, they also need to know the cultural dimensions that may confront them within any given culture. An alternative for leader coaches to undergoing a formal assessment of their own cultural orientation is to do an honest self-appraisal of where they reside in Bennett's framework.

Cross-Cultural Coaching Principles

Leader coaches who are already working cross-culturally in your organization are experiencing much of what this chapter describes. We encourage thinking of cross-cultural coaching as another application of that skill, out into the service of developing others. To that end, we offer some principles to help guide coaching work across cultures:

- *Build the relationship, and take whatever time is needed.* Be prepared to demonstrate commitment to the coaching relationship, and don't assume that your coachee will simply accept a statement of commitment. An expression from the field of Total Quality Management, "faster is slower," also applies to cross-cultural coaching. Coachees will forgive, overlook, and may not even notice if you use a less-than-perfect coaching technique if the relationship between the two of you is strong. What gets communicated is that you have the coachee's interests at heart—and that builds trust. Coachees will disclose much information and invite insight and feedback when the coaching relationship is strong and bounded in appropriate ways that are understood and agreed to by the coach and coachee.
- *Take more time with the assessment process.* View it as an opportunity to discover the unique person that your coachee is. Take more time to build the rapport and get to know the coachee as a person. The more relationship oriented the culture is, the more this will be important to your coaching work together.
- *Don't rely on assumptions, and ask when uncertain.* Communication is difficult enough when two people from the same country speak the same language. Take advantage of cultural differences to seek clarification and nuanced meaning in what the coachee tells you. Ask questions. Ask your coachee to give examples and be specific. Nonverbal behavior also communicates powerfully. Personal space and eye contact, for example, are two cultural body language behaviors that can convey different meanings.
- *Familiarize yourself with multiple cultural and leadership models.* An inexperienced leader coach may know one or two models and try to force-fit all

situations into them. The more models you expose yourself to as a coach, the greater your capacity is to adapt your approach to the coachee's situation.

• *Learn the coachee's context, especially if he or she is working in a part of the organization or in a location that is less familiar to you.* Speaking the language of the country in which you are coaching isn't sufficient. For example, a coach who learns French in school and yet is ignorant of the impact of *grande écoles* in France on its organizational culture and the composition of the organizational elite may be at a loss when it comes to coaching a French manager in a French multinational.

• *Pay closer attention to your language, especially if you are coaching in English and your coachee's first language is not English.* Avoid jargon and references your coachee may not understand, like sports analogies and sports terms, and especially U.S.-centric terms that most non-U.S. coachees do not understand.

• *Check frequently for understanding, especially if you are coaching in a language that is not the coachee's native tongue.* It is not uncommon for coachees to be a little embarrassed that they do not completely understand what their coach is telling them. This is especially true in hierarchical cultures and in those high on the power-distance dimension (see Exhibits 5.1 and 5.2). The same word can have a very different meaning in another language. For example, *large* means "big" in English but "wide" in French. Even American English and British English have crucial distinctions. To "table an issue" in British English means to bring it up for discussion; in American English, it means to remove it from discussion. Imagine the misunderstanding that could occur with more complex concepts.

• *Learn to be comfortable with silence.* In some cultures, like some of the Nordic or Asian cultures, silence is valued, and conversation is not rushed when discussing issues. Allow for silence even if the pace of the conversation seems slow to you. For some coachees in certain cultures, silence may serve as additional processing time that allows them to understand what you are saying, especially important if the coachee is not speaking in his or her first language.

• *Develop the ability to embrace a high degree of complexity and ambiguity.* Avoid quick solutions, certainty, and definitive conclusions. No one is an expert at everything, and as a cross-cultural coach, you may be frequently confronted with situations or issues that can confuse you as much as they confuse the coachee. The ability to embrace that ambiguity, work it over with your coachee, and at the same time maintain your credibility as a coach is a skill that's challenging to develop. A less experienced coach may be tempted to quickly draw conclusions or assist the coachee who wants a solution in making a quick assessment. To work with the creative tension of not knowing and to use a working hypothesis while encouraging your coachee to do the same requires discipline and the mind-set of a learner.

- *Do an honest appraisal of your cultural sensitivity and mental models.* It's difficult to know what you don't know about yourself. But you can assess the breadth of your experiences, note your level of comfort when operating in a different environment, and ask for feedback on whether you understand the coachee's perspective. This is a companion to your checking for understanding, but in this case, the focus is on you and your effectiveness as a cross-cultural coach.
- *Be coachable, and accept coaching from others, especially your coachee.* Coachees are quite forgiving of cultural mistakes when they see the coach as genuinely authentic and open to comment. Acknowledge your limitations, specifically around cultural blind spots, and invite your coachee to help you learn more.
- *Exercise a high degree of mental and behavioral resourcefulness.* Because cross-cultural leader coaches are frequently confronted with unusual situations, they need confidence in their creativity. They may need to forge new developmental pathways and in embracing creativity still help their coachees accomplish their goals.
- *Improve your global business knowledge.* Effective cross-cultural coaches are aware of business on a global scale and understand what is different from country to country in terms of laws, regulations, and ways of doing things. They stay current with the latest business and global events, and they understand global trends and their implications for organizations and the people who work in them.
- *Demonstrate high levels of empathy and respect for differences.* The ability to put yourself in the shoes of another person from a different culture with different ways of behaving and thinking and the ability to engage comfortably in local traditions and activities, including different eating and drinking habits, without judging them to be bad or wrong, makes the difference between an effective coach and a less effective one.

Conclusion

In evaluating where and how well leader coaches can apply the components of CCL's coaching framework model across cultures and where they might need to adapt its principles or where they might seriously be challenged, the biggest differences appear to be in two areas: relationship and assessment. In any coaching circumstance, if the relationship is not solid and assessment is flawed, coaching as a developmental activity may not be very effective. When culture comes into play, those elements take on extra significance.

A track record of effective coaching doesn't guarantee success when crossing cultures. It's daunting to imagine developing the knowledge of such complex variables as different cultures, different leadership models, different and equally effective ways of interacting, and the multiple approaches that global organizations have developed in their operations around the world. But by increasing your attention to stretching, even transcending, your own cultural beliefs and behaviors, you can help to develop stronger, more resilient global leaders. Global forces, be they economic, political, or social, are accelerating the contacts between people from different national cultures. Current technological advances, which increase speed of interactions and communication, may for the foreseeable future outpace the human tendency to prefer what is familiar and comfortable. Embracing the discomfort of continual learning is a key global competency for both global managers and the leader coaches who serve their development.

Coach's Bookshelf

Adler, N. J. (1997). *International dimension of organizational behavior* (3rd ed.). Cincinnati, OH: Southwestern College Publishing.

Carte, P., & Fox, C. (2004). *Bridging the culture gap.* London: Kogan Page.

Hampden-Turner, C., & Trompenaars, F. (2000). *Building cross cultural competence: How to create wealth from conflicting values.* New Haven, CT: Yale University Press.

Lewis, R. D. (1996). *When cultures collide.* Yarmouth, ME: Nicholas Brealey Publishing.

Lombardo, M., & Eichinger, R. (2004). *For your improvement: A guide for development and coaching* (4th ed., pp. 567–612). Minneapolis: Lominger Limited.

McCall, M. W., & Hollenbeck, G. P. (2002). *Developing global executives: The lessons of international experience.* Boston: Harvard Business School Press.

Rosinski, P. (2003). *Coaching across cultures.* Yarmouth, ME: Nicholas Brealey Publishing.

Ting, S., & Hart, E. W. (2004). Formal coaching. In C. D. McCauley & E. Van Velsor (Eds.), *The Center for Creative Leadership handbook of leadership development.* (2nd ed., pp. 116-150). San Francisco: Jossey-Bass.

Trompenaars, F. (1993). *Riding the waves of culture.* London: Economists Books.

CHAPTER SIX

COACHING SENIOR LEADERS

Ted Grubb
Sharon Ting

CCL's work with senior-level executives typically includes those with more than fifteen years of management experience and leadership responsibility for five hundred or more people. They include C-level executives and those ascending to that level. These individuals, survivors of many organizational storms, have honed their management talents through self-reliance, boldness, ambition, and a high degree of motivation. They have demonstrated superior intelligence, intuition, drive, and a desire for mastery, and they have been rewarded consistently for those traits.

On the flip side, by the time these executives reach the top levels of their organizations, they may appear to some as feedback-proof and unwilling to change. Even if they feel something is missing in their leadership, they are often unable to get others to confirm or talk openly about that possibility.

Traditionally, these leaders might have received coaching only if they were seriously failing in their positions. But in the past ten or fifteen years, coaching has become more commonplace for senior leaders. This growth has promoted an awareness that coaching senior executives is different in many ways from coaching managers at other ranks in the organization, and the skills required often transcend those of the typical leader coach.

Senior executives have special coaching needs by virtue of their unique roles, positions of influence, and broad scope of responsibility. Their place in the hierarchy can inhibit access to honest feedback, which they need to assess and improve their own performance. Their opportunities for trial-and-error learning are severely constrained because the price of mistakes can be ruinous, both personally and for the organization.

This chapter serves as a road map for the subtle and complex developmental terrain that lies ahead for leaders operating at this level. Based on our experience coaching senior leaders, we describe their typical characteristics, common coaching issues, and ways in which CCL's coaching framework plays out in this context. We also discuss the attributes coaches need to work successfully with senior leaders. Our intended audience includes senior leader coaches responsible for developing other senior leaders in their organization, along with professional HR and external coaches who work at this level. Where applicable, we describe differences in the roles and relationships for leader coaches and professional coaches.

The Role of Senior Executives as Leader Coaches

Many senior executives, despite the level they have achieved, are still in ascension mode. That is, they aspire to even more senior jobs within their own company or similar roles at larger or more complex organizations. Even when promotion to a higher level is not at issue, senior leaders can continue to develop and improve their leadership effectiveness in their existing role. The prevailing practice in many organizations is to use external coaches for senior executives because of the power dynamics and political sensitivities of using coaches who reside within the organization. Although much of this chapter is directed to external coaches, we believe it can be equally helpful to leader coaches because they have an important role in coaching other senior executives.

Within the senior executive's own organization, the potential leader coach might be the CEO, COO, an executive vice president, or even a member of the board if the coachee is a C-level executive. In these situations, a senior leader coach can help ascending executives anticipate the challenges and rewards that can be expected if and when they too move into the highest ranks of organizational leadership. Sometimes that means helping them understand the difference between being intellectually ready and emotionally ready for more responsibility (Bunker, Kram, & Ting, 2002).

Because this is a more select group with fewer opportunities for coaching relationships, the leader coach is sometimes a peer outside the executive coachee's organization. Executives who once worked together move on to different organizations but remain in contact, or acquaintances made through professional organizations develop into more lasting friendships. Along the way, business, leadership, and personal experiences are shared and discussed. Although executives in these situations may not describe their relationship as coaching, in practice they serve as coaches to one another around specific challenges that arise. These peer coaching relationships work well because each person has empathy and understanding of the other's world but not the competition that accompanies peer relationships within the same organization.

Senior leader coaches often have a deeper understanding of particular organization and business issues, which, in addition to the advantage of business expertise, enhances their credibility and influence with a coachee. They might recognize themselves in this chapter's discussion. By recognizing and gaining clarity about their own developmental journey, they may better coach and guide others in their organizations.

What the View from the Top Means for Coaches

Top executives do not enter a first-line management job with "future CEO" tattooed on their foreheads. The particular mix of innate ability, job challenge, learning opportunity, and just plain luck that leads to the senior executive level is quite varied, just as the individuals and their circumstances are in many ways unique. Sometimes the developmental journey looks remarkably similar for those who ascend to the top and those who don't. We do know that the ability to learn from experience is one crucial skill seen in executives who succeed (McCall, Lombardo, & Morrison, 1988). At the same time, we haven't observed a universally successful pathway up the organizational ladder. It is important not to oversimplify the characterization of top executives because there is enormous diversity in their personalities and behavior. That being said, over the years professional coaches—including those at CCL—have identified familiar themes and patterns among senior executives, which we describe below. Any one executive may not show all these characteristics, but among top executives these qualities are commonly found.

Experience

Senior executives are usually older and have more personal and professional life experience than do midlevel executives. (The average age of senior executives we work with is forty-seven. We are seeing a growing number who are younger than forty and many who are in their fifties.) If successful executives learn from their experiences, having more experiences means they've had more opportunities to learn. The fact they have continued up the promotional path implies they were able to retain and apply a fair number of those lessons.

Age doesn't guarantee wisdom, but senior executives do rely on firsthand knowledge gained from various organizational roles, project assignments, cross-functional duties, and often from having worked in multiple industries and multiple organizations. They are also inclined to attribute credibility to others with whom they share a street-smart approach born of hard work in the proverbial trenches.

Ambition and Mastery

Top-level executives are strongly driven to succeed, take on new challenges, and achieve mastery. Kaplan calls it *expansiveness* and defines it this way: "To be expansive is to possess a very considerable drive to achieve and to advance. The executive job requires someone who can move an organization forward by overcoming the inertia in any institution" (1991, p. 5). *Ego strength, self-confidence, resilience, determination,* and *drive* are all words used to describe this character trait.

For some senior executives, the need for accomplishment is virtually addictive. It is highly rewarding and self-reinforcing. Having built on their successes, senior executives hold little interest in repeating the past and eagerly look for new challenges. Many executives will tell you that when ambition's "fire in the belly" begins to wane, when their current role no longer seems to hold excitement or challenge, it is time to move on, do something new, or retire. Conversely, retirement or lack of advancement is difficult for those who still have the fire with no place to direct it.

Power and Control

Senior executives like to be in charge or at least have their ideas prevail. In addition to a need for dominance and control, senior-level people tend to be less interested in the relational aspects of their performance than in the more measurable aspects of making their numbers. Kiel, Rimmer, Williams, and Doyle write that "many even hold a fair amount of distrust and disdain for the 'soft' side of leadership. When push comes to shove, most executives habitually turn to leveraging the hard side—they focus on numbers and the bottom line and, in general, rely on the formula that worked in the past" (1996, p. 68).

In our work with senior executives, we see this need for power and control play out in their behavior, and we hear about it from their colleagues. One senior executive we worked with, who committed himself to the goal of establishing more positive relationships with colleagues, acknowledged that to do so would require "giving up my high need for control and sense of superiority."

Leadership Stature

Perhaps partly a function of age but certainly characteristic of many senior-level executives is a high degree of polish and bearing, or what might be called executive image. The senior leaders we encounter aren't arrogant or haughty; indeed, supreme graciousness is quite typical. It is a bit hard to describe precisely, but there is something in the body language, tone of voice, sense of presence, and confident manner of senior executives that sets them apart. In fact, the occasional lack of executive image in an otherwise successful senior executive is always noticeable and is a useful avenue to pursue in feedback and coaching.

Resistance to Change

By definition, making it to the top of the pyramid means an executive has been far more successful than not. So it's reasonable for senior executives to wonder why they should make changes when what they've done so far has worked so well. This perspective is common to most successful executives, and it's one of the most difficult and important challenges to address in coaching.

Most executives make it up the ladder by virtue of their ability to get the job done. Over the course of an executive's career, the rewards for certain kinds of behavior linked to certain kinds of success constitute an almost Darwinian selection process (who gets promoted and who doesn't) that reinforces "successful" leader characteristics while paradoxically strengthening potentially maladaptive qualities that become quite resistant to change. That process hides a potentially debilitating or at least limiting outcome: that strengths overused or misused become weaknesses (Kaplan & Palus, 1994).

At the top levels, old skills and strengths often have limited application to meeting new challenges. At best, executive self-reliance and overuse of a standby strength are inefficient and effective only within a limited reach. At worst, they impede others and limit the executive's own learning and growth. A senior leader's impact spans multiple layers across diverse functions, and successful execution depends far less on completing tasks than on exerting influence on others. It is a skill set beyond and perhaps even contrary to that which gets most executives promoted in the first place. Even for executives who continue to perform well overall, persistent sameness can lead to unintended and unseen side effects, such as overshadowing and limiting the potential of others to participate, learn, and grow, or an unswerving commitment to an idea or course of action that precludes flexibility and adaptability.

Interestingly, even when executives hear clear feedback about aspects of their behavior that need improvement, even when they correctly answer the question, "Why should I change?" with "Because what got me here isn't going to keep me here," even when they are sincerely committed to changing their actions, their response seems almost hard-wired into them: *Do what has worked in the past.* It's important for coaches who come upon this perspective in their coachees to make a distinction between "resistance to change" and "unwillingness to change." A coachee may be willing to change, but it's still difficult to make the change. Some of that difficulty is connected to the executive's ambition and mastery, which yields an expectation, grounded in real experience, that he or she knows how to solve whatever problem arises. But what happens when the old solution or approach doesn't work and the executive has no other tools in her tool kit, and does not know how to acquire them? Making change even more difficult is the reluctance and discomfort that senior executives feel when they ask for help.

Chris Argyris addresses this from a learning perspective. He writes, "Put simply, because many professionals are almost always successful at what they do, they rarely experience failure. And because they have rarely failed, they have never learned how to learn from failure. So whenever their single-loop learning strategies go wrong, they become defensive, screen out criticism, and put the 'blame' on anyone and everyone but themselves. In short, their ability to learn shuts down precisely at the moment they need it the most" (1991, p. 100). In reinforcing the idea that this is a pronounced problem at the uppermost executive levels, he adds, "Those members of the organization that many assume to be the best at learning are, in fact, not very good at it. I am talking about the well-educated, high-powered, high-commitment professionals who occupy key leadership positions in the modern corporation" (p. 99).

M.O.O.

It may appear slightly comical in its written form, but the acronym points to a very real phenomenon: the Myth of Omniscience and Omnipotence. This psychological blind spot results from an unintended and largely unconscious co-conspiracy between senior executives and the collective members of the organization. It goes something like this: top executives are among the best and brightest people in the organization; they have a track record of success; they hold the reins of power; they are paid handsomely to get results; they should know the answers; they should be able to make results happen. Many executives accept and try to live up to the myth that they should be all-knowing and all-powerful, and too many organizations expect their executives to be card-carrying members of the legion of superheroes.

Let's be clear in our intent. This isn't about arrogant executives with highly inflated egos. Even the most humble, self-effacing executives fall prey to the myth. It is an unwritten contract that serves a steadying and reassuring function for the organization. When successful executives become even mildly aware of a problem, they get to work immediately trying to solve it. They don't wonder if they alone know the answer or who other than themselves are in the best position to influence a successful outcome. Rather, they make a sincere, honest, well-intentioned effort to do their best (on their own) to figure it out. After all, they are in charge; it's up to them.

Organizations contribute powerfully to this mind-set. If a coach were to ask senior executives how safe it is for them to be franker and more open about their own weaknesses, the areas where they could benefit from learning more and from seeking the help of others, the answer would likely be, "You've got to be kidding." The risk that a senior executive might be perceived as weak or incompetent is not to be taken lightly. We once explored with a very senior executive management team member for a large financial services firm the possibility of his approaching the CEO to ask for greater clarity and support around his leadership development needs. He paused, gave us an odd look, and said, "Remember, this is Wall Street." The organization expects its senior people to know what to do and how to do it. And so the myth continues.

Air Is Rare

The notion of rarefied air at the top is no myth. In fact, there are some very real circumstances working at this altitude that coaches need to keep in mind. Senior executives certainly do. It takes time to adjust to the elevation, and as executives adjust, changes in their attitude and behavior are likely. For example, top executives are always short on time. As one executive complains, "Because I'm so busy, I'm always in relationship deficit mode with somebody." Better time management, prioritization, and delegating are reasonable and fairly standard approaches, but they don't eliminate the problem.

One of the adjustments we see in many executives is their exquisite sensitivity to and distaste for time wasters. Many senior executives work diligently toward ridding themselves of things (people, activities, ideas) that have little or no real importance or value. One executive told of his extreme frustration with direct reports who had an alarming capacity to "get distracted by all the bright shiny objects." If you want to upset a senior executive, just try to force him to spend (waste) time on something where there's no discernible return on that investment. Senior leaders would usually rather err on the side of excluding rather than including marginal possibilities: even if there's a small chance of a nugget in there, they'll pass and look for the next one if the time and energy demand is too costly.

Hierarchy Effect

David Campbell describes another predictable phenomenon that occurs as people move up the executive ladder, which he calls the hierarchy effect: the higher a person is in the organizational hierarchy, the more likely he is to have a satisfied view and positive assessment of the organizational climate. Campbell offers two plausible reasons for the hierarchy effect, noting that they are not necessarily conflicting but may actually be complementary. First, life at the top is good: "They have more control over their destiny; they are better informed about what is happening; they have a greater voice in organizational policies; they have more opportunities to try out their own ideas; they live in more elegant surroundings; they have greater access to organizational resources; and they are paid higher salaries and are more likely to benefit from extended compensation plans. Why shouldn't they be happier?" (Campbell & Hyne, 1995, p. 108).

Campbell's other explanation for the hierarchy effect is that happier, optimistic people are more likely to gain promotion to the top of their organizations. "It may not be 'the higher you are, the happier you are,' but rather 'the happier you are, the higher you will go'" (Campbell & Hyne, 1995, p. 108). Regardless of the reasons for the hierarchy effect for any particular executive, it is clear that senior executives tend toward a more positive view of their organization than those further down the ladder.

Wealth

We've alluded to the salary and other perks that top executives enjoy, but it's worth paying specific attention to compensation and its impact on senior executives. Albeit unpredictable in its influence, the wealth effect is almost always a powerful one. Executives readily acknowledge that "money is the scorecard" in corporations, at least American ones, and the pain of incredibly long work hours and time away from personal and family pursuits is mollified by their pay package.

Where a high degree of trust has been established in the coaching relationship, top executives are sometimes more open about the powerful influence that wealth plays in their lives and the choices they make. Coaches should keep this factor in mind, even if the executive coachee does not openly discuss it. In addition to functioning as a measure of success, wealth may represent the means to personal freedom and autonomy. Senior executives also acknowledge that it prompts a broader sense of responsibility to family, often extending into future generations, community, and society. Combined with the legacy issues we discuss in the next section, it may also lead to philanthropic endeavors.

There are important challenges and potential downsides to the powerful influence of wealth. Sometimes the lure of enormous bonuses can place the executive's own well-being in competition with the best interests of the organization. We have seen more than one organization reward top executives with major payouts tied to short-term financial benchmarks that were well publicized to shareholders. We have also observed (but didn't coach directly) top executives at one company who managed to hit short-term earnings targets by ruthlessly cutting costs, including significant layoffs in a number of areas deemed critical to the organization's mission by mid- to senior-level managers. This raised strong doubts internally as to the long-term viability of some of the company's key strategic initiatives, but top executives were widely praised from outside the organization and the stock price was boosted (at least temporarily) when ambitious earnings goals were met. What those senior executives didn't hear were the comments we heard from their subordinates, such as: "We agree there was fat that needed to be cut out, but we've definitely cut into muscle and bone at this point." Of equal concern from a leadership perspective, it was not uncommon to hear thinly veiled suspicion and cynicism that the "big bonuses" promised to the top team were driving its business decisions. Lower-level leaders responsible for executing the strategy came to see it as tainted by the top leaders' compensation, and their enthusiasm for carrying out the strategic plan was greatly reduced.

At worst, one might conclude that selfish personal gain will sometimes override the best interests of the organization and the long-term value to shareholders, and there are certainly enough ghastly stories of executive greed and malfeasance in recent years to lend credence to that view. But even apart from egregious abuse (which coaches are unlikely to witness directly), there may be an important "wealth effect" that never approaches an Enron level of abuse, but nonetheless has an impact on judgment and decisions when personal and organizational interests are potentially at odds. For example, aversion to risk is heightened when personal fortunes are at stake, even when such risks might ultimately serve the organization. If nothing else, coaches need to stay mindful of what is at stake and to inquire appropriately about potential dilemmas that place an executive's personal interests at odds with those of the organization.

In some cases, the most poignant consequence of the money effect is when the executive chooses (or has allowed to develop) a lifestyle that becomes self-reinforcing or even addictive. It becomes a coaching issue when the executive begins to realize or consider the price of the trade-offs: time away from personal interests, family, and friendships. The balance between work and personal life is among the most compelling concerns for senior executives.

Legacy

The psychologist Erik Erikson and colleagues identify eight human developmental stages. He uses the term *generativity* to describe the seventh stage, when the mature adult begins to think and act with a focus toward the future, toward creating a legacy for the next generation. As Erikson sees it, to create such a legacy is an altruistic, unselfish form of love and caring for others. It is achieved in dynamic tension against (or conflict with) its opposite pole: stagnation and self-absorption (Erikson, Erikson, & Kivnick, 1986).

In actual practice, this legacy quest may have positive or negative outcomes. Making strategic decisions for the future well-being and stability of the company and planning carefully for the development and succession of the next generation of leaders are highly desirable. Often it is at this stage that senior executives become most interested in coaching others. Coaches are wise to tap into the executive's reservoir of duty to those who come after.

On the negative side, there may be such reliance on the executive's particular brand of leadership, the persona, and strength of character that it creates inertia against change. Executives may hang on past their level of maximum effectiveness, with the mistaken belief that their departure would leave the job undone or risk chaos and failure to the organization. Or the search for a replacement may place too great an emphasis on trying to replicate the strengths of the departing leader. The level of respect, affection, or deference to the top executive may also make it difficult to provide her with the kind but painful feedback that it is time to go.

The former CEO of Quest Diagnostics, Kenneth Freeman, chose to step down at age fifty-three. He noted that he might have extended his tenure if he had been sixty-three and close to retirement, but he realized "then there would have been the risk that, when I turned sixty-five, the board would have extended my contract for another three years and, as so often happens with a CEO, I'd have become a predictable part of the furniture" (2004, p. 59). Freeman writes persuasively that "the CEO's real legacy" is to plan early and well for the succession of the next CEO: "It's hard to give up the reins. But a chief executive who initiates and manages his own succession can add enormous value to the company" (p. 51).

Using the CCL Coaching Framework with Senior Executives

Any attempt at a linear or cookbook approach to coaching top-level executives is particularly risky. Taken simply as a framework of ideas, CCL's straightforward approach is useful because it's not overly complex or convoluted. It's a self-correcting tool the leader coach may apply to any coaching engagement, a way to gauge the coaching engagement as it unfolds in order to identify gaps or make necessary adjustments and corrections.

Relationship

The importance of establishing and maintaining a good relationship with top executives cannot be overstated. When we have seen top-level coaching go awry, it is almost always due to a problem in this area. The central tenets of the relationship—collaboration, rapport, and commitment—certainly hold for senior executives. We discuss each of these briefly.

Collaboration. The collaborative aspect of relationship is probably foremost for senior-level executives. They are used to making decisions; they are fairly autonomous and self-contained; they won't respond well to a coach who promotes wholesale changes in their attitudes or behaviors.

Even when it is apparent that some significant behavior change or shift in their perspective would be beneficial, senior executives prefer to have a dialogue with someone who can challenge their thinking and assumptions. They want expertise less for the purpose of being told what to do than for knowing the coach is prepared to have a point of view, one that broadens their own.

To this end, a coach's credibility is always at issue. Like trust, it is lost more easily than it is gained. Part of it comes from a sufficient level of experience and knowledge so that senior leaders see they can learn something new or different by talking to a coach. As Witherspoon and White remind us, "A coach who misunderstands basic business issues or makes impractical suggestions will not be able to gain the trust of and build rapport with a business executive" (1996, p. 15). Coaches may usefully borrow from and refer to past experience with other senior-level executives, although examples need to be woven in naturally and where relevant.

Credibility requires coaches to have confidence to challenge and offer opinions that may differ from the executive's own. In fact, regardless of whether they acknowledge it and even if they don't particularly like it, top executives expect their coach to fulfill the key role of truth teller. Whether it comes from interpretation of 360-degree feedback data, interviews with colleagues, or the coach's own observations of the executive, a coach at this level must be willing and able to tell it straight—both the positive and the negative. Sometimes that means acknowledging the executive's feelings while reframing alternatives.

To perform this role as a coach, you need to be comfortable with bad news. In fact, your own comfort with bad news (serious, thoughtful, but nonetheless comfortable) helps instill trust not only in you personally, but also in the hope for finding solutions going forward. Keeping expectations hopeful and realistic is vital. It's better not to overpromise or underexpect what changes may occur.

Senior leader coaches may have an edge over professional coaches with the credibility of personal experience, and if they avoid the trap of offering only advice, they can stimulate significant change in the coachee's thought processes. However, because they also live in the organization and politics and power are significant factors at senior levels, trust may be harder to come by than credibility.

Associated with collaboration is the coach's capacity for siding with the executive coachee (as support, for example) but not against the organization or the people and challenges the executive faces. It is crucial to maintain deep and genuine interest, but not overinvestment, in the executive's success. Executives are in charge of their behavior and decisions, answer to their constituents, and own their successes and failures. Because the stakes are so high, the need for healthy boundaries between coach and executive (and the pressures that work against them) is magnified.

Rapport. Rapport is usually ascertained early in the coaching engagement, for practical reasons. Given their penchant for not wasting time, executives will likely size up the coach quickly for a reasonable degree of fit and compatibility, which may include energy level, sense of humor, common background and interests, perceived thinking style, and pace. While rapport might be successfully nurtured over time, senior executives (more so than leaders at other levels) are not inclined to make that investment, no matter how convinced the coach may be that it will work eventually. If there are problems with rapport, executives will not necessarily be direct or take the initiative to say, "I don't think we have good chemistry." They may simply say they don't need or want to pursue further coaching at this time, or their interest or commitment may just fade, evidenced by such markers as a failure to return calls and canceling or abbreviating coaching sessions at the last minute. Coaches should directly address a perceived mismatch.

Commitment. Coaches need to be clear and affirming and make promises they will keep with regard to availability, speed in returning telephone calls, and similar actions. It is also important to assess the executive's level of commitment. Sometimes a lack of commitment exists even when rapport seems positive. For example, an executive may overextend herself and then cut back on coaching as the most affordable time commitment to give up. Occasionally executives are coaxed into the engagement by others in the organization and never really make the personal investment themselves. Obviously those engagements are rarely productive, and there's not much point in going through the motions.

In circumstances such as these, it's better for the coach to respect the executive's current low motivation or commitment and suggest a discontinuation or postponement. Offering something like, "It doesn't appear that coaching is a very high priority for you right now; should we discuss best options going forward?" may be useful. It's sometimes hard for coaches to think about giving up a coaching engagement with someone very senior in the organization, but it's better to stay on a positive note than to hold on too long and create a negative association with you personally or with coaching. This allows the door to stay open for future opportunities if circumstances change for the executive.

If your coachee exhibits signs of low commitment, you may encourage this person to talk to other executives who have used a coach. Commitment to coaching may require a few planned trial-run sessions to allow the executive to evaluate whether coaching is worth putting on his priority list. Remember the demands of top-level leadership: every time something goes on the priority list, something else has to come off.

Assessment

From our observation of executive coaching practices, assessment is an area that is often underemphasized. We have seen (and sometimes felt ourselves) the pressure to move quickly, especially in stand-alone coaching situations, when supposedly there is a clear developmental issue that needs to be addressed. In fact, the more senior the executive is, the greater is the pressure to start "working the problem" immediately. Coaches should slow the process down enough to ensure that an adequate assessment is completed and that a reasonable delineation of goals emerges from the assessment process. Completing an adequate assessment takes time and is essential for a successful long-term result. Giving the executive an honest appraisal up front about the nature and time frame for the assessment process lays a healthy groundwork for the start of a coaching initiative. Lasting change takes time; it's counterproductive to operate as a coaching SWAT team with high-intensity, emergency solutions.

Leader coaches typically don't conduct such formal assessments on their own. They usually have the benefit of accumulated knowledge of the executive coachee from direct observation, reputation, ongoing performance results, and periodic performance reviews. While this offers some of the best forms of assessment, leader coaches should not assume that they have all the necessary information and neglect to consider what else they need to know about the coachee. In times of expressed urgency, the coach needs to balance several things: acknowledging and validating the need to move the process expeditiously, setting realistic expectations for the nature and time line of an adequate assessment, and proceeding as deliberately as necessary to ensure completeness of the initial assessment.

The initial assessment may often be quite detailed and formalized; although subsequent assessments are usually less detailed or time intensive, there is an iterative process to assessment that is important to keep in mind throughout the coaching engagement. We use the term *initial assessment* quite intentionally—not to promote interminable addiction to ever more numbers and graphs, but to emphasize that assessment is not just a one-time event. With top-level executives, it is particularly beneficial to help them internalize the value of assessment as a routine and ongoing process, especially about, by, and for themselves as leaders.

An important shift for top executives is not just to do things differently, but also to think differently about themselves and their ongoing development as leaders and change agents in their organizations. Leadership is, of course, about what you do, not just what or how you think; but the best way to sustain adaptive and effective leadership behavior is for leaders to learn to think differently about themselves and about how they do what they do. It is a learning process, not an event or a specific behavior, and continued assessment is fundamental to learning.

There is no one-size-fits-all list of assessment tools or approaches for this level of coaching. Kaplan and Palus (1994) maintain that standard feedback does not address performance at the level that is important to senior-level executives. Whereas traditional 360-degree feedback for most levels of management tries to get at identifying strengths and weaknesses based on performance ratings from peers, superiors, and subordinates, senior executives require a richer form of feedback. This may include detailed verbatim descriptions, observations from family and friends, psychometric measures of personality and motivation, and an extended coaching relationship. These intensive assessment methods are used in CCL's Awareness Program for Executive Excellence (APEX), and a modified and somewhat less detailed assessment is used in CCL's Leadership at the Peak (LAP) program. With virtually all senior executives, we use 360-degree multirater feedback, personality and work style inventories, and interviews.

We often use the term *whole life* to describe the differentiating characteristics of assessing senior executives. Sometimes this means that interviews are conducted with key individuals in the executive's personal life such as spouse, grown children, and personal friends. In addition, the assessment process examines the historical origins of values and interests, contextual examples of executive presence, impact on team effectiveness, and organizational climate. Senior leaders cast long shadows, and it is important for them to understand and assess their influence across multiple levels.

The context component is sometimes more elusive and subject to interpretation, but the contextual influence is enormously important for senior executives and their coaches to consider. Right or wrong, fair or unfair, top-level executives receive causal attribution from people below them based on how things are going in the organization. Sometimes the executive gets to take advantage of the fact things are going very well. Whether the executive really made a difference or was lucky enough to be in the driver's seat when the checkered flag was waved, she gets credit and her performance ratings tend to reflect that attribution. Conversely, even great executives can be victims of circumstances well beyond their control. If things aren't going well, it's natural for people to identify someone to blame, and the top seat is usually also the hot seat. Attribution takes a nasty toll in those cases. As a common example, consider the frequent stories in the daily sports pages that describe managers and coaches being fired because the team isn't performing up to expectations.

One executive we coached suffered the adverse effects of having her leadership strengths reevaluated in the light of a new job assignment and the new context in which she operated. Jenny had the enviable reputation of being the "go to" executive: if a project needed to be done well, on time, and under budget, she was the one to do it, and that played no small part in the accelerated promotional path she enjoyed. No one was more determined, dedicated, or hard working than Jenny. Sometimes her success seemed to come from sheer force of will in making things happen.

Jenny's track record earned her the opportunity to take over a turnaround business unit that was underperforming and lagging on several quality indicators. But at this new, more senior level and with a more complex set of challenges, Jenny's forceful behavior—within a very different context—did not appear so universally positive. Almost a year into her new job, the unit looked about the same and Jenny was frustrated; moreover, her performance assessments and respondent interviews were well below what she had come to expect. The story behind the assessment was that all of Jenny's positive attributes were still there, but a new story was emerging. Jenny had alienated many senior managers in the business unit by virtue of a "can do" attitude that struck some as overzealous or even immature; some felt insulted and blamed, believing they were now seen as incompetent and in need of help from this outsider.

Part of the problem was indeed about and because of Jenny, and part of the problem was about others and their unwillingness or inability to meet her halfway. There were other factors operating too. Few would say so directly, but Jenny's being a woman seemed to increase the resentment from the mostly male management staff. Perhaps even more significant was the hard business truth: the unit had been poorly run and underresourced for a long time and had been overtaken in the marketplace by skilled competitors, so it was likely that anyone taking over the reins would have suffered a similar fate. For Jenny, all three of the above dimensions (her behavior as a leader, the needs and behaviors of her colleagues, and the organizational and business context) had to be examined to make sense of the assessment data now before her.

As a final thought on assessment for this special population of coachees, it's wise to understand that inadequate assessment can lead to inefficiency and frustration with coaching because issues that could or should have been identified earlier may exert their influence but may not be captured clearly or in a form that allows direct examination and exploration. Even when a full battery of instruments and interviews is completed, the coach should retain a healthy respect for that which remains to be uncovered. Assessment is best seen as an ongoing process of discovery and clarification rather than an end point of final clarity. In the final analysis, the executive coachee holds key pieces of the assessment, and time spent understanding her will offer the most valuable information.

Challenge

The personal qualities and circumstances that set top-level executives apart from those at lower levels also describe the key challenges for coaches to address or at least keep in mind while working with them. For example, as we touched on in our discussion of assessment, the focus of coaching is often less about what an executive does behaviorally—at least in the immediate moment—and more on how the executive thinks about and processes things going forward. By challenging previous assumptions and giving the executive new ways to consider a variety of issues (his leadership effectiveness, the needs and preferences of colleagues and clients, the analysis and planning process for business decisions), coaching can yield more significant and enduring effects.

When it comes to coaching executives (senior and otherwise), it is important to take a mature and complex view of emotions, to examine how they influence thoughts and actions, and certainly not to avoid them or pretend they don't exist. At its best, coaching helps top executives become better learners and promotes cognitive flexibility and increased emotional complexity that enhance possibilities for lasting and important change. It is the integration of intellectual and emotional awareness and change that is the true challenge of coaching top executives. That doesn't mean a coach needs to employ psychotherapy to untangle complex childhood trauma or to ameliorate clinical pathology. However, there is often a level of depth in the self-analysis and recalibration of behavior with top-level executives that surpasses initial expectations and can exceed what is commonly seen with midlevel executives. It is not surprising that top-level executives have a distinct level of intellectual and emotional depth; it's what got them to the top. So the nature and intensity of a coaching intervention must, in essence, match the personal qualities of the person being coached. This is not always easy, but it is a process that, to be successful, virtually always requires a challenge to the executive's intellectual and emotional habits, assumptions, and behaviors. (A useful perspective for understanding the challenge of coaching senior executives is the adult development frame of Robert Kegan, which is described in Chapter Twelve, along with a discussion of those concepts as applied to coaching.)

Separating cognitive from emotional changes is conceptually useful, although these may appear less distinct or separate in practice. The emphasis in any particular case may lean more toward one dimension or the other, but when we see executives change their mind-set, there is usually a corresponding change in their "emotional-set" as well. One executive we coached was a highly successful attorney who won his spurs and reputation in the courtroom: he was seen as a litigator's litigator and eventually became the managing partner in his large law firm. He had also become increasingly troubled, however, that his aggressive and adversarial style was present whenever and wherever he asserted his influence. He could effectively look over his own shoulder in relationships with colleagues, family, and friends, and he did not like what he saw. He accurately dissected his behavior, recognized the adverse reaction it elicited from others, but couldn't bring himself to behave like the "nice guy" he believed himself to be—at least not when some dispute or difference of opinion, however slight, was at stake.

His rather enlightened self-analysis was almost purely intellectual—necessary to be sure, but not sufficient to get him where he wanted to be. It became evident there was a crucial polarity in his thinking and, even more important, an inhibiting emotional association that drove his behavior. His experience had always combined and reinforced a link between aggressive, adversarial intensity and winning. The accompanying association, which he had not recognized, was that to behave other than aggressively risked losing—and that triggered fears of disempowerment and loss of competence that threatened his abiding sense of self, his personal identity. It wasn't the desire to win that was so powerful; it was the fear of losing.

Through coaching, this executive was able to examine his own worst fear (clearly more an emotional issue than an intellectual one) of being a loser and to challenge his unconscious and unrealistic belief that his identity was therefore at stake. The healthy and successful alternative for him was to define and practice assertive behavior that did not cross the line into being aggressive, choose his battles more selectively, and allow some losses in which others' opinions prevailed over his own. Maintaining and strengthening relationships became a domain where he could truly win, while lost arguments became largely disconnected from his self-worth. Importantly, he was able to internalize a new definition of himself, although not until after some initial hesitation in trying new behavior. He had to risk the new behavior and actually experience the emotional satisfaction and acceptance from others that followed it. Both intellectual and emotional change came together to allow lasting behavior change.

Disequilibrium, stretch, and obstacles look very different for senior leaders than they do for managers lower in the organization. Rarely is a senior executive totally surprised by assessment feedback. Closing the gap in perception, which can create a powerful unfreezing process for most junior and midlevel executives, is not the typical motivator for change to a senior-level manager. These executives are usually not engaged in coaching to close a gap in leadership skill so they can get the next promotion. Their primary obstacles are more often internal than external. They are looking less for affirmation than they are for subtle and nuanced feedback that can help them make decisions about their personal leadership style. At this stage in their development as a leader, they are less likely to assess themselves against a set of leadership competencies or a particular leadership model. They are creating their own personal model of leadership and assessing themselves against this personal ideal.

Support

Senior executives may sometimes minimize the importance of social and emotional support. Their view is often reinforced because, like so many other kinds of information and feedback, the opportunities for social and emotional support grow smaller as an executive rises in the organization. Not only is support less available in the executive's daily work environment, it is not something the self-contained and often proud senior executive thinks about or feels a need to put into place. A coach is often in a unique position to provide such support for a top-level executive where his feelings of vulnerability can be managed in a more private setting. It can be useful for coaches to remind executives that, especially at their level, changes are likely to be more incremental than dramatic—although even incremental change can have enormous effects throughout the organization.

It is useful to encourage executives to create and maintain external sources of support within their natural environment. Some of that may come by addressing and demythologizing their power and sense of responsibility. Simply put, executives need to learn that it's okay to ask others for support. The support may also take a form that is less personally nurturing or emotional than how we often think of it. Many executives say they feel very supported and invigorated simply by staying connected to others through shared goals and accomplishment.

Coaches can help executives anticipate challenges and mentally rehearse potential problems and responses, based on what they already know about their own particular preferences, strengths, and weaknesses. That is also a function of the more complex intellectual and emotional integration that very senior executives have attained. This ability to know themselves well enough within their own context that they can introspect and project themselves is like a game of mental and emotional chess in which they operate as one of many pieces on the board, relative to the world. More than just planning how to counter others' moves, successful executives create a kind of self-supporting and sustaining reservoir of strength by recognizing their intellectual and emotional frames and sensibilities, appreciating what they're likely to think and feel under certain circumstances, and considering how they might improve, expand, or even alter their repertoire of behaviors. Proactive behavior has enormous supportive and sustaining value over reactive behavior.

Interestingly, despite behaviors that often suggest strong ego and even egotism, senior executives may feel self-conscious about the very idea that they need to receive or create support in any direct way. It may carry connotations of being selfish, needy, or dependent. For some, this is a potentially critical blind spot that warrants further examination. It seems almost ironic that people at the highest levels, who in some sense have the most to lose, appear to have previously spent so little time on purposeful reflection about the choices of where, how, and with whom they invest their most precious resources of time and energy. One coaching tactic to encourage reflective practice as a means of support is described in Exhibit 6.1.

Results

Top executives tend to set goals and measure results with a broad, whole-life perspective; traditional measures of success remain important but are complemented and enhanced by yardsticks that are somewhat more elusive, qualitative, and internally held. In many business and professional contexts, self-measured outcomes are rightly viewed with skepticism due to errors of bias and limited perspective. Although some of that also applies to measuring developmental changes of top executives, the inherently internal or subjective aspects need to be accepted and even embraced.

Senior people typically hold themselves to a very high standard anyway, so incorporating that ingrained habit and perhaps influencing and shaping it is a useful avenue for coaches to pursue. Similar to many other aspects of the coaching relationship and process with senior-level executives, the best advice we can offer is to focus less on the detailed "how to" of defining goals and measuring results and more on facilitating a shift in framework—or the

EXHIBIT 6.1. A WAY TOWARD SELF REFLECTION AND SUPPORT.

One form of support and accountability that CCL uses with senior executives is writing a letter to themselves. The letter serves as a reminder, when it is mailed back to the executive, of their motivation for and commitment to achieving their goals. Following is a portion of one such letter:

> Dear Frank,
>
> Well, you've really gone and done it to yourself, old buddy. You took that course at CCL and it has sliced you open to the core, and now you've got to do something about it. You came into this program thinking it would help make you a better leader at work, and I'm sure it will, but it's opened up a much larger and more important issue, and that's leadership in your life. From your 360 scores and peer feedback, you definitely are skilled at aligning constituents and motivating and inspiring others. Frank, the issue for you is setting direction, and I've got news for you, it's not setting business direction for [the company], it's setting direction in your life. You're at the crossroads. You have done very well in your career and you have some wonderful opportunities ahead, opportunities that others in the organization would give their right arm for. But with all this good fortune, you've been struggling internally for the past couple years. . . . It's a question of direction and only you can decide. . . . You do just fine; don't be so hard on yourself. . . . Just open up and be yourself and stop worrying about what others think. . . . You should believe in yourself. Good luck.
>
> Your friend, Frank

---

philosophy—of what it means for executives to measure their development and evaluate the results of changes in their leadership. In the negative extreme, this approach perhaps runs the risk of veering off into happy navel gazing, devoid of any reasonable standard to determine whether meaningful change is occurring. But we believe it is necessary to consider a different or at least more flexible standard for measuring results in the context of coaching and facilitating cognitive and emotional developmental change. One such measure, particularly at the most senior executive levels, is a climate survey.

Determining the coach's impact or the executive's effectiveness using strictly objective measures (like bottom-line numbers) potentially rules out entire domains of crucial and relevant inquiry. This is not a recommendation to try and move the executive into a safe zone, where numbers no longer matter. But it is often very useful for executives to expand the nature and type of gauges they use to measure results, both for themselves as leaders and with regard to others for whom they are the evaluators. Psychologists remain a long way from being able to satisfactorily measure either existing or evolving states of cognition and emotion, much less the behavioral impact of those changes, but that does not preclude valuable exploration and influence within those areas.

For senior executives, we find it is most useful when they adopt a balanced, multifaceted consideration of results. There is currently no gold standard against which to calibrate the accuracy of any particular measurement. Introspection and self-analysis yield one important source of data. Close discussion with a trusted confidant and adviser provides another useful source. When the executive learns to self-assess and collaborate with trusted advisers, some reasonable windows can be opened, and kept open, on the hidden cognitive and emotional frameworks they use and the changes they are making. Subjective reports about things "feeling better" (or not) or "working well" (or not) do not provide the final and only answer, but they certainly should be given credence. Repeated multirater feedback, cultural assessments, and interviews can also be helpful, although broad assessments may be less helpful at later stages in the coaching process than more targeted questions related to the executive's distinguishing leadership characteristics and influence.

Coaching Themes for Senior Executives

Earlier in this chapter we described common qualities of senior executives. In this section, we highlight some common coaching themes that surface in our work with them. It's worth noting that the personal themes are similar to those we encounter with executives at all levels, but at senior levels they are more intense. The professional themes tend to be more characteristic of senior-level roles. Whereas coaching at lower levels tends to target specific management skills, senior-level coaching generally aims at more complex or high-level systemic issues.

Deepening Relationship and Influencing Abilities

It's no accident that improving relationship and influencing skills emerges as a common issue for senior executives. To achieve their position, senior executives have had to continuously demonstrate skills in running the business and getting results. So those capabilities are less often in question. It's not that senior executives lack relationship and influencing skills. More often than not, those skills are not as well honed or developed as their business skills. Compound that fact with the reality that these executives are, more than ever before in their careers, dependent on others to achieve their goals. There is a premium on how well senior executives understand and develop others, tap into their motivations, create a vision others can embrace, and ensure superior implementation of organizational strategy.

Leading the Organization Through Transition

Leaders at every level and in every industry are faced with leading and managing people through change. (Chapter Eight delves deeply into this issue.) What makes this issue different for senior executives is their proximity to the process and their role in triggering or managing the change event. They are more likely to be in a position to influence what and how things change. They are often the final decision makers. Part of the coach's role is to provide senior executives a sounding board for their doubts, concerns, and inspirations surrounding the change and transition. The coach may also help senior executives think through effective ways to lead the organization through the change and transition in a way that validates any distress they feel, while helping them maintain their optimism and productivity as they move to the new state.

Creating Cultural Change

Senior executives have a broad interest in maximizing their impact on the organization's climate and culture. They realize that the organization's values, resources, and core competencies have to align to maintain competitive advantage. They need to create the conditions where change, risk taking, and learning are embraced. In addition, they need to be role models for the desired new state.

Making systemic change is daunting. Coaching can help senior executives see how their personal behaviors and attitudes enable or hinder the desired cultural shift. In addition, senior executives usually need to explore how the senior leadership team operates relative to the desired organizational culture. Someone from outside the team, such as a coach, brings a fresh perspective to the process.

Building Future Leadership Capacity

Succession planning is an assumed component of a senior executive's role. However, often that role is delegated to the HR executive and managers until the executive's departure appears on the horizon. Coaches may prompt top executives to be more forward looking and deliberate toward succession and the development of key leaders.

This is also a time when the senior executive's role as leader coach can be addressed more directly. Is the senior executive providing sufficient guidance, tapping the best capabilities of others, and helping them confront their own developmental challenges? Take the case of one senior executive who is within five years of retirement and has identified a direct report as her likely successor, but realizes he is weak in many leadership skills. From working with her own coach, she recognizes that her emphasis on business skills has inadvertently contributed to his leadership gaps. As a result, she commits herself to developing her direct report's leadership skills and works to improve her own coaching skills to achieve that goal.

We have seen many organizations undertake costly, broad-based initiatives to coach and develop their next generation of leaders. One of the most important factors in the success of these initiatives is the modeling at the top. The CEO sets the tone, and if she doesn't become visibly and directly involved in the process (actively coaching others and, ideally, being coached), it sends a mixed message to those further down in the organization.

Reassessing Personal Trade-Offs

It's well understood that executives, and senior executives in particular, make significant sacrifices in their personal lives to achieve their levels of responsibility. It's not uncommon for the coaching dialogue to focus on weighing the price they have paid and exploring opportunities to rebuild or rediscover these relationships and balance between work and personal life. For midlevel executives and senior executives whose families are still young, that discussion is more likely to revolve around ways to find more balance or incorporate that issue into their current career decisions. For very senior executives and those whose family lives are at a more mature stage, the discussions are more a reflection of past choices—coming to terms with those choices and making sense and meaning of their lives today in that context.

A CEO engaged in coaching confessed that his greatest concern in receiving feedback was not what work colleagues would report but rather what his children and wife would say. He was most anxious to learn if, in his children's eyes, the sacrifices he made to support his ambitions and their lifestyle were worth it. And with regard to his wife, he speculated nervously whether enough of their original relationship remained to survive their now empty nest.

The outcomes of these coaching scenarios are varied. Some end with wonderful stories of reconnection and renewal, and others end in sadness over opportunities lost and the need to begin anew. Regardless of the outcomes, the chance to give senior executives space to reflect and receive feedback on the impact of their leadership choices at home, as well as at work, is valuable to them and rewarding to us as coaches.

Reclaiming Self and Achieving Authenticity

Implicit in our coaching with senior executives is the expectation that change happens when they become more self-aware and retain openness to learning. It also means they embrace who they are rather than struggle to redefine or re-create themselves in some fundamental way. Bunker (2005) argues that authenticity in leadership is more than sincerity and good intentions, more than being true to self. Authenticity implies a deeper understanding of what is really going on in oneself and in others. It's grounded in genuine openness to feedback and growth and a refusal to collude in self-deception.

In this process of becoming clearer and more accepting of self, warts and all, senior executives find themselves questioning choices they've previously taken for granted and valuing different choices. These executives are able to incorporate others' perceptions of them into their own awareness without having to choose one as the truth.

Consider the story of one such senior executive, who was competing for the CEO position at the time he engaged in intensive coaching. He received his aggregate feedback nearly simultaneously with learning that he had not been selected. After reflecting on his own self-assessment (including his goals and the company's needs) as well as others' feedback, he concluded the right choice had been made. While initially hurt and disappointed, he came to realize that he wanted the CEO job because it was the obvious next step. He never stopped to question how compatible the demands of the role were with who he was. As a result, he made the decision to stay with the company, proposed a new senior role that leveraged his strengths, and privately began to design his exit plan, which he successfully implemented when the timing was right.

Leading Self Through Transition

Transition for senior executives can take a number of forms: new role, new career, new phase of life. Sometimes the three are intertwined, with the executive leaving to pursue personal interests or define a new professional arena. Each form of change is usually accompanied by some degree of internal reflection, churning, and uncertainty. Few undergo this type of change without alternating and, at times, conflicting thoughts and feelings.

For personal transition issues, senior executives value coaching that helps them rediscover their passions, think through options and timing, and manage their energy toward new possibilities. One coaching challenge is to help senior executives balance between anticipating new interests, while sustaining necessary devotion to existing work issues and people who rely on them.

Conclusion

This chapter emphasizes the characteristics of top-level executives, and all the qualities we have identified are coachable. The challenge for a coach is to understand the issues and adapt methods that apply generally to senior-level people, while continuing to respect each executive's unique history and circumstances. This requires a high level of coaching sophistication, flexibility, and experience. The coaching role for top executives may be filled by other senior leader coaches or by professional coaches from inside or outside the organization. While the complexity and demands of coaching at this level can be significant, the end results are often quite rewarding for both the coachee and the coach.

Senior executives are sometimes perceived as gruff and difficult, but we more often find them personable and eager to learn. With or without the more obvious rough spots, what these executives have in common is a keen interest in maintaining their winning edge—to meet stakeholders' and their own expectations and to benchmark and sharpen themselves for new challenges. They realize that the tenure of those at the top of the hierarchy is becoming increasingly shorter. Of course, the survival imperative, in and of itself, rarely translates directly to improved leader behavior, and executives are increasingly seeking coaching and support for staying at the top of their game.

PART THREE

COACHING FOR SPECIFIC LEADERSHIP CHALLENGES AND CAPACITIES

Ask leaders what their key leadership challenges are, and you could spend hours listening. The very nature of leadership entails managing numerous daily challenges that range from quick firefighting to long-term strategic planning and systemic change. Part Three discusses two topical areas that will continue to figure prominently in the development and practice of leadership.

One of those areas is acknowledged as an essential leadership skill that can make the difference between good and superior company performance: the development of high levels of emotional intelligence. Chapter Seven discusses what is meant by emotional intelligence (as it has been defined by the work of Daniel Goleman), why it matters, and how to coach for development of increased emotional intelligence. This chapter discusses how important it is for coaches to have developed high levels of emotional competence in order to discern and coach for those aspects of emotional intelligence that may require further development in coachees.

Chapter Eight deals with a second topical issue: managing and leading others through the constant change that is now the norm in business. This chapter discusses the emotional impact of change and transition and how leaders can effectively coach others through change. A key discussion point for leader coaches is how they face their own emotions around the change they are asking others to adopt. Learning to coach others through change requires an examination of your own response and the ability to coach yourself or let others coach you.

Chapter Nine addresses the issue of physical well-being and fitness as a leadership challenge. Some readers may question whether this topic exceeds the boundaries of traditional leadership coaching. After all, some physical conditions are linked to genetics and other factors beyond the coachee's control. CCL's coaching principles adhere to a focus on those attributes that a leader can learn and develop and on those developmental areas with which a coach can appropriately assist. We firmly agree that coaches should set and respect boundaries around those issues that may be of such a personal nature that the coachee should best address them through types of professional support other than leadership coaching. This chapter acknowledges the validity of those questions. It also offers some valuable insights, based on CCL's research and experiences and on the work of others, into the relationship of physical fitness to leadership, some possible signs that may indicate it needs attention, and appropriate ways that a coach can support a coachee's recognized need in this area.

CHAPTER SEVEN

COACHING FOR EMOTIONAL COMPETENCE

Kathy E. Kram
Sharon Ting

In order to effectively meet the challenges posed by an increasingly turbulent global environment, leaders must have the capacity to understand and manage themselves, and they must have the social skills to manage relationships with customers, employees, suppliers, and other critical stakeholders (Bar-on & Parker, 2000; Cherniss & Goleman, 2001; Goleman, 1998). These capabilities, now commonly referred to as emotional competencies, become increasingly important as individuals advance in an organization and assume positions of greater authority and responsibility. Today leaders and coaches are generally in agreement about this strong link between emotional competence and high performance.

Numerous empirical studies completed at CCL and elsewhere have demonstrated that leadership failures are often related to the lack of critical emotional competencies (Cherniss & Goleman, 2001; Sala, Drusket, & Mount, 2006; Goleman, 1998). For example, high-potential young executives are found to mismanage relationships with their peers, failing to build the support needed in order to implement significant business strategies. Similarly, recently promoted managers fail to appreciate the behaviors required in their new roles and continue to employ tactics that were successful in their previous positions but do not translate to their current ones. Their failure to learn and adapt to new challenges results in inappropriate actions that reduce their credibility and effectiveness (Bunker, Kram, & Ting, 2002). Finally, mobilizing others—both direct reports and peers—becomes increasingly important in senior positions. Some leaders lack the empathy, influence skills, and collaborative skills to make this happen. Although many, if not all, of these individuals were adept at running the organizations and exercising their technical competencies with skill, common to each of these examples of derailment is the absence of critical emotional competencies.

This chapter explores how coaches help individuals develop the emotional competencies required to be successful at work and in life. It is our observation that many coaches, whether leader coaches or external professional coaches, have been doing this work (without labeling it as such) for a long time. However, in making this work explicit and identifying the factors that contribute to success in this domain, leader coaches, HR coaches, and external coaches will be in a better position to assess the effectiveness of their work and enhance it. We examine coaching objectives, strategy, and approach, as well as ways to assess outcomes and the effectiveness of the effort.

We make several key assumptions in this chapter. First, we assume that although there are various approaches to coaching, all have in common at least one or more of the following objectives: to improve individual and collective performance, change specific behaviors and attitudes that will enhance performance and satisfaction, work toward specific personal or professional goals related to satisfaction and well-being, and enhance the individual's learning agility (and in particular, the capacity to learn on the job without the regular assistance of a coach) to foster ongoing development.

Second, consistent with CCL's coaching framework, we assume that several core principles underlying the coaching alliance are critical to the success of this developmental tool:

- The alliance should advocate and promote self-awareness.
- The work helps the coachee learn how to learn from experience.
- Through the five factors of the coaching framework—relationship, assessment, challenge, support, and results—the coaching alliance offers a safe and challenging environment in which to practice new behaviors.
- The coach always begins with the coachee's agenda.
- The coach models the attitudes and behaviors that the leader needs to develop.

Finally, and of equal importance, we believe that all coaches can be effective in this work only if they regularly assess, reflect on, and continue to enhance their own emotional competencies. At a minimum, empathy is essential for creating a safe environment in which a coachee can be vulnerable and risk trying out new behaviors and attitudes. In addition, a primary way that coaches help leaders learn new behaviors is through modeling; thus, if as a coach you are unable to model direct feedback or handling of uncomfortable feelings, it is unlikely that your coachee will learn to do so. And as we have learned from convening groups of coaches to reflect on their practices, collective reflection of this kind enables coaches to see how their own biases and personality preferences shape and limit their approaches to the work. This self-awareness prompts reassessment and continuous learning that ultimately serves coachees well.

Advances in neuroscience show that emotional competencies are developed differently from technical knowledge and skills (Bar-on & Parker, 2000; Goleman, Boyatzis, & McKee, 2002; Sala et al., 2006). Therefore, we first summarize what we know about the specific emotional competencies underlying self-awareness, self-management, social awareness, and social skills—the basic elements of the Goleman model (1998) that we use in this chapter to frame our discussion—and how these are developed. Then we present a case study to illustrate how the coach enables the coachee to enhance the emotional competencies, as well as the variety of approaches that can be employed at each stage of the engagement. And we consider how coaches can improve their own practice through periodic reflection and shared inquiry with other coaches. We conclude this chapter with implications and guidelines for those interested in coaching for emotional competence.

What We Know About Emotional Competence

In the past decade, several conceptual models and empirical measures of emotional competence have been developed (Bar-On & Parker, 2000; Cherniss & Goleman, 2001). Fortunately, there is considerable agreement among scholars and practitioners regarding the key building blocks of emotional competence, as well as how these are developed over time. For the purpose of this chapter, we use Daniel Goleman's descriptions, which he developed in collaboration with the Consortium for Research on Emotional Intelligence in Organizations. (See Exhibit 7.1 for a review of his descriptions.)

EXHIBIT 7.1. DANIEL GOLEMAN'S MODEL OF EMOTIONAL COMPETENCE.

Self-Awareness	Self-Management	Social Awareness	Social Skill
• *Emotional self-awareness:* the ability to read and understand your emotions as well as recognize their imact on work performance, relationships, and the like • *Accurate self-assessment:* a realistic evaluation of your strengths and limitations • *Self-confidence:* a strong and positive sense of self-worth	• *Self-control:* the ability to keep disruptive emotions and impulses under control • *Trustworthiness:* a consistent display of honesty and integrity • *Conscientiousness:* the ability to manage yourself and your responsibilities • *Adaptability:* skill at adjusting to changing situations and overcoming obstacles • *Achievement orientation:* the drive to meet an internal standard of excellence • *Initiative:* a readiness to seize opportunities	• *Empathy:* skill at sensing other people's emotions, understanding their perspective, and taking an active interest in their concerns • *Organizational awareness:* the ability to read the currents of organizational life, build decision networks, and navigate politics • *Service orientation:* the ability to recognize and meet customers' needs	• *Visionary leadership:* the ability to take charge and inspire with a compelling vision • *Influence:* the ability to wield a range of persuasive tactics • *Developing others:* the propensity to bolster the abilities of others through feedback and guidance • *Communication:* skill at listening and sending clear, convincing, and well-tuned messages • *Change catalyst:* proficiency at initiating new ideas and leading people in a new direction • *Conflict management:* the ability to deescalate disagreements and orchestrate resolutions • *Building bonds:* proficiency at cultivating and maintaining a web of relationships • *Teamwork and collaboration:* competence at promoting cooperation and building teams

Source: Goleman (1998).

Each of these clusters contains several specific competencies. While neuroscience shows that individuals are hard-wired with a certain amount of emotional intelligence from birth, recent studies clearly indicate that all of these can be developed with regular practice and feedback (Cherniss & Adler, 2000; Kram, Ting, & Bunker, 2002). However, research also reveals that emotional competencies are acquired quite differently from technical knowledge and skills. Whereas the latter can be developed through reading and practice in a relatively short period of time, emotional competencies such as empathy, conflict management skills, and leadership skills require self-awareness, the motivation to learn about oneself, support and encouragement from others, and repeated practice over time combined with regular feedback. New habits must be developed and new neuropathways established, all of which takes time and repeated practice (Boyatzis, 2001).

It is not necessary to score high on all of the specific competencies within a cluster to behave in an emotionally competent way. But proficiency in at least a subset of the cluster is necessary in most leadership situations. For example, a leader may be quite proficient at communicating an exciting vision to his constituents and sensing the political climate of his organization as he promotes change and transformation. He may be less competent at managing his own impatience with change or unable to empathize with the fear and resistance that some organizational members experience. Which competencies are essential to the work at hand are situationally dependent.

The practice required to develop new responses and behavioral habits occurs primarily back on the job in everyday situations involving relationships with bosses, peers, and direct reports, as well as with suppliers, clients, and customers. It is reflecting on these everyday experiences in meetings with a coach that individuals systematically analyze the impact of their new approaches and whether further adaptation of their responses is necessary. This combination of repeated action, feedback from the environment, and reflection enables the development of personal and social skills.

As outlined in Chapter One, this book assumes that coaching involves intervention at the level of behavioral change and insight into personal drivers. Change begins from the inside and moves out. Assessment facilitates self-awareness, including how individuals' behaviors affect others, as well as the personal drivers that shape assumptions and behaviors at work. It is only after such self-awareness is achieved that coachees have a clear picture of the appropriate next steps they face. While all aspects of self-management, social awareness, and social skills require diligent practice and feedback, some are harder to develop than others. Behaviors that are tightly linked with personal values and core beliefs are likely to be the most difficult to modify.

The coach is there to help coachees prioritize, set realistic goals, model effective alternatives, provide encouragement, ensure a safe environment in which to test out new behaviors, and help to collect meaningful feedback down the road in order to assess progress and future learning agenda. In addition, the coach can play a vital role in helping coachees identify individuals and potential relationships on the job that can serve as part of the individual's developmental network. Ultimately coaches should work themselves out of a job by encouraging coachees to build a learning infrastructure that they can rely on as they continuously learn and develop new competencies.

How to Coach for Emotional Competence

The process of coaching for emotional competency is complex and can feel challenging to coaches because it calls on them to understand, discern, and model those skills. And because coachees are usually a complex mix of technical, business, and leadership skills with varying levels of emotional skills, the coach has to begin by clarifying where emotional development is needed. Consider the following case:

"He's driven to get results." "You can't manage corporate professional staff the same way as field operations." "I don't think he even realizes when he's gone too far. He doesn't notice that everyone has gotten quiet." "He gets impatient and irritable when we don't do things his way."

These are remarks about a manager we will call Henry, an action-oriented leader who spent the early part of his career in operations in the aerospace industry. He is highly regarded for his drive and dedication to the business. Having had multiple successes in managing large-scale operations projects, senior management has asked him to assume a new role in corporate where he would be responsible for a multidisciplinary professional team that works in a highly matrixed environment. The hope is that he can bring the same discipline and results focus to this group of smart, independent-minded, highly autonomous staff.

However, within nine months of his arrival, two staff have resigned, a few others are considering offers or internal transfers, and the remaining staff are laying low, waiting for the storm to blow over. Henry has never felt so at a loss for solutions. In a meeting with his boss, he confesses, "I've never felt so inadequate as a leader. I don't know what to do."

His boss, Dave, is more optimistic and assesses the situation in the following way. "Henry thinks this is like a huge project where he can lay out a plan, set milestones, monitor performance, and fix problems as they arise. But this is less about technical skill than the softer skills of coaching and managing people. Sure, he's inherited some difficult and defiant staff who are used to doing things their way and now they need to change. But Henry's been like a bull in a china shop in his handling of the situation, his staff, and the difference in cultural norms from his previous job in manufacturing. He hasn't taken the time to understand their perspective. There were other and better ways to manage them that would have gained the respect of his other direct reports."

Henry's boss has described a classic example of a leader who lacks a number of emotional competencies. Despite Henry's deficiencies, Dave is right to be optimistic. Henry doesn't need to reinvent himself. He has already demonstrated his strength in a number of emotional competence skills, including trustworthiness, achievement and service orientation, and conscientiousness. People believe Henry is fundamentally well intended and not self-focused or overly ambitious. However, even Henry realizes it is time to reconsider many of his assumptions about what constitutes effective leadership and to develop new skills that add to his current style and strengths. The question is, How can Dave, Henry's leader coach, help Henry develop and practice these new skills? Exhibit 7.2 provides some answers and also serves as a guideline for leader coaches in other situations.

EXHIBIT 7.2. COACHING FOR EMOTIONAL COMPETENCIES.

- Model emotional competencies early and often.
- Be prepared to acknowledge your own strengths, weaknesses, and emotional fluency.
- Be disciplined about asking questions that reinforce the emotional competencies frame.
- Assist the coachee in building a network of developmental relationships.
- Offer coaching tools that can be internalized and self-managed.
- Remind the coachee that developing emotional competency is an iterative process.
- Encourage optimism.

Self-Awareness

An assessment of one's strengths, weaknesses, orientations, emotions, and internal states is essential to developing self-awareness. Assessment can take two forms: internal and external. The internal assessment process involves encouraging the coachee to access information he already knows about himself through past experiences, current work context, and personal arena and to stand outside himself and reflect on how these attributes might be perceived as strengths or shortcomings by others, especially those who are different from himself. In this process, it helps if the coachee can articulate his emotions and those that pose the greatest challenge to his effectiveness and ability to manage. In Henry's case, he concluded that his greatest challenge was learning to manage his extreme action and results orientation. That combination caused him to feel impatient, which he couldn't hide, when direct reports didn't make progress quickly enough on project assignments.

The second form of assessment is external and uses a wide range of assessment tools such as interviews, personality style surveys, and performance appraisals. This process is particularly useful in confirming self-perceptions and identifying areas less known or understood to the coachee about his impact on others. Feedback from others is also useful in identifying emotions that may underlie the coachee's behaviors. Often coachees are surprised that others sense their emotions, particularly those that detract from their leadership effectiveness. They may not know the origins or the triggers, nor do they need to, but typically they can describe well the behavior and the impact on them and others. The coachee may place a high value on not showing emotions, confusing that with not managing emotions well. In fact, leaders who are able to share their emotions in an appropriate and authentic manner are viewed more effectively than those who hide emotions. This is particularly true in situations with conflict.

Henry is an example of this dynamic. In the first few months of coaching, Henry struggles to identify his emotions during a meeting or while in the midst of solving a manufacturing problem. It takes a lot of reflecting and prompting from his coach to find the right words to describe his emotional state or reactions. Henry was used to jumping from his feelings to an action; hence, he received feedback that he tended to act too quickly or to overreact.

Some of the immediate benefits to Henry in simply learning how to identify his emotions were the enhanced quality of his family life and his improved capacity for later implementing a significant reorganization and downsizing within his business unit.

The leader coach can support the coachee's development of self-awareness in a number of ways:

- *Facilitate self-assessment through dialogue.* Individuals often already know what they do well and what they do not, but they may not have been willing to acknowledge or examine the ways in which they bear on leadership effectiveness. When the coach asks questions such as, "What do you see as your strengths? Weaknesses?" "What would others identify?" "In what ways would theirs be different from your list?" "What would you like to do differently?" "What do you think others would prefer you to do differently?" the coachee is prompted to draw on his own knowledge and experiences to form alternative views for how his actions might be perceived.
- *Guide the coachee in gathering external assessments.* External coaches routinely use formal assessment processes to gather additional data for the coachee to consider. Leader coaches can facilitate a similar process, usually through HR, or access existing data if they are available and current. In any event, the coach should help the coachee decide if additional data are needed, and if so, what type of data will be gathered, who from, and what process will be used.
- *Collaborate in forming an integrated picture of the coachee's leadership.* A difficult task for coachees is to accept new information about themselves, especially if it does not reinforce their self-image or if it requires them to alter that view. Part of the process of increasing self-awareness is deciding which perceptions are meaningful and how to incorporate them into a desired self-image. The leader coach can help the coachee sort through these perceptions from an organizational and a personal perspective.
- *Demonstrate links between proposed areas of emotional-competency development and leadership performance.* These links can provide an incentive for a coachee's investing time in reflecting on her personal strengths and weaknesses and skill at managing emotions. For instance, if a manager understands that her inability to exhibit confidence and optimism when undertaking a challenging project diminished her team's performance because they were reluctant to engage, give full effort, and contribute new ideas, then she might be more motivated to work on improving her attitude and behaviors.
- *Challenge and support the coachee in selecting goals for improvement.* The purpose of increasing self-awareness is not to overwhelm a coachee with new or different

perceptions but to help coachees make more strategic and holistic choices about what skills to develop. The coach can make decisions about where to focus developmental energy by helping the coachee articulate her professional and personal aspirations.

- *Help the coachee expand his emotional vocabulary.* Managers who predominantly use rational and objective processes may have overdeveloped analytical skills and an underdeveloped range of emotions that they can identify and access. Helping coachees to understand the subtlety and complexity of their own emotions in a given situation is the first critical step to their learning how to use them effectively. Leader coaches can facilitate this growth by noticing the emotions that surface in their coaching conversations, making them an explicit topic of discussion, and getting the coachee to attach descriptors to those emotions.

Self-Management

Helping a coachee learn to manage his internal states, emotions, and impulses can feel a bit like telling someone who has arachnophobia not to be afraid of spiders. He might agree, but he is unlikely not to jump or react violently the next time a spider surprises him.

In a leadership context, this process of emotional hijacking comes in many forms. The common images are those displayed in Henry's case: obviously negative emotions such as anger, overcompetitiveness, and arrogance that may result in behaviors such as shouting, belittling others, or interrupting. In a leadership context, we hear often of these types of self-management issues, but there are also more subtle versions.

For example, the leader who fears not being liked might withdraw in the face of perceived conflict or might appear indecisive by agreeing with each person's perspective but not stating his position. A more self-contained leader may feel ignored in a meeting with high-energy and opinionated colleagues and disengage from the meeting or withhold important information that the group needs to make a good decision. In the last two examples, the results may not be as publicly disruptive, but the loss of productivity or quality performance nonetheless is a consequence of the individual's inability to identify and manage the emotion. Consider the story of Jack.

Jack is a well-liked senior executive who cherishes his good guy image because most of the other senior leaders have reputations as having questioning, challenging, and micromanaging approaches. A major systems conversion project for which Jack is ultimately responsible, and is critical to the organization's strategy, is significantly off track. The project leader, Marla, is capable and hard working but over her head. Jack's difficulty managing his discomfort with any form of negative expression or conflict had two adverse impacts. First, despite progress reports clearly showing huge problems and delays, he accepted assurances from Marla that everything was okay. Second, at a session to prepare for the quarterly board meeting, the CEO unmercifully grilled Marla and critiqued her on her poor performance. In both cases, Jack got feedback that others wanted him to step up: first, to hold Marla accountable and second, to diffuse what appeared to others as excessive criticism from the CEO. To his coach, Jack admitted that his fears of drawing out anger or hurt from others paralyzed him in these situations, where his leadership was needed most.

Coaches can help their coachees learn these skills if the coachees demonstrate enough self-awareness about the emotions and situations they want to learn how to manage better and are willing to use a disciplined process, because repetition and reflection are key to success in this arena (Cherniss & Adler, 2000). Leaders who are coaching other leaders sometimes forget that behavioral change can be more immune to external force and influence than business problems. We would like to believe that awareness is sufficient to motivate change, but all of us who have managed, led, or coached others or ourselves know that awareness is only the first step in a long journey.

In Henry's case, his disruptive emotions were typically triggered by what he perceived to be a lack of action, decision, forward activity, and rigorous analysis. When his staff wasn't reaching solutions fast enough, Henry would get frustrated, impatient, and overbearing. He lacked self-control in critical situations and had limited adaptability. Henry's lack of self-control nearly nullified his strengths (he was seen as very emotionally competent in the dimensions of conscientiousness and achievement orientation).

Leader coaches working with coachees who want to develop competency in the self-management area can work along these lines:

- *Help the coachee identify as precisely as possible what the disruptive emotions are that reduce or interfere with his or her leadership effectiveness.* Be careful not to land on a behavior or an emotion that does not capture the true feeling. For strongly analytical and logical coachees, it may be more useful to ask them to use a word or short phrase to describe their internal state. Because this step can trigger strong feelings of vulnerability, a coachee may need support from the coach in validating and role-modeling empathy.

• *Explore the triggers: the situations, specific people, and issues that provoke the emotion.* You can help your coachee identify warning signals, which are often physical, like a knot in the stomach or a warming sensation, and describe the specific situations and people that trigger the emotion. It's through telling the story that the answers become clear.

• *Positively challenge your coachee to identify times when she successfully managed the emotion.* Discuss what she did, how she did it, and how to replicate it. The techniques described in Chapter Eleven can be particularly helpful at this juncture, especially the use of the "exception" question.

• *Encourage your coachee to develop options in addition to accessing previous successful experiences.* Some of these might include developing new or using latent skills such as taking another's perspective; focusing on desired outcome and not presenting an irritant; reframing the issue or situation; enlisting support from another colleague; creating a personal distraction such as engaging in physical movement or getting a drink of water; self-coaching (inner dialogue); accessing a powerful reminder, motivator, or soother such as an image, physical object, mantra, or meaningful quotation; or declaring the emotions (after identifying them internally).

These techniques require varying degrees of sophistication in order to implement, and some will feel more doable for coachees depending on their personal styles and strengths. The more varied and numerous the approaches used, the greater likelihood for success is (Dalton, 1998). There will be times when the coachee is unable to improve his management of a particular set of disruptive or destructive emotions because the triggers are too powerful. These situations likely reflect a need for coaching at the level of root causes, and they fall outside what is appropriate for a leadership-focused coaching relationship. The best support to offer for such cases is referral to a professional whose practice is focused on individual psychological therapy or counseling.

Social Awareness

A key part of social awareness is the ability to sense others' emotions, understand their perspective, and take an active interest in their concerns (Goleman, 2000). Two of the questions we ask about leaders who participate in CCL's formal coaching are, "How well is the executive able to empathize with others?" and "How well does he or she sense and respond to others' needs?" Interestingly enough, respondents frequently say that the executive is able to empathize but seems to choose not to factor that in or respond based on that awareness.

There is an important link between the raw ability to empathize and a willingness to show and demonstrate interest. For many leaders, this dilemma lies at the heart of this particular developmental challenge. There may be a conscious choice on the coachee's part to discount its importance or, worse, interpret this capacity as weakness, not strength, because he or she imagines that showing empathy means not holding people accountable (Bunker & Wakefield, 2005). Thus, an area that a coach may need to explore early on with coachees is what value they place on the skill of empathy and how they understand its role in leadership. And the leader coach too may need to explore his or her own views about this.

In Henry's case, he struggles to understand what it would look like to express empathy for others and their hopes, dreams, and disappointments. His coach asks him about his son's decision to reluctantly engage in competitive swimming and how Henry responded to his son's first loss. Henry recognizes how much he (as well as his son) was invested in winning. He resisted the urge to downplay the loss, to talk his son out of feeling bad, and to offer helpful suggestions for the future. Instead, Henry said he saw such a profound sense of disappointment in his son that instinctively, and counter to his normal reaction, he simply asked his son how he was feeling. When his son told him through tears how disappointed and discouraged he was, Henry said he understood and felt his disappointment. The notion that he could respond in a similar way to people at work seemed enlightening to Henry. Henry used this lesson months later when the company went through a major reorganization and he had to communicate layoff and demotion decisions to a number of staff. Henry decided no matter how uncomfortable he felt, he would give everyone at least thirty minutes to talk. He found that after moments of silence, each person, regardless of whether he or she fared well, wanted to talk about how he or she felt, to discuss the stress and the future. Henry says this is one of the most important experiences he has had in his career and how glad he was not to have avoided the discomfort of being with people's emotions during this tough time.

There are several things a leader coach can do to support development of social awareness competencies in coachees:

- *Make the business case for social awareness.* Be prepared with meaningful and relevant examples of situations in which those skills were critical to the productive functioning of a group, business unit, or organizational initiative.
- *Help your coachees incorporate these skills into their personal values and discover ways to enact them authentically.* This is an important step because once the coachee

builds the need for these skills into his personal value system or leadership model, it becomes easier for him to adapt his leadership style accordingly. The motivation to make change is now internally and externally driven.

- *Once your coachee agrees that improved understanding and empathy for others is a development need, identify the specific aspects of or situations in which she is challenged to employ these skills.* By identifying the situations where the coachee tends to lose access to her ability to empathize, the coachee can develop early warning signals and coping and compensating mechanisms. It's equally useful to help the coachee identify situations where she has demonstrated empathy so she can replicate those behaviors.
- *Help your coachee anticipate and calibrate what "too much" and "too little" empathy might look like.* Consider how that skill might play out in the absence of or in conjunction with other attributes, such as being adverse to conflict or ambitious, and be construed as negative.

For self-awareness and social awareness, leader coaches can support their coachee fairly well within the boundaries of a traditional coaching relationship. Developing the full range of emotional competency skills requires a lot of practice, reflection, and feedback (Cherniss & Adler, 2000; Kram, Ting, & Bunker, 2002). These skills are fundamentally about social interactions and require experience to solidify learning. What is learned within a one-to-one coaching relationship has limits. Coaching must move into a public arena if the coachee is to gain feedback beyond her own perceptions and discussions with the coach. One benefit for the leader coach in this respect is an ability to observe coachee interactions frequently and in a variety of settings.

Here are some specific techniques that a leader coach can use to support these efforts.

- *Help the coachee find learning partners at work.* Partners can be people who share some similar challenges or are involved in the coachee's specific situation but are reasonably objective. These individuals can offer behavioral feedback from a personal perspective and what they observe about the group's actions.
- *Practice perspective taking.* Have your coachee identify current conflict or emotionally laden situations where she can practice empathy and reflection.
- *Offer information on active listening and questioning skills.* The coachee can use that information to increase his or her empathy or demonstration of empathy.
- *Explore issues that block the coachee's empathy or cause her to disregard opportunities to demonstrate empathy.* Issues might include underlying assumptions and be-

liefs about the world and people, life experiences, or personality and work style preferences that might naturally deemphasize or overshadow the development of empathy.

- *Get specific.* Have your coachee identify a meaningful ongoing situation, organizational issue, or colleagues in which or with whom he would like to achieve specific improvements or changes in his display of empathy.

Social Skills

The skills in this area of emotional competence closely align with accepted definitions of leadership. Like the social awareness skills, they have an outward focus (Goleman, 1998). This cluster can be thought of as the culmination and successful integration of the three previous clusters of skills.

More so here than with the other competencies, the leader coach acts less as a sounding board and guide and more as a companion and partner (particularly if coaching a senior-level executive). For example, Henry's boss and coach, Dave, serves as a guide not only because he has walked some of the same roads but because he is living some of the same challenges that Henry faces, particularly the organization's strategic and cultural changes. Dave functions as the interface with senior management and relies on Henry and his peers to make recommendations and communicate decisions to the troops. While Dave coaches Henry on how to lead through his first major reorganization, occasionally Dave allows Henry to coach him. These moments occur when Dave feels he is too removed from the front-line staff, forgetting how anxious they are feeling, and instead of empathizing becomes annoyed with their complaints or constant need for reassurance. Henry communicates that scenario as feedback, which helps Dave regain his perspective and compassion.

The complexity of organizational challenges that the coachee is responsible for or has undertaken determines the skills, tools, and knowledge with which the coach needs to be equipped. In this area of developing emotional competency, leader coaches can use several approaches to fulfill their roles:

- *Clarify with the coachee where, how, and the extent to which she desires to have impact and create positive change.* Another way to frame this is to get the coachee to articulate her vision for what she hopes to achieve for her part of the organization. This may have both a current and long-term focus.
- *Focus your efforts.* Help the coachee identify one of the skills within this cluster of emotional competencies that would be productive to focus on.

- *Marshal resources.* Identify what the coachee's personal learning infrastructure and network of developmental relationships would look like and how that might be constructed. (This tactic assumes that coachees who excel in the qualities contained in this cluster of social skills have superior ability to build long-term positive relationships and alliances.) As noted in Chapter Six, the higher the level of the executive coachee, the more challenging it can be to construct an internal network of trusted developmental partners. Frequently it's necessary for the senior-level coachee to add relationships with peers outside the organization to his or her developmental network.
- *Broaden assessments.* In addition to the typical assessment tools used for individual leader development assessments, organizational and team climate assessments can be useful in measuring the coachee's social skills. Such surveys say a lot about the coachee's ability to effect change on a large scale and facilitate development of culture and climate.

In coaching for emotional competence, the relationship between coach and coachee and others in the coachee's developmental network is key. It serves as the first arena for the coachee to practice modified or new emotional competencies. The coach serves primarily in the role of helping the coachee access existing skills that can be modified or leveraged into new skills. The leader coach can also function as a sounding board for coachees to self-assess and explore options. Role modeling is especially critical, particularly around self-awareness and self-management skills. The coachee of a coach who is not well developed along these dimensions of emotional competence might easily question the validity and value of emotional competence as a development focus.

Applying the CCL Framework to Emotional Competence Development

Up to this point we have discussed applying the CCL coaching framework to developing leaders' emotional competencies without linking specific coaching practices to each of the critical dimensions of the framework. In this section, we make the link between framework and practice more explicit.

Relationship

Relationship is at the core of coaching for emotional competency. In fact, there are two relationships: one is between the coach and coachee, and the other is the broader network of relationships that the coachee cultivates as a way of practicing and expanding emotional competencies. Hallmarks of the coach-coachee relationship include its reciprocal nature and the importance of role modeling by the coach. The leader coach doesn't need to be perfect to be effective, but does have to understand the four clusters of emotional competency (self-awareness, social awareness, self-management, and social skills) and practice its underlying principles. Coaching these skills requires thought, commitment, and emotional maturity. With regard to the relationship's reciprocal nature, there is always in the process opportunities for the leader coach's continuous self-improvement. With regard to emotional competency, there are ample occasions for leader coaches to refine their own skills, particularly those in the self-awareness, self-management, and social awareness clusters.

The quality and depth of the coaching relationship is quite important in coaching for emotional competency because the coaching deals with emotions, and for leaders that is often unfamiliar territory and can elicit feelings of vulnerability and exposure.

The other relationship, the one between the coachee and others, ultimately becomes the focus of the coaching engagement. While the coach and coachee's relationship can be a laboratory for that learning, ultimately the coachee's ability to relate, understand, and influence others is the full measure of emotional competency. The proof of progress is the quality of relationships that the coachee builds with others, how effectively the coachee develops networks of alliances through those relationships, and how well the coachee uses those relationships to facilitate positive change in the organization.

Assessment

Leaders with high emotional competency are assessing continuously. They do that by explicitly asking for feedback from individuals and their part of the organization. They also do it implicitly by scanning their environment and paying attention to subtle indicators from people around them. These are leaders who don't need a formal climate survey to know how others in the organization are feeling. They are comfortable with feedback, both getting it and giving it, and they know that information about themselves and their leadership impact comes in many forms.

Most managers and leaders have not developed their emotional competency to that level, and so they have to be deliberate in assessing themselves. Leader coaches do a great service to their coachees by helping them develop self-assessing skills and networks of quality feedback. Assessment practices that enable coachees to facilitate ongoing development of emotional competency are reflecting in action (using internal dialogue about their behavior while they are in the midst of it), taking time at the end of each day or week to assess what they've learned, and asking for feedback informally and formally from people they've identified as part of their developmental network. With regard to accessing others for feedback, the leader coach can guide and reinforce the use of ongoing, informal assessment as a natural outgrowth of developing relationships with peers, direct reports, and bosses. Leader coaches should be prepared to serve as one of the sources of assessment when they have relevant observations to share.

Challenge

While some leaders will derail as a result of inadequate emotional competency skills, the more common outcome of underdeveloped emotional competency is that the leader and organizational unit may perform well but won't achieve excellence. The good news is that many leaders display a degree of emotional competency, and few are devoid of it completely. In most cases, coaching for emotional competency is about refining and improving an existing capacity, especially in the areas of emotional awareness and management (both of self and others). Leaders with underdeveloped emotional competency have often moved through a number of promotional gates, relying largely on technical skills and analytical acumen. Often it's not until they reach a senior level in the organization that the presence or lack of emotional competency begins to define their careers (Bunker, Kram, & Ting, 2002).

The coaching challenge often arises because it's difficult to find a compelling reason for convincing leaders to engage in developing this set of skills. After all, they can rise fairly far up the organization without them. Leader coaches play a significant role in making their coachees aware of the concept and stimulating coachees to be more deliberate about developing emotional competency.

It's not unusual for coachees to initially question the value of working on what are commonly seen as soft skills (as opposed to the hard skills honed in the analytical rigor of business schools). Consider again Henry's story. He resists and externalizes his frustration with the weak performance of his unit onto a few problem direct reports. It is not until he exhausts all of his usual problem-solving approaches, and his leader coach confronts him, that he is willing to entertain the idea that the problem is in a different arena. Henry's experience is more typical than not. A primary challenge to coaching in this specific context rests with the coachee's and the coach's surfacing their own assumptions and biases around incorporating emotional competencies into their repertoire of management skills, a challenge exacerbated by the obstacles that may exist within the organizational culture.

Support

We have already described tools and approaches that leader coaches can use to support their coachees' developing emotional competency. In the context of CCL's coaching framework and its four components of support (maintaining motivation, accessing resources, celebrating wins and managing setbacks, and creating ongoing learning agendas), the third and fourth are most critical for the leader coach's work. Developing emotional competency is a long and sometimes uncomfortable process of unlearning and relearning new behaviors that often sit at the core of how the coachee views and relates to the world. Many executives express feelings of awkwardness when practicing new behaviors, and "falling off the wagon" is a common occurrence with leaders who are developing and refining these skills. Add to that discomfort the fact that organizations rarely reinforce the importance of emotional competency. The leader coach can supplement the coachee's personal motivation to develop these skills by acknowledging small gains and highlighting for the coachee the direct link between the use of emotional competency and positive organizational results.

Helping the coachee develop a relational network is key. Once the coachee has this, she becomes less dependent on the leader coach for providing support. She can select individuals within her network who have particular skills, interest, and availability to support her.

Results

It may be easiest and simplest to measure emotional competency development in behavioral terms, such as getting feedback on how well coachees manage their emotions, how well they understand their own strengths and development needs, how well they empathize, and so on. More important, however, is the overall effectiveness of the leader. A key assumption behind the purpose of coaching for emotional competency is that it can improve individual and collective performance as well as satisfaction. Given that perspective, leader coaches can measure results in a holistic rather than compartmentalized fashion. Leader coaches are in a strong and unique position to assess the overall improvement of their coachees' individual performance and the performance of the unit they lead or are a member of, and to determine the extent to which improvements along the emotional competency dimensions contributed to that performance. The leader coach has the frequency of contact and observation to provide the ongoing and in-the-moment assessment, challenge, and support that coachees need while experiencing the growing pains of developing a greater capacity for emotional competency.

Conclusion

The leader coach must have a baseline of emotional competence to effectively help others develop personal and social competencies. In order to serve as role models for their coachees, coaches should build alliances characterized by trust, encouragement, honesty, and challenge; they should have a good understanding of their own strengths and weaknesses (self-awareness); be able to monitor negative emotions such as impatience, frustration, or anger (self-management); pose supportive questions and listen well (empathy); and have the ability to build quality relationships (social skills). Ideally, it is through the coaching relationship that coachees develop learning agility so that they can continue to develop self-awareness and enhance particular personal and social competencies long after the coaching engagement is complete.

Our purpose in this chapter has been to demonstrate how leaders can develop critical emotional competencies in coaching relationships. Whether one is a coach or coachee, or both, there is great potential in a coaching relationship for enhancing self-awareness and practicing empathy, self-regulation, and a variety of social skills that are essential to effective leadership. For the leader coach, working within this historically undervalued developmental arena can ultimately boost individual effectiveness and satisfaction, as well as organizational performance.

Classroom learning can help an individual get started with developing self-awareness (Goleman, 1998; Cherniss & Adler, 2000; Kram et al., 2002). However, developing the other personal and social competencies required of leaders in today's complex and turbulent environments requires repeated risk taking, practice, feedback, and support. This can't be accomplished in one week of off-site training, but instead requires a learning infrastructure back on the job that provides opportunities, guidance, and support (Kram & Cherniss, 2001; Hall & Kahn, 2001; Higgins & Thomas, 2001). Coaching offers the ideal vehicle for this challenging work.

When it comes to coaching for emotional competency, a common pathway toward results has emerged. It starts with self-awareness, with knowledge about one's strengths and weaknesses and the impact one has on others in the workplace. From this starting point, individuals, with the help of a coach, can define personal goals that are meaningful and motivating and can be accomplished in the time frame and context established. Through role modeling, practice, reflection, feedback, encouragement, and follow-up, individuals have the opportunity to try out new approaches, revise their mental models, and enhance their leadership style over time.

What is less obvious is the variety of forms that coaching for emotional competence can take. Both coachees and the leader coach shape how the coaching alliance unfolds. For example, an introverted coachee prefers private meetings with the coach to practice new behaviors before using them in real work situations. In contrast, extraverted coachees bring recent encounters on the job to the coaching session for reflection, review, and a plan of action going forward. Some focus on social skills related to managing conflict and disagreement, while others may focus on developing the capacity for empathy. In all instances, the coachee's development needs drive the process; how the work is accomplished depends on coach and coachee values, beliefs, and career history.

The organizational context also shapes coaching alliances. Approaches range from one-on-one coaching as a follow-up to off-site training, peer coaching within the context of off-site training, training for the manager as coach, peer coaching and supervisory coaching on the job, group coaching among peers and seniors who face similar business challenges, and internal or external professional coaching. The range of available alternatives is rich and promising. The challenge is to choose the appropriate coaching approach based on the organization's strategy, culture, available resources, and development systems and practices already in place.

It's not possible to prescribe the right approach for all organizations, but several basic tenets seem relevant to all settings. First, any coaching initiative—

including one focused on developing emotional competency—should be explicitly linked to an important strategic objective; thus, for example, an organization may recognize it has thin bench strength when it comes to future leaders in its business units, and those with potential are lacking critical emotional competencies. Second, once a primary objective has been identified, how these individuals can benefit from coaching alliances should be defined. Some organizations have taken the approach that potential leaders can best refine their emotional competencies by coaching less experienced managers. Others have hired external professional coaches to work with these high-potential people one-on-one. Finally, the introduction of any coaching initiative should be positioned as a pilot so that interim evaluations can measure how well the approach is meeting the identified development need.

Multiple approaches to coaching are likely to have more impact than a single approach. This is based on recent research that indicates that individuals benefit from multiple developmental alliances (Higgins, 2000; Higgins & Thomas, 2001) and that a learning infrastructure comprising several coaching relationships with peers, mentors, and others can be far richer than one relationship alone. However, many individuals are not able to build such networks without the initial exposure to the value of relational learning in the context of leadership training or one-on-one coaching.

The value of coaching multiplies as individuals reflect on their experiences with others who are doing this same work. In an organization, it is very useful for leader coaches to convene regularly to reflect on their experiences of serving as coaches to people in their organizations (see Exhibit 7.3). Here, they have the opportunity to expand their repertoire of coaching tactics and to get assistance in dealing with particularly difficult situations with specific client managers. Similarly, peers who face similar challenges (for example, marketing managers from across an organization) can benefit from reflecting on their approaches to addressing these situations together, and in doing so become coaches to one another.

Coaching for emotional competence enables both coach and coachee to refine personal and social competencies. Best practices for this work now exist as outlined in this chapter, and the variations of its practice are yet to be fully discovered. It is up to each leader coach and coachee to find the approach that works best.

EXHIBIT 7.3. HOW LEADER COACHES CAN DEVELOP THEIR OWN EMOTIONAL COMPETENCE.

The mental models that leader coaches bring to their coaching relationships are quite varied and often not clearly articulated. The opportunities to learn from successes and failures are minimal due to the solo nature of the work. Even when a conscientious leader coach makes time for personal reflection in order to gather the lessons learned, the breadth and depth of their learning is limited by their own biases, blind spots, and experiences. It's much the same for everyone.

CCL has sponsored reflection sessions of twenty coaches. The participants were asked to come prepared to talk about a coachee situation that was particularly challenging and where developing emotional competence was part of the learning agenda. Participants listened to others' stories, probing as each coach reflected about what had transpired, and collectively they identified new insights about their mental models, how they went about their work, and alternative interventions that they could add to their coaching repertoire.

These reflection-on-practice sessions offer a number of learning opportunities. They are designed to foster mutual learning within the group, improve coaching, and bolster organizational learning and performance over time.

But what actually occurs in these sessions that produces new emotional competencies in participants? Some of the coaches saw their own experience reflected in another coach's story and learned through this mirroring process. Other coaches offered approaches that the storyteller had not even considered due to their personality preferences or prior intervention practices. Collectively, after exploring each participant's story, they defined what they had learned about when and how particular emotional competencies might be improved through coaching.

It was not uncommon for participants to see more clearly the range of opportunities that they had not yet put to use. For example, helping a coachee to develop more effective skills in handling conflict situations could encompass an assessment tool that characterizes the coach's stance toward conflict, a role play within the coaching relationship, systematic reflection with a coach on a situation that happened at work, an opportunity to practice doing it better, experimenting with the new approach back on the job, and soliciting feedback from learning partners on the job as well as from one's coach. One key lesson that regularly resurfaced was the fact of a range of alternative actions, rather than one best approach, that could facilitate development of emotional competence.

Another key lesson derived from collective reflection is that the appropriate choice of approaches depends on the personality preferences of both coachee and coach, their innate talents, their values and beliefs, their life experiences, and the

EXHIBIT 7.3. HOW LEADER COACHES CAN DEVELOP THEIR OWN EMOTIONAL COMPETENCE, Cont'd.

particulars of their coaching relationship. For example, introverted coaches tended to be more patient with coachees who did not readily express their feelings about a challenging situation because they were able to empathize with the difficulty of doing so. Alternatively, extraverted coaches could offer examples of how they probed their coachees to facilitate reflection and expression and provided a role model for their coachees to follow. From these discussions, coaches frequently established new personal learning objectives for themselves that would enhance their coaching practices going forward.

These sessions demonstrated that several emotional competencies can be enhanced in the course of a single coaching intervention. For example, in the course of reviewing and interpreting 360-degree feedback data for the purpose of enhancing self-awareness, a coachee begins to develop deep motivation to practice active listening and empathy with peers and direct reports, and at the same time the coach models how it's done. After such a session, the coachee finds herself listening more, encouraging more, and sensing the concerns of direct reports more easily.

Leader coaches should encourage their coachees to build relationships that can become part of their overall learning infrastructure. The same holds true for leader coaches who are committed to enhancing their emotional competence. While solo reflection is certainly useful, shared reflection multiplies the learning possibilities.

Coach's Bookshelf

Argyris, C., & Schön, D. (1996). *Organizational learning II: Theory, method and practice.* Upper Saddle River, NJ: Prentice Hall.

Boyatzis, R. (1995). Cornerstones of change: Building the path for self-directed learning. In R. Boyatzis, S. Cowen, & D. Kolb (Eds.), *Innovations in professional education: Steps on a journey from teaching to learning.* San Francisco: Jossey-Bass.

Collins, J. (2001). *Good to great: Why some companies make the leap . . . and others don't.* New York: HarperCollins.

Douglas, C. A., & McCauley, C. D. (1997). A survey on the use of formal developmental relationships. *Issues and Observations, 17*(1/2), 6–9.

Goleman, D. (1998). *Emotional intelligence.* New York: Bantam Books.

Hughes, M., Patterson, B., & Terrell, J. B. (2005). *Emotional intelligence in action: Training and coaching activities for leaders and managers.* San Francisco: Pfeiffer.

Schön, D. (1990). *Educating the reflective practitioner: Toward a new design for teaching and learning in the professions.* San Francisco: Jossey-Bass.

CHAPTER EIGHT

COACHING LEADERS THROUGH CHANGE AND TRANSITION

Kerry A. Bunker

Executives and senior managers don't need to be told that change is rapid and transition is constant. They are experiencing waves of change, one change cascading on another. Leaders are reacting to and influencing new technologies and new strategies; they confront economic and political change and juggle new projects, new organizational structures, new markets—all simultaneously. Even the language of change management is getting stale, with managers so steeped in change that it has become the status quo.

Rapid change and constant transition create an agitated emotional dynamic in organizations. Change for many executives constitutes letting go of established skills and preferred patterns of behavior while simultaneously tackling challenging problems that require the use of unfamiliar and uncomfortable learning processes (Bridges, 2001). Stress and emotion are everyday companions in such settings. Research shows that both are inherent elements of any potent learning experience (Bunker, 1994; Bunker & Webb, 1992).

Leading is categorically different when people's emotions are stretched and stressed. This makes it both more critical and more difficult to focus simultaneously on managing the business and providing effective leadership to the people. Attending to the people side of the equation is the piece that most often gets lost in the shuffle.

Effective leadership in times of transition requires the ability to coach others as they struggle to stay on track in the face of the emotional turmoil that accompanies change. Leader coaches in this situation have to understand their own emotional reactions to change and transition before they can effectively coach others in how they might respond. Developing and releasing effective coaching skills in leaders often demands that they first identify, accept, and cope with their own emotional responses. That process opens the door to genuine empathy and the capacity and willingness to engage and coach others during transition. This chapter addresses two aspects of coaching during change and transition: the challenge of coaching leaders on understanding and coping with the emotional fallout from transition, and the related challenge of learning to coach others as they live through the process.

When transformational initiatives fail to reach fruition, it's typically not because leaders have failed to address the structural challenges and mechanics of implementation. Rather, it is because organizations underestimate (or fail to be proactive in providing) the help their leaders need to respond to the emotional fallout that blocks their ability to learn. Many models and resources exist for addressing the mechanics of initiating and implementing the structural aspects of change. The subtler and more daunting challenge involves developing leaders who possess the emotional competencies required to guide and coach themselves and others through the learning and loss side of a potent transition experience.

In their rush to make change happen, organizations often go in search of the best practices for avoiding or doing away with thorny emotional issues. But the answer isn't in leadership as implementing best practices; it is in leadership as a way of being. Successful transitions require ongoing stewardship from leaders who are themselves living through the change in a genuine and authentic manner.

Despite a lack of organizational support, many executives already accept the idea that they need to learn how to address the difficulty of transition within this new context of change. They are familiar with the work of Daniel Goleman and Cary Cherniss and can recite the fundamental tenets of emotional competence and the need to deal with the emotional fallout of change and its impact on the organization (Cherniss & Goleman, 2001; Goleman, 1998). This kind of learning requires executives to wade into the murky emotional water of change—virgin territory for many executives.

Failing to address the emotional component of change often has significant negative consequences for the individual executive and the organization. The risk that leaders face in minimizing or ignoring the human dynamic that plays out in the context of change and transition is twofold. First, they may prevent or undermine the structural and strategic goals by failing to gain sufficient acceptance and commitment from workers. Second, ignoring the emotional issues can destabilize the organizational culture and erode the trust and values that engender dedication. Loyalty and trust give way to insecurity and fear, as productivity and enthusiasm are displaced by withdrawal and skepticism.

Executives can learn to be more effective in dealing with the emotional elements of transition, but it requires a more significant intervention than simply reading the latest best-selling metaphor on change or attending the typical change management seminar. By coaching managers in concert with pivotal change experiences, leader coaches can create the space, direction, and support necessary to help managers recognize and appreciate when and how they might be overlooking the impact of emotions during times of change. Furthermore, the coaching process can help them develop the skills that underlie the process of becoming more authentic and empathic leaders.

The knowledge in this chapter derives from two distinct and ongoing CCL learning experiences: Leading People Through Transition, a developmental initiative that emphasizes professional and peer coaching in the context of a developmental intervention, and the Awareness Program for Executive Excellence (APEX), an intensive coaching experience for top-level leaders. The emphasis in both is on strengthening a leader's effectiveness around the people side of transition.

This chapter examines the powerful role that leaders who are coaching other leaders can play in enhancing the capacity of executives to lead themselves and others through extraordinary times. It begins with some background on the watershed events that have made constant change an ever-present condition, along with a revealing sketch of the extraordinary organizational environment that emerges from the resulting transitions. It then discusses the seven key components to be addressed between the leader coach and coachee and examines the process from the perspective of CCL's coaching framework. A coach's primer that illuminates the particular challenges and qualities required for this type of coaching and provides some guidelines for coaching leaders in transition rounds out the chapter.

Transitions on the Rise

Significant historical and economic factors have contributed to the increase in the amount of change and transition that managers are experiencing. The breakup of AT&T in January 1984 was of particular historical significance. At the time, I was a young psychologist studying executive stress in the organization, and it fell to me to "fix the morale problem" that inevitably resulted from the breakup.

In hindsight, the court-ordered divestiture was a pivotal event in the unraveling of the prevailing psychological work relationship in the North American culture—a relationship built on the expression of hard work, commitment, and loyalty in exchange for the promise of job stability and lifetime employment. As David Noer wrote in 1993, "Organizations that used to perceive people as long-term assets to be nurtured and developed now see people as short-term costs to be reduced" (p. 16). The psychological covenant between the organization and the individual was permanently broken, replaced by the imponderables of constant change.

The breakdown of this contract produced shock waves that rocked the very foundation of organizational life. Neither employees nor their employers have completely recovered from the undermining of the established basis of loyalty, trust, and commitment in organizations. To make matters worse, the imperatives for contemporary workforces are different and more challenging than they used to be. The modern manager must be more flexible, more adaptable, and, perhaps most important, more able to learn quickly. Ironically, one outcome of the erosion of the old psychological contract and the growing emphasis on flexibility is that young managers have come to believe that performing successfully for a single organization over a longer period of time is not necessarily a positive career strategy. Short-term situational commitment is encouraged and rewarded, and the pace of management has become grueling.

This environment creates an interesting paradox. An increasing number of bright, young managers with unusually high levels of talent, intellect, and ambition are rising to significant levels of responsibility on an accelerated career path. Effective managers but not seasoned leaders, they often arrive with gaps in their development that can be traced back to the absence of the critical experiences needed to hone them into authentic, mature, and emotionally competent leaders of change and transition. Not surprisingly, they often excel in strategic analysis and bottom-line results, but they struggle to operate effectively with peers and direct reports who are more seasoned, better connected, more politically savvy, and more grounded in terms of self-awareness and emotional maturity. The fallout from this fast track comes when these talented but developmentally immature managers find their way into executive positions. The roles demand deep leadership capacity, but these fast-rising managers often are more focused on individual achievement and recognition than on building a leadership team or working with and through others. In short, they are emotionally clueless (Bunker, Kram, & Ting, 2002).

Considering how the demise of the psychological contract has been coupled with the emergence of these emotionally clueless managers, it is easy to see why organizations wrestle with the challenge of implementing and managing rapid and continuous change. Individuals struggle to make sense of the need for constant change and to make peace with associated feelings of uncertainty, loss, and violation. An ongoing challenge for the leader coach is to create and implement interventions that close the gap between these seemingly divergent responses to change and transition.

Extraordinary Times and the Human Dimension

One way to think about the leadership pressures created by ongoing change and transition is "leadership in extraordinary times." Paradoxically, the dynamic of extraordinary times is becoming the norm in most organizations. And because most leaders confront and have to deal with the implications of extraordinary times at various points in their careers, the choices they make on how to lead become critical. Extraordinary times create unique organizational environments, and when organizations are ailing, they tend not to address the emotional fallout that is prevalent in those environments but sweep it under the rug.

Certainly, crisis and unusual difficulty can create extraordinary situations. Leadership in today's world seems unusually challenging. But more telling than the level of challenge or trouble is the emotional pitch of the organization or situation. Extraordinary times are triggered when some sort of event or transition (new roles, a restructuring or downsizing, a merger or acquisition, for example) hits people emotionally while demanding high performance. Leaders in extraordinary times face intense pressure to achieve results and therefore push themselves and the organization to change, adapt, and succeed.

As an illustration of how this plays out, consider the experience of Mitchell:

Mitchell is the director of R&D for a small, highly successful biotech firm that was recently purchased by a major pharmaceutical company. He and his colleagues are relieved that they will remain as an intact unit of the larger organization and that no one has been laid off. Even so, the transition is not going the way Mitchell expected. The purchase was driven by the perceived value of his unit's work, but after just three months, headquarters and the larger R&D function in the organization are pushing Mitchell's group to change its focus.

Mitchell finds himself as the go-between, supporting and speaking for "his" people while negotiating the new environment. While he, like his R&D team, sometimes misses the days where he could just "do the work and not worry about politics," Mitchell is eager to make the transition successful. He's willing to explore the implications and benefits of changing course, but is also comfortable pushing back and speaking openly to the "powers that be" in the parent company. He thinks things will get better when his colleagues stop comparing the situation to the past. And given some more time, he's confident "we'll get our groove back and work together to influence the outcomes."

The leadership pressures that Mitchell faces are characteristic of the challenges presented by leading in extraordinary times. The acquisition of Mitchell's company has pushed the people in his unit out of their emotional comfort zone. In the face of rigorous demands that a leader must face just to survive in an organization, it is no wonder that there is a tendency to relegate the human dynamic, the emotional fallout, to the end of the to-do list. Many senior-level managers who excel in the structural aspects of leading change—creating a vision, reorganizing, restructuring, and so on—are derailed by their failure to exert strong leadership around the human side of change—grieving, letting go, building hope, and learning. These managers either don't see it as necessary, or they don't know how to relate it to the other difficult strategic and analytical decisions they have to make.

For leaders to harness and maintain the talent and commitment needed to benefit from organizational change, they must operate from a place of emotional maturity and authenticity. This posture, though complex and demanding, generates trust. And from a position of trust, a leader can more effectively guide others through change and transition.

The Seven Important Elements to Coach for During Times of Transition

A key principle in CCL's philosophy of coaching is that if you want to lead people somewhere new, then you need to meet them where they are. It is a simple phrase that gives rise to a challenging agenda with demanding expectations and widespread implications. It assumes a readiness and capacity for self-awareness and sensitivity to others. It implies active listening and a willingness to be empathetic to the position of others. It requires insight and courage to insert yourself as a leader coach between the demands of constant change and the time, effort, and emotional energy required to make that change palatable enough to come to fruition.

Coaching leaders on the human dynamics of learning, stress, and transition (Bridges, 2001; Bunker & Webb, 1992) is an effective way to help them deepen their awareness and empathy for the emotional demands of growth and change. It also fosters their ability to connect to their own emotions and experiences of transition and to learn from those experiences. The role of the coach is to guide the coachee toward self-awareness and understanding of the important elements of transition leadership:

- Authenticity
- Resilience
- Acceptance of change
- Influencing with vulnerability
- Emotional learning
- Active listening and empathy skills
- Balance

Each of these elements can enhance the capacity of executives to meet people where they are and lead them through transition. They represent the areas in which the leader coach and his or her coachee can expect to experience the highest levels of learning and growth. The role of leader coach is to guide the coachee toward an understanding of these elements as important to building their capacity to lead in times of transition.

Coaching for Authenticity

Authentic leaders pay careful attention to their inner selves. They are attuned to their emotions, expectations, struggles, motivations, preferences, frustrations, and even the contradictions they may hold.

In coaching for authenticity, the coach's role is to guide the coachee in discovering who he or she is, how he or she came to be that way, and how he or she is experienced by other people. Bill George (2003) describes this first step in the process of becoming an authentic leader as being good at being yourself. Similarly, Robert Terry (1993) encourages people to be true to themselves and adds the acid test of comparing one's self-assessment to how one is assessed by others. Good intentions are necessary but not sufficient criteria for authentic behavior. An authentic leader is not one who sees herself as motivating, challenging, and a stickler for high-level performance but is routinely characterized by her direct reports and peers as abusive, overly controlling, and egotistical. The underpinnings for authenticity are genuineness, communication of respect, sincere empathy, and capacity for self-disclosure. Moving a coachee toward these perspectives will make a big difference in how that person leads during transitions.

The Role of Trust. Leading with authenticity is essentially about creating and maintaining trust. And trust is the prime ingredient for effective leadership, particularly during transitions (for an example of trust building well done, see Exhibit 8.1). Leaders who are not trusted may get a minimal level of compliance from others in the organization (they do hold the power of rewards and punishment, after all, not to mention control over continued employment), but they will not receive the commitment, confidence, and effort the organization requires to implement and capitalize on the change. The challenge of creating and maintaining trust during periods of transition is heightened by the fact that emotionally charged employees are hypervigilant to any evidence that their leaders are behaving in ways that are less than authentic. Trust in a leader is a vital but fragile commodity. It's a challenge to earn and difficult to repair once damaged.

Masking. At work, people typically feel compelled to "wear masks" to protect themselves and others from what they are feeling inside. The pressure to

EXHIBIT 8.1. A STORY OF TRUST.

Here's a story about one of the best CEOs I've ever met, one whose work has inspired the trust of his coworkers. He excels at both driving change and coping with the complexities of transition. Jay runs an enormous, sprawling organization with a long history and an entrenched bureaucracy. Yet he has challenged the organization to be a different and more competitive business.

As a true visionary leader, Jay's thinking is way ahead of everyone else's in the organization. He champions new ideas, new strategies, and new ways of working with clarity, passion, and intensity. But alongside his push for change, Jay respects the organization's roots and is committed to helping his people cope with the fallout of that change. Always honest and direct, he readily talks about the emotional and practical difficulties employees face given the pressure to change. Over and over again, he makes the case for change. He lays out the imperative and then says, "I know it's not easy, but we're going to help you. Here are some things that will help us work through it."

Jay is personally engaging, telling stories of his own experience, offering metaphors, examples, and encouragement. He has invested in leader development programs and formal mechanisms to acknowledge and facilitate transition; more important, he models the behavior he is asking of others. Jay's authentic approach to leadership remains quite constant in good times and bad. The behaviors described were characteristic of Jay even before the recent changes. Thus, he entered the time of turmoil with established credibility and trustworthiness that positioned him well to lead the emotionally charged transition process.

In many respects, he is a model of leadership as a way of being. Leaders who enter into periods of heavy change already bereft of credibility and trust will be hard-pressed to earn it on the fly regardless of how much coaching they receive. The moral of Jay's story: don't put off the development of the leadership skills you need during times of transition until you are in the middle of one.

Jay's example shows us that paradoxically, the inward focus and seemingly self-oriented development of the authentic leader ultimately serve to generate a broadened perspective and a drive that extends well beyond individual ambition. An authentic leader elevates advancement of the mission above promotion of self and makes integrity and long-term organizational sustainability a focus. Such a leader responds to the intrinsic rewards of work with a clear, accurate view of himself, his organization, and the situation. He is committed without illusion and without cynicism and despair. Personal ambition and ego are subsumed by confidence, commitment, and a genuine desire to develop leadership in others.

put on a good face increases as a leader gains responsibility and authority. Masking affects the ability of leaders to be authentic (particularly the younger, successful superstars). Leaders who wear many masks often:

- Try to be superhuman in the face of fatigue and shrinking resources.
- Act positive, upbeat, and optimistic on the outside while having doubts and feeling overwhelmed or uncertain on the inside.
- Remain blind to personal learning gaps or act defensive about managerial blunders.
- Ignore the spillover of consequences onto others such as colleagues and family.

Many executives and senior leaders think their masking behavior is the required or natural behavior of someone in their position. They perceive masking as the way to act like a leader. But masking has negative consequences for the leader as an individual and for the organization trying to adapt to change. The masked leader typically:

- Feels alone during a difficult time.
- Allows self and others to get stuck in prechange attitudes and practices.
- Creates an image lacking in authenticity that inhibits the healing process.
- Provokes a dysfunctional buildup of anger and resentment.
- Contributes to a breakdown in the revitalization process at the key level of leadership.

The leader coach can help the manager become more authentic by helping him or her build trust among direct reports, peers, and other stakeholders and by helping the manager set aside masking behaviors. Specifically, coaches can work with their coachees to enhance these authenticity-strengthening capabilities:

Deep reflection—expanding self-awareness, focusing on learning and growth, assessing meaning and focus of life and work

Responsibility—examining role beyond individual career and achievements; assuming responsibility for those who will follow

Acceptance—owning one's limitations and derailing behaviors as easily and completely as one's strengths

Assurance—becoming more grounded and genuinely self-assured; connecting more easily and fully with others

Coaching for Resilience

Because constant change has taken on such prominence, it is critical that managers learn to be resilient, to be able to bounce back from adversity. Executives or leaders who manage by hunkering down or muscling through are acting as if they are leading a one-time event. Rather than pushing change to get to the other side, leaders and their organizations are better served by incorporating strategies and tactics for enhancing resiliency and the ability to learn in themselves and others.

During the coaching process, managers have access to a powerful developmental tool when they examine their personal experiences that triggered their ability to bounce back from adversity. (For an example of that power, see the story in Exhibit 8.2.) When people share their hardship stories, they can search for the common threads that run through most resiliency experiences. A number of studies have demonstrated the qualities that allow people to bounce back from adversity (Coutu, 2002; Pulley & Wakefield, 2001). Coutu cites the following critical elements of resiliency in hardship situations:

Making meaning: Building bridges between current difficulties and a better future state.

Improvisation: Making do with what you have. Being creative. Learning.

EXHIBIT 8.2. A STORY OF RESILIENCY.

The old saying about judging a book by its cover has more to do with people than it does with books. Consider this story. A group of government public servants expressed outrage at an army general when he admonished them during a powerful transition experience to "stop whining and look after yourself." But they softened with understanding and support when he later described being dropped off at an orphanage at age eleven because his immigrant parents didn't speak English and couldn't find work to support the family. The empathy of his colleagues allowed the general to examine the downside of overdoing his self-reliant approach to resiliency and to accept feedback on why his response was perceived as cold and insensitive.

Relationships: Drawing on the support and resources of others. Reciprocating their contributions.

Facing down reality: Accepting the limitations of current circumstances. Balancing optimism with realistic assessment.

Coaching for the Acceptance of Change

Resisting change causes people to get stuck in transition, refusing to accept the current reality. This undermines their adapting to the current reality and makes it more difficult for them to be flexible and adaptable to subsequent changes that are sure to come.

Still, change overwhelms many people. They can often handle the transition from one or two major changes or from several smaller ones, but dealing with layers of change, limited control, and complex, unknown situations (typically woven into work life, but also in family and personal lives) can crush the spirit. Leaders who have not come to terms with the ubiquity of change are powerless to help those around them accept change themselves.

William Bridges (1980, 2001) makes a distinction between change and transition, which is useful for the leader coach to keep in mind when helping the coachee confront the challenges of accepting change. *Change* is the situation or event that is new or different; *transition* is the process of psychological and emotional adaptation to change. Confronted by change, people go through a time of transition—a process of letting go, grieving, rebuilding, and learning. The key for managers going through this process and for the leader coaches who are working with them is to recognize that this cycle of adapting to change occurs at a different pace and in various ways depending on the circumstances and the individual. The manager's responsibility is to understand and invest in the process of transition while simultaneously energizing and managing the change. Leader coaches can help them understand the distinction between change and transition and assist them in learning to facilitate both simultaneously. Mental models are major roadblocks to accepting change. Mental models are deeply rooted, habitual expectations and beliefs. Without our realizing it, they become our operating assumptions. Most of us have strong mental models of what leadership means and how other people should react to our leadership and our decisions. Sayings such as "never let them see you sweat" or "when the going gets tough, the tough get going" represent mental models of strong leadership. Mental models such as these tend to generate an expectation that others comply on the leader's timetable when she makes a decision. When compliance lags or isn't forthcoming at all, the leader may wonder aloud why employees won't "get with the program." She may be scornful of those who ask for help or question her decisions, all owing to her mental model of leadership. Our mental models play out continuously in our daily lives and are heightened when stress levels increase. Stress triggers our strongest coping mechanisms. Human nature leads us to default more quickly to the assumptions and strategies associated with protecting ourselves against our fears and worst-case scenarios.

Coaching executives to understand the implications of mental models in themselves and in others can be a pivotal step in helping them develop into more effective leaders. By becoming aware of the assumptions that have shaped their personal style, leaders can make enlightened and conscious choices about how they want to operate in the future. Left unexamined, however, they have a tendency to repeat patterns that may or may not be serving them well and frequently have unintended consequences for the organization. In cases like this, the role of a leader coach requires challenging the mental models that underlie a coachee's resistance to change.

Coaching for Influencing with Vulnerability

When mental models are revealed, masks are taken off, and the emphasis shifts from driving change to fostering resilience, the result is vulnerability. Being vulnerable is an unfamiliar and uncomfortable experience for most executives and senior leaders. Many have not approached this level of self-reflection and openness for decades, and countless others have experienced the feelings without acknowledging them. Nearly all express the fear that revealing their inner concerns will open the door to a perception of weakness. Certainly people look for strength and courage in their leaders, but they also want them to be human enough (and vulnerable enough) that they can relate to the feelings of others. It is easier to commit to change when you are confident that your leader has walked in your shoes and understands what you are experiencing. It is also empowering to know that you can trust a leader to share the bad news as well as the good, the hurdles and obstacles as well as the promising new vision, and the missteps as well as the successes. Vulnerability doesn't undermine competence and confidence; rather, it multiplies the positive impact and opens the door to the creation of genuine trust and commitment.

Powerful intervention techniques are required to create a readiness for learning and a safe space to explore the power of vulnerability. CCL has drawn on the power of its Leading People Through Transition program to provoke vulnerability by immersing leaders in real-time transition experiences and in its open-enrollment APEX, which uses a mountain of interview data gathered from observers in the leader's work and nonwork life (coupled with personality and preference data). The leader coach doesn't have ready access to these kinds of approaches; however, much of the power in those interventions comes from the peer coaching that occurs between the leaders who participate. By relying on trust, honesty, confidentiality, and the strong belief that the coachee defines the process, leader coaches can confront and challenge their coachees in much the same way, creating a learning environment that is insightful and potent.

Coaching for Emotional Learning

Change and transition are emotionally charged processes because they bring together coping with stress, responding to uncertainty and change, and the challenge of tackling powerful learning experiences. Significant change almost always comes coupled with increased stress and heightened demands for the ability to learn. Significant learning triggers powerful emotional reactions, both positive and negative.

The coach's role is to provide the context and learning vehicles that will allow coachees to examine their patterns of behavior and their emotions tied to change. The goal is to raise the coachee's self-awareness around the emotional aspects of powerful learning opportunities and sensitize the coachee to the patterns and behaviors that enhance the ability to learn in challenging situations and those that are getting in the way of developing as leaders.

One way leader coaches can be helpful is to share with coachees their own experience with change and transition. Leading through transition is not something learned by reading a book or attending a lecture. Most often, learning about the emotional impact of change is best accomplished by examining how one thinks, feels, and behaves when operating in the midst of it. Coaches can help leaders come to terms with their emotional experiences and thus show others, through their own example, how to cope with change and transition. The result for coachees is that they can connect to those whom they lead and can be comfortable about sharing their emotions, even when they appear to be in conflict with their decisions.

Coachees also often need guidance and support in overcoming the tendency to employ previously successful strategies and tactics that are ineffective or even dysfunctional in the face of a changing environment. Life conspires to keep people doing what they already know how to do. It's easier, safer, and more comfortable to keep doing what has worked in the past, even when it prevents others from doing what they have demonstrated that they know how to do. Overcoming the inertia that accompanies emotional learning typically requires a great deal of support and coaching.

Coaching for Active Listening and Empathy

One of the important aspects of learning to lead through transitions is the ability to step outside oneself and recognize that each individual in the organization is experiencing the change in the context of his or her own life situation and history of learning. Each has a bank of preferences, mental models, and learning experience. Each looks at the transition experience through a set of personal lenses, shaped by a lifetime of learning (or not) and a unique set of skills, values, and motivations that ground his or her approach to change and uncertainty. People deal with the same situation in very different ways because of who they are and where they are in life.

An authentic leader must deal with transitional events not only for herself, but also to some degree for the people around her. She must have (or develop) the active listening and empathy skills that will allow her to assess and respond to how a common situation may be experienced differently by those around her. The leader coach can use this knowledge to form peer-based storytelling sessions between coachees. This is a particularly powerful technique to help coachees develop the skill of active listening and for enhancing their development of empathy skills. The role of the leader coach is to set rules of engagement that allow coachees to be comfortable in sharing examples of overcoming hardship or facing up to a challenging change initiative. Practicing these skills in a facilitated group experience can prepare coachees to carry them back to their work units.

Coaching for Balance

Life outside the comfort zone is the norm for those going through change and transition. The incompatibility between the pressures and demands of the coachee's job and the requirements for leading transitions creates a significant imbalance. Finding a tenable position between structural leadership and people leadership is the goal. By seeing how the hard and soft sides of leadership can, and must, coexist in times of change and transition, coachees can develop the broad and flexible approach that is required to lead in extraordinary times. Leader coaches can provide beneficial guidance to coachees who are responsible for implementing change to find ways to answer both sets of demands without sacrificing either.

Effective leaders accept and appreciate that their role encompasses numerous behaviors, many of which may appear on the surface to be contradictory. In coaching their development of a balanced approach, leader coaches can help coachees come to terms with the need to manage this dynamic tension by focusing on twelve competencies that contribute to effective leadership in times of transition. Six of the competencies are structural and tied to strength and commitment; the other six represent people- or transition-related abilities and are tied to emotional competency, learning, and resiliency. Figure 8.1 illustrates these twelve competencies. In the figure, the black line represents an approach that is balanced and about right. The gray area of the circle represents when a competency is overdone, such as when a leader might be too tough during times of transition. The white area of the circle represents when a competency is underdone, such as when a leader doesn't communicate a sense of urgency about the change that his team or organization needs to make.

Together, the twelve competencies create a positive, dynamic tension that fosters the effective, authentic leadership needed during times of change. All of the twelve are important and need to be expressed, but any of them can also be exaggerated, neglected, or in balance. Overdoing or neglecting any one capability tends to skew the opposing capability toward the other direction (exaggerating one competency can mean neglecting its opposite).

- *Catalyzing change.* This capacity involves the ability to champion an initiative or change. A leader who is skilled at catalyzing change consistently promotes the cause and seldom misses opportunities to encourage others to join or to reinforce those who already are. Such leaders are highly driven and eager to get others engaged in any new initiative.
- *Coping with transition.* This capacity involves the ability to recognize and address the personal and emotional elements of change. Leaders who are able to cope with transitions are in touch with their personal reactions to tran-

FIGURE 8.1. TRANSITION LEADERSHIP WHEEL.

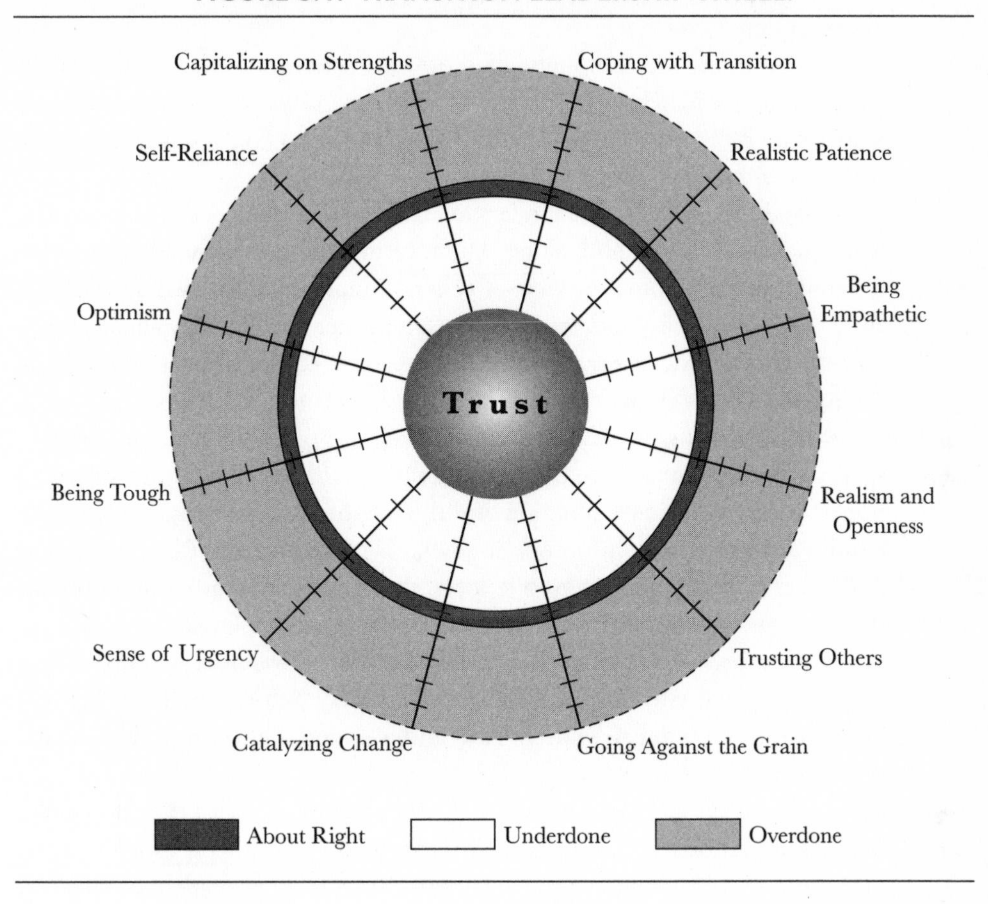

sition and change and make use of that emotional information. They lead by example.

- *Sense of urgency.* This competency relates to the ability to take action and keep things rolling. A leader who has a strong sense of urgency moves on issues quickly and pushes others to work at a rapid pace. This kind of leader values action and knows how to get things done.
- *Realistic patience.* This skill involves knowing when and how to slow the pace down to allow time and space for people to cope and adapt. A leader who displays realistic patience appreciates that people learn and deal with

change differently and does not judge them based on her own style, preferences, or capabilities.

- *Being tough.* This competency requires the ability to make the difficult decisions about issues and people with little hesitation or second-guessing. A leader who is comfortable being tough is not afraid to take a stand in the face of public opinion or strong resistance.
- *Being empathetic.* This skill refers to taking others' perspective into account when making decisions and taking action. Leaders who are empathetic try seeing things from the point of view of others, enhancing their own perspective.
- *Optimism.* The ability to see the positive potential of any challenge is key to leading people during transitions. A leader who communicates and conveys optimism to others encourages them to feel the same.
- *Realism and openness.* This capacity relates to having a grounded perspective and a willingness to be candid. Leaders who are realistic are clear and honest about assessing a situation and the prospects for the future. They are candid and open in communicating what is known and not known. When managers exhibit realism and openness, they speak the truth, don't obscure the facts, and are willing to admit personal mistakes and foibles.
- *Self-reliance.* The capacity for this skill involves a willingness to take a lead role and to personally do the work when necessary. Self-reliant leaders have a great deal of confidence in their skills and abilities. They are willing to take on most new challenges.
- *Trusting others.* This skill involves being comfortable with allowing others to do their part of a task or project. A leader who trusts others is open to input and support from colleagues and friends. Such leaders respect others and demonstrate trust through a willingness to be vulnerable.
- *Capitalizing on strengths.* This competency entails knowing one's strengths and attributes and having the ability to confidently apply them to new situations and circumstances. A leader who knows how to capitalize on strengths trusts the abilities that have generated success, rewards, recognition, compliments, and promotions in the past and uses them in new situations.
- *Going against the grain.* This skill relates to the willingness to learn and try new things, even when it's uncomfortable. Leaders who can go against the grain are willing to tolerate discomfort if it leads to learning.

While the transition leadership wheel is a useful way for thinking about the complex demands of leadership in times of change and transition, true development as a leader takes place when ideas turn into action. This is where the coachee's experience with change and transition meets CCL's coaching framework.

Change, Transition, and the CCL Coaching Framework

Part of the leader coach's job is to create a learning experience that encourages the coachee to look deeply at the complexities of leading in extraordinary times and to reinforce learning, monitor behavior, and support positive change. Due to its highly personal and emotional focus, coaching for transition is largely an organic and evolving process rather than a series of steps or a set of tools. Nevertheless, through years of work with executives and groups facing these kinds of circumstances, CCL has identified techniques that coaches can use to trigger deep personal learning and strategies for putting that learning to use. By applying CCL's coaching framework (relationship, assessment, challenge, support, and results) to a coaching-for-transition situation, leader coaches build a road map for the process and as a gauge of coaching effectiveness over time.

Relationship

In coaching to lead transitions, many relationships are key. The relationship between the coach and the coachee is paramount, and the relationship between peers—especially if peer coaching is involved—also plays a vital role. The success of leading people through transitions is rooted in trusting, open relationships. During times of change and transition, relationships trigger and support powerful insights and meaningful growth.

Commitment, rapport, and collaboration are the three pillars of coaching relationships. Commitment is particularly salient for a coachee in a transition situation. When the coach makes contact routine, stays consistent about endorsing simple messages, and doesn't throw in the towel when the going gets rough, it spells stability for an otherwise besieged coachee, a small island of support amid a swirling sea.

Leader coaches may experience the relationship as a special challenge because they are going through much of the same turbulence. But it also creates a special opportunity in that they can use personal experience to grow through transcending their own pain in order to support their coachees. This is also a time for the leader coach to solidify relationships with others by coaching them through a shared difficult experience. Cindy McCauley (McCauley & Douglas, 2004) gives the name of *companion* to a specific kind of developmental role. This concept resonates well with the unique elements of the leader coach's relationship to the coachee in the context of change and transition because the coach is neither apart nor exempt from the experience and turmoil. Indeed, the leader coach is typically experiencing (but often masking) his or her own version of the discomfort caused by the change. Enlightened transition coaching emerges when a leader coach succeeds in melding the positional access to information and control with the influencing power of self-awareness, vulnerability, and empathetic listening. Such coaches have impact because they share their insight through a bond that says, "We are in this thing together." That is one reason that coaching through change and transition often takes the form of peer coaching. As individuals, we have a tendency to underestimate how helpful we can be to one another as coaches. But there is enormous power in simply sharing one's perspective and insight as a participant in a challenging adventure.

Assessment

Assessment during the coaching process is built from information about the coachee's performance, person, and context. In the case of transitions, understanding context is critical because the specific change being initiated becomes a meta-context. The more personal aspects of context can be helpful in guiding the coach toward understanding the impact the change has on the coachee—on his or her role, position, work content, lifestyle, and even compensation.

Stress is a close companion to change, and individuals can frequently take a step backward when under stress (see, for example, Quenk, 2000). In these moments, we are often not at our best because our less capable self hijacks us. So if the leader coach doesn't have a full appreciation for how the change affects the coachee's context, then he or she may not make a correct assessment, looking only at performance reviews or 360-degree survey feedback.

That isn't to say that traditional feedback can't be helpful. Meaningful data presented in a powerful way stimulate people to think in new ways. Feedback can shake up assumptions, mental models, and the status quo. Given in a safe and protected coaching environment, such a jolt can raise the level of personal and interpersonal awareness and stimulate a climate of learning readiness. In the context of change, these data may help the coachee realize the full significance of the emotional impact of change.

For leaders with broader responsibility, we encourage the use of climate surveys to offer a glimpse into how effectively they may be leading others through the change and transition. If also using interviews, the leader coach can ask a few direct questions about how the coachee is handling the change personally and how he or she is helping others through the process.

Challenge

Leaders often want challenges. More than most other developmental situations, learning to lead in extraordinary times involves extraordinary challenges. Learning to lead authentically is largely an experiential process. It begins with the coachee recognizing and acknowledging that the change has moved him out of his personal comfort zone. Many coachees at this stage may prefer to focus on their perception of the discomfort and angst that others are expressing. This presents a challenge for the leader coach, who may need to first serve as a role model by acknowledging how the current change (or a similar one in the past) moved her out of her comfort zone, before expecting the coachee to make himself vulnerable in that way.

The stretch, or what we often refer to as "going against the grain," has additional meaning for the coachee in transition and is intimately linked with the obstacle component of challenge. The typical leader understands that possessing the ability to learn from obstacles is a developmental asset. However, the obstacles confronted during extraordinary times are on a much larger scale, with implications that failure to adapt could mean an end to a career. It is not just a matter of improving a particular performance. It is more like facing off against massive corporate reorganization and surviving within the environment it produces. The real challenge in this situation is that the coachee is asked to consider the large-scale environmental changes in terms of his or her own situation and then confront them with soft skills such as empathy, active listening, and patience. These are the kinds of skills that leaders often push to the background when their organization presses to implement a significant change.

The other obstacle for coachees in this situation is an internal one: the fear of taking the deeper dive into the sea of emotions that surrounds any significant change. Coaching someone to engage in the emotional and relational complexities of transition is asking this person to take a large risk. Coaches need to applaud and respect the courage that coachees show under these circumstances.

A key role for the leader coach during this process is to help the coachee see options and outcomes that are less catastrophic than what the coachee imagines would happen if she opens the door to the emotional implications of change. Executives often equate managing emotions and people needs during change as weakening their ability to achieve the desired performance outcomes of the change. When we ask leaders what they think will happen if they show vulnerability, they often say that the people in their organization will fall apart. They imply that, like Humpty Dumpty, once they show any signs of cracking, they can't be put back together again. To help their coachees set aside that perspective, coaches need to simultaneously challenge and support.

Support

Creating a safe environment that enables the coachee to give voice to authentic feelings during times of change is at the heart of the leader coach's support role. Most coachees have the inner resources to cope once they articulate their emotions. (For a more detailed view of the strength of inner resources, see Chapter Eleven.) But they may need help in accessing those inner resources and skills. The leader coach becomes but one among many others including peers, friends, and family members, who can offer support through these extraordinary times.

Support for the coachee in transition is strongly related to the coaching relationship. Constancy is essential. The coach's role is to understand the unique nature of the developmental challenge, be prepared to develop a personalized coaching process that addresses it, and stick with the coachee and support him until he develops a self-sustaining process.

Coaches can also help the coachee gain access to other external sources of support. Perhaps a coachee is too overwhelmed by the circumstances, and a referral to outside professional support is warranted. Or the coach may suggest that the coachee attend a formal development program that addresses specific aspects of managing transition.

Results

Leaders want results. When leaders invest hard work, show vulnerability, and take risks, results take on added significance. Results of coaching leadership in extraordinary times are tied to (1) examining behaviors and emotions tied to change, (2) establishing and protecting trust, and (3) finding a balance between structural leadership and people leadership. New awareness and the ability to bring balance into one's leadership repertoire are valued and valuable outcomes. In essence, a primary and universal outcome for coaching others through transition is developing the coachee's emotional maturity as a leader. From this perspective, improvements along the structural side of the business are seen as the result of personal growth and improved relationships.

A Leader Coach's Guide to Extraordinary Times

Coaching executives on leading transitions differs from other coaching situations in terms of the intensity and depth of focus required to tap into the intrapersonal and emotional aspects of learning and change. Coachees face high expectations relative to their ability to understand, empathize with, and address a diverse range of individual responses to the demands of change and transition. This section deals with general challenges the leader coach encounters in these circumstances, sets out specific qualities leader coaches can aspire to when coaching others through change and transition, and describes additional guidelines to keep in mind when coaching managers in those situations.

The Coach's Challenge

In the post-9/11 world, leaders are expected to be simultaneously strong and vulnerable, heroic and open, demanding and compassionate. Furthermore, becoming adept at emotional competence and maturity is riskier and more difficult than developing other leadership capacities because the coachee must be willing to get in touch with personal emotions and reactions. Leaders need to wade in the water of transition if they hope to understand the impact of change on others.

It is one thing to understand the emotional side of transition at a conceptual level; it is quite another to live and model resiliency in day-to-day leadership situations. As a leader coach working in this kind of environment, you face unique challenges. You will be coaching someone who is taking on a significant and emotional challenge. This person may be resistant to your guidance, and almost certainly does not have a full awareness of the personal and emotional journey that is required to lead change and transition.

To have any hope of engaging the coachee in this endeavor, you must be able to model the desired competencies and behaviors. You can't pretend. To help your coachee achieve desired results, you need to be confident in your own emotional maturity, vulnerability, and authenticity. Going through the motions of a scripted coaching session or a prescribed model will be transparent to the coachee and won't get the job done.

Given the unique dynamic of coaching others through transition, it's often the case that senior executives and top leaders benefit most from the process. Leaders at this level tend to set the pace and the process of change and transition in their organizations. Because of their responsibilities and influence, transition coaching for top managers has the most impact on the organization. At this level, most leaders are bright and talented. Many have a conceptual understanding of the emotional impact that difficult times have on the organization and its people, but are wrestling with how to connect this to their work and leadership. (For a more detailed discussion of coaching top-level leaders, see Chapter Six.) Among this group may be managers who have been rapidly promoted due to their talent and performance but who lack the emotional maturity and authenticity that develop over time and with experience. This particular challenge is likely to last well into the future as organizations rapidly prepare managers to meet the demand created by a departing generation of leaders.

The Coach's Qualities

In all developmental coaching, the effective and ethical coach possesses a solid knowledge of the issues and the frameworks that can be applied to make sense of them. But coaching leaders through transition puts an even deeper demand on the leader coach. The coach is asking the coachee to be authentic and vulnerable and to develop a level of emotional intelligence that facilitates connection to others in an authentic and human way. For this to work, the coach too must be able to genuinely reflect and model this type of behavior. Coachees need to see that the coach is living and breathing the values he is advocating for others as he leads his part of the organization through transition. Neither the coach nor the coachee can fake authenticity. People may not know precisely how to define what an authentic leader is, but they recognize it when they feel it and they rebel when they notice its absence.

Knowledge. There are a few baseline texts and theories that are useful for leader coaches working in situations of transition. Associated mainly with the idea of emotional competence, several works reinforce the ideas in this chapter and are accessible to nonscholar leader coaches (see, for example, Bridges, 2001; Bunker, 1994; Goleman, 1998; and Pulley & Wakefield, 2001). Leader coaches can use these sources to get the basic information needed to set up an effective coaching process. Ultimately you will need to decide how much or how little you need to use these resources and how you can use them to gain knowledge and skills.

Experience. Because coachees can experience feelings of vulnerability and discomfort during times of change, coaches must possess the experience and understanding required to reassure coachees that the learning journey will be a safe and productive one. Your ability to model effective leadership behavior carries more weight than providing specific content on leadership behavior. You will need to practice nondefensiveness, vulnerability, and responsibility in the face of assertive pushback and emotional outbursts. Coaches who handle such conditions more effectively than others tend to share most of these characteristics:

- Experience and credibility from having been involved in significant transitions in the past
- Flexibility and confidence to adapt to changing conditions
- One-on-one feedback skills
- A sense of humor

Authenticity. The leader coach is an integral part of the interpersonal and emotional dynamic of transition experiences. You can't remain above the fray or detached. Transitional events demand that leaders share in the experience and model the ability to adapt and learn on the fly. To remain effective in challenging and supporting the coachee, you must model authenticity by being psychologically and emotionally resilient, aware of your own emotional transitions, and able to incorporate paradoxical trade-offs in your own behavior (those described in Figure 8.1).

Additional Guidelines for the Leader Coach

Coaching leaders through transition is not for the faint-of-heart. An effective leader coach in this situation grasps the coachee's situation and challenges and creates or leverages the coachee's readiness to connect to the problem in an authentic, emotional, and developmental way. The main tasks the coach faces are to help the coachee go beyond intellectual awareness to emotional awareness and acceptance, and then to connect that learning back to the daily challenges of transition. Along the way, here are some key points to keep in mind:

- *Expect pushback.* Successful senior leaders are generally strong-willed people who are used to getting their own way. They may overvalue the structural side of leading change and resist anything beyond an intellectual appreciation for the complexities of leading the human side of transition.
- *Stay focused.* During times of change and transition, the coaching role is more intense and more demanding than in many other circumstances. It is an organic, process-oriented, and relationship-driven process. If you fail to listen carefully or otherwise tune out, you fail to model the behavior you are teaching.
- *Remain aware of the coachee's context.* Managers can come from any part of an organization, and change affects each individual and each work unit differently. To have an impact, you must understand the very different challenges any manager's particular group faces and what his or her role in the group is during the change.
- *Consider using a professional coach.* The external perspective of a professional coach ensures unbiased and nonpolitical feedback. This allows unmasking, practicing vulnerability, and developing greater authenticity. If the situation warrants it, you can take a support role and let an external coach create the safe environment your coachee needs to develop the capability to lead transitions.
- *Know the line.* It's difficult to help people understand the emotional side of transition without exploring who they are and how they came to be that way. Focus on behavior, and examine the coachee's cumulative life experience and preferences for indications of how that leads to their behavior during transitions. But coaching in this way is not therapy, so know your own capacities and limitations and be prepared to refer the coachee to a therapist if necessary.

Conclusion

Displaying emotional authenticity and sustaining trust are key for leader coaches working in extraordinary times. Their goal is to help their coachees regain equilibrium and acquire those same capabilities. With that, leaders can build and maintain a high-performing staff, even during chaotic times. And they acquire a set of adaptive skills that will serve them a lifetime.

Developing this capacity asks that coachees step out of carefully crafted comfort zones rooted in self-reliance and invulnerability. Because such learning doesn't come naturally or easily to most executives, it takes a personal, emotional, and experiential process to learn to lead transition effectively.

Coach's Bookshelf

Bunker, K. A. (1997). The power of vulnerability in contemporary leadership. *Consulting Psychology Journal: Practice and Research, 49*(2), 122–136.

Bunker, K., & Wakefield, M. (2004). In search of authenticity: Now more than ever soft skills are needed. *Leadership in Action, 24*(1), 16–20.

George, B. (2004). The journey to authenticity. *Leader to Leader, 31,* 29–35.

Goleman, D. (2002). *Primal leadership: Realizing the power of emotional intelligence.* Boston: Harvard Business School Press.

Van Velsor, E., Moxley, R. S., & Bunker, K. A. (2004). The leader development process. In C. D. McCauley & E. Van Velsor (Eds.), *The Center for Creative Leadership handbook of leadership development* (2nd ed., pp. 204–233). San Francisco: Jossey-Bass.

CHAPTER NINE

COACHING FOR PHYSICAL WELL-BEING

Sharon McDowell-Larsen

Leadership makes heavy demands. It takes creativity, vision, and often working outside one's comfort level. Add to this the daily agendas of nonstop meetings, heavy responsibility, and wearying travel. James Quick writes that "executives who enjoy good health in all its dimensions are unquestionably better equipped to focus their energies on high performance" (2000, p. 35).

All this takes energy, lots of energy, and can lead to premature fatigue. Good athletes understand that recovery is as important as training. Good leaders need to understand this as well: that periods of recovery are just as important as periods of intense efforts, that recovery of energy is as important as expenditure of energy. Many leaders try to push through the fatigue on sheer willpower (Loehr & Schwartz, 2001). This might work in the short term, but over time, undue fatigue compromises performance. Figure 9.1 illustrates the relationship of leadership demands to recovery and performance.

The point here is that leadership is not just about time management but also about energy management. Managing energy means managing one's physiology: taking care of health, sleeping well, getting regular exercise, and eating a proper diet. These are the behaviors that enhance health and performance, yet they are often neglected for the cause of work. Loehr and Schwartz (2003), in their work on the relationship of energy management to leadership, argue

FIGURE 9.1. RELATIONSHIP OF LEADERSHIP DEMANDS TO RECOVERY AND PERFORMANCE.

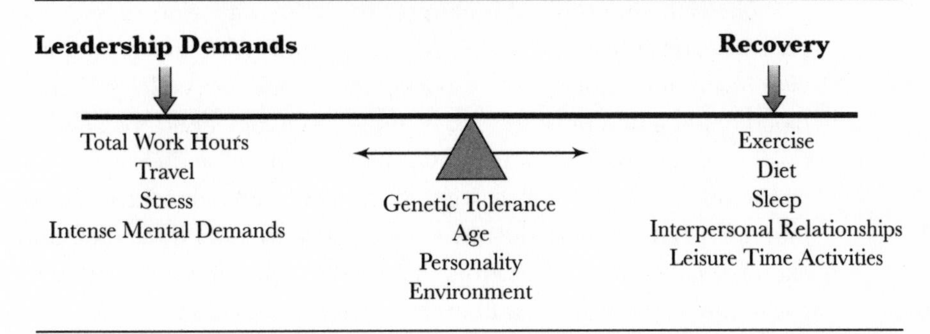

that the primary issue affecting corporate America today is disengagement of the workforce. So many leaders, faced with extreme demands, disengage from their jobs, their families, and communities in order to conserve energy. Being fully engaged means that one is fully alive, firing on all cylinders, and marshaling full energy for the task at hand. When individuals are not able to manage that energy properly, breakdowns in health occur, and careers are threatened. The implications are serious for leaders and organizations.

The downward spiral can seem benign. I once heard a talk given by former vice chairman of the Joint Chiefs of Staff, General Peter Pace. Someone asked him, "What keeps you up at night?" He responded that nothing kept him up at night. He said sleep was important to him; without it, he couldn't think clearly or have the energy to do his job. I appreciated his response; many leaders I have worked with try to get by on only four or five hours of sleep a night and are chronically sleep deprived. When one is fatigued, it is hard to eat and exercise right. Poor diets and lack of regular exercise lead to poor sleep and more fatigue, in the process reducing the ability to deal with stress.

This chapter demonstrates that the state of health of leaders can and does affect their performance and ultimately the performance of their organizations. Leader coaches can identify the areas of well-being that are being compromised and help coachees make concerted efforts to improve their health and marshal their energies in those areas. Although fitness may not come immediately to mind as a part of developmental coaching, this chapter makes the point that it needs to be explored and addressed as an important element of the leadership development process. Lack of fitness can be a pernicious yet almost invisible factor in an executive's life and can have stunning consequences.

The information in this chapter draws on data and experiences from CCL's Leadership at the Peak (LAP) program. During that program, we provide health and fitness data to participants. Data are collected on body fat, blood lipids, blood pressure, stroke and heart attack indicators, and information on exercise routines. Participants receive reports on their health status and recommendations for improving their physical well-being. Our database contains information about the fitness levels of more than three thousand senior executives. As a whole, this group has better health indicators and is more engaged in the fitness process than the average population.

Given what we have learned from these participants and their experiences with addressing fitness as a developmental goal, this chapter can provide direction to leader coaches about what is important to know when helping others with physical fitness issues and how to integrate this aspect of development into their plans for coachees.

Why Coach for Fitness?

Consider the story of Maurice, a leader coach who has become gravely concerned about Joe, one of his direct reports whom he is coaching:

Maurice has observed Joe huffing and puffing when he climbs stairs, and after a recent business trip he was sick for a week. First and foremost, Maurice is concerned for Joe's physical well-being, but he is also concerned about Joe's decreased performance and what that might mean to the department's goals. Maurice's problem is that he isn't sure if he should approach the topic with Joe, or what he would do or say even if he could. Would Joe regard his intervention as interference in his personal life and that it had nothing to do with his developing as a leader?

Maurice might start with the perspective that Joe may not realize how his health issues are affecting his performance. Maurice has worked with Joe long enough to remember him as healthier in the past. If Maurice discerns that health issues are a deterrent to Joe's performance, then he can assume that addressing the health aspects of Joe's performance goals is a valuable aspect to his developmental coaching.

Coaching for physical fitness does not always assume that there are negative health factors. It can also play a role when the coachee is fit. Like other developmental activities, it can help with maintaining or improving a satisfactory position. CCL data show that executives who exercise are rated as more effective leaders and work fewer hours per week. Individuals who are already performing well and feel well probably already know that some work on their part is required to maintain optimal fitness. Within this sphere, the leader coach has opportunities to coach on the issue of fitness. Leader coaches are privy to the conditions under which their coachees work, how others perceive them, what their performance issues are, what the stresses and demands are, and what keeps them awake at night. Even leader coaches who are not fitness experts (which is highly likely) can use their perspective to help coachees face important health and fitness issues that can have a major impact on their ability to perform, or they can support coachees' healthy lifestyle choices and fitness maintenance when other conditions are unaccommodating. (Leader coaches can use their influence to push their organization to provide fitness rooms that employees can access, for example, or to work out discounts at health clubs or set up health committees that offer advice on nutrition, activities, and even exercise equipment.)

In short, coaching for physical fitness can enhance or maintain performance. By gaining awareness, information, and skills related to coaching fitness, the leader coach can present a positive, supportive link to these kinds of health issues. Before bringing up this subject with coachees, however, leader coaches will want to know the particular issues and caveats that may arise within the coaching context. Some aspects of health and fitness are better left to exercise and nutrition experts, and it is important for leader coaches to know where the boundaries lie. This chapter deals with those concerns, but first it defines what physical well-being means in the context of developmental coaching.

Defining Physical Well-Being

Physical well-being means different things to different people. Some people focus on a proper diet, while others focus on the activities they perform to benefit their health. On a practical level, being fit means having the ability to perform daily tasks and engage in leisure-time pursuits without undue fatigue. For the purposes of this chapter, I define it as a measure of physical fitness, particularly aerobic capacity and endurance. *Aerobic capacity* is the ability to exercise at high intensities (such as on a treadmill or stationary bike). *Aerobic endurance* is the capacity to work for a long period at less-than-maximum intensity. I chose these two aspects because most fitness tests (such as a cardiovascular health assessment) are designed to measure them.

Both capacity and endurance are important for optimum physical health, and each works in tandem with the other. Exercising at higher intensities results in higher aerobic capacity and is related to improvements in cardiovascular function. Exercising at below-maximum intensity for longer durations improves aerobic endurance and is related to improvements in muscular function. Both bring improvements in the body's ability to burn fats and sugars and can improve lipid profiles such as triglycerides and HDL cholesterol.

Certainly there are many other aspects of physical well-being not addressed by aerobic capacity and endurance. This chapter does not cover all of the aspects of poor fitness that can affect performance, such as obesity and lack of sleep. Instead, it uses those two aspects of physical health and links them to an area of fitness that commonly plagues leaders: stress. Stress exacts a considerable toll on executives' psychological and physical health. It is the most visible complaint for the executive and the most recognized by coworkers. It is the primary, though not the only, cause for executive burnout and degraded energy. Exercise is an effective counterpoint to stress, helping to alleviate the effects and enhance recovery. Leader coaches can serve their coachees debilitated by stress by offering them ways to address their physical well-being through exercise.

Stress: Aftermath and Answers

The average LAP participant works more than sixty hours a week and is on the road for up to a third of the year. These participants often say that their health is compromised by the relentless stress that accompanies their responsibilities. The demand to produce is high, while resources are often lacking.

These LAP executives are certainly not unique. One study estimated that stress-related absence accounts for 60 percent of all workplace absences and affects one in five employees in the United Kingdom (Cartwright, 2000). But is stress always bad? For some individuals, it can provide a competitive edge: they thrive on stress. Others, however, wilt under it. The difference lies in controlling the stress, which relates to the interplay between individual resources and the severity of the demands, moderated by genetic factors and social support systems. When perceived demands exceed perceived resources over an extended period of time, something has to give. More often than not, it is our physiological systems that are harmed. Heart disease, asthma, diabetes, allergies, autoimmune disorders, and even obesity have all been linked to prolonged levels of stress.

Some people's physiological systems are more prone to failure than those of others during periods of stress. Those predisposed to suffer from prolonged stress are the immune system, muscular system, cognitive functions, emotional systems, and the nervous system. Examples of symptoms if the immune system is affected are allergies, cold sores, flu-like symptoms, and frequent colds. Muscular symptoms include backache and joint pain. Cognitive symptoms may be memory problems and difficulty in concentrating. Emotional and nervous system effects include sadness, depression, fatigue, sleep disturbances, and digestive problems. If these symptoms are evident, the person suffering them must either reduce the extent or degree of the strain or make the system stronger so that it is more resistant to the ill effects of stress.

The leader coach can take heart from this piece of information: personal control appears to play a large role in determining the intensity and quality of responses to stress, and this is where executives and other top managers seem to have an advantage over people in lower-ranked jobs (McDowell-Larsen, 2002; also see Exhibit 9.1).

People in jobs that allow them to use creativity and initiative (such as executive positions) produce epinephrine in response to mental stimuli but at the same time show lower levels of cortisol (Frankenhaeuser, 1991). This type of

EXHIBIT 9.1. COMMON SOURCES OF STRESS CITED BY SENIOR EXECUTIVES.

- Desire to succeed, excel
- Family relationships
- Work/family/personal life balance
- Fear of failure
- Features of the job itself
- Meeting others' expectations

response tends to be less harmful on health than a response in which levels of both hormones are elevated because an elevated cortisol level can lead to increased appetite, which in turn can lead to weight gain. Both hormones increase in those whose jobs impose unpredictable demands, leave little room for individual discretion, fail to use skills and abilities to full potential, and lack personal control—a situation typical of lower-ranking managerial jobs. Such individuals are prone to stress-related illnesses.

Although personal control appears to have an advantageous effect on response to stress, it is by no means a universal antidote for stress. For instance, one study showed that people with borderline hypertension do not benefit as much from personal control as do people with normal blood pressure (Bohlin et al., 1986). Yet another study documented gender differences in stress-response patterns. Women managers reported having less control at work than did men, but they appeared to benefit more than men from the control they did have (Frankenhaeuser, 1991).

A strong social support system and physical fitness increase resiliency to stress. Similar to how the strength of a bridge or building can be improved using supporting devices and using stronger materials, so individuals can bear heavier loads by having support and being physiologically stronger. Studies have shown a correlation between mortality and having a social support network: friends and family help individuals live longer (Marmot & Syme, 1976).

When practiced early and often in an executive's career, exercise can relieve immediate stress and improve physical stamina and resiliency over the long term. The catch is that stress itself may keep people from exercising regularly. In the next sections, I use the structure of CCL's coaching framework to describe the benefits of exercise, how to recognize when a coachee needs to make it a practice, and how to approach the question as a coach.

The Benefits of Exercise

Our physiological response to stress prepares us for physical exertion. Exercise helps to dissipate hormones, glucose, and lipids released as a result. Exercise itself is a stressor (it diverts blood flow and increases heart rate), but it decreases psychological stress by acting as a diversion and an outlet. The rhythmic nature of aerobic exercise produces a tranquilizing effect, increases calmness, and decreases depression. One study documented that people who walked showed decreased electromyographic activity (a measure of anxiety-tension), while a group on tranquilizers did not. The same study discussed how regular exercise can replace maladaptive behaviors such as smoking, poor dietary habits, and alcohol consumption, which are often typical responses to stress (Rostad & Long, 1996).

Data that CCL has collected from senior executives show a positive correlation between regular exercise and leadership effectiveness. Executives who exercise regularly (regardless of how little or how much) are rated higher by their observers on various attributes of leadership effectiveness. Not only are those who exercise rated higher on their leadership performance, they also work fewer hours per week (about two fewer hours per week) than nonexercisers or sporadic exercisers. Although these data do not imply cause and effect, they do suggest that exercise need not be given up at the expense of leadership performance.

In one example of how those kinds of ratings play out in the real world, an executive we know was told by his doctor to exercise or he would suffer severe health problems. He made a choice to go the gym each morning at 6:00 A.M. rather than carry out his usual practice of getting to the office at that time. He made it clear to his team that there would be no meetings called before a specific time. Though he was getting into work later, he found he could handle the stress of work better, he was more patient with coworkers and direct reports, and he performed better.

Aside from physical benefits, exercise increases brain function and results in clearer thinking, better problem solving, and improved creativity. Leaders often report that they use their exercise time to problem-solve and plan their days. This is especially true if the exercise is rhythmic in nature, such as walking, cycling, or running.

Exercise can bring benefits to the emotional side of life as well. It can bring a sense of increased control over life, increasing optimism and self-confidence. It can act as a release or outlet for emotions or physical tensions. Another individual I know suffered from periods of depression and was too shy to join a health club. I coached her to start a walking program, which gradually progressed to a running program. A year later, she ran the Pikes Peak Ascent, a thirteen-mile run up to the top of Pikes Peak, a feat she never would have believed she could achieve. In the process, she transformed herself into a cheerful, optimistic, and confident woman. She reported that her newfound confidence transferred to her performance at work and that she felt she could meet any challenge. Exercise doesn't always create striking results like this, but even small improvements to a person's emotional state can have a dramatic impact on the quality of life.

The physical benefits of exercise are obvious. It increases energy, improves muscle tone, and improves cardiovascular endurance and capacity. Physical fitness has also been shown to be protective even in the presence of other risk factors. For example, people are better off being overweight and fit than lean and unfit and better off having high cholesterol and being fit than having normal cholesterol and being unfit. This flies in the face of the images portrayed in popular media, which assume thinness means health. No one should ignore such risk factors as obesity and high cholesterol levels, but regular exercise that promotes physical well-being can provide a measure of protection.

Stages of Exercise Behavior

There are five stages of exercise behavior: precontemplative, contemplative, preparation, action, and maintenance (see Figure 9.2). These stages are derived from a theoretical model of behavior change that has been applied to a wide variety of health behavior problems, including smoking cessation, alcohol abuse, and weight control (Prochaska & Velicer, 1997). That model focuses on individuals' decision-making pattern. Behavior change is often construed as an event; for instance, one smokes and then quits. This model argues for change as a process, involving progress through a series of stages. CCL has used the model in LAP to determine where a particular individual is in regard to his or her capacity for exercise.

The stages help leader coaches assess the level of physical activity of their coachees. With that information, coaches are better prepared to conceptualize and suggest an exercise program (in broad terms, that is; we don't expect leader coaches to be fitness experts). We recommend proceeding with this step before embarking on a fitness coaching initiative. The following sections describe the stages. Figure 9.3 is a more formal decision tree that can help coaches assess a coachee's exercise stage.

To give leader coaches some idea about how to work with coachees when they are at specific levels, Table 9.1 makes relevant links between exercise stages and CCL's coaching framework. (The framework reappears later in the chapter in the broader context of leadership and fitness.)

FIGURE 9.2. A MODEL OF EXERCISE BEHAVIOR.

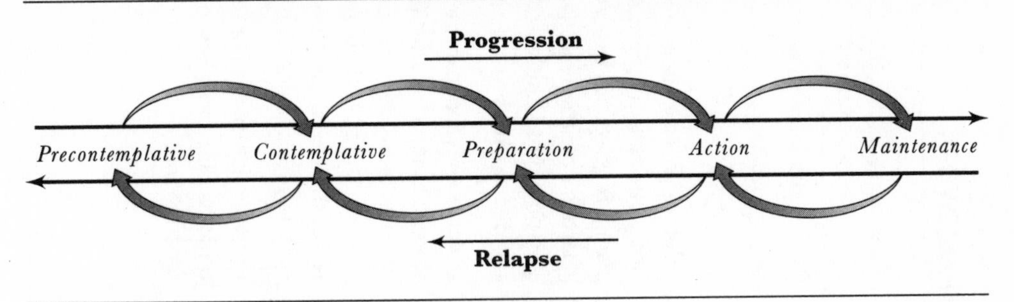

Source: Adapted from Prochaska & Velicer (1997, pp. 38–48).

FIGURE 9.3. ASSESSING STAGE OF EXERCISE BEHAVIOR.

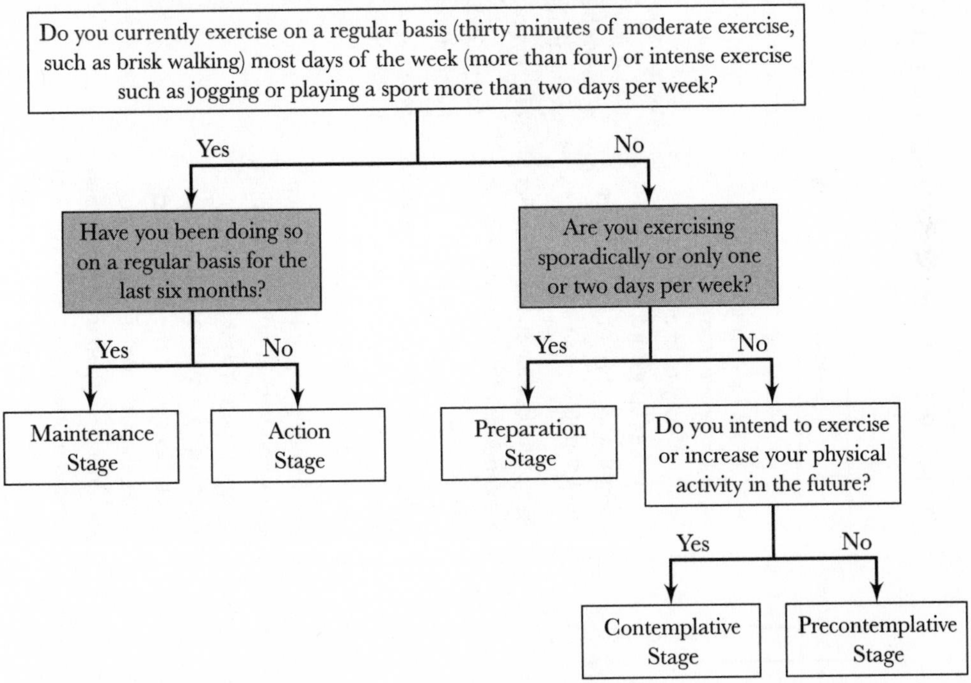

Do you currently exercise on a regular basis (thirty minutes of moderate exercise, such as brisk walking) most days of the week (more than four) or intense exercise such as jogging or playing a sport more than two days per week?

Yes → Have you been doing so on a regular basis for the last six months?

- Yes → Maintenance Stage
- No → Action Stage

No → Are you exercising sporadically or only one or two days per week?

- Yes → Preparation Stage
- No → Do you intend to exercise or increase your physical activity in the future?
  - Yes → Contemplative Stage
  - No → Precontemplative Stage

TABLE 9.1. EXERCISE STAGES AND CCL'S DEVELOPMENTAL FRAMEWORK.

	Leader Development Framework		
Exercise Stages	**Assessment**	**Challenge**	**Support**
Precontemplative	Help your coachee define any health risks he or she has that would improve from exercise: family history of heart disease, high blood pressure, excess weight, diabetes, or high cholesterol count, for example. Ask your coachee to list his or her perceptions of the health benefits of exercise. Ask your coachee to list the reasons that he or she doesn't exercise and what he or she sees as barriers. From your perspective as a coach, think about what other underlying reasons there might be for your coachee to remain at this stage. What does he or she think constitutes exercise? What is his or her experience with exercise? Are there deeper, underlying drivers (view of self, or family issues, for example)?	Challenge some of your coachee's notions as to what exercise is and how much needs to be done. Encourage your coachee to think about creative solutions to some of his or her barriers to exercise. What are alternatives to this view of exercise? Ask your coachee to list reasons in favor of exercise or what the perceived benefits of exercise would be for him or her.	Listen, and listen some more. Ask questions before jumping to solutions. Educate yourself about exercise and its benefits to physical well-being. Be prepared to answer your coachee's questions with information on fitness if the coachee invites the discussion. Become knowledgeable about external support sources (trainers or nutritionists, for example) so that you can offer those resources to coachees who ask for guidance outside your personal expertise. Use your influence to present a business case for fitness to your organization.

Contemplative	Talk to your coachee about behaviors he or she can change to make time to exercise. What does the coachee need to happen, or what needs to be in place in order to start an exercise program? Responses might include the need to set up an exercise room at home, join a health club, buy equipment, buy walking shoes, find a partner, hire a personal trainer, or hire a sitter. The coachee's goal is to figure out how to make fitness possible, not to define a fitness outcome. Other questions you can explore with your coachee: What kinds of things prevent him or her from exercising on a regular basis: lack of priority, schedule, injury, fatigue, lack of opportunity, or no facilities? What sort of exercise has the coachee done in the past? What does the coachee currently believe about exercise, and how much does he or she think is needed? Are these current conceptions realistic, appropriate?	Challenge your coachee to change the way he or she thinks about exercise. What are ways to overcome the perceived barriers? The most common barrier is a lack of time. Frequently, the reasons coachees give for not finding time to exercise are all legitimate. Challenge your coachees to think about who owns their schedules and about the choices they make about how to spend their time. As a coach, you want to help them understand that on some level, these are choices, not obstacles. Try challenging your coachee with the notion that ten minutes of exercise is better than none. To most people, ten minutes doesn't seem worth the time. True, ten minutes won't bring weight loss or significant health benefits, but finding ten minutes feels possible. A coachee who can get into the habit of finding ten minutes can build that into the habit of finding more time. Exercise time can evolve to twenty minutes, and that is enough time to deliver health benefits.	Support at this stage involves helping the coachee identify personal motivations to engage in fitness. By acknowledging that he or she would like to exercise in the future, the coachee demonstrates an understanding and interest in achieving improved fitness. What the coachee likely needs is a jump-start. Reinforce the reasons to do this. Help provide some accountability for what the coachee agrees to do. Assist with finding resources. Are there ways, for example, the coachee can allocate workloads in order to leave work earlier or get to work later? Are there ways to have the exercise time serve a dual purpose?

TABLE 9.1. EXERCISE STAGES AND CCL'S DEVELOPMENTAL FRAMEWORK, Cont'd.

	Leader Development Framework		
Exercise Stages	**Assessment**	**Challenge**	**Support**
Preparation	Find out what your coachee's perceived exercise needs and beliefs are. Is there the perception that exercise is all or nothing? ("I don't have an hour to work out or time to play tennis with my friends, so it is not worth doing.") What prevents this person from being consistent? What derails him or her? What can your coachee do to make exercise time feel less like a burden?	Tap into what you know about what makes your coachee tick. Challenge your coachee to find times and routines that work for his or her personality preferences and are consistent with how he or she tends to operate in other arenas. For example, CCL's data on individuals in the maintenance stage show that introverts have a slight preference for exercising in the morning but extroverts are more likely to exercise in the evening. Start working with your coachee to identify the desired outcomes of the exercise.	Help your coachee connect with the benefits he or she has noticed thus far. They may be subtle, such as a bit more energy during the day or sleeping better at night. Celebrate those small wins, and help your coachee manage any setbacks. Your task is to help the coachee convert an intermittent behavior into a habit. Talk with your coachee about other times when he or she was able to establish a new habit. How can those conditions be re-created? Have your coachee reflect on the typical distractions and eliminate or mitigate those as a means of removing obstacles. Continue to guide your coachee toward recognizing and focusing on short-term and long-term benefits. Continue to hold your coachee accountable for what he or she agrees to do.

Action	As a leader coach, your main task at this stage is to be supportive of the new exercise program. How well is the program going? What benefits does the coachee see? What changes has the coachee made to have time for exercise?	Begin to guide your coachee toward a focus on long-term goals. What does he or she want to get out of the program? Is the goal to get fit, increase endurance, lose weight, get stronger, run a 10-kilometer race, or ride a bike tour? Depending on the desired outcome, it might be time to seek the help of an expert fitness or athletic coach.	Help your coachee sustain his or her achievement. Through dialogue, surface what works for the coachee to help make the process more conscious. From that point, your coachee can sustain and self-correct more easily. If an expert fitness or health coach is part of the process, partner with both the coachee and expert coach in achieving the desired goal. Continue to encourage, and help the coachee hold himself or herself accountable.
Maintenance	Individuals at this stage are highly motivated, and they do not likely need coaching on exercise. The coach's task may be only to monitor. Is the coachee happy with the results of the program?	Help your coachee determine if the level of exercise is appropriate to the desired result by arranging for an evaluation from a trainer or other kind of fitness professional.	If your coachee wants to raise the level of the exercise and fitness program, it's appropriate to refer him or her to a fitness professional.

Precontemplative. Individuals in the precontemplative stage ("I don't currently exercise, and I don't plan to in the future") are few and far between. Data on senior executives show that only 2 percent of males and 4 percent of females are in this stage. Most nonexercisers recognize that exercise is good for them and have every intention of starting to exercise in the future, so it is surprising to encounter someone in this stage. A common feature among such individuals is that they dislike exercising. They might have exercised in the past, but their list of reasons not to exercise is longer than any reasons they can think of as to why they should. They often operate under the notion that some people were just not made to exercise and they are among them. The pressures of work life, lack of time, and other obstacles strengthen their case.

To coach someone at this stage, the coach should consider that the goal is simply to move that person into the next stage (*contemplative*). To get there, the coachee has to agree that exercise is something to consider doing in the future, that it is important because it will have an impact on long-term health and perhaps job performance. Few coachees at this stage would disagree that exercise is good to do, but they may, with a coach's guidance, be able to think about why it is good for them.

Contemplative. CCL's data show that 13 percent of executives (both male and female) attending LAP are in this stage ("I don't currently exercise, but would like to exercise in the near future"). Individuals at this stage are not currently exercising but think they probably should because it is good for them. They might want to be more physically fit, but for various reasons haven't made it a priority. They intend to change and are aware of the advantages of change but are also aware of the challenges. This tension between the costs and benefits produces ambivalence and can keep them stuck here. The goal of a coach leader working with someone in this stage is to get the coachee to start thinking about ways for making room for exercise—to move on to the preparation stage.

Preparation. About a third of senior executives are in this stage ("I don't currently exercise regularly, but would like to exercise regularly in the future"). They know how to exercise and may even do it, but sporadically. They have a health club membership, a workout room at home, running shoes, a tennis racquet, and proper clothing. But things come up at work, travel intrudes, illness and injuries happen. They would like to be more regular in their exercise program and do try, but they haven't made it a regular part of their lives.

The goal of a coach when working with individuals in this stage is to help them set aside time on a regular basis so they can move into the action stage.

Action. Individuals in this stage ("I currently exercise on a regular basis but have been doing so only for less than six months") have started to exercise. They have a program and have figured out how to fit exercise into their day. It might not be as much as they think they should be doing, but they have been consistent. They have started to experience the benefits. But their exercising hasn't become a habit, as natural as any of their other activities.

The coach should provide plenty of support to coachees at this stage, working with them to set long-term health goals and help them assess their progress so that they can make physical well-being part of their daily routine.

Maintenance. CCL's data show that executives in this stage ("I currently exercise and have been doing so for more than six months") have figured out when, where, and how to exercise. Their reasons for exercising have more to do with positive effects (health, enjoyment, feeling good, energy) than with ameliorating negative factors (weight loss, health crisis recovery). Their routines are time efficient. Exercise is a priority for them, and if they miss a workout, they feel it.

How the Exercise Stages Play Out in Coaching

To give leader coaches a clearer idea of the value of these stages as a means of coaching for improved physical well-being, the story of a particular coachee proves helpful:

Bill's coaching process began when he entered LAP as a participant. From the information he provided, he was clearly in the precontemplative stage. This assessment was reinforced by observations that he was visibly overweight and from self-disclosed information that he had high blood pressure. On the first day of the program, he admitted that he hated to exercise and would present a real challenge to that part of the program. True to his word, he did not attend any of the exercise sessions during the week. However, during the fitness presentation, coaches observed that he listened carefully when presenters detailed the possible consequences of his decision not to exercise.

At that point Bill must have realized he needed to do something because he requested an individual coaching session to pursue his thoughts. He and his coach brainstormed about what his resources were, what he needed to get into place to start exercising, and what conditions he needed to create to get started. His goal at the end of the LAP program was to start to exercise regularly. After the program, CCL continued to send him information about blood pressure and how to control it better through diet and exercise. He communicated to us about starts and stops in his exercise program; then he stopped communicating, and his coach assumed that he had found the challenge too difficult.

About a year later, his coach was surprised by a visit from Bill and his wife. They were on vacation and had stopped by to let his coach know he was exercising regularly. He described working with a personal trainer twice a week and said he felt good, had more energy, and was performing better at work. Even during vacation, he and his wife were taking time to go to the gym—something they had never done in the past on their vacations. Then he leaned over and said to his coach, "Just between you and me, I still don't like to exercise."

The point of this story is that a person doesn't suddenly go from "never intending to exercise" to "exercising." It is a process that takes time (it took Bill almost a year). During his attendance at LAP, he moved from precontemplative to contemplative. Then he took tentative steps toward preparation. By joining a gym, he figured out what worked for him and what didn't. He relapsed along the way. But he finally got to the point where it was a regular routine—something he missed when he didn't do it.

If Bill's coach had begun his work with Bill by telling him that he needed to get out and do certain activities for exercise, Bill isn't likely to have made any progress. The value of seeing exercise as stages is that it lets the work begin where the coachee stands in terms of his or her attitudes and capacities for exercise.

Even armed with the perspective of exercise as developmental stages and a process that takes time, it is a tricky proposition for a leader coach to know when and how to suggest an exercise program to a coachee. The following section describes some of the issues coaches may face when making this decision, and offers some guidelines to aid in the decision-making process.

Issues for the Coach

There are some specific points to keep in mind when entering this area of coaching. These issues touch on such matters as the decision to coach, the definition of illness, the coach's own health, the coach's comfort level with fitness coaching, and the coach's knowledge of the field. (See also Exhibits 9.2 and 9.3 for additional points.)

EXHIBIT 9.2. WHEN TO COACH FOR EXERCISE.

Exercise is a key element in managing the stressful demands of leadership and maintaining physical well-being. Coaching on this issue is appropriate when:

- *The coachee expresses interest in health or fitness topics.* This interest may be expressed as a result of the coachee's receiving results of a physical or other health assessment when the results are not as positive as they could be. Less formally, the coachee may complain about gaining weight, not getting enough exercise, or not sleeping well. Under the best conditions, the issue comes up because the coachee is committed to fitness and wants to ensure that she is able to maintain that level of health. She may wonder if the organizational culture will support her priority around fitness as she takes on greater responsibilities.
- *There are subtle or not-so-subtle signs that lack of exercise is affecting work performance or health.* These include fatigue, low energy, inability to deal with stress, weight gain, trouble sleeping, recurrent upper respiratory illnesses, or even impatience with direct reports and peers. The leader coach has to bring a lot of awareness and sensitivity to these kinds of signs. Poor physical well-being is rarely the sole cause of a performance issue, but it can be a compounding factor or even a symptom of some other cause.
- *There are signs that poor eating habits or lack of exercise is negatively affecting the way peers, direct reports, or bosses view the coachee.* CCL research reveals that executives who do not exercise regularly are rated lower by their observers on energy, resilience, productivity, optimism, and calmness. Self-ratings on these factors are also lower for the nonexercisers. Factors such as poor posture, excessive weight, cigarette smoking, or low energy can all harm credibility and leadership stature.

The Decision to Coach

Coaching on health and fitness can touch on intensely personal issues. The prevailing view is that health is a private issue, so the question as to whether to raise the issue of fitness can create a quandary for leader coaches. While few people would argue about the benefits of fitness to health, not many would consider it a leadership competency and so not a leadership coaching issue.

The health and fitness of a leader is not usually a primary consideration when it comes to performance, but the perception of fitness often influences how others judge a person's capacity to lead. Although it is unlikely that poor fitness will make or break a leader (unless there is an extreme case of

EXHIBIT 9.3. WHEN NOT TO COACH FOR EXERCISE.

Despite an abundance of popular magazines promoting health and exercise, television shows of exercise routines, and other cultural influences, many people consider health and physical well-being a personal affair. Coaching on this issue is inappropriate if:

- *It is prescriptive.* It is not a leader coach's job to prescribe a particular diet or exercise program. If a coachee wants to bicycle a hundred miles, it is not the leader coach's task to help or even advise how to go about training for this. If someone wants to go on a diet to lose weight, it is not the leader coach's job to prescribe or advocate a particular diet. The leader coach's role is to help the coachee identify these as goals or assist in finding an expert to help him or her reach those goals.
- *The coachee sees it as a personal issue and doesn't want to discuss it.* It may seem obvious that a lack of health and fitness is an issue with a coachee. But as with any other coaching relationship, the coachee has to agree that this is an issue for which coaching can play a part.

poor health), leadership does include an element of managing personal energy to meet high demands and high levels of stress, and that includes managing one's physiology. When poor physical well-being does not contribute to that energy, it affects performance—and so falls within the domain of coaching. It is also in the realm of coaching to help coachees anticipate the impact that increased responsibility may have on their physical well-being and to encourage coachees to build and maintain a commitment to fitness under these circumstances.

Illness and Its Perceptions

Jan Krupp, of Executive Health Watch, has been quoted (Romano, 1994) as saying, "Employers have a right to expect their key people to get a checkup and be in the best possible health" (p. 40). That statement implies that not only should leaders be concerned about their health for personal reasons, but their health and well-being should concern employees and stakeholders. Their ability to perform effectively has a direct bearing on the health of their organizations. Leaders are expensive to replace. Evident poor health in a leader can result in instability and uncertainty. After Roberto Goizueta, CEO of Coca-

Cola, died at the age of sixty-five, Coca-Cola's stock suffered a 15 to 20 percent decline. Goizueta did not safeguard his health, was a chain-smoker, and had other known health risks (Rippe, 1990). A broader perspective increases the leader's responsibility to stay healthy.

Most people do not want to spend time thinking about illness. Executives are confident about their odds for not getting sick. According to one article, "illness is an imperfection most would not consider happening to them" (Romano, 1994). The prevailing notion is one of invulnerability: "I can work seventy hours per week, not sleep or eat well, and exercise only sporadically, but it won't happen to me."

The Coach's Health

A leader coach with a reputation of alienating colleagues is not a suitable candidate for guiding others in the area of improving peer relationships. In the same way, a coach who is out of shape, eats junk food, or smokes or drinks to excess will not have much authority when it comes to coaching in the area of physical well-being. The leader coach does not have to be the perfect specimen of health and fitness but should have some personal commitment to being healthy. Before coaching in this area, leader coaches need to examine their own views and values. This may even offer an opportunity for reciprocal coaching, in which coach and coachee agree to support one another's commitment.

The Coach's Comfort Level

It is important to ask how far a coach who is not trained as a fitness specialist can go in this area. Some coaches might feel that it is so outside their area of expertise that they cannot be comfortable at all coaching it. Other coaches, who themselves may be fitness advocates, may overstep their bounds and try to coach too far outside their primary focus on leader development. What are the boundaries, and when is it appropriate to coach in this area?

According to CCL data and other published research (Rippe, 1990), the number one motivator given by executives as a reason to exercise is not improved productivity but health benefits. We all want to be healthy; we are all motivated by a desire for pleasure and fulfillment. This should comfort coaches who are concerned about overstepping their bounds when raising the issue of physical well-being.

It is beyond the boundary of leader development coaching to coach toward specific outcomes, such as running a faster marathon or benching three hundred pounds. That kind of specific fitness coaching is better left to the experts. It's not appropriate to recommend a certain amount or level of exercise (see Exhibit 9.4 for general guidelines), although being familiar with current guidelines would be helpful.

EXHIBIT 9.4. WHAT KIND OF EXERCISE?

If your coachee is interested in exploring exercise as a means of developing physical well-being, what kinds of guidelines regarding types of exercise can you provide? Assuming that you are not a fitness expert, it's probably best to stick to some general information that will help your coachee get started on the right track. Research shows a clear benefit to being fit: the higher the fitness level, the lower one's risk for cardiovascular disease.

You and your coachee should start with defining his or her current fitness level. Highly sedentary individuals can improve their fitness with walking. For some people, however, walking at a leisurely pace won't improve fitness. More vigorous efforts, such as walking hills or stairs, are needed. Well-trained individuals need high-intensity workouts to improve aerobic capacity (they are unlikely to be seeking your guidance in the first place).

For the benefit of physical well-being, structured and lifestyle activities are important. Structured exercise includes such activities as walking, running, lifting weights, taking an exercise class, or participating regularly in a sport. Lifestyle exercises can include taking the stairs at work, cleaning the house, or engaging in a physical hobby such as gardening or woodworking.

Always consult with a doctor before beginning any kind of exercise regimen. Exercise recommendations for reducing the risk of cardiovascular disease include:

- Expending more than 1500 (men) or 1200 (women) calories per week in aerobic exercise
- Getting thirty minutes of moderate exercise (brisk walking) most days—if not every day (U.S. Department of Health and Human Services, 1996)
- Exercising twenty to sixty minutes, three to five days per week at an intensity of 55 to 90 percent of maximal heart rate (American College of Sports Medicine, 1998)
- Exercising sixty minutes per day for weight loss; to maintain weight loss, sixty to ninety minutes per day may be needed (Institute of Medicine, 2002).
- Accumulating ten thousand steps per day.

The leader coach is on firmer ground when simply raising the issue, shining light on the fact that the coachee should consider fitness a part of the bigger leader development picture. The role of raising awareness is not much different from coaching on other issues related to changing perspectives and behaviors. In the area of physical well-being, the leader coach can focus on helping the coachee change behavior, set specific goals, and garner support.

The Relationship of Health, Fitness, and Leadership

Recent CCL data have shown a positive correlation of regular exercise to ratings of leadership performance (McDowell-Larsen, 2003). In three 360-degree instruments, when observer ratings of senior executives who exercised were compared with ratings of those who exercised only sporadically (or not at all), the exercisers were rated higher on such characteristics as energy, organization, calmness, resilience, productivity, credibility, results orientation, and optimism, to name a few. This positive correlation was found for three different groups of executives, suggesting that the findings were not out of the ordinary. In addition, the exercisers worked fewer hours per week, which suggests that regular exercise need not come at the expense of work.

Solid quantitative research that links exercise to improved performance is sparse, but strong public anecdotal evidence makes it hard to ignore such a connection. Richard Snyder, chairman and CEO of Simon & Schuster Publishing, is quoted as saying, "The healthier and stronger I am, the more relaxed I am, the better it is for the company." Kenneth Otto, senior vice president of Tenneco, has said, "My thinking is clear, and I'm not mentally exhausted. So my exercise program has been one of the best things I've ever done" (Rippe, 1990, p. 128).

Jim Loehr and Tony Schwartz of LGE Performance Systems, who have worked with both elite athletes and hundreds of senior executives and managers, are strong advocates of physical fitness and the importance of managing energy. They describe peak performance in business as a pyramid, the basis of which is physical capacity—one that increases endurance and promotes mental and emotional recovery. It is on this foundation, they argue, that emotional, mental, and spiritual capacity is built (Loehr & Schwartz, 2001).

Applying CCL's Coaching Framework to Physical Well-Being

If you've decided you want to coach for fitness and health, CCL's coaching framework can guide you. But before applying the framework, you will need to decide how the subject of physical fitness can be introduced into the coaching process.

When the Coach Introduces the Issue of Physical Well-Being

Leaders, like most other people, want to be healthy. They are also interested in performance and are driven to be successful. Coaches can best introduce the issue by asking questions and letting the coachee articulate what difference he or she wants to see in life. If the signs such as undue fatigue are there, you might ask if this is something that concerns your coachee. If it is, is he or she concerned enough to change some of the behaviors that produce fatigue? Work with the coachee to determine which behaviors need to be changed. Keep in mind the stages of exercise, and encourage the coachee to think of physical fitness as a process, not another burden to carry.

When the Coachee Self-Declares a Desire for Increased Fitness

In this situation, the focus remains on what needs to be adjusted in the coachee's life in order to find time to exercise. He or she may need to delegate some work to direct reports to find time to meet the fitness goal—a tactic that also helps coachees develop the leadership capacity for empowering others. By helping the coachee figure out the answer to scheduling and time, the way is often cleared for developing and practicing a fitness routine.

Relationship

As with any other kind of coaching, the relationship between coach and coachee is crucial for achieving positive results. The coachee's perspective toward physical fitness defines the role that relationship plays when coaching for physical well-being. His or her perspective is often tied to one or more of three instigating factors: (1) the coachee expresses a need for developing better physical fitness, (2) the coachee's performance appears to be affected by health issues, or (3) feedback provided by others through a formal assessment process indicates that the coachee is perceived as a less effective leader because of the state of his or her physical well-being.

In the first case, coaching is less relationship dependent. The coachee has given permission to discuss and acknowledged that lack of fitness is affecting his sense of well-being or even effectiveness as a leader. In this situation, the leader coach can begin the discussion and work with the coachee to explore resources.

In the second case, relationship is key to the coach's ability even to broach the subject. It's important for the coach to measure the depth of the coaching relationship and the level of trust she has with the coachee and let that guide her in when and how to surface the concern. If a high degree of trust exists, the coach can address the issue from two perspectives: genuine personal concern and the potential impact on performance and productivity. If the relationship is still evolving, the coach is better off focusing on perceived performance or productivity issues and allowing the coachee to respond with his views on what is affecting his performance. As part of the exploratory discussion, the coach could appropriately ask how other non-work-related issues are affecting performance, inviting disclosure.

In the third case, the coach relies on third-party feedback to help the coachee build awareness about how others perceive him or her. Feedback givers often describe their perceptions about energy, appearance of health, and fitness. The coach can use these remarks to open the discussion with the coachee in a way that preserves the relationship between them because the information is coming from outside the relationship and the responses to that information are part of the relationship-building process between coach and coachee.

Assessment

Assessing a coachee's orientation toward fitness and exercise is fairly straightforward. In most cases, coachees will be transparent about how exercise fits into their lifestyle. What may be less apparent is how the coachee's fitness is affecting his work. There are at least three ways for coaches to assess that impact: (1) ask the coachee for her views and desired state, (2) use a 360-degree assessment instrument that includes a dimension on fitness and energy, or (3) in a structured coaching process that uses interviews, invite respondents to provide anonymous written feedback and include a question specifically about health, physical well-being, and energy.

Consider how a feedback-rich assessment changed the leadership course of one high-potential manager who attended LAP:

Jeanne was already receiving developmental coaching as a process to prepare her for greater responsibility. Her peers and direct reports told her coaches: "We think she is one of our best hopes for the future. But we wish she would look more like a senior leader. She needs to lose weight and present herself as an executive."

Jeanne took the feedback to heart and achieved two goals over the following year: she lost significant weight, and she engaged the help of a professional to work with her on dress and demeanor. Her colleagues noted both accomplishments and reported to her developmental coach that their confidence in her had increased and that they noticed a greater degree of self-confidence in her as well.

Challenge

Convincing coachees that physical well-being is a valuable attribute and that it would benefit them to start or maintain an exercise program does not usually pose a challenge. Motivation and momentum to exercise regularly often come to coachees in the form of a negative health test result or from observing the negative result of poor physical fitness in a loved one. The coaching process is likely to uncover more specific obstacles, such as figuring out how to incorporate exercise into a busy schedule, understanding how the organizational culture hinders or helps a coachee achieve fitness, and potentially even the coach's own mixed signals related to balancing priorities between exercise and work demands (leader coaches especially must be mindful of not unintentionally creating obstacles to their coachee's goal of physical well-being).

Support

Leader coaches can support their coachees' work toward physical well-being in numerous ways, including the tactics used to support other developmental efforts. For physical fitness, there are five crucial devices:

- Validate in words and actions the coachee's commitment to fitness.
- Help the coachee maintain motivation with regular discussions as a reminder of why he or she undertook the goal of exercising.
- Help the coachee access external support such as personal trainers, nutritionists, and other professionals as needed.
- Use your influence in the organization to build broad support for physical fitness and good-health policies.
- Become a role model. Illustrate your own commitment to physical well-being and engage in a reciprocal supportive relationship with your coachee.

Results

More than any area of coaching, determining desired results for fitness is entirely driven by the coachee. Leader coaches and their organization have less voice in setting goals and measuring outcomes when coaching for fitness. That does not make discussing results less valuable. The coach's role is best served in helping the coachee set reasonable and tangible goals. Encouraging the coachee to treat fitness as she would any other developmental goal means getting her to state the goals as specific actions, such as "run a 10-kilometer race" or "walk before dinner three times a week."

Conclusion

The physical demands of leadership are often overlooked and little understood. Long hours, stress, heavy responsibility, and wearying travel all take a physical toll. Many senior executives know from personal experience that waning performance has a direct relationship to declining health. They realize that their recovery time and ability to work effectively with low energy levels lessen with age. In response, many have turned not only to healthier lifestyles but regular exercise to maximize their energy levels.

Under all of this, stress is a primary driver. The job of leader coaches is to help their less experienced coachees understand this dynamic. The midlevel manager coachee is often younger than the leader coach and may be more focused on the next promotion and willing to tolerate long hours and extensive travel. Younger managers may not feel so acutely or immediately the physical effects of neglecting fitness, and they may not believe they can afford the time to devote to fitness.

Leader coaches can help these managers see themselves as athletes playing a long game and coach them to manage and conserve their energy. They can identify staff with stress-related performance issues and gently approach the idea of exercise as a means of mitigating the effects of stress. It's a challenge for the coach to enter this area, and it requires sensitivity. With a firm set of guiding principles, such as knowledge of the stages of exercise behavior and awareness of benefits and obstacles, the leader coach can help coachees reap unexpected performance rewards.

Coach's Bookshelf

American Heart Association. (2002). *Just move.* Retrieved July 7, 2005, from www.justmove.org.

Barnes, D. (2004). *Action plan for diabetes.* Champaign, IL: Human Kinetics.

Benyo, R. (1998). *Running past 50.* Champaign, IL: Human Kinetics.

Blair, S. N., Dunn, A. L., Marcus, B. H., Carpenter, R. A., & Jaret, P. (2001). *Active living every day: Twenty weeks to lifelong vitality.* Champaign, IL: Human Kinetics.

Brown, R. (2003). *Fitness running* (2nd ed.). Champaign, IL: Human Kinetics.

Carmichael, C., & Burke, E. R. (1994). *Fitness cycling.* Champaign, IL: Human Kinetics.

Center for Science in the Public Interest. *Nutrition action.* Retrieved July 7, 2005, from http://www.cspinet.org/nah/index.htm.

Chmiel, D., & Morris, K. (2001). *Golf past 50.* Champaign, IL: Human Kinetics.

Clark, J. (1992). *Full life fitness: A compete exercise program for mature adults.* Champaign, IL: Human Kinetics.

Evans, R. G., Barer, M. L., & Marmor, T. R. (Eds.). (1994). *Why are some people healthy and others not? The determinants of health of populations.* Hawthorne, NY: Aldine de Gruyter.

Iknoian, T. (1998). *Walking fast.* Champaign, IL: Human Kinetics.

Incledon, L. (2004). *Strength training for women.* Champaign, IL: Human Kinetics.

Jacobson, M. F., & Hurley, J. (2002). *Restaurant confidential.* New York: Workman Publishing.

Loehr, J. (1997). *Stress for success: The proven program for transforming stress into positive energy at work.* New York: Times Business.

Loehr, J., & Schwartz, T. (2003). *The power of full engagement: Managing energy, not time, is the key to high performance and personal renewal.* New York: Free Press.

Nelson, M., & Wernick, S. (2000). *Strong women stay young* (Rev. ed.). New York: Bantam Books.

Ornish, D. (1998). *Love and survival: The scientific basis for the healing power of intimacy.* New York: HarperCollins.

Page, P., & Ellenbecker, T. (2005). *Strength band training.* Champaign, IL: Human Kinetics.

Philbin, J. (2004). *High-intensity training.* Champaign, IL: Human Kinetics.

Schoenfeld, B. (2002). *Sculpting her body perfect* (2nd rev. ed.). Champaign, IL: Human Kinetics.

Tesch, P. A. (1998). *Target bodybuilding.* Champaign, IL: Human Kinetics.

Tribole, E. (2003). *Eating on the run* (3rd ed.). Champaign, IL: Human Kinetics.

Weil, A. (2000). *Eating well for optimum health: The essential guide to food, diet, and nutrition.* New York: Knopf.

Wellcoaches Corporation. www.wellcoaches.com.

Wellness Councils of America. www.welcoa.org.

Westcott, W. L., & Baechle, T. R. (1998). *Strength training past 50.* Champaign, IL: Human Kinetics.

Willet, W. C. (2001). *Eat, drink, and be healthy: The Harvard Medical School guide to healthy eating.* New York: Free Press.

PART FOUR

COACHING TECHNIQUES

Leader coaches rely on many traditional and proven techniques in helping their coachees develop as leaders. They can supplement those efforts by broadening the array of techniques and methods they use and tailoring them to the coachee's needs. The chapters in Part Four offer three approaches that can be integrated with a coach's natural style to help coachees reach a successful outcome.

Chapter Ten explores how techniques that we usually associate with the arts and tend to confine to our personal lives can be applied to leadership coaching. The arts are a powerful means of stimulating thoughts and emotions. Most leader coaches already use artistic forms in coaching as they tell stories, use metaphors, quote from pieces of effective writing or from a popular movie, or ask coachees to visualize or imagine an outcome or state. This chapter takes a more comprehensive look at artful techniques and draws on what Chuck Palus and David Horth call "neglected leadership competencies" in their book *The Leader's Edge.*

Chapter Eleven discusses the application of solution-focused therapeutic approaches to leadership coaching. While the terminology is not often specifically referenced in coaching literature, most coaching in fact relies heavily on these principles. Solution-focused techniques offer a structure that helps coachees draw on their own resources and positive experiences to increase their effectiveness as leaders. This chapter reinforces CCL's position that coaching is fully accessible to leaders at all levels of their organizations because the premise of solution-focused concepts is to draw on the coachee's knowledge and resources rather than rely on or assume the coach has specialized training. This chapter walks the reader through the specific techniques, shows how to use them, and explains why they work.

Chapter Twelve examines the work of Robert Kegan and constructive-developmental theories of adult development. It offers coaches a view on why change is difficult even when coachees and coaches are motivated. It also raises important considerations about the coach's own stage of development and what impact that may have on how she or he coaches.

CHAPTER TEN

ARTFUL COACHING

Charles J. Palus

Artful coaching is a genre of practices and perspectives that applies abilities, media, and methods from or related to the arts to the coaching of managers, leaders, and other professionals. It works by enhancing the perception and meaningful reconstruction of developmental challenges and their solutions by coachees, using artful media such as stories, metaphors, and images; body language and movement; self-narratives and scenarios; and the material context of artifacts and environments.

Several characteristics describe the process, content, and implementation of artful coaching:

- Artful coaching is not a stand-alone approach; rather, it is typically combined into a diverse repertoire of coaching methods. Artful coaching is especially effective in promoting synthesis, that is, at helping the coachee perceive and assemble large amounts of input in ways that build coherence and meaning. Thus, artful coaching is complementary to analytical methods such as assessments and 360-degree feedback.
- Artful methods can be practiced by leader coaches in one-on-one situations and in groups. Basic competence as a leader coach is assumed in much

of the discussion in this chapter, although some of the perspectives and tools can be applied without prior formal experience as a coach.

- Artful coaching, like other coaching forms, aims to improve the coachee's performance, learning, and development.
- Artful coaching is about bringing the whole self to the coaching experience and engaging the whole self of the coachee. Artful media typically allow people to bring more of their experience, intuitions, and wisdom to bear on developmental challenges.
- Artful coaching does not necessarily have to be used in difficult situations or for deeper or more complex issues. Leader coaches can use it at various levels and with varying degrees of skill and sophistication.

This chapter describes the history and characteristics of artful coaching and the drivers for it. It outlines three levels of artful coaching, discusses the relationship of artful coaching to the CCL coaching framework, and ends with some cautions and tips for coaches interested in using these techniques. (The term *artful coaching* is used by the Adler School of Professional Coaching and predates my use of the term. Our meanings are compatible. I use it as an umbrella for a family of perspectives and practices. The Adler School of Professional Coaching uses it in more specific ways as part of a certification process.)

About Artful Coaching

Artful coaching as an explicit topic is newly emergent (two organizations exploring it are the Adler School and The Banff Centre), yet it has its roots in well-tested practices in counseling and therapy (Bandler & Grinder, 1975; Erikson, 1998; Perls, 1992) and is related to recent insights about creative leadership (Palus & Horth, 2002) and management amid uncertainty and complexity (Nissley, 2002; Vaill, 1989).

The media and methods of artful coaching fall into six basic categories:

- Creating, perceiving, and interpreting images such as drawings and photographs
- Making, telling, and listening to stories
- Becoming aware of and crafting metaphors

- Dialogue around artifacts from people's work and personal lives, including their creative endeavors
- Becoming aware of and crafting the environments in which coaching occurs
- Becoming aware of and reshaping body movement, posture, kinesthetics, and voice

Why this particular list? First, it's what effective coaches who work consciously with artful methods say they use. Second, this list includes most of the artistic media available to us in our work and social lives for making meaning out of our opportunities and predicaments—what Eric Booth (1997) calls "the everyday work of art."

As an example of how artful coaching techniques integrate with the coaching process, consider the case of Chris:

Chris is the director of a corporate research center specializing in advanced polymers used in consumer products. Because of rapid changes in the industry, Chris's company has tried to become a learning organization, and Chris's role has come to include the coaching of his direct reports in ways that emphasize participative leadership and shared learning.

It is time for performance appraisals, and Chris sits down with Ki-Hun, a senior scientist. Ki-Hun is Korean and one of the many professionals in the organization for whom English is a second language, which adds cross-cultural issues to the complexity of the work. To prepare for the meeting, they have reviewed Ki-Hun's objectives and accomplishments for the year (part of a Management-by-Objectives system the organization uses). In spite of Ki-Hun's many achievements for the year, neither of them is happy with the performance appraisal process, finding it stilted and somehow unable to capture the highs and lows of Ki-Hun's contributions and motivations. Language and culture differences also seem to get in the way.

This time, Chris tries a different approach. After looking at the MBO forms, Chris pulls out a box of diverse images clipped from Web sites and magazines. He says, "Ki-Hun, I feel that there are a lot of important things about your work and your role that we aren't getting at with this list of objectives. What do you think? How about if we each pick several pictures that somehow represent the positive things about your work this year, and several more that get at your frustrations this year? Then we'll share the pictures we each picked and talk about them." The ensuing conversation flows freely and is surprisingly candid. They laugh a lot, especially when Ki-Hun admits he felt like "this fat goat" when his project tied up the electron microscope for a month without anything to show for it.

Chris was being an artful coach when he brought out the box of images and changed the nature of their dialogue. He was able to say some tough things to Ki-Hun, while also expressing in a vivid way his perception that Ki-Hun was potentially a star performer. And Ki-Hun remembered for a long time afterward the picture Chris chose of an eagle in flight and what it meant to be a star performer who is somewhat isolated from his peers.

Why Artful Coaching?

Why would a leader coach engage in artful coaching? For Chris, it was because he was dissatisfied with the limits of formulaic, management-oriented procedures as applied to human relationships. And there are many other drivers to using artful coaching for leader development. Successful artful coaches report six basic categories of drivers:

- Supporting desirable leadership qualities
- Creativity and innovation
- Information processing
- Whole-person functioning
- Rapport
- An expanded coaching repertoire

Any single artful coaching intervention typically is done with several of these acting in concert.

Supporting Desirable Leadership Qualities

Artful coaching addresses many qualities and competencies that are desirable in leaders. "Business leaders have much more in common with artists . . . and other creative thinkers" (Zaleznik, 1977). For example, good leaders tell stories, and they are astute listeners of other people's stories. Thus, it seems natural that coaching should use storytelling as a way to create and apply insight. Leadership is also about creating vision, grasping and communicating scenarios, and painting the big picture.

Creativity and Innovation

Artful coaching fosters creativity and innovation in coachees. This often includes an organizational competency aspect and a personal aspect. Many organizations cite creativity as a desirable competency and yet have few means for building it. Artful coaches assume that everyone is creative in a significant way and that they can find a foundation for further creativity development if they look in the right places. Thus, a productive line for coaching to take is to explore the coachee's inner resources for creativity and apply those to dilemmas in work and life. Many coachees are in some sense stuck or experiencing some sort of threshold that may benefit from a more creative approach.

Information Processing

During a coaching engagement, the coach and coachee deal with huge amounts of potentially relevant information, including diverse sources of data, observations, emotions, and knowledge. Much of this is implicit rather than explicit, intuitively accessed, and subject to blind spots and other kinds of misperception (Nonaka, Takeuchi, & Takeuchi, 1995). The techniques described in this chapter can be enormously helpful in placing knowledge in context. The use of metaphor, for example, is often used in coaching to surface implicit knowledge and to see connections. Human beings naturally assimilate meaning from stories more effectively than from piles of data. One way to understand art is that it is how people create meaningful themes and patterns within turbulent streams of information.

Whole-Person Functioning

People in organizations typically draw on a narrow part of their skills and abilities, to the detriment of their developing adaptability and resilience. Coaching addresses the whole person. Artful coaching supports that process by giving coachees the chance to draw on resources they might otherwise keep out of sight and to connect all of those resources in a developmental, transformational way.

Rapport

Coaches practice artful coaching to enhance rapport with coachees. This means being attuned to subtleties like use of language, hidden talents, body language, and contextual clues about underlying issues. Once attuned in these ways, the coach can steer the coaching in ways that feel authentic to the coachee.

An Expanded Coaching Repertoire

Leader coaches can derive great satisfaction in expanding their repertoires to include artful coaching techniques. These practices let the coach move beyond narrow, analytical approaches. In working with their coachees, leader coaches can themselves learn to be more creative and whole, able to process large amounts of complex information.

Practicing Artful Coaching

How does a coach build artful coaching into his or her everyday coaching with direct reports? The three-level stepwise approach detailed in Table 10.1 offers a useful path. These levels were derived from my interviewing artful coaches with different levels of experience and expertise (Palus, 2004) and from research on the practices of creative leaders (Palus & Horth, 2002). There is a consistently identified starting place for creative work of many kinds, and for artful coaching that place, level 1, is *paying attention.* That sounds simple but it's not. Artful coaches and creative leaders consistently point out the difficulty in adequately paying attention (perceiving, noticing, apprehending) in complex interpersonal settings such as developmental coaching. These coaches and leaders turn to various forms of art as a partial defense against the enemies of careful attention: stereotyping, boredom, snap judgment, and overanalytical detachment.

As coaches move from paying attention to using tools, they move into level 2 artful coaching. Coaches make this move often because they are looking for a creative response to regaining momentum in a coaching initiative. The choice of tool is highly individualistic: some coaches seem especially drawn to photography, for example, others adopt storytelling, and others explore techniques related to using metaphor. For the leader coach who is aware

TABLE 10.1. THREE LEVELS OF ARTFUL COACHING.

Levels of Artful Coaching	A: Coach	B: Coachee	C: Coaching Encounter
Level 1: Attention (entry): Initiation of relationship/ beginner as artful coach—*Supporting active perception by coach and coachee*	Coach "reads" (pays careful attention to) the coachee, situation, and environment by listening to and looking for stories, metaphors, images, artifacts, and so forth.	The client is supported in paying attention to ("reading") self, relationships, and environment, using an expanding repertoire of senses and devices.	The context is one of rapport building. The environment provides opportunities for each party to pay attention. The notion of artistry is implicit rather than explicit and involves attending to artifacts rather than creating art.
Level 2: Tool use (instrumental): Intermediate/ experimentation—*Using tools and media for the creation of meaning*	The coach helps the coachee deliberately construct and shape various kinds of meaningful artifacts such as self-narratives, personal metaphors, and scenarios.	The client is actively constructing various kinds of representations and perspectives using any of a variety of media.	The encounter involves more explicit use of artistry. Artful tools and methods are at hand and offered depending on readiness and need. An environment of shared sense making and reflection is provided or created.
Level 3: World making (mastery): Mastery/integrated artful practice—*Remaking the relationship of self and world*	The coach has a refined sensibility and philosophy for using artistic means in service of human transformation, including experience and competence in a variety of media and tools.	The client explores and develops his or her own competency as a world maker or artist with respect to the transformation of self, relationships, and environments.	There is a sense of risk associated with exploring the unknown and commitment to transformation. All creative resources are fair game for application toward further development.

of these techniques, selecting a tool often requires reflection: What is my art? What artistic media do I enjoy using or appreciate? What artistic approaches do I have talent for? What kind of art often gives me new insights?

At level 3, coaches typically attain mastery by discovering or inventing a set of artful tools in a particular domain and deepening their knowledge about how to use them and where they can lead. In almost every case, such coaches come to value the transformative potential in working with an artistic sensibility, and they choose to master some domain in order to effect transformation more adeptly. Coaches working at this level often have a history of personal passion for their chosen media and a history of risk taking; they might even test their skills with coachees. Master artful coaches grow into their unique expert practices, which include storytelling, metaphor work, voice development, designing creative environments, and other practices.

Level 1: Paying Attention

The first move in artful coaching is paying attention, which is a close cousin to the skills of observing and attending that are foundational components of coaching. Of course, everyone pays attention. What's at issue here is how and to what one pays attention. Artful coaching expands and deepens attentive possibilities for the coach and coachee. Artful coaches and their coachees attend to artful media in specific ways, and artful coaches also pay attention to the same things all good leader coaches pay attention to: assessment data and interpretive formulas, behaviors, emotional tenor, nonverbal behaviors, competencies, personality, and goals, for example.

Many forces operate in everyday life to narrow and dim our attention, such as pressures to make snap judgments (Edwards, 1989) and blind spots produced by stress and anxiety (Goleman, 1985). Both coach and coachee tend to see what's in front of them through lenses created from the mental models they carry with them (those formed out of culture, for example, or from personal values). Artful coaches deliberately work to make their own and their coachees' attention accommodate multiple perspectives, with the purpose of making it deeper and ultimately more accurate.

What coaches pay special attention to are coachees and their contexts and challenges. The premise of artful coaching is that coachees and their challenges are composed and revealed in significant ways by use of artful media. Thus, artful coaches pay special attention to the stories coachees tell and to the metaphors and imagery they use. They pay special attention to the environment of the coachee and to artifacts from life and work. They pay attention to the physical being of the coachee, including how he or she moves and speaks. Finally, they attend to the gestalt or overall unity of how these media are used by the coachee in "composing a life" (Bateson, 1989).

One of the main benefits of art—making it as well as viewing it—is that it can invite the best of our powers of perception. Harvard University's David Perkins has studied how the discipline of looking at art can discipline the way we think within the broader territories of life and work (1994). He identifies four principles of paying attention characteristic of what he calls "the intelligent eye"—ways of looking at art that transfer to intelligent ways of looking at people, things, and experiences in the world:

- Give looking time.
- Make your looking broad and adventurous.
- Make your looking clear and deep.
- Make your looking organized.

These principles accurately describe how effective artful coaches pay attention to the six categories of media described at the start of this chapter, separately and combined, while working with coachees. When paying attention to complex, meaningful subjects—whether works of art or the work and lives of the people you coach—following these four principles can help you see better and think better. For leader coaches just starting to delve into artistic techniques, it's helpful if they think of Perkins's principles as a sequence or cycle. With practice, they become a set of attitudes that overlap each other and pervade every moment. Let's look at them one at a time and how they build on one another:

- *Give looking time.* Typical managerial attention is rapid-fire and staccato. Good managers zero in, judge and act, and quickly move on. But good managing is not the same as good coaching. A key to artful coaching is regularly slowing down and lingering over the nuances of things that at first glance may be familiar, boring, complacent, or painful.

Almost anything that people can hold in their hands and examine is potentially a good vehicle for slowing looking. Something tangible that invites close examination counters the disposition to take a quick read and move on.

For example, coaches know that detailed reports from feedback instruments can slow down attention in positive ways. In the previous story of Chris and Ki-Hun, a collection of images and a process of finding meaningful ones amid all the others and looking at the details slowed a difficult conversation and invited deeper insights.

Pay attention to what your coachee keeps in his or her office. One coach interviewed for this chapter describes using objects this way: "I pay attention to the physical objects I see when I enter. If we get stuck in the data or run into tough feedback, I pull out of it and comment on what I see around me. I might ask, 'What's that object? Where did it come from?' It might seem to them as random, or a tension breaker—but I am looking for another avenue into who they are and what they are about."

• *Make your looking broad and adventurous.* One of the pitfalls of coaching is that if you let the process become too formulaic, you can omit possible solutions for developmental challenges. This happens if you are coaching an individual and ignore parts of who he or she is and what this person can do, or when working with a group and too narrowly define the problem and the available resources. This is part of what the CCL framework means when it says to assess the person and the context. There is pressure in some organizations to narrow in on a list of competencies and behaviors in the name of focus and efficiency. Therefore, one of the moves of an artful coach is to make looking broad and adventurous and to admit the possibility of surprise.

• *Make your looking clear and deep.* This principle involves focusing, asking probing questions about what you are seeing, and forming and testing hypotheses. "Time and broad thinking can still just skim the surface," Perkins says, and we need to pursue lines of inquiry by which to see into the image, artifact, or other object.

Most leader coaches try to see clearly and deeply when looking at various kinds of assessment data. In artful coaching, they would extend this same kind of rational scrutiny to a different kind of information. They might, for example, ask coachees to bring to a coaching session mementos of some time and place in their lives when they felt truly creative or when they experienced the roots of their own leadership. By making time to tell stories about these mementos, the leader coach encourages a dialogue that often becomes broad and adventurous. The leader coach can provoke deeper attention by asking specific, rational questions:

"Why is this picture glass cracked, and when did it happen?"

"Who made this? Where did you learn how to do this?"

"Who are the people standing with your father in this photograph? What year and place is it?"

"What happened on the project after you received this award? Why?"

"And why was that?"

"Okay, and why was that?"

("Asking *why* five times" is a technique that helps make attention clear and deep.)

• *Make your looking organized.* Leader coaches can develop comprehensive strategies for organizing their attention in order to direct it and integrate the results for the benefit of the coachee. A desirable outcome of paying attention is that separate perceptions cohere into a whole and take on added significance. This principle employs dual, integrated approaches to coherence: topical and emergent. Topical approaches use categories to cover all the territory of interest. An example of a topical approach is the five-part developmental planning model of career, self, family, community, and spirit (Sternbergh & Weitzel, 2001). CCL's leader development framework (assessment, challenge, and support) is another example. In practice, such a topical structure might provoke a leader coach to ask such questions as, How does the coachee adequately perceive his or her support network? How does he or she map it? How does he or she imagine it changing?

An emergent approach to coherence focuses on the gestalt, the configuration or pattern of elements so intertwined and unified that the properties of the whole can't be adequately captured by simply summing up its parts. Artful coaches pay attention directly to the coachee as a complex but unified whole person. As a leader coach, that means becoming immersed in all of the information and context surrounding the coachee and attempting to perceive the whole picture—the gestalt—directly or intuitively.

A leader coach interviewed for this chapter describes how she organizes her looking using the data at hand, before meeting the coachee for the first time: "I wait for a sense of the gestalt of the person to frame itself in my mind. It often comes with an intuitive sense of the connections among the issues they express, their biographical information, their key attributes, and the subtle patterns in their behavior. I have a sense of unreadiness to begin the coaching process until I get that sense of the gestalt."

Leader coaches take their first steps in paying attention themselves, without actively engaging the coachee's attention. But they soon find their way toward actively shaping their coachee's attention. At that point, coaching becomes a collaboration of attention between coach and coachee (and can even encompass groups, teams, and entire organizations). One leader coach from the Netherlands describes the kind of collaborative attention that is possible:

> If I am sitting in a person's office, I talk about what they have in the office. I was with somebody who has lots of wooden pieces in his office. It turns out that he is working for a wood technology institute. He is accustomed to working with wood. He also has sailing pictures in his office. Later I asked him, in the context of his career: "If you changed course one degree, where would you go?" At the start of a coaching conversation, even though we work together, I tell my background and ask theirs. I ask, "Do you have any hobbies?" Things in their hobbies are interesting. Take this as a start. Then you have a relationship, and later you can compare work to hobbies.

Level 1 of artful coaching is about paying attention in certain ways. It is an entry point, a sensible place to start an artful coaching engagement. The emphasis at this level is on reviewing certain kinds of media according to principles guiding the skillful perception of art. All leader coaches can use this approach without special tools. And after gaining some experience, they can add tools and move to level 2.

Level 2: Tool Use

The tools that leader coaches have available in a level 2 artful coaching practice are structures, processes, and devices. What sets this level apart from level 1 is that the coach is involved in choosing, naming, and shaping media in a structured and sustained way rather than only looking at it. At this level, the coachee realizes the coach is doing something different. Coachees may show some resistance because this step requires more vulnerability on their part (and from the coach).

At level 2, leader coaches need a certain amount of familiarity with the media, competency in techniques and the underlying principles, and knowledge of the tool itself. This chapter is only a tour of artful coaching tools. In practice, learning to use these tools happens through experience, much as artistry is learned—by apprenticeship, imitation, feedback, mistakes, and immersion in particular media. This section starts with a look at three principles behind tool use and tool invention. It then looks at a number of tools that artful coaches use and how coaches manage the coachee's experience of those tools. It also explores in more depth the media within which the tools are used.

Principles for Tool Use. Four important principles of tool use for artful coaching are:

- Putting something in the middle
- Adapting to the circumstance
- Shared sense making and meaning making
- Serious play

Putting Something in the Middle. Dialogue is a form of conversation that allows underlying assumptions, meanings, and emotions to be surfaced in service of shared understanding and effective action. According to Peter Senge (1990), it's one key to learning in organizations, and it is often cited as a feature of effective coaching (Marsick, 2002). Yet dialogue can be difficult to practice.

One way of enhancing dialogue is to have one or more tangible objects serve as a kind of conversation piece. There is enormous value in having something that can be seen and touched, held, examined, and passed around. Such objects carry meaning that can be symbolic, metaphorical, or literal—or all three. For example, a physical prototype of a product or process provides a centerpiece for a probing conversation. Likewise, images or personal mementos can be anchors for paying attention and scaffolds for fresh interpretations. We call this "mediated dialogue" (Palus & Drath, 2001), or "putting something in the middle."

Adapting to the Circumstance. Nothing about artful coaching is a cookie-cutter or one-size-fits-all experience. Because these tools evoke hidden assumptions and deeper meanings, coaches must use them in ways that are responsive to what's happening in the room, with the coachees and their challenges. Consistent with CCL's coaching principles, artful coaching centers on the coachee, not on the coach, and much depends on how coachees pick up the tool and where it takes them.

To deal with changing circumstances, artful coaches sometimes invent their own tools, but more often they adapt something they have used before. With experience, leader coaches can become increasingly improvisational and flexible in choosing and in applying tools as they adapt to the coaching experience.

Shared Sense Making and Meaning Making. The tools used in artful coaching help make complex information available to the physical senses—vision, hearing, and touch—and to the internal sensing of kinesthesia ("body sense"), emotions, and intuition. Adequate sensing is necessary for logical and reflective thinking (Kolb, 1984; McCarthy, 1996). This powerful combination of sensing plus reflection is what we call *sense making*—in other words, making sense of complexity (Palus & Horth, 2002; Weick, 1979). When people do it collaboratively, as in coaching, it is shared sense making.

Ultimately the tools used in artful coaching help to integrate the sense made of complex input into broader frames of meaning, such as values, vision, mission, morals, ethics, and spirit. This processing of information all the way from sensing into integrated, higher-order meaning is meaning making and is an essential component of leadership (Drath & Palus, 1994). Human beings share a drive toward meaning making above and beyond the mere compilation of information (Kegan, 1982). This principle addresses two partially incorrect and thus misleading stereotypes about using art in coaching. The first stereotype is that the main purpose of art is to express emotions. A related stereotype is that the main purpose of art is self-expression. Managers typically reject any process that stops at the mere expression of emotion or stops at self-expression without going on to address complex challenge in meaningful ways—a truer goal of artful coaching. Artful coaching is not window dressing, nor is it just an icebreaker or used for merely setting a creative mood.

Serious Play. This form of play helps people learn. Serious play involves putting something in the middle and then bending, testing, and exploring it, even to the point of having some fun (Gergen, 1991; Palus & Horth, 2002; Schrage, 2000). A coach interviewed for this chapter describes using a big paper desk pad as a kind of playing field: "I want the coaching sessions I do to be playful work. I put data and ideas on the pad between us, in this neutral place, and we play with it until the person can take it in. If I were barreling numbers at them, they don't get to that relaxed place. Having a neutral place to play in makes it easier to have humor. Then the humor is not located 'in' you, not directed 'at' the person, but rather it is in this neutral place. It is between us and becomes like a ballpark, like a bridge, like Switzerland."

Artful Coaching Media and Associated Tools. The media introduced in this chapter are the ones artful coaches report as using to perceive, portray, explore, and reconstruct developmental challenge with their coachees: images, stories, metaphors, environments, artifacts, and body/kinesthetics, as well as the gestalt of all of these.

Metaphor. Metaphor has been called the foundation of all conscious thought (Jaynes, 1976) and the poetic basis of mind (Hillman, 1996). Such descriptions don't necessarily mean much to busy managers whom leader coaches work with. The whole notion of metaphor transports some people back to school and grammar lessons. The coach might do best by not overexplaining the tool is but just using it. The fact is that metaphor is basic to human thought, and people use it more or less naturally, without much thought as to what it is or how it can be talked about.

In essence, metaphor is a comparison of one thing to another, and it acts as a springboard to new knowledge. A fruitful metaphor is one that propels people into fresh perspectives and insights and forms a scaffold for new behaviors (Erikson, 1998). Another helpful feature of metaphors is that they tend to travel well: people remember and communicate them because of their uniqueness and imagery. Coaches talk about metaphor as a friendly means of establishing rapport with a coachee. Metaphors often play a key role in invention and design and as such are called "generative metaphors" (Schön, 1983). The root meaning of the word *metaphor* is "moving across," and metaphor tools are often used to get unstuck and depict transitions.

A useful kind of metaphor is a root metaphor, one that captures some aspect (not necessarily all) of a person's identity, down to the roots (Horth, 1993). For example, a coach interviewed for this chapter describes working with a coachee who had lost a sense of who he was:

> He had a high position. He was trying to be what other people wanted him to be. So I talked to him about what made him unique in the past. For him it was a passion for photography. So we began exploring his situation using photography as a metaphor: "What do you want in the foreground? What is lighted, and not lighted? What is in the background?" It opened a lot in our conversation. It was a nice way in. When you get a sense of what makes their heart sing and what makes them cool and unique, they want to stay with that. But often they have set that aside.

Some coaches take coachees through a process of forming metaphors for current state, transitional state, and future state. For example, one coach interviewed for this chapter often leads her coachees through a metaphor process she has created. She uses it only after there is a good level of trust, often when the coachee appears to be stuck. She offers it as a choice, and tells this story of its use:

> Jack was a financial vice president at a large manufacturing organization. Having been a "hatchet man" at another company, he was brought in to streamline, flatten, and modernize accounting. Jack was very controlled, hyperrational, unemotional, and extremely private. People were afraid of him. He demanded compliance, and his people were kept at a distance.
>
> So we started the metaphor process. His current metaphor was himself as God directing people to build the temple. In the same session we arrived at a metaphor for the future: himself as a bishop, among other bishops. In this image, the people were not quite as afraid, there was not as much distance, and he was getting more done.
>
> Three months passed, and Jack was successful. He had been tapped to help them go international. In order to do that, he needed to be freed up from his first task of streamlining accounting. The middle managers were his greatest resistance, and he needed their buy-in. So I did another metaphor in the sequence, which I call *next future.* His next metaphor was himself as a basketball coach. He said, "Now I see myself on the sidelines. I love seeing the team perform in the moment. We have practiced, and they can do it." I asked him to "find some things that will remind you of this new basketball image." He wound up with a basketball in his office. Later I did a survey on people with whom I did this kind of metaphor

work. Jack said he thought about his metaphor every day, and that the metaphor had been very influential for him reaching his goals.

Images. Artful coaches often use images as the something-in-the-middle to support dialogue with individuals and groups. Recall the earlier case of Ki-Hun's performance appraisal: a variety of printed images provided material to slow the conversation, provide a favorable medium, and focus on hard-to-express topics. Images used in coaching include photographs, schematics, drawings, collage, paintings, video, and maps. To bolster its power as a coaching tool, use an image that is tangible to eye and hand so you and your coachee can handle it, examine it, return to it after a while, and so on. Some coaches work with mental imagery but reinforce it with a tangible object.

The notion of drawing is readily accepted by many coachees. For example, people with science and technical backgrounds are used to sketching all kinds of things. A coach from the United Kingdom interviewed for this chapter said, "Many managers in the U.K. are used to drawing, and to the idea of 'sketch that out for me, give me a visual.' It's used a lot in action learning."

Almost everybody can and does draw using some mode or other. Talent or skill in drawing is not an issue. Simple stick figures, graphs and flowcharts, or just impressionistic doodles can all play a part as image tools. Artful coaches tend to keep paper, sticky notes, pencils, and markers at hand. Returning often to drawing pads, white boards, and easel sheets during a coaching session can uncover useful modes of visual representation and shared sense making between the coachee and the coach. A coach interviewed for this chapter describes how he attends to his coachee's drawing and uses it as a springboard to deeper insight: "How things relate to each other is interesting in a drawing. I am interested in their experience—strong lines or weak, the mood of the drawing. What's happening to them in it? And then what shifts as they draw? What images do they use?"

Sometimes working with images can be as simple as saying to a coachee, "Tell me what image you have of that situation. What does it look like? Imagine what happens next. Imagine there were no barriers, and tell me what happens next."

Metaphors chosen by coachees can be made into tangible pictures or objects. One coach interviewed for this chapter uses a metaphor process to help her coachees picture a current state, future state, and transitional state. She uses a professional artist to render images of the coachee's metaphors. At the coaching session, the coachee reviews the images to see how well they match the metaphor. Once perfected, these artistically rendered images become touchstones to the coaching engagement.

Stories. Effective leaders tell stories. This means three things for coaches. First, coachees have an underlying propensity to tell stories. By evoking these stories and paying attention to them, coaches have a way into a coachee's world-view and the language he or she uses to express it—a window onto the person and context. Second, leaders listen to and generally remember stories, so a repertoire of good stories is invaluable for a coach. Finally, getting coached in the art of storytelling is a valid undertaking for many coachees because it makes them more effective in leader roles.

One coach interviewed for this chapter makes a useful distinction between pull stories and push stories. She defines the use of a pull story as a way to help the coachee reflect, in a sense, pulling the story out of himself or herself and experiences as a way of remembering and understanding. A push story is designed to have an impact out in the world, as if the coachee were pushing an idea into a new arena.

Almost every artful coaching tool described in this chapter pulls for stories. Any time the leader coach points to an object, image, metaphor, or artifact and asks the coachee, "Tell me more about what you mean by that," the result is storytelling. But that's just half of the tool. The other half is listening to the story with close attention. Doug Lipman (1999) describes some important questions that ultimately should anchor the listening as well as the telling of a story: Where exactly in this story do I respond emotionally? What are those emotions? What are the images that stand out for me?

Steve Denning (2004), a former executive at the World Bank, adds another question to these: What are the key messages in the story that you intend as the teller or that you receive as a listener? He argues that push storytelling is "the only thing that worked . . . [for] persuading a group of managers or front-line staff in a large organization to get enthusiastic about a major change."

Environment. Level 2 artful coaches go beyond paying close attention to the environment and actively shape and use the environment as a source of support for the coaching process. One coach interviewed for this chapter refers to the power of the environment as "the place as coach." Think of the coaching environment in terms of three categories of places where coaching sessions are conducted: my (the coach's) place, your (the coachee's) place, and the third place.

Level 2 artful coaches often put a lot of thought into the design of their own place for conducting coaching sessions. In no small measure, the coach's place is designed to help the coach be centered and confident in the course of difficult work. The coach's place is also set up to send a deliberate message to the coachee: the place (and, by extension, the coaching relationship) is safe, inviting, private, warm, interesting, thoughtfully prepared, and comfortable. These qualities are often held in tension with other qualities that suggest development: the coach's place is not the equivalent of business as usual but may express creativity and offer the possibility of expansion into a larger or unfamiliar territory.

The second category of coaching environment is the coachee's place. A level 2 coach will actively seek to understand the coachee's environment, paying attention to the details and the gestalt, and then bringing this awareness into the content and process of the coaching. There is a lot a coach can learn from and expand on in a coachee's place. For example, a coach interviewed for this chapter talks about a particular coachee's place and how she used it in coaching sessions:

> It was important for me to see this coachee in her own space. When I came for our appointment, she had me wait in a guest office. Her former boss had used the office in a similar fashion, and a lot of his belongings were still sitting out. I confronted her about this: "Why do you have this stuff? It's as if he is still here. How does this affect you?" One of her issues was that this boss had squelched her and kept her in a subordinate position. I also gave her the feedback that her office looked very nonexecutive, with piles of stuff all around, as if she were overburdened and didn't delegate. We got a lot of insight from this line of discussion, and as a result, she streamlined her office and put in more visuals relevant to her own corporation. Then she renovated the guest space for group gatherings. As a result, more people came to her space for meetings, and she was able to show her new look to others.

The last category of coaching environment might be called the "third place": a place that is not the quarters of either coach or coachee but is chosen because it offers fresh sources of inspiration and insight into the coaching process. In the same way that groups and teams often retreat from the organization's site to seek new ideas, so a coach and coachee can move to a new environment to encourage the facilitation of new thinking and behaviors. Level 2 and level 3 artful coaches typically are mindful and deliberate about the choice of such third places and the objectives in going there.

Another coach interviewed for this chapter describes the possibilities in having a leisurely meal with a coachee in an interesting restaurant: "In many cultures outside the United States, it may be impolite to do any coaching without having food first. It is a traditional setting for getting to know one another. The setting of the meal offers a chance to relax and take different perspectives. It creates possibilities—with different courses, we can change subjects. And there is a beginning and end, and that is good too."

Artifacts. Level 2 artful coaches invite dialogue with coachees by soliciting various kinds of artifacts into the middle of the dialogue, where the artifacts become the objects of shared sense making. Previously I discussed how an artifact can be the physical embodiment, reminder, and model of a larger story.

A typical level 2 coaching technique is to ask the coachee to come to a coaching session with some artifact of his or her own creativity from the present or past. If the coachee pleads that she isn't creative, the coach can ask her to bring something that is a memento of a time when she made something with a special level of quality or pride of workmanship. Inevitably, the coachee brings something that invites exploration and depth of insight.

One coach talks about making bridges from a personal or even private creative pursuit into another realm of their lives where they are looking for a breakthrough: "Sometimes I say to a coachee that one area of creativity helps another—and their eyes light up." Specific artifacts thus can be seen as tangible parts of and pathways into some larger whole in the life of the coachee, such as creative ability, leadership style, work life, career, or personality.

Body Movement and Kinesthetics. Artful coaches at level 2 typically practice deliberate awareness of their own as well as their coachee's physical and emotional being. The physical body is not only a source of information, but an arena for change when the awareness is made explicit in the coaching relationship.

One coach interviewed for this chapter cultivates an awareness of the physical presence of her coachee and frankly brings that awareness into the relationship: "This person I was coaching looked always ready to leave. His whole vibe was 'I want to get out of here.' I told him directly, 'I observe that when you come into the room, you slouch. You lean way back in your chair, and you act slightly bored. You don't carry yourself like the others in this company.' So then I had him move his body and feet differently. We practiced what it is like to sit in a state of relaxed attention."

Level 2 coaches often use guided imagery to deepen rapport and help coachees slow down, relax, and allow their imaginations to open up. One coach, after establishing a trusting relationship with her coachee, uses her own body movement and voice to achieve this state with the coachee:

> At this point, I am using an easy, soothing rhythm in my voice. I borrow some of their words and phrases. I pattern my voice on their own rhythms but usually slow it down and even it out. Posture-wise, I also match them but again tending toward slowness and relaxation. When they [begin to relax], you can see it in their faces. Their pace of speech will slow down; they use more silence and more pauses; their voice is quieter; their posture goes relaxed; they stop fidgeting and settle down. Breathing is deeper, maybe a yawn or sigh. They may stop intensively looking you in the eye as they are accessing their imagination.

Level 3: Mastery

Level 3 indicates a high degree of mastery in one or more of the six artful coaching media. Coaches working at this level are adept, innovative, and comfortable in their chosen media and can adapt a variety of tools in the moment to the needs of the coachee. There are many routes to mastery, but level 3 coaches consciously test and extend the limits of their own particular art without losing their learning orientation.

Level 3 coaching has two important aspects based in the masterful engagement of artful media: (1) appreciative inquiry (creating a positive integration of the past and a generative vision of the future) and (2) world making (transforming the core meanings by which the individual or group perceives and acts).

Appreciative inquiry is an approach to learning and change that emphasizes the leveraging of strengths and aspirations rather than focusing on problems and deficits (Cooperrider & Srivastva, 1987). Level 3 coaches often report that the exploration of a coachee's special talents is a route to profound insight and growth. Such special talents in people are inevitably expressions of artistry—of levels of expression, composition, and execution, aesthetically informed, that go far beyond mere technique. But many people are unaware of the nature of their own artistry, and so its contribution to their lives and work is less than it could be.

Level 3 coaches often use artful media to help their coachees transform their personal and social reality. We understand this as world making: viewing, engaging, and constructing reality in more effective and satisfying ways through the invention and use of symbol systems and artistic modes of representation (Goodman, 1978). Level 3 artful coaches collaborate with their coachees to remake their personal and organizational worlds.

As an example of level 3 coaches engaged in appreciative inquiry and world making, consider the case of the Medic Inn as reported by Barrett and Cooperrider (2001). The authors were coach consultants to the senior team of this 380-room hotel complex. The team had to reinvent its work after being acquired by a health care center and receiving a new mission: to become a four-star hotel. The organization had the technical skills to pull this off, but they were riven by long-standing interpersonal and interdepartmental conflicts. The senior team had sunk into pessimism and cynicism and lacked any positive vision for how it might succeed. But instead of problem solving, the coaches saw that the task was "to break out of the current frame altogether."

In what they call the Generative Metaphor Intervention Process, the coaches combined appreciative inquiry and world making in a four-step process. The first step was a journey into metaphor. In this case the coaches proposed the metaphor: the Tremont Hotel, a successful four-star hotel. Attention was thus temporarily pulled away from their obvious predicaments and into "conversations that resonated with a sense of excitement, adventure, and positive anticipation about the journey to come." Step 2 was poeticizing the world. The team (after much preparation) spent five days at the Tremont in an appreciative mode, "learning how to perceive organizations as creative constructions, as entities that are alive, vital, and dynamically emergent." Step 3 was cocreation of possibility. The group focused its attention on possibility and what might be. Their language shifted away from one based in problems to one based in values and aspirations. Step 4 was a return to the original domain. The managers on the team faced the hard work of returning to their problems and attempting to live out their aspirations. The authors reported an overall transformation of interpersonal relationships as a result of the continuing learning journey. Members now had shared scripts for confronting differences and pursuing a vision. The mission to achieve four stars was changed into one crafted to their unique status: a hotel supporting a health care center. Their new vision generated much success.

From an artful coaching perspective, it is important to note that this journey was one of world making rather than one of merely problem fixing or competence building (though these things also happened). At its best, world making is artfully done; the authors observe, "The group had become an aesthetic forum for sharing and crafting new meaning" (Barrett & Cooperrider, 2001).

Artful Coaching and the CCL Coaching Framework

The tools and techniques of artful coaching can be used to good benefit within the scope of CCL's coaching framework. Both the artful tools and approaches discussed in this chapter and the ideas collected in the coaching framework accommodate a whole-person perspective that coaches can use to work with coachees more effectively. Used together, they allow the coach and coachee to move back and forth between analysis and synthesis, exploration and discovery, expansion and focus. This rhythm of divergence and convergence is essential to creative processes of all kinds, including coaching (Gryskiewicz, 1999). Following are specific aspects within artful coaching where aspects of the framework may be informative to the process. In Exhibit 10.1, some cautions and tips for leader coaches considering these kinds of approaches are discussed.

Relationship

Coaches build rapport in their coaching conversations when they pay attention, use a metaphor or simile, or reference a piece of art or music that has relevance to or illuminates the coachee's situation. This does not require an unusually trusting relationship; however, if the coach intends to use artful methods to uncover or draw attention to a more challenging issue, help the coachee get unstuck, or explore an uncharted developmental arena, then the nature and quality of the relationship may become critical. Using more artful coaching parallels the evolutionary process of developing a relationship, which takes time and is usually based on a series of interactions that allow rapport, collaboration, and commitment to grow. Part and parcel of that process

EXHIBIT 10.1. CAUTIONS AND TIPS FOR THE ARTFUL LEADER COACH.

- Watch out for the "expressing our feelings" trap. There is a common caricature that the main purpose of using art in coaching situations is to express feelings. The real power of these techniques lies in their ability to integrate thought, perception, feeling, and action.
- It's not about "getting artsy." It's about the coachee, the coachee's context, and the coachee's challenges. It's about making sense of the complexity of it all.
- When using artful methods, connections and disconnections of attention are the vital signs. Stay attuned to your coachee's visual and verbal cues. If the coachee starts to talk about himself or herself, you've hit a chord.
- Artful coaching requires willingness to play; to improvise, test, and bend; to explore boundaries; and even to have fun. Figure out what play looks like to you and to your coachee, and together push to the edges of your willingness to play.
- Attain and retain a good rapport with your coachee before going deeper with artful methods. It may take some coachees several sessions to go down another path than the strict analytical path.
- Like a good exercise session, artful coaching needs a warm-up. It may take 30 or 40 percent of the coaching session's time to reach a relaxed enough place to use metaphors and other artful tools.
- Follow through to the underlying meaning produced from using artful media. Too many people use creative techniques and don't allow time to process what comes from the work. That's a waste of time.

is taking risks with one another and letting the relationship guide the level and type of risk the coach takes. More often than not, we would expect the coach to initiate and invite the coachee into an artful coaching process.

Assessment

By its nature, artful coaching techniques and approaches avoid relying too heavily on analytical assessments such as 360-degree feedback and psychological testing. But that information can be seen through artful eyes and is often useful when combined with artful coaching techniques. Artful coaching can be particularly helpful in understanding the human element of assessment.

Coachees often have a particular interest in a specific art, which a leader coach can use to round out his or her understanding of the coachee. Some other specific ways that artful coaching can add robustness to the assessment process include these:

- Fostering reflection on underlying drivers
- Making sense of large amounts of data by seeing patterns and connections
- Exploring the depths and uniqueness of the whole person
- Using artful media (artifacts or stories, for example) to provide a form of "soft" assessment data
- Using artful media to produce informal assessment and self-generated feedback as a complement to formal assessment and external feedback
- Integrating objective data with the coachee's subjective perspective
- Sensing issues that the coachee has not articulated and maybe cannot articulate
- Revealing other dynamics that underlie behaviors that may not be discernible through an instrument because it does not fully address context
- Enabling the coachee to put different language to his or her development needs in a way that makes the need and subsequent actions clearer
- Offering a more holistic, and in some cases less threatening, way to crystallize the coachee's leadership style or impact on others

Challenge

Developmental challenges are often not as they first appear. Seeing challenges in their true light does not come from analytical data alone. Artful coaching provides means to explore and make sense of the challenges faced by the coachee. A key step in facing complex challenges is to pay attention from a variety of perspectives and to see with fresh eyes. At level 1, coaches are learning to pay attention and to guide the coachee's attention to the challenges at hand in ever more skillful ways. At level 2, coaches deliberately use artful tools to engage the challenge, not only to see it but also to create and test scenarios for creative action. Active framing and reframing of the challenge are taking place. Coach and coachee collaborate on putting the challenge in the middle of their dialogue in order to see it differently. Level 3 coaches may go on to help the coachee experience a challenge as a transformative opportunity. Coaches use artful media to more fully experience the patterns as well as the tensions and contradictions in their situations in support of significant learning. Developmental challenges are faced through creating whole new ways of understanding and acting in the world.

Support

In CCL's coaching framework, support is about motivating, finding resources, and celebrating successes and managing setbacks. Artful coaching often works because it locates deeper motivations and neglected resources for meaning making in the face of both setbacks and success. The stories coachees make and tell about who they are and where they are going help clarify what support might even look like on such a journey. Ultimately, artful coaching is about the kind of support provided by making meaningful connections in a chaotic world.

Results

Artful coaching can be thought of as the complement to coaching that settles on a narrow set of objectives within an analytical framework. For example, it invites the intuition of the coachee to be active and inform the range of desirable outcomes. Whether this achieves results depends on how relevant the intuitions are to the challenges at hand. In our experience, the engagement of both sides of human abilities, the analytical and the artful, leads to a more informed and balanced approach and more satisfying results.

Conclusion

When managers can access more and different options for developmental experiences, they often improve in unexpected ways or break loose from obstacles that confine their perspectives. Leader coaches who show coachees how to use such techniques as storytelling to get a grasp of the narrative of their work situation or body kinesthetics to become aware of the physical image they are projecting report significant rewards and successes with coachees.

These outcomes rely on the skill of the coach to meld a traditional array of such tools as 360-degree feedback instruments and goal setting with a choice of nontraditional approaches, such as using metaphors and deep attention to achieve meaningful reflection. The leader coach is responsible for knowing that these options are available, determining how to use them in conjunction with traditional development tools, and being able to work out a development program for each coachee that gets results.

Coach's Bookshelf

Adler School of Professional Coaching. http://www.adlercoachsw.com/ccp.htm.

Arnheim, R. (1969). *Visual thinking.* Berkeley: University of California Press.

Austin, R., & Devin, L. (2003). *Artful making: What managers need to know about how artists work.* Upper Saddle River, NJ: Pearson Education.

Bacon, S. (1983). *The conscious use of metaphors in Outward Bound.* Denver: Outward Bound School.

Banff Centre. http://www.banffcentre.ca/departments/leadership/.

De Ciantis, C. (1995). *Using an art technique to facilitate leadership development.* Greensboro, NC: Center for Creative Leadership.

Denning, S. (2004). *Squirrel Inc.: A fable of leadership and storytelling.* San Francisco: Jossey-Bass.

Drath, W. H. (2001). *The deep blue sea: Rethinking the source of leadership.* San Francisco: Jossey-Bass.

Harris, C. (Ed.). (1999). *Art and innovation: The Xerox PARC artist-in-residence program.* Cambridge, MA: MIT Press.

Kelly, T. (2001). *The art of innovation: Lessons in creativity from IDEO.* New York: Currency.

Schwartz, P. (1991). *The art of the long view.* New York: Currency.

CHAPTER ELEVEN

BRIEF SOLUTION-FOCUSED COACHING

Michael Wakefield

Perhaps you have tried coaching people before, with varying degrees of success. Like most other managers, you may have wondered whether your coaching efforts were worth the time it took to prepare and have the sessions. From the training you've had in coaching and from what you have read, you can probably explain why coaching is a good practice in any organization and recite the fundamentals: use good listening skills, create an open climate for discussion, grant an implied degree of discretion, and so forth. Still, you wonder if coachees can really change for the better as a result of your efforts.

This chapter describes a set of coaching techniques that leader coaches can use to help coachees consider new meanings and options to their current thinking and actions: brief solution-focused coaching (BSFC). This approach is predicated on beliefs that adults possess many resources of which they are not consciously aware. The techniques available to leader coaches who adopt this approach are relatively simple, time efficient, and effective.

BSFC has proven to be effective in a variety of settings with different configurations of people in leadership roles. Consider this exchange by one of those configurations—between a boss and a direct report:

Bill: I must admit that I haven't been able to fully commit to that project. I'm doing okay, but I know I'm only complying and giving only what we need to get by.

Coach: (Bill's manager): What's getting in your way?

Bill: Time, of course. And, you know, Joyce is not the easiest person in the world to work with.

Coach: I knew you two weren't best friends, but—

Bill: If she only would—

Coach: Bill, I'm sorry that I interrupted you. I realize it is not simple and that there is some history between you two. But I don't want to get distracted and start talking about Joyce right now. Perhaps at another time. What if we stay with what you could do to improve the situation. You told me that you weren't fully committed. Let's see if there is something you have control over that we could work with.

Bill: Okay, but she is part of it.

Coach: If you were to plot your current working relationship with Joyce on a 1 to 10 scale, with 1 being fraught with significant conflict and distrust and 10 representing a nearly ideal collegial relationship, where would you rate it now?

Bill: About a 4. It's not like I don't respect her and what she contributes. It's just that she—

Coach: Wait. We almost drifted into talking about her. Let's stay focused on what you can do. You are also part of that 4.

Bill: Okay, okay, I get it. But I'm not in this alone. It's not all my doing.

Coach: Agreed. It is a bit of a dance. And what can you do to improve it? What could you do to move that rating from a 4 to a 5?

This exchange typifies the kind of dynamic that can occur when a leader coach uses BSFC techniques. Bill's manager keeps the conversation targeted on a specific action. Bill comes out of this conversation focused not on the negative aspects of his relationship with Joyce but on his behavior and what he can do that will make a difference in the future. He thinks about what he can do to improve his effectiveness, which may even change his attitude about working with Joyce.

BSFC techniques encompass a series of tactical questions that get at an observed behavior and work on a quick result. The skillful application of these questions by the coach starts a change process that allows individuals to see their own behavior differently and become more aware of how they affect others. That process is the first step in creating change; disrupting the coachee's established pattern is a major objective.

BSFC techniques stem from a widely used therapy model that has produced success with individuals, couples, and families (see Exhibit 11.1). A key tenet of that model holds that solutions to prickly interpersonal problems are accessible with the right prompting by the therapist. BSFC has adapted the principles and techniques that define the use of that therapy model so that leader coaches without a background in therapy can apply them and integrate them with other coaching skills in their repertoire.

How can behavioral therapy techniques be relevant and useful for coaching leaders? The conventional wisdom is that therapy takes a long time, requires frequent contact, and produces solutions gradually, if at all. How can anyone expect professional managers from a variety of business backgrounds to apply such therapeutic techniques in their coaching interactions? Part of the answer lies in the similarity of their goals. A fundamental goal of developing leaders through coaching is to help the coachee become more effective in dealing with the challenges of life and achieving desired changes—a goal

EXHIBIT 11.1. ROOTS OF BRIEF SOLUTION-FOCUSED COACHING.

Much of the research and practice that has evolved into BSFC tactics originated with the work of the Mental Health Research Institute in Palo Alto, California (De Shazer, 1988). That group pioneered work on problem formation and subsequent success (or lack of it) in arriving at solutions. The work showed the profound effect that problem re-formation has on problem resolution. Reframing problems frees up potential solutions that were not considered before.

As De Shazer describes these ideas, he indicates the next step in their evolution rested with Milton Erickson and his colleagues, who carried out research to develop alternative ways of communicating. A major contribution of this work showed how many of the traditional barriers that limit people's efforts to change can be circumvented (1992).

CCL has incorporated BSFC into its coaching efforts, adapting its techniques and assumptions for use in some leadership development programs. The adaptations, when applied within the appropriate context, make BSFC techniques available to managers who are not mental health professionals.

shared in part by therapeutic techniques. The principles and techniques of BSFC essentially help entice a person to do something differently so as to get a different result when his or her behavior interferes with effectiveness or is not sufficiently developed. Two assumptions about BSFC are pertinent here. First, the momentum for change can be triggered in an instant, and that change can trigger more activity, change, and momentum. Second, it is counterproductive to believe that change takes a long time. BSFC makes use of limited, strategic coaching sessions of shorter duration—manna for the time-challenged executive.

BSFC also enjoys the advantage of flexibility. Its techniques can be used in a planned stand-alone coaching session, elements of it can be employed off-the-cuff in such settings as hallway conversations and business lunches, and it can play a part in a wider organizational coaching effort. It is appropriate for handling many kinds of workplace behaviors and contexts and for all levels of leaders. BSFC has certain universality in that its techniques can be adapted to all levels of employees, it can be used at any time, and it is not constrained to specific time limits or rules.

This chapter acquaints the reader with BSFC and shows how it can become a part of everyday coaching interactions for leader coaches and others. It also serves as a guide for engaging in long-term, explicit coaching. I begin with the guiding principles of BSFC and follow with a discussion about the orientation of the coach. The chapter then covers the essential tools of the practice (six evocative questions), relates BSFC to CCL's coaching framework, and addresses the sticky issue of resistance.

Principles of Brief Solution-Focused Coaching

Understanding and applying principles that support BSFC is actually more important than mastering its tools and techniques. There are endless ways of challenging and supporting the coachee within the boundaries of these principles. Most managers have a substantial array of information and skills that are applicable to coaching. For instance, earlier supervisory training and on-the-job experiences may have taught techniques such as effective listening skills, open-ended questioning, and techniques for giving effective feedback. The guiding principles affiliated with BSFC will help the coach to select the appropriate skills already in their repertoire that can be applied effectively.

BSFC Is Future Focused

BSFC discards the notion that change requires in-depth examination of past problems. Promoting change takes precedence over clarifying the past or gaining insight into the existence and meaning of nonproductive behavior. A leader coach using BSFC starts with the coachee's future, not with the coachee's past. The goal is to help the coachee find more effective ways of dealing with the tasks at hand. That usually requires changing patterns of behavior to create more effective patterns. BSFC tactics enable that change without a reexamination of the past.

The BSFC approach aligns with concepts of positive psychology. Those concepts reflect an optimistic future focus and presuppose intrinsic capabilities that can help people move toward their goals and intentions (Seligman & Csikszentmihalyi, 2000). The future focus of BSFC helps make coaching more palatable for leaders who see the coaching process as psychologically intrusive.

The brief dialogue between Bill and his coach at the start of this chapter illustrates the future focus principle. Bill's coach thwarted his efforts to cite past history and avoided any character examination of Joyce (Bill's colleague). Instead, the coach kept the focus on Bill and his future behavior.

Change Can Begin Quickly

BSFC tactics are attractive to leaders—those coaching and those being coached—because they are just that: brief and solution focused. Coaching with this approach emphasizes the process of changing, with small changes leading to larger changes. This creates a sense of always moving forward that appeals to coachees. As capabilities evolve, new resources and options constantly emerge to improve. This model contends that the beginning of desired change can happen fast. Each session should start with this principle in mind.

BSFC's characteristic of providing relatively quick change is particularly well suited for busy leaders. With the limited time they usually devote to their development, they often need at least subjective evidence that something is happening in order to maintain their motivation. Staying focused on behavior change over time is not easy for most people. Catching themselves engaging in new observations and behaviors, even small ones that are addressing a problem, is an intrinsic motivation—the most important kind. Seeing evidence that their behavior is having different effects on others is also critical to reinforce their effort. The more quickly the coaching discussions turn into useful behavior, the better.

Know the Coachee's Inner Resources

For coaches to make best use of BSFC techniques, they should examine their beliefs about their role. These beliefs contribute to the choices of techniques and practices that coaches adopt, such as self-discovery, expert, analytical, and behavioral. For example, is it necessary that a coach provide expert advice to change a coachee's behavior or beliefs? Not if, as the BSFC approach asserts, the coachee has sufficient internal resources to behave and even believe differently. However, if a coach believes the coachee's development requires the coach to explain what and how, the BSFC approach suggests that the coachee has not yet connected the correct knowledge and skill to address the problem.

How does a leader coach know if the coachee has enough self-awareness and impulse control to monitor his or her behavior? Can the coachee catch himself or herself before continuing a pattern of behavior? Can the coachee choose to act in another way? All adults have these capabilities to some degree, and the coach has to work from a perspective that trusts that such capabilities are within the coachee's control. The BSFC approach relies on the fact that all adults possess large amounts of information and are capable of making creative connections of which they are not aware (that is, they are not conscious of making the connections). When working with leaders, it is reasonable to assume they are smart and have many skills that helped them achieve their positions.

One coaching objective that is part of BSFC is helping the coachee to make use of his or her own capabilities (discover and rediscover) to behave differently. The coach helps the coachee find the information he or she knows and the processes that have served him or her to think and act differently. Not only does the coachee's learning history provide information to consider, it also provides many experiences to draw on for examples of changing and adapting.

For some coaches, trusting the internal resources of the coachee may require a leap of faith. They may be very comfortable keeping the locus of control in themselves and not in the coachee. But there is ample evidence that an internal locus of control is important for the coachee's participation, buy-in, and follow-through (Rotter, 1966). It is often easier or more comfortable for the coachee to get an answer from the coach, but it is not better for development. Ting and Hart (2004) called this the inside-out process, marked by the presumption that coachees are most capable of directing and building their own learning. This principle is long-standing and broadly understood, like the aphorism (known similarly in many countries and cultures) about giving a person a fish is food for a day but teaching a person to fish is food for a lifetime.

Imagery Facilitates Change

If you are encouraging people to think into the future, you are encouraging them to see a positive circumstance, to create a mental image in their imaginations. A growing body of study on the effects of mental imagery shows it to be quite effective (see, for example, *Journal of Mental Imagery*). The premise is that mental imagery stimulates the neurological system and in turn stimulates feelings and physical sensations. Essentially feelings follow images. Try this quick experiment. Recall a scene and sounds of a circumstance that you found particularly enjoyable and relaxing. Scan the environment in your mind. Notice people, textures, and sounds in your imagination that catch your attention. Then focus on the feelings you are experiencing while you are imagining. Repeat the sequence, this time focusing on an unpleasant circumstance. In your mind's eye, see and hear that situation. Notice the people, the sounds, and so forth. What are you feeling? People can commonly experience the effects of imagery with this simple demonstration.

A leader coach who engages the coachee to see himself or herself doing something in a different way sets into motion the process of disrupting a pattern that may have limited the coachee's responses. It can also provoke unconscious capabilities the coachee can apply to reach a better outcome than by relying on past strengths. It does not require anything more than conversation to stimulate such imagery. We do it all the time in our storytelling. Simply relating an experience provokes imagery in the teller and the listeners. This tactic is well within the capabilities of leader coaches.

Imagery in and of itself does not necessarily create lasting changes in behavior patterns. But it can have a profound unfreezing effect on ingrained patterns. It can encourage coachees to attempt new behaviors. Those attempts are the first steps toward replacing old, ineffective patterns of behavior.

There Is Choice

The coach is a catalyst—challenging and supporting the coachee's considering alternatives. Rarely, if ever, does a coach want to suggest that the coachee eliminate a particular behavior from his or her repertoire or take any tools from his or her toolbox. CCL research says that a primary contributor to limited growth as a leader is overreliance on a proven strength (Bunker, Kram, & Ting, 2002). Reliable skills become a liability by overuse, typically when applied to the wrong task. As the saying goes, "If you only have a hammer in your toolbox, every job looks like a nail."

It is a thorny developmental challenge if a coachee attributes much of his or her success to a particular skill. The skill has been rewarded and reinforced many times. It is natural the coachee would rely on it, particularly under pressure. But that does not make it effective in all or even most cases. It is not comfortable to let go of a favorite tactic or try a new one. Those who attempt a different approach often revert to old, default patterns out of habit and comfort, even when the new approach is successful. Integrating a new pattern requires attention to strengthen it until it becomes comfortable.

The Coach's Orientation

The guidelines just discussed are built on some generalizations that are useful to know when engaging in BSFC. The following discussion provides further recommendations that apply specifically to the coach's mind-set and orientation. They are useful because they encourage the leader coach to examine mental models and beliefs about the process of coaching and the situation of the coachee.

Examine Your Beliefs About Change

Effective application of BSFC requires both the leader coach and the coachee to reconsider their own beliefs about behavior change. One such belief is abandoning the notion that people must untangle the past in order to change. Switching gears about basic beliefs is not as easy as it appears. Most people are aware of many theories of learning, personality, and people in general that explain the hows and whys of human change. We learned such things from our parents, churches, our culture's stories, universities, and executive training programs. We have all heard the cliché that the best predictor of future behavior is past behavior.

There are also other notions commonly associated with behavior change that may be difficult to reorient to: change takes a long time and requires many repetitions; a person must unlearn some things to learn to do new things; change must be painful or at least very difficult; change requires a lot of reading, study, or training. The list goes on. True, some of life's important lessons don't come easily. However, the principles that support BSFC recognize the almost instantaneous connections caused by subtle shifts in perspective. Awareness by itself cannot displace entrenched behavior patterns without consistent application over time. But getting started with different behavior can begin immediately.

Discern the Right Level of Coaching

Leader coaches are often concerned about the hazy line between coaching and counseling or therapy. As discussed in Chapter One, CCL's view of coaching accommodates three levels of coaching: behavior, underlying drivers, and root causes. Coaches must consider at what level they want to work with a particular coachee on a particular issue.

As in any other adult interaction, both parties are responsible for the quality and the depth of the interaction. But it falls to coaches to stay aware of the level or depth of change they and their coachees are working at to avoid violating that line. Most people would agree that behavior is the end product of the drivers and root causes that influence our actions. The temptation to explore these levels in the hope of freeing the coachee to make needed changes is seductive. Fight that urge. At the very least, do not pursue the issue for the sake of finding the root cause. That is inconsistent with BSFC principles, and it is an especially slippery slope for leader coaches, who often do not have the requisite backgrounds to address psychological drivers and root causes.

BSFC practices purposefully minimize examining the past. Because of its future focus on doing something differently, coaches and coachees are less likely to get hooked into discussions of root causes. Still, using BSFC principles does not eliminate the possibility that the coachee will confront deeply held beliefs with strong emotional ties. A change in behavior or a shift in perspective that may help the coachee address a particular workplace circumstance may also have a broad range of applications in his or her personal life. He or she may realize that a limiting behavior or belief is rooted in deeper patterns established earlier in life. But even when the coachee chooses to examine such a topic, a focus on the future decreases the likelihood that the coachee will become a "patient."

Identifying deeply seated events, beliefs, and feelings that are not at the conscious level may require the services of a professional therapist if the coachee concurs (see Chapter One). Many contemporary companies have employee assistance programs or affiliations with other professionals who are trained to address such situations. The level at which a coach works is based on role, not just on training. Leader coaches can find reassurance in that perspective (good coaching does not require therapeutic training) and find encouragement: good coaching practices are accessible to the leader coach.

Practice Curiosity and Respect

Effective application of BSFC techniques requires the coach to operate from a perspective of curiosity about and respect for the coachee. To integrate this philosophical element into a coaching style requires self-awareness and patience on the coach's part. It requires the coach to recognize how to be effective without the need to be the expert, which is easier said than done. This belief does not preclude the coach from making inquiries, exploring assumptions, or even doing some teaching. The key point to remember is that BSFC work is based on a philosophy of utmost respect for the coachee that invites the coach to assume a "not-knowing" stance.

In many cases, coaching from this perspective means the coachee is teaching the coach about what kinds of actions or changes might work. Socrates employed the same method thousands of years ago. Solutions emerge from these kinds of dialogues. Coachees often "remix" information from their experience to help the coach understand the viability of a solution they've imagined, paving the way for change and provoking the coachee into creative new options to consider.

Listen Actively and Reframe Problems

A critical element of BSFC strategy involves how the coachee constructs his or her problem. Embedded into descriptions of problems are descriptions of goals—essentially, a problem is defined by what isn't being accomplished. The leader coach who listens for these embedded statements performs a great service for the coachee.

For example, a manager might say to her coach, "I don't know what to set as a goal. The only problem is that people don't understand me. It seems so many times I am in an argument even when trying to explain the simplest things. What can I do so they can better understand me?" After interviewing some of these people, the coach finds that they did not think she heard their ideas. The problem moved from "not being understood" to one of focusing on simple attending and listening. The leader coach reframed from problems that rested with others ("they don't understand") to something she could do something about (listen better). After practicing these behaviors, the manager was amazed at how much better people understood her and her perspective.

The solution behavior must always be about the coachee. For example, say you are coaching a manager who is having a "personality conflict" with a colleague that was keeping them from working collaboratively. Your coachee's first tendency might be to want the other person to behave differently. But such is life; we have little or no control over others except perhaps by manipulating them with reward or punishment. In this case, you might challenge your coachee: "What is one thing that you could do that would move you two a bit closer to each other?" Reframing the problem can give the coachee access to different options and possible solutions.

Coaching Leaders Using BSFC Techniques

Before applying the tools of BSFC (explored later in this chapter), there are some things for the leader coach to consider that can help ease the way in. For example, goal setting is a critical element and important first step. Determining progress and giving direction are also crucial, and both depend on clear, specific, behavioral goals and assignments (see Exhibit 11.2).

Getting Started in a BSFC Context

Even expert BSFC practitioners differ in their opinions on how to start the initial coaching session. One group suggests a solution-oriented question as an opening such as, "What will tell you that participating in coaching has paid off for you?" Such a question requires a positive outcome answer. But others advocate a simple, "Why coaching?" or even, "What problem would you like to work on?" (Walter & Peller, 1992). Although questions such as these open the door for the coachee to address his or her shortcomings and problems (a direction BSFC strives to avoid), they allow coachees to express themselves in ways they believe necessary for the coach to help them. Coachees often expect

EXHIBIT 11.2. GOALS AND SHORT-TERM ASSIGNMENTS.

Goals set the intention of development, defining the result. They are also applied as assignments, which can tie coaching sessions together. In either case, there are a few points for the leader coach to keep in mind.

Goals should be framed positively and stated as behaviors. In other words, they should not describe what the coachee wants to stop doing, but instead should focus on what behaviors the coachee wants to do. For example, a coachee who states, "I want to stop being so quick to judge the ideas of my direct reports," will do better by reframing the goal: "I will engage my direct reports more by allowing time and discussion around their ideas." A positive frame may seem to be a subtle point, but it makes a world of difference as the coachee begins to imagine the new, intended behavior. A positive outcome statement stimulates the coachee to "see" the solution.

Most managers, including leader coaches and their coachees, know a variety of planning schemes. Forming goals, objectives, and action plans are commonplace for them. When it comes to setting goals, the coachee should lead the way, with managerial guidance only in the form of making the goal's expression consistent with BSFC principles. Assignments that coachees will focus on between sessions don't need to be documented in triplicate and measured precisely. Don't discourage coachees with more paperwork, but work with them to make it clear what determines progress, effort, and other outcomes.

Another element of effective goal setting is that it be stated as a process, not just an outcome. The focus is on execution and the impact of desired behavior. A statement such as, "I will be more patient," would be more effectively stated as a process and in more behavioral terms such as, "I will listen more and check out my understanding before responding." This statement suggests there will be an ongoing sequence of behavior, not just a state of being. Consistent and persistent execution of specific behaviors will become integrated patterns with time.

Effective goals need to be specific, calling to mind succinct, observable action. Crafting specific behavioral indicators is not always easy. Most people have much more practice at making assumptions and generalizations. Sometimes the specifics are more personal, revealing actions or lack of action that are nothing to admire. But letting coachees work in generalizations makes it difficult for them to recognize progress and to build on small improvements. Approach goal setting as a process to allow adjustments and upgrades as the coachee's struggle to apply specific behavior gives way to the integration of new patterns.

to contribute background information. They almost insist on it. The advocates of this starting position contend that coachees will be distracted from attending to solutions until they at least state their problem and contributing circumstances at least once. It satisfies their expectation of their role in the coaching process and also reveals the perception the general population has about change: that you must understand the background in order to change the future.

Coaches applying BSFC strategies must respect the idea that most people they coach will have similar ideas about change. BSFC is different. Although you must allow the coachee to apply his or her own knowledge and experience, you don't want to reinforce an expectation that problem evolution is the focus. Try to redirect to a solution focus as soon as you think your coachee is satisfied that you know enough to be of help.

In addition to opening questions, leader coaches can begin by building on change that precedes the coaching. Research reveals a fascinating phenomenon regarding the internal resources of coachees. Important progress on problem resolution occurs between the time the coachee chooses to pursue help and the time of the first coaching appointment (Talmon, 1990). Leader coaches can build on the supposition that people begin to move toward solutions as soon as they have committed to talking with a coach. They will subtly, perhaps not consciously, begin organizing their thoughts in preparation for the coaching session. They often begin to do the sorts of things that are required to address the issue at hand.

Several explanations might account for these initial steps toward change. For example, by making a challenge public by calling in a third party (a coach), the coachee is redefining the challenge. A second explanation is that in some cases, the act of seeking help leads coachees to do something different. Simply making room in their busy schedules for coaching causes a shift that can disrupt ingrained patterns of reasoning or behavior, which blocked their access to more productive action or perspectives. Coachees often move toward their own solutions because of these precoaching preparations.

Because one of the supporting principles of BSFC is a high regard for people to organize past information and experiences in new and novel ways, the leader coach can probe for precoaching change with provocative questions such as: "What has improved since we agreed to meet?" or "What have you already done that has helped resolve the problem?" The coachee's responses can set the tone for a positive, future focus. At the same time, the leader coach implies that problem-solving strengths are already within the coachee's repertoire and acknowledges that the coachee is in control of the change process—powerful developmental motivations.

This dynamic can also operate between scheduled coaching sessions. As time approaches for a session, the coachee usually will collect information (usually based on the assignment from the previous session). This often provokes appropriate action on the part of the coachee.

The core mechanics of the BSFC lie in a six-question set, which is summarized in Exhibit 11.3. Perhaps the most essential characteristic of these tools is their property of being able to focus attention. One of the BSFC guiding principles rests on breaking patterns of behavior so that coachees can take a different view or behave differently. Often people can break patterns simply by changing their attention patterns. Each of us has our own patterns, our mental models that influence what we pay attention to and what we don't. Challenges arise when our models or our actions don't accomplish what we wish. As the saying goes, "You can't get out of a problem with the same thinking that got you into it."

EXHIBIT 11.3. BSFC'S SIX CATALYTIC QUESTIONS.

Miracle question: Elicits behavior-based outcome goals.

Exception question: Identifies skills the coachee already has.

"What else?" question: Used with other questions to get more information.

Scaling question: Establishes a subjective point of reference.

Coping question: Reveals positive aspects of the situation.

Relationship question: Shows how another would feel in the same situation.

This list is not meant to suggest a linear order to asking the questions that are at the heart of BSFC techniques. Circumstances, short- and long-term goals, and the relationship between coach and coachee steer the use of the questions. In addition, the questions and the use of topics, metaphors, language, and other factors will differ depending on whether a leader coach is working with a vice president of a major international company, for example, or a principal of a local high school.

The Miracle Question

This question elicits behavior-based outcome goals. It focuses the coachee and the coach on behaviors that are solution oriented. The question takes this kind of form (addressed to the coachee): "While you are sleeping, a miracle happens and solves the problem. Because you were sleeping, you are unaware of this miracle. When you awake, what will you notice that you are doing differently?" Such a question provokes future-focused, positive imagery.

Leader coaches first exposed to this BSFC question often remark that such a fairy tale–like statement would turn off the typical executive and damage the coach's credibility. That's a legitimate reaction, but consider these two thoughts. First, it is important that the selection of language, metaphor, and other elements in this question be consistent with the essential style of the coach. Authenticity is king. So as a leader coach, construct your version of the miracle question in your own way. Useful alternatives might include: "Imagine you are performing more effectively. What are you actually doing?" and "What would you be doing if your new behavior was working?" Second, set aside doubts, and simply try the technique. Judge the results for yourself.

The compelling nature of the question lies in its unusual presentation. It is different enough to stir attention and transparent enough for the coachee to understand what to do. It also provides opportunity for describing the "miracle" as behaviors, which can evolve into goals. In CCL's use of this question, later stages of long-term coaching relationships can benefit from a simple reference to "miracle" or "when you go to sleep." These phrases prompt the coachee to examine future-focused, positive imagery. Furthermore, the coachee often uses the question alone, taking the tool the coach has offered and using it as needed.

Exception Questions

This kind of question gives the coachee opportunities to recognize he or she is already successful handling the challenge or some part of it. The coachee and coach can identify effective skills the coachee has but may not be aware of. Even the most capable leaders often frame problems in absolutes: "I'm incapable of learning the new system," "She always makes it more complicated than it needs to be," or "He can't say no." Often such absolute statements are products of frustration and not meant to be literal. When the leader coach prompts the coachee to recognize that this absolute statement is unlikely, the coachee can often free himself or herself to consider the dilemma differently.

Exception questions reinforce your coachees' capabilities and help them reform the way they see their developmental challenge. It's easier for them to see options when they are considering adjusting a current behavior than it is to create a capability that doesn't even exist.

Some examples of exception questions or prompts are: "Are there situations when you are able to deal with . . . ?" "Are there times when bits of 'the miracle' occur now?" If you ask a closed-ended question such as these, follow with a prompt, such as: "Tell me about one of those times." By identifying positive exceptions, the coachee increases his or her developmental potential: if this person can perform well sometimes, he or she can perform well at other times.

After the coachee names some positive exceptions to the behavior he or she wants to change, the prescription is evident: do more of it. The leader coach can simply let that recognition of effective behavior become the assignment. Prompt the coachee to pay attention to opportunities to use the behavior that has worked. Again, the shift in attention (looking for opportunities) can reframe the circumstances and allow the coachee to apply behavior differently. After all, he or she has done it once, and it has worked. Your coachees may find it hard to believe it can be that easy. They may have a vested interest (saving face) to resist such a simple assignment. As a leader coach, this is your time to encourage the coachee to give it a try. Most coachees are surprised that such a subtle intervention can lead to progress.

Coachees quickly pick up the ideas behind exception questions and often apply those ideas outside regular coaching sessions. The result is a reduction in their limiting, absolute statements, which increases their choice of action. Consider the example of Bill that began this chapter. Here's how a coach might use exception questions during a session:

Bill: Another problem with Joyce is that she always has to study things to death before she will make a statement about anything!

Coach: I can see that would be a problem. But, truthfully, Bill, haven't there been times when Joyce has made decisions or given you the go-ahead without having "studied it to death"?

Bill: Yes, of course.

Coach: Tell me about one of those times, and what was different.

Bill: Well, I certainly didn't hang around long enough for her to change her mind. I got right on it, and it worked out great for all of us.

Coach: Besides acting swiftly, what else might have been different that allowed her to "not study it to death"? Can you remember anything that you might have done to contribute?

During this brief exchange, the coach has subtly shifted Bill's attention to useful behaviors that he can apply to continue improving his working relationship with his colleague.

"What Else?" Questions

Leader coaches can use this kind of question repeatedly with variations of the other questions. It prompts the coachee to continue generating more solution-focused options. This question and its variations let the coach show curiosity and confidence in the coachee's inventory of connections, options, and untapped ideas.

Practitioners of Six-Sigma training and other quality tools have come to appreciate the learning associated with repeatedly asking, "Why?" Although it is a subtle difference, CCL promotes *what* questions instead because our experience is that they more often result in behavioral or action responses, but *why* questions more often invite rationalizations and justifications. Consider this example:

> "Why did you do . . . ?" *becomes* "What did you expect to happen by doing . . .?"

Once a leader coach has established "what" instead of "why," it is simple to add "and what else." After a few exposures to this question, coachees can begin catching themselves in limiting, absolute statements and start challenging their own perceptions.

Scaling Questions

This kind of question establishes a subjective point of reference for coachee and coach. The coach prompts the coachee to plot his or her current experience in a given situation on a 1 to 10 scale, with 10 representing the best the experience has been or could be. Coaches may find it useful to use scaling questions in regard to such issues as the severity of past or current challenges, the degree to which the coachee is willing to work on solutions, the amount of progress the coachee thinks he or she is making or has made, the amount of effort being put forth, and the coachee's confidence in improving.

Here are a few examples of scaling questions:

> "To what degree can you be candid giving feedback to others on your team? The scale is 1 = cautious, political, anxious to 10 = very open, unguarded, as if no risk exists. When the team was performing at its best, what would you have rated it? How would you rate it at its worst?"
>
> "Your direct reports indicate in your 360-degree assessment that they want more direction from you. Where would you plot your activity on that, with 1 = very little attention to it, leaving them too much on their own, and 10 = I communicate the goals, and other information so each person understands and I am available to give supportive and corrective feedback?"

When using scaling questions, it is useful to follow up responses with queries such as, "What was different about the way that you were behaving when circumstances were better?" and "What could you do to move that rating just one point on the scale?" Often coachees see small changes that can lead to more small changes as more realistic and possible than dramatic quick fixes.

An additional benefit to using scaling questions is that they can be revisited to see how a coachee's ratings have changed—possibly because of his or her own development. The difference in ratings can suggest progress and reinforce the change or provide insight into a more effective action.

Coping Questions

Coping questions can illuminate capabilities or encourage perseverance from seemingly hopeless or very frustrating situations. Some examples include: "What do you do to keep going?" "How have you been able to cope?" and "What has prevented this from getting worse?" These questions often elicit acknowledgment of things taken for granted but not honored. From their responses, coachees recognize they have and are demonstrating resilience and that they are getting useful learning despite the drudgery. Coping questions often provide opportunities for the coach to lend support for efforts that the coachee does not recognize. Coping capabilities can often be aimed at viable solutions, and coachees can transfer them to behaviors that are part of a solution.

Returning to our example of Bill, here's how his coach might use coping questions during a session:

Coach: I heard about the setback to your project. Are you frustrated with that?

Bill: You have no idea. It took forever to get the funding approved. Damn politics! And now we find out IT cutbacks are going to delay it even more. I don't know how I can keep the team together, much less excited.

Coach: This has been a concern before this IT problem. What have you done to keep them hopeful so far?

From this point, the coach can probe for actions Bill has taken in the past that worked to keep the team engaged. It may take a couple of "What else?" questions to prompt Bill to recognize the more subtle things he had been doing and perhaps taken for granted.

Relationship Questions

These kinds of questions invite the coachee to consider solutions from an outsider's perspective. They further challenge the coachee to focus on positive behavior. For example, a leader coach could follow up on a miracle question with:

"When you do that, who else might notice something different about you?"

"What would your boss notice?"

"If I was a fly on the wall watching the meeting, what would I see that is different?"

For best effects, leader coaches should weave the six BSFC questions into conversations at appropriate times. The guiding principle is to keep the coachee focused on a solution. With the exception of the miracle question, variations on all the others can be used repeatedly throughout a single session. With experience, coaches will learn a variety of ways to engage the coachee with the essence of these questions. We provide some tips for applying BSFC techniques in Exhibit 11.4; however, it is a mistake to think of BSFC as just a

EXHIBIT 11.4. TIPS TO APPLYING BSFC TECHNIQUES.

- Learn to weave the BSFC questions into conversation. They are simply entrees into developmental dialogue. Integrate them into your repertoire of skills for coaching, teaching, self-reflection, and managing.
- BSFC techniques do not replace the fundamentals of effective communication. Being fully present with the coachee without distractions, listening to both the content and the feelings in the coachee's messages, and reflecting what you heard to make sure you have understood are all prerequisites to effective application of BSFC skills.
- Experiment with different ways to use the BSFC questions. Authentic, congruent delivery far outweighs the importance of mimicking someone else's words. If the setup of the miracle question feels uncomfortable, try a variation that works for you. If "What else?" isn't the best way for you to challenge the coachee to consider other options, try asking, "And?" or some other verbal signal to continue.
- Match your style with that of the coachee. You are in a dance that is most effective when both of you are in a relationship that allows assessment, challenge, and support. Coaching is a process, with ebbs and flows. The relationship that holds it is worth paying attention to and, occasionally, even discussing.
- Stay clear about your purpose as a coach. What is your intent? It may seem trite to remember that you are a vehicle for others' learning, but the tactics you use stem from that purpose.
- Beware of early overuse. Integrating new skills into your repertoire requires practice. Leader coaches new to the use of BSFC techniques often announce what they are doing, which often proves distracting to the coachee.
- Get your coachees to see, name, or describe the behavior they want to improve. They often will talk about the outcome of their efforts. You need to get them to see and name what they actually did or will do. Their behavior is what they have to choose from to be more effective.
- Fight the urge to participate in "problem talk." Minimize the amount of time spent on complaints. Don't ignore analysis of complex circumstances that may influence the coachee's choices, but remember that ultimately it is different behavior on your coachee's part that makes the difference. Try to keep the conversations on behavior that contributes to a different outcome from the one that spawns complaints.
- An intriguing question to help coachees consider their strengths and capabilities to apply toward a solution is, "What has been your success formula?" The question presupposes competence and an optimistic future and invites positive imagery of

EXHIBIT 11.4. TIPS TO APPLYING BSFC TECHNIQUES, Cont'd.

capabilities that can be used. It may also expose the overuse of strengths, which could stand in the way of effectiveness.

- People act or do not act based on the image of who they want to be. If you craft an assignment that is inconsistent with the coachee's self-image, he or she will be less motivated to pursue it than if the assignment is more congruent with who he or she wants to be. Finding out about your coachee's broader, long-range ambitions will help you help your coachee.

collection of techniques or questions. The real power of these techniques lies in the fundamental, respectful trust that the coachee is the actual driver of any change that can happen. By communicating respect, coaches help coachees to lower their defenses and their need to rationalize, defensive behaviors that often get in the way of their development.

BSFC Techniques and the CCL Coaching Framework

Techniques of BSFC, like all other coaching techniques, weave throughout the coaching process. Because CCL's coaching framework is iterative and not sequential, a single BSFC technique or question may facilitate multiple elements of the framework simultaneously.

Relationship

A strong, trusting, and respectful relationship is critical to providing effective coaching. One of the benefits of BSFC is that it is less relationship dependent; that is, relationship remains important, but BSFC techniques can yield highly effective results at various degrees of relationship. This is a valuable aspect of this coaching approach. It's doubtful that a leader coach can reach the same level of trust with every direct report, peer, or boss. Effective use of the BSFC approach is less dependent on developing a close personal relationship in part because it doesn't assume that coachees will dwell on their inadequacies or past mistakes nor does it require that of them. BSFC does, however, require a high degree of collaboration because the coach is drawing on the coachee's knowledge and experience.

Assessment

BSFC underplays diagnosis but does not devalue the use of assessment tools in collecting feedback for development. Leader coaches need to gather perceptions that others have of the coachee to guide their effective crafting of solutions. Most important, assessment can help the coachee set goals, which is a key part to BSFC.

What's different about the role of assessment in the BSFC context? Because BSFC techniques can be used at any stage of the coaching process, it is less dependent on a formal and in-depth assessment process occurring beforehand. Through skillful questioning, available performance data, and the firsthand knowledge that the leader coach has about the coachee, BSFC can lead to highly effective outcomes, especially if the coachee has a high degree of awareness and motivation. Formal assessments that become particularly useful when used in conjunction with BSFC techniques are 360-degree behavioral surveys or interviews using behavioral examples from the coachee's environment. Because BSFC focuses on the future and behavior, not on the past or root causes, assessment data that provide behavioral feedback are more valuable and useful than other forms of feedback.

This does not mean that other forms of assessment, such as personality inventories or style-indicator instruments, are not valuable. Many coachees find it useful to understand how "hard-wired" some of their behavioral styles are because it helps them better identify strategies and situations where they are able to behave differently. However, most leader coaches will not have access to these data nor will they have the training and skills needed to interpret and use the data appropriately. Coaches who are unable to include those forms of assessment should not feel handicapped to engage in high-quality coaching because BSFC techniques make the need for those types of surveys less relevant or essential to the assessment process. Coaches who do have these kinds of assessment data available to them should avoid the compulsion to form a "diagnosis." That mind-set often causes the coach to focus too much on what the coachee is not doing well and not to focus enough on eliciting the coachee's strengths and inner resources.

Current context is relevant; past context is less so. This reduced focus on context is consistent with the BSFC principle of future orientation. Coaching with these techniques means not dwelling in the past except to the extent that such exploration meets coachees' needs and expectations.

Leader coaches will do well to remember that information gathered through other people or through assessment tools can be used to restrict or expand options. BSFC strategies would apply any assessment data to expand options for the coachee. There is room for the use of many change techniques if the coach does not lose sight of the context: future-focused, coachee-driven, and solution-oriented behavior. The practice of curiosity, respect, and specific goal setting continues to be part of the process.

Challenge

Challenge in the CCL framework comprises disequilibrium, stretch, obstacles, and the opportunity for learning and change. In a BSFC approach, disequilibrium may have preceded the start of the coaching process, especially if the coachee enters with a clear sense of what he or she would like to do differently or can articulate a problem. Something or someone may have unsettled the coachee enough to motivate him or her to engage in exploring the issue, even if not immediately agreeing to personal change.

BSFC techniques can by themselves cause the disequilibrium. One of its key tenets is that the momentum for change can be triggered in a moment. This is essentially a form of disequilibrium, albeit it may occur without a lot of fanfare or "Aha!" insight.

In a BSFC context, stretch often overlaps with goal setting and results, and it is illuminated through the miracle and scaling questions.

Obstacles receive less attention, or different attention, because of the positive future focus of BSFC. Instead of anticipating ways in which the coachee's development might be sabotaged, a coach using the BSFC approach would apply positive behaviors and call for reflection when the coachee and coach notice that desired behavioral change is not occurring or is occurring at an unsatisfying pace for the coachee.

Support

BSFC advocates would find their approach compatible with the aspects of support that the CCL framework highlights: maintaining motivation, accessing resources (internal and external), celebrating wins and managing setbacks, and creating a sustainable personal learning agenda. Of those four aspects, accessing resources, specifically the coachee's internal resources, is paramount.

This element of support is a key principle underlying BSFC. This does not diminish the importance of the other support elements or of the role of the coach in providing personal support. The internal resources of the coachee function like a hub from which the other aspects of support radiate. The role that the leader coach plays reinforces the idea that his or her ultimate goal is to help the coachee create a self-regenerating learning agenda.

Results

BSFC's approach to results maps closely to the framework. Three elements in particular bear directly on results: goal setting, the miracle question, and the scaling question. BSFC recognizes that the overall impact and effectiveness of the process relies on clear problem formation (or reformation) and goal specificity. The miracle question essentially helps coachees articulate what results they'd like to see. Overall results can be measured through a reassessment process after some period of time has passed and coachees are constantly being assessed through the BSFC questioning process. For example, scaling questions can be an ongoing means of getting the coachee to reflect on progress ("How far do you believe you've moved on the scale since you identified the desire to . . . ?").

Conclusion

There are many philosophical models of human behavior. Most managers are exposed to several during their careers. Those that are consistent with their preexisting mental models make sense and are easily accepted and integrated into their understanding. Those that are not consistent are questioned or rejected outright.

Because mental models are continuously evolving, it is valuable for leaders to examine their current mental models of change and influence. Think back to the beginning of your career and on what you believed drove people to learn and change. What key events changed your beliefs? What psychological and philosophical models did you subscribe to? What readings or training programs influenced your beliefs? What previously held models no longer satisfy you? It is valuable to revisit from time to time the ideas that drive your actions and choices. Challenging, provocative, reflective questions such as those used in BSFC will help you keep the contextual integrity of your work intact and fresh.

Much of the elegance of BSFC lies in its simplicity. Steve de Shazer (1988) holds simplicity (which he refers to as parsimony) as a core element of its effectiveness. However, simplicity is not the same as simplistic. BSFC techniques are effective because they have simplicity of focus, not because they serve simplistic ends. Leader coaches who put these techniques into practice acknowledge the complexity of coaching relationships. There is much we don't understand about the human animal.

Coach's Bookshelf

Douglas, C., & McCauley, C. (1997). A survey on the use of formal developmental relationships in organizations. *Issues and Observations, 17*(1/2), 6–9.

Douglas, C., & Morley, W. (2000). *Executive coaching: An annotated bibliography.* Greensboro, NC: Center for Creative Leadership.

Fish, R., Weakland, J., & Segal, L. (1983). *The tactics of change.* San Francisco: Jossey-Bass.

Frank, J. (1961). *Persuasion and healing: A comparative study in psychotherapy.* Baltimore, MD: Johns Hopkins Press.

Goldsmith, M., Lyons, L., & Freas, A. (Eds.). (2000). *Coaching for leadership: How the world's greatest coaches help leaders learn.* San Francisco: Jossey-Bass.

Goleman, D. (1998). *Working with emotional intelligence.* New York: Bantam Books.

Goleman, D., Boyatzis, R., & McKee, A. (2002). *Primal leadership: Realizing the power of emotional intelligence.* Boston: Harvard Business School Press.

Guthrie, V. (1999). *Coaching for action: A report on long-term advising in a program context.* Greensboro, NC: Center for Creative Leadership.

Hall, D. T., Otazo, K. L., & Hollenbeck, G. P. (1999). Behind the closed doors: What really happens in executive coaching. *Organizational Dynamics, 27*(3), 39–53.

Hammond, D. (1990). *Handbook of hypnotic suggestions and metaphors.* New York: Norton.

Hargrove, R. (1995). *Masterful coaching: Extraordinary results by impacting people and the way they think and work together.* San Francisco: Jossey-Bass.

Kouzes, J., & Posner, B. (1993). *Credibility: How leaders gain and lose it, why people demand it.* San Francisco: Jossey-Bass.

Lankton, S., & Lankton, C. (1983). *The answer within: A clinical framework for Ericksonian hypnotherapy.* New York: Brunner/Mazel.

Lombardo, M., & Eichinger, R. (2000). *The leadership machine: Architecture to develop leaders for any future.* Minneapolis: Lominger.

Lombardo, M., & Eichinger, R. (2004). *For your improvement: A development and coaching guide* (4th ed.). Minneapolis: Lominger.

McCall, M. W., Jr., Lombardo, M. M., & Morrison, A. M. (1988). *The lessons of experience: How successful executives develop on the job.* Lanham, MD: Lexington Books.
O'Hanlon, B. (1999). *Do one thing different.* New York: Morrow.
Thomas, F. (1996). Solution-focused supervision. In S. Miller, M. Hubble, & B. Duncan (Eds.), *Handbook of solution-focused brief therapy.* San Francisco: Jossey-Bass.
Watzlawick, P., Weakland, P., & Fisch, R. (1974). *Change: Principles of problem formation and problem resolution.* New York: Norton.
Wilber, K. (2000). *A theory of everything: An integral vision for business, politics, science, and spirituality.* Boston: Shambhala.

CHAPTER TWELVE

CONSTRUCTIVE-DEVELOPMENTAL COACHING

Wilfred Drath
Ellen Van Velsor

Every coach, whether a leader coach working in an organization or a professional coach working with a specific executive, has likely experienced a situation in which the person being coached seemed resistant to changing even the most ineffective behaviors. In this difficult coaching situation, even when the coachee tried to change, something held her back—something that seemed as important to her as the fact of her ineffective behavior. This situation can be as frustrating for the coach as it is for the coachee, leaving the coach feeling inadequate in his skills and the coachee feeling that the change goal may be impossible to reach. Although it is relatively easy to facilitate development when the coachee is ready and willing to change, it is much harder to be an effective coach for someone who seems stuck or unable to change.

This chapter explains a framework that we have found useful for coaching in any situation, but particularly when it seems that the coachee is having difficulty changing despite a stated desire to do so. We explain constructive-developmental theory (which we will refer to as c-d theory) and provide some practical guidelines for using the framework to become a more effective coach. Reading the chapter will help the leader coaches who know little or nothing about c-d theory use the theory to enhance their skill in coaching for development. After a general orientation to the main ideas of c-d theory and how they fit with CCL's coaching framework, the chapter describes specific c-d-based coaching practices and refers to sources for learning more. In addition, the chapter discusses a number of issues in coaching from a c-d perspective.

The Basics of Constructive-Developmental Theory

The main ideas of c-d theory go back to the foundational work of Jean Piaget (as cited in Kegan, 1994). Unlike Freud, who was primarily interested in what the developing child thought about, Piaget was primarily interested in how the developing child thought. In a now famous experiment, Piaget showed a preschool child two identical containers holding the same amount of water. The child would agree that there was the same amount of water in each container. Piaget would then pour the water from one of the containers into a much taller, thinner container and ask the child to compare the amount of water in the two containers now. Usually the child would say that the taller container held more water, even though no additional water had been added; after all, it looked as if it had more water in it.

To Piaget, this demonstrated that a very young child sees and thinks about the world in a completely different way from an adult, a way that has its own distinctive forms and organizing principles. By now, we have come to accept this discovery of Piaget as common sense. We are familiar with the idea of developmental stages in the growth of the child, and we think nothing of saying that the way a child thinks and feels is the result of "a stage—he'll outgrow it."

Before children can become adults, they must progress through several of these distinctively different stages, or ways of thinking. Such development is not just a matter of a gradual growth of what the child knows, but also involves major shifts in how the child knows what she knows. For example, a child older than five will likely understand that the amount of water has not changed, regardless of the size and shape of the container into which it is poured.

The five year old is becoming able to reflect on the fact that her perception makes it look as if there is more water in the taller container, and she will be able to make judgments about such a perception ("My eyes are fooling me here"). She is awakening to a world independent of her perceptions, and she is beginning to recognize her perceptions as something she has, something that she can be aware of, manage, and make judgments about (Kegan, 1982). In c-d terms, she has developed. The child's perceptions have moved from being something that she was subject to (and that therefore controlled her) to being something she is aware of, can manage, evaluate, and make decisions about.

Key Ideas

The essential quality of development according to c-d theory is this transformation from being subject to some way of understanding oneself and the world to being able to hold that way of understanding (or mental model) as an object of reflection and judgment, thereby being more in control of the way that it affects one's feelings, behavior, and decisions. We often describe this transformation as akin to wearing (but eventually changing) a well-fitting, comfortable pair of glasses with exactly the right lens. If a pair of glasses is a comfortable fit, a person loses the awareness of wearing them. She sees through them but doesn't realize, moment to moment, that she is using the glasses to see. However, over time, the lenses may dull or the person's vision may worsen, making her more aware of the glasses themselves and also bringing in focus the limitations of that particular lens. The person at this point would likely take off the glasses, examine them, and decide to trade them in for a new pair, more adequate to her current needs. Developmental movement is much the same: the beliefs that for a time feel so comfortable that we may not be fully aware of them somehow reach the limits of their effectiveness for us and begin to get in our way. It is at this point, and only at this point, that we become ready to take them off, examine them, and evaluate whether they are still useful in our lives.

Another key idea in the c-d framework is that a developmental shift does not immediately dispense with the earlier way of knowing. First, these shifts do not occur overnight or permanently with a blinding flash of insight. Rather, glimpses of a new way of knowing gradually emerge as a person is confronted with new and more complex life challenges. Second, even after a developmental shift has fully taken place, one can remember and relate to earlier ways of understanding (the child still sees that there appears to be more water in the taller container and the child sees the difference between what her eyes tell her and the water's independent property of volume). Development is thus always a matter of transcending some earlier way of knowing and including it in a newer, more complex way of knowing, much the way a larger Russian doll encloses smaller dolls. While the child will no longer believe that her perception and the reality are one and the same, she can now understand how it is that her younger brother sees it in that way, as his way of understanding will feel familiar to her. And this sense of having "been there" can enable an empathetic response from her. We will return to the importance of this point in coaching adults later in the chapter.

The kind of developmental transformations that we have come to understand in the child do not stop when the child matures beyond adolescence. Adults continue to grow and develop in just this same way, only with increasingly more complex internalizations and increasingly more complex developmental shifts. We believe leader coaches can enhance their practice by helping coachees become more aware of their current developmental challenges in terms of the c-d framework. As we will see, this does not need to involve the coach's using a formal assessment to measure developmental stage or feeding such data directly back to the coachee. It is not necessary, and certainly could be confusing, for a coach to educate a coachee on the theory itself, nor is it important for the coachee to have a "diagnosis" as such of his or her developmental stage. But it is useful for the coach to gain a sense of what is challenging for the coachee about his experiences given the coachee's current way of constructing or understanding things—that is, by understanding what underlying ways of thinking and feeling the coachee is currently using and perhaps working to change.

From "Stages" to "Webs of Belief"

Traditionally, the ways of thinking that people develop as they mature have been referred to as stages. Many people are familiar with this term, especially in relation to children ("It's just a stage").

The term is problematic, however. In the first place, because it is associated with child development, there is a reluctance to apply it to adult development. Second, the primary definition of *stage* is that it's one of a series of positions or stations, and it carries the meaning that these positions are arranged one above the other. This common definition implies to some people that later stages are superior to earlier stages. It can suggest that "more developed" automatically means better or superior. In c-d theory, "more developed" actually means "more complex," which may or may not be "better" depending on circumstances (for instance, the demands of a situation, the people with whom one is interacting, the culture of one's organization).

As life becomes more complex (for example, as we take on the additional roles of spouse and parent or higher levels of responsibility at work, or both), development is both called forth and required for continued effectiveness—called forth in the sense that new, more complex sets of challenges invite us to look at the limitations of current ways of knowing self and others, and required in the sense that until and unless a person does develop more complex and more fully adequate ways of knowing self and others, he is limited in how well he can deal with new, more complex challenges. Kegan (1994) describes the demands of contemporary work in terms of the need to invent or own one's own work; to be self-initiating, self-correcting, and self-evaluating; to be guided by one's own vision; to take responsibility for what happens to oneself; to be an accomplished master of one's own work role, job, and career; to conceive of the organization from the outside in; and to see one's relationship to the whole. When development lags behind what is being demanded by life situations, as it usually does for most of us, we can feel as if we are in over our heads, that is, unable to cope with the complex demands we face.

One final note about the term *stage* is that it often connotes a resting place, an area where growth and development level off for a time. In c-d theory, most people are in developmental motion most of the time, so the idea of a resting place can be misleading.

For all of these reasons, there has been an effort to replace the term. Several alternatives are available. Ken Wilber (2000), whose work is compatible with c-d theory, uses the term *meme* to denote a particular set of values related to development stage. Mike Basseches (1984) has used *mode* to describe ways of being in the moment. Robert Kegan (1994) uses *order of consciousness* to refer to the degree of complexity of a person's awareness and knowledge of self and the world.

Although all of these proposed terms have benefits, they also have drawbacks. In this chapter, we use the term *web of belief.* We suggest that belief be thought of in terms of a habit of thought that provides a reliable guide to action (Peirce, 1877). A web of beliefs (as our proposed substitute for the term *stage*) would thus be understood as interconnected and mutually reinforcing beliefs forming an overall habitual way of thinking that guides a person's understanding, as well as his actions. Development—changes in the structure of a person's thinking and thus in the nature of his actions—could then be understood as the process of reweaving such webs of belief. The interpretation of development as reweaving avoids the idea that development dispenses with prior beliefs (significant portions of the earlier web are incorporated in the newly emerging web), that subsequent developments are necessarily better than earlier ones (the new web is a more complex arrangement of beliefs, whose "betterness" is tested against the effectiveness of the actions they support), and the idea that development results in resting places (people continually reweave their webs in the face of life's challenges).

If beliefs are habitual and reliable guides to action, then webs of belief can be thought of as leading to or supporting patterns of behavior. Because much of a coach's work with a coachee involves facilitating her desired behavioral change (her actions), this framing allows the coach to think of a coachee's behavior as a web of belief in action and points to the need to understand the web of belief in order to facilitate the change in behavior effectively. Later in this chapter, we describe a coaching process based on this idea of helping people to change behavior by facilitating this naturally developmental and belief-focused process.

Three Adult Webs of Belief

Because this book focuses on managerial and executive coaching, we are primarily interested here in three webs of belief that are central to development in the adult years. These three webs are important for how adults form their sense of self and understand their place in the world. To make these webs of belief easier to understand and remember, we adopt a metaphor of the self as a kind of book (Van Velsor & Drath, 2004).

Self-Reading. Adults begin their journey in adulthood with a web of beliefs that centers on "reading" the "book of the self" from within their most important interpersonal and professional relationships. An adult who knows himself by using this web of beliefs primarily understands himself through the reactions, responses, praise, blame, judgments, and evaluations of others. His understanding of himself is a composite of those significant others' views. This is the self-reading web of beliefs. Anyone who remembers the way it felt to be a teenager can relate to this way of knowing self. The identity of teenagers is for the most part determined by their parents' views (whether the teenager accepts or rejects them), the views of other significant adults (perhaps relatives and teachers), and the way their peers see them. As these others' views shift (and they frequently do), teenagers are regularly thrown off balance about who they are. They do not yet have a firm identity they can call their own, on which to base actions and decisions, no matter how much parents may demand it of them. Yet as we shall see, the self-reading web of beliefs maintains its usefulness, to some degree and for most people, well beyond the teenage years. Many teenagers are fully embedded in this web and begin to see its limitations only during the college years. But seeing the limitations and truly growing beyond those are two different things. Reweaving a web of beliefs is like building a bridge to cross a river. To feel fully safe and grounded in traveling across that bridge, people need more than a glimpse of the far shore. They need the safety of knowing their bridge is well anchored on both sides (Kegan, 1994). It takes time to build that bridge and then to be fully ready to journey across it.

The Move to Self-Authoring. The adult process of development continues as a person gradually reweaves the self-reading web of belief. Self-reading beliefs are often strongly challenged as people move into roles that make more complex and competing demands on their attention. Take, for example, the young manager recently promoted to a role where he supervises former peers, has a demanding boss, and has just started a family. Let's say this person has begun to see the limitations of the self-reading view, in that he no longer fully depends as he once did on others' views to know himself and to make decisions. However, he still feels torn by the strong and often conflicting demands he feels from his boss, his direct reports, and his family. The perspective most often relied on by the self-reading manager will provide few resources for managing these competing claims on his attention. He does not assume, as a fully self-authoring manager would, that the claims of others can be subordinated to a set of personally owned priorities and perspectives. The manager who still relies to some degree on the self-reading perspective will feel that conflicting demands are very difficult to reconcile, and tremendous stress can be a result. As this manager comes to see that he can understand and evaluate himself separately from how others view him (that he has his own independent point of view about himself), he will begin to have a stance that he fully owns to drive decisions about competing priorities. Rather than being torn and perhaps paralyzed by others' demands, he is more likely to see others' views as playing an informing role, helping him to understand what they need from him, but not necessarily setting the terms for his behavior. Instead of reading the book of himself in others, he begins to write his own book of the self, to reweave the web of beliefs from those of self-reading to self-authoring.

Often this developmental move is referred to as identity formation, or "figuring out who you really are." But this construction ignores the fact that before this developmental move is made, when a person is self-reading, he does have an identity and does know who he "really" is—but in terms given to him by important others. With the move to self-authoring, it is the way he understands his identity and the way he knows who he is that changes. Of course, changing the way he knows also changes what he knows. Once a significant ability to take the self-authoring perspective has set in, the manager in our example knows how to balance competing demands on a day-to-day basis by reconciling them to priorities that are his own.

Research into adult development has shown that in the United States, most professional adults (including managers and executives) are at a point of development that is somewhere between self-reading and self-authoring (Kegan, 1994). In other words, most adults have begun to reweave the self-reading web of beliefs they acquired in their teenage and early adult years, but have not yet become fully self-authoring. The journey from self-reading to self-authoring is indeed a long and difficult one. Later in this chapter, we discuss the nature of this move in more detail to help the leader coach understand how best to facilitate this movement in the coachee.

The Move to Self-Revising. The last stage of the adult journey of development (at least in c-d theory) begins with the reweaving of the self-authoring web of belief, which is again stimulated by experiencing life challenges that cause us to become aware of the limitations of a self-authored perspective.

So what kinds of experiences might challenge the self-authored manager to experience the limitations of her web of beliefs? When a manager has achieved the ability to be self-authoring, has a place to stand that she can call her own, and feels clear about her stance or her priorities, it can be difficult to work in a way that brings her own goals, viewpoints, or priorities into alignment with those of others. One reason managers derail at senior levels is due to strategic differences with higher management—being unable to let go of one's own stance even when it means having to leave the organization or be fired.

Few adults ever fully experience the limits of a self-authored view and move on to reweave their beliefs into a new web of beliefs we will call self-revising. This web centers on the understanding that the very self one has worked so hard to author and in which one instills so much integrity and wholeness is actually a construction that is somewhat arbitrary, built from available materials, so to speak, and not necessarily the only right and true self. The process of self-authoring is very much an ongoing project based on ideas, experiences, and relationships experienced within clan, culture, society, community, and profession. In reweaving from self-authoring to self-revising, the self one believed to be fully independent and to have its own distinct integrity comes finally to be understood as fully embedded in an ethos, and one's charge is to work and rework the self from the materials of that environment in one's own unique way, as new challenges surface the limitations of the existing self. In short, one comes to see oneself as an ongoing, self-generated, creative revision of received elements, including language, ideas, values, disciplines, and all the other elements by which one relates to others and to the world. As you might imagine, being able to move toward this web of beliefs supports a manager's ability to fully develop important capabilities such as cultural adaptability. And it is only when we begin to glimpse the possibilities inherent in reweaving our webs of beliefs in a self-revising way that we become, for the first time, truly able to "reinvent" ourselves.

Developmental Transition

These three webs of beliefs are ordered sequentially. It is in the process of becoming aware of and questioning the self-reading beliefs that a person becomes able to take on the self-authoring beliefs, and it is in the process of calling the self-authoring beliefs into question that a person becomes able to take on the self-revising beliefs. Table 12.1 summarizes the self-reading, self-authoring, and self-revising webs of belief.

Since most adults, and thus most managers, are doing their developmental reweaving somewhere between the self-reading and self-authoring webs of belief, it is this developmental transition to which we will pay the most attention in this chapter. In his book *In over Our Heads* (1994), Robert Kegan underscores the danger of assuming that every educated professional person, such as a highly placed manager, is or should be a fully self-authoring person and thus working at becoming self-revising. "If a great many of us are working with dignity and difficulty at the gradual transformation from [self-reading to self-authoring]," he asks, "how can we be expected to appreciate or understand a critique of the limits of [self-authoring]?" He goes on to say that "misattributing the nature of people's mental challenges jeopardizes our capacity to receive the actual people we hope to support. Misattributing the nature of the real mental transformations people are seeking makes us good company for the wrong journey" (pp. 336–337).

TABLE 12.1. THREE ADULT WEBS OF BELIEF.

Belief	Takes for Granted as True Beyond Question	Is Able to Reflect on and Call into Question
Self-reading	That identity can be understood by reading it in the way important other people respond	Childhood assumptions that the self is identical with one's needs and desires
Self-authoring	That one creates one's own identity according to self-generated standards	The role played by other people and important ideas and values in making a person who he or she is
Self-revising	That while being the author of an identity, one is responsible for continuously re-creating it in alignment with one's environment	The idea that a person can create a fully adequate identity once and for all from standards that are completely self-generated

It is our hope in writing this chapter that we can help leader coaches avoid being "good company for the wrong journey" with their coachees. Good coaches know that they must meet their coachees "where they are." Yet too often the assessment of "where they are" is limited to an assessment of the effectiveness of the coachee's behavior, sometimes with a behavioral goal in the coach's mind that may or may not be appropriate to the current web of belief most often used by the coachee. We return to the topic of assessment in more detail a bit later in the chapter.

One more important point: it is a mistake to think of the three categories we are describing (self-reading, self-authoring, self-revising) as distinct categories into which any adult can be placed developmentally. Development is more like the range of hues on a color spectrum, with each individual's web of beliefs incorporating or spanning several shades of a color at any one point in time. We've all seen teenagers who, although they mostly know themselves only through the eyes of significant others, are suddenly able to find and stand on their own convictions for a period of time or in the face of certain issues. The same phenomenon can be seen with adults. Managers fairly far along in the process of reweaving self-reading belief systems may, in many situations, be able to set direction for their units, manage competing priorities at work and at home, and handle other challenges that might typically overwhelm a person not as far along in the process of reweaving a self-reading identity.

However, such a person may get in over his head when asked to join a team of senior executives—let's say a team whose behavior or competencies he may not respect. Given that he has not fully moved to a self-authored stance developmentally, he may have doubts about whether he could join and make a contribution to this team without becoming "one of them." Although normally operating from a perspective that is almost wholly self-authoring, the individual with an incompletely rewoven web can experience a range of reactions and feelings in different situations and can exhibit a range of behaviors.

The process of developmental progression is a lengthy one that often involves taking two steps forward and one step back. As we will see, coaching can play a key role in both challenging an individual to press forward and in understanding and supporting those backward steps.

Linking Constructive-Developmental Theory to CCL's Coaching Framework

Constructive-developmental theory complements CCL's overall coaching framework. In this section, we discuss how c-d theory fits with this framework and point out some ways that we believe c-d theory can contribute to it.

CCL views coaching as having three important aspects: the context of the relationship in which the coaching occurs; the core elements of assessment, challenge, and support from CCL's leader development model; and the results that the coaching process aims to achieve. We begin at the core with a discussion of assessment, challenge, and support from a c-d perspective and then move on to discuss the aspects of relationship and results.

Assessment

Assessment is described by Ting and Hart (2004) as "an 'unfreezing' experience that enables a coachee to see herself differently or become more aware of how she affects others. Having a full picture of the coachee's current skills and perspectives, from her own view and from the perspective of others, is crucial to helping her decide what goals she wants to set" (p. 122). Assessment can be formal or informal. Examples of well-known types of formal assessment are multirater leadership instruments and personality assessments such as the Myers-Briggs Type Indicator. When we talk about informal assessment, we are often referring to the kinds of feedback one might get (or seek) on a more regular basis from colleagues, direct reports, or coaches—the in-the-moment answers to, "How am I doing?" whether solicited or unsolicited. The key to assessment's effectiveness is that it illuminates a gap between the person's current behaviors and some desired state or ideal capacity level (Van Velsor, 1998). Recognizing this gap is assumed to both motivate a person to change and to give him or her important resources for change.

From a c-d perspective, assessment can be formal or informal as well. A formal c-d assessment can be accomplished by using the "subject/object" interview (Lahey, Souvaine, Kegan, Godman, & Felix, n.d.) or the Loevenger Sentence Completion Test (Loevenger, 1976). While it might seem ideal for a coach to have a formal assessment of the web of belief from which a coachee is operating, the formal assessments currently available are cumbersome and fairly theoretical at best. We have experimented with a less formal process in which the coach enlists the coachee in a conversational process aimed at articulating a particular kind of question that seems to the coachee to be critically important to answer and at the same time strikes the coachee as being particularly difficult, if not impossible, to answer. We describe this process in more detail later. Another approach to helping people articulate their embedding web of belief without formal assessment is the "four columns" method developed and practiced by Robert Kegan and Lisa Lahey (2001).

An astute leader coach can use a good grounding in c-d theory and good listening skills to get some intuitive idea of the web of belief most often used by their coachee. For example, in reviewing feedback from a multirater survey, managers are confronted with differing views of important rater groups (boss, peers, direct reports, customers) on a set of leadership skill categories. When all competing views seem important, the manager using primarily a self-reading framework will often ask the coach which is the most important perspective to pay attention to. The individual seeks the coach's expert advice to relieve his or her anxiety about dealing with conflicting views. Anxiety may come from lacking a firm, self-authored view through which to filter and evaluate all other views. We say "may come" because we want to make clear here that unless there has been a reliable, formal assessment done (which we do not necessarily recommend), the coach is forming hypotheses about the framework being used by the coachee, without ever having complete certainty. But some understanding and a good working hypothesis is enough to improve a leader coach's practice and the results for those being coached.

Let's take a second example: another manager also being coached around some multirater feedback. This manager's reaction is different. Instead of wondering whose responses to pay attention to, she seems to act as if this is all good information but more in the sense that it helps her to see what small adjustments she could make to be more effective given who she is—her style, priorities, and skills. This is more the voice of a self-authored manager receiving feedback. She may interpret negative feedback as "just that person's view," something to be used to be more effective with that person or (if she is prepared to examine the limits of her current stance) as something to be perhaps better understood.

From a c-d perspective, assessment of the effectiveness of specific behaviors plays a role in the coachee's beginning to recognize concrete limitations in his current web of beliefs. Consider another example, a manager whose assessments reveal that she is hard to give negative feedback to. Her boss's ratings on this are especially low. Her coach might plausibly assume that this is feedback that is both important and relatively easy to respond to. A new and perception-changing behavior would be simply to ask her boss for feedback more often, to listen attentively, and then thank him for the feedback. The coach might even envision helping the manager see feedback as a learning opportunity, as a gift.

But if the manager makes sense of herself from the self-reading web of belief, she may not be able even to imagine the change that the coach has in mind. Negative feedback from her boss may be for her a direct and immediate attack on her very being, not a criticism of what she does, but a negative evaluation of who she is, which she absorbs with some anger and pain. Recognizing that understanding feedback in this way is only one way to understand it, that there are other possible reactions she might have, including one of gratitude, and that there is a gap between the way she feels now and the way she might feel, may not be possible for her. She cannot imagine having any other response to negative feedback, because she believes that the opinions and judgments of other people who are important to her reflect who she is. A belief is by its nature something that a person accepts as true, and therefore, before she can even imagine a different way to feel about negative feedback, she will have to learn to question the very truth of her current belief (that she needs to own someone else's view). From a c-d perspective, the value of the behavioral assessment (that is, eliciting the view that she is difficult to give feedback to) is that, with good coaching, it can play a part in helping her begin to recognize that her current beliefs impose limits on her effectiveness. For this to happen, the coach would need to explore the belief behind her being unable to hear negative feedback rather than asking her to simply change her behavior and solicit more feedback. Certainly, without coaching, the feedback would be hurtful and would not likely result in sustainable behavior change in the present.

The role of assessment from a c-d perspective is to help the person become more explicitly aware of the capacities and limitations of her current ways of thinking—her current web of belief—so as to enable her to move beyond those one day. This is slightly but significantly different from the equally important step of recognizing a gap between current behaviors and desired future behaviors. The important point is that a person may not be able to desire or pursue a new way of behaving that cannot currently be fully imagined or understood. We have all experienced this phenomenon—the good ideas we have so much trouble putting into practice.

Unlike an assessment of skills, an assessment (whether formal or informal) of the web of belief is not immediately or directly actionable. Knowing that one is somewhere between being self-reading and self-authoring is not especially useful knowledge in and of itself, and the goal of assessment is not to offer to a coachee any such labels. Being able to apply a label to one's current beliefs doesn't lead to ways to question those beliefs; it offers no way to begin feeling different feelings or thinking different thoughts. Assessment from a c-d perspective is less about identifying actionable gaps between current behaviors and desired future behaviors and is more about becoming aware of or articulating specific beliefs and their connection to specific limitations the person experiences in facing new challenges, achieving difficult goals, or changing behavior.

The assessment process has two goals: (1) for the coach and the coachee to be able to frame a useful level of challenge and (2) to provide the coach with a basis for meaningful support. Assessment is thus tied directly to challenge and support.

Challenge

The nature of challenge from a c-d perspective is directly related to the nature of belief. A person's web of belief is not a convenient set of ideas that can be applied or not as the person sees fit, but the very ground of what is true and real. Challenge in developmental terms involves the introduction of doubt and discomfort into the web of belief. These can come from an interaction with a coach or introduced through other types of challenge (a job assignment, for example). Too little challenge, too little doubt, and a manager will continue to cling to her current web of belief. Too much challenge, too much doubt, and the anxiety and threat of meaninglessness will drive the manager back to her accustomed and comfortable current beliefs. The purpose of assessment is to find the beliefs whose questioning will produce a level of challenge that is just right: beliefs that are usefully questionable though hard to question.

For example, suppose an IT manager has difficulty reconciling the demands of his boss for rapid results with the needs of his technically oriented staff to delay results until they get everything right. He feels torn between these conflicting demands. The outcome of this torn feeling is that his direct reports see him as making unreasonable demands on them in order to please his boss, while his boss sees him as making excuses for his staff and being unwilling to confront performance problems. From a purely behavioral point of view, it could be hard for him to see how he should change: get tougher on his direct reports and please his boss at the cost of further alienating them? Or align himself more solidly with his direct reports at the cost of further confirming his boss's judgment that he is not tough enough to be a good manager? By articulating what is most in conflict for him about these demands—that, for example, it is his way of looking to both his boss and his direct reports for affirmation of his effectiveness—he can better understand why the demands are conflicting. Because he has not questioned whether his boss's evaluation and the evaluations of his direct reports are synonymous with his effectiveness, he believes that who he is can be read in others' judgments of him. For this manager at this time, an appropriately challenging question might be: What would it mean for him to become less dependent on either his boss or his direct reports for affirmation of his effectiveness? Or what would it mean for him to have his own standard of effectiveness? From a coaching perspective, if he were able to establish his own self-generated sense of the right balance between speed and quality, he would be establishing his own measure of effectiveness and would feel less torn between two external views. From that point of balance, he could more effectively manage both his boss's expectations and his staff's needs and performance. He could comfortably state his sense of priorities and engage in a dialogue about how his own standards fit with the needs and expectations of others. As a result, he would likely be seen as exercising more leadership, having more leadership stature, and being more decisive.

This question, based on an assessment of the manager's web of belief, is presumably just challenging enough to facilitate development. It neither asks the person to move toward new feelings, thoughts, and beliefs that he cannot imagine, nor does it take his current feelings, thoughts, and beliefs as fully adequate to his situation. It enables the manager to begin experimenting with some new and potentially more useful beliefs about who places demands on him and why. He might, for example, begin by simply paying more attention to the way the judgments of others influence his judgments of himself. In time this might lead him to recognize some ways in which his own judgments of himself are independent of the judgments of others. Gradually framing these self-judgments as increasingly important to him in time might help him take the judgments of others more as judgments he can reflect on and evaluate. In the end, he might come to change his beliefs about the demands of his boss and his direct reports, seeing them more as possibly legitimate views that he can subordinate to his own. Not only would he then feel less torn, but he might also have developed as a manager who is better able to handle conflicting demands in general, because his beliefs about the claims that conflicting demands necessarily place on him have changed.

Support

The second goal of assessment in c-d theory is to provide a basis for support. As described elsewhere in this book, support exists as a supportive environment. Leader coaches can meet their coachee's need for support by helping the coachee to identify motivators that will sustain a commitment to growth and sustain the coachee through the sometimes uncomfortable learning process, to recognize small wins and manage setbacks or lulls in growth, and to identify and access resources and tactics necessary for success. Clearly a coach needs to be supportive of the coachee in these critical aspects. However, the leader coach with a c-d perspective understands another critical aspect of support that is directly related to the need to find the right balance between not enough challenge and too much.

This is the need for the coach to fully appreciate the coachee's current web of belief. We have already discussed the tenacity with which a person clings to her beliefs, understanding them to be no less than the ground of her being. What is often referred to as resistance to change is in this light not so much resistance to taking on new beliefs as it is the very practical reluctance to give up current beliefs. Development, when conceived as the reweaving of beliefs, always involves a distinct loss—the loss of the wholeness and integrity of the web that is being rewoven. The old web gives truth and value; the new web, as yet unwoven, is of unknown truth and value. If I change, the coachee has a right to ask, "What will I lose?" Definitely, for some period of time, some measure of certainty, some sense of comfort, and some value will feel lost. The coach working from a c-d perspective provides support by becoming intimately aware of the cost to the coachee of changing her beliefs and by communicating this awareness to the coachee in ways that show the coach's appreciation for the coachee's current beliefs and the difficulty of the journey. This supportive stance avoids the danger of allowing the coach's zeal to facilitate change to result in the coachee's feeling that her current beliefs are unworthy or that she is being pushed across a bridge that is still dangerously under construction. Remember that although the coachee may see that her behaviors are limiting or inadequate, the beliefs that act as reliable guides to those behaviors are real and true. Calling those beliefs into question, even contemplating changing them, is not only painful but involves actual loss—the loss of meaning, of rational justification, of values. To provide support from a c-d perspective, the coach must be aware of this loss in specific terms; the coach must know exactly what the coachee stands to lose in the process of development. Without this kind of support, any level of challenge sufficient to motivate development is likely to be experienced as too much challenge by the coachee. Support of this kind—as appreciation for what the coachee stands to lose—is the key factor in balancing the amount of challenge.

From a c-d perspective, the core elements of assessment, challenge, and support fit together as follows: assessment points to the most useful beliefs to call into question, those that are most important currently for the coachee's development; challenge is about exploring the limits of current beliefs and creating enough disequilibrium to call forth change; and support provides the balancing counterforce to challenge, keeping it from being too much for the person to handle.

Relationship

Ting and Hart (2004) make a critical point with respect to relationship: "If the coach becomes overly invested in maintaining a harmonious relationship or the relationship becomes too personal, the coach may find himself reluctant to challenge the coachee, or the coach may be infringing on boundaries that exceed the scope of the coaching relationship" (p. 120). From a c-d perspective, this important point surfaces the issue of the coach's web of belief as compared to that of the coachee.

There are many possible goals for a coaching relationship. Sometimes the goal of coaching is for the coach to give the coachee the benefit of the coach's more extensive knowledge of some area of expertise. Or the coach might aim mainly at giving the coachee the benefit of the coach's more extensive experience in the organization, helping the coachee navigate the formal and informal systems, the career opportunities, and the politics of the organizations. In such cases, the extent of the coach's personal development in comparison with that of the coachee is not important. Only the coach's greater knowledge and experience count. If the goal of the coaching relationship is to facilitate the development of the coachee, that is, to help the coachee grow and mature as a person, the coach should be considerably more developed (understand self and others more complexly) than the coachee.

In c-d terms, being considerably more developed than the coachee translates to the idea that the coach, assuming the coachee makes sense of himself mostly from the self-reading web of beliefs, should make sense of herself and her world mostly from the self-authoring web of beliefs. And if the coachee operates mostly from the self-authoring web, the coach should operate mostly from the self-revising web. This is not to say that people operating from the same web of beliefs cannot be helpful to one another in their growth and development: it is almost always helpful to have someone to talk to about the issues and conflicts in life that are difficult to deal with. But if the relationship is to be something more than the sympathetic ear of a friend or colleague—something more like mentoring, providing guidance, and helping the person make important judgments and decisions—then the coach should be significantly more mature than the coachee.

It is important for the coach in these circumstances to understand what is difficult for the coachee from a more developed (more complex) perspective than the one the coachee uses to understand his difficulties. If the coach cannot see the challenges the coachee faces from a more complex perspective, she is unlikely to be able to add much to what the coachee already knows. Remember that a change in web of belief is a change not just in what a person knows but a change in how the person knows. This is often just exactly what the coachee needs most: a different way to think about the challenges he is facing—not just more information about those challenges or advice about them, but a whole new approach to them. Because the coach has already built and crossed the very bridge the coachee is trying to build and travel, she sees the coachee's challenges from the other side of the river. From that vantage point, things look quite different, and she can use this difference in perspective to help the coachee anchor the bridge firmly on both sides.

Results

According to CCL's coaching framework, results occur in three areas: behavior change, personal and professional development, and learning agility. From a c-d perspective, the relationship between the first two (behavior change and development) depends on the meaning of the behavior within the person's current web of belief. We already discussed an example of a self-reading manager who is not seen as open to feedback. However, it is also possible for a manager who firmly believes that his identity is self-authored to be seen by his peers as not being open to feedback. Perhaps this is because, consistent with his self-authoring beliefs, he relies almost completely on his own evaluations of his behavior. In response to information that his peers are dissatisfied, however, he can change this behavior and even begin to solicit feedback from his peers. He can do this while holding to his self-authoring belief simply by framing feedback from peers as their legitimate independent views telling him what he needs to do (given who he is) to be more effective with his peers.

If we take this same behavior change and apply it to a manager who firmly believes that her identity is read in the judgments of others, the issue of being open to feedback from peers is likely to be more emotionally charged, as in the example described earlier. In this case, a change in behavior (attempting to seek more feedback) is likely to call forth a reweaving of the manager's web of belief, to involve the issues of developmental loss, and to be difficult and painful. A coach who is unacquainted with developmental frameworks might interpret the first manager as being "open to change" and even characterize him as possessing "learning agility" because he appears to be better able to incorporate the feedback directly into new behaviors. As this example shows, such characterizations, while true enough, may point more to the developmental phase that a person is moving through than it does to any enduring characteristic of the person. The lesson for leader coaches is that when a coachee seems to be "resistant to change," she may be experiencing the called-for behaviors as threats to her sense of what is right, valuable, and true—in short, as threats to her current web of belief. This is where the coach's support—the appreciation for her current beliefs and for the cost to her of even contemplating a change in those beliefs—is especially helpful.

Unlike some other approaches to coaching, coaching from a c-d perspective means being less focused on immediate results in the form of behavior change. Although sometimes immediate changes are highly appropriate and need to be made, the coach cannot be sure that such changes will be accompanied by a change in the coachee's web of belief. As such, immediate changes are not developmentally charged and may not be as significant for building long-term leadership capacity. When working from a c-d perspective, the leader coach has an interest in facilitating the process of reweaving the web of belief in areas connected to behaviors that limit the coachee's effectiveness. A person can begin to significantly reweave his web of belief without making any changes to his behavior at all. The process of change takes place at first in the meaning of his behavior. Gradually changes in the meaning of behavior begin to bring about changes in the behavior itself. Thus, results from a c-d perspective can be immediate in the form of questioning and reframing beliefs, and they can be immediate in the form of behavior change. But immediate behavior change is less important in the long run than the process of reweaving the web of belief.

To ground this discussion of c-d theory, here is a brief case study of coaching from a c-d perspective. The leader coach in this case is not a professional HR coach and uses no special methodology.

Developmental Coaching from a C-D Perspective: A Case Study

Muriel is Alex's former boss. Alex has been having a great deal of difficulty in his new job, which has him working side-by-side with high-level managers, attending high-level meetings, and in many ways performing executive-level tasks—but without an executive title. Alex is still a director, whereas everyone he interacts with as virtual peers is a vice president. He knows he shouldn't let this bother him, but it does. Alex feels embarrassed by his "one-down" status; in addition, he believes that it is basically unfair to be asked to do executive-level work without the executive title; finally, he is stung by being excluded from some executive activities, such as the monthly vice president–only luncheons. In general, he feels that he is being used, and he has become increasingly resentful.

Muriel was always someone Alex felt he could talk to. She is about twenty years his senior, has more years with the company, and when she was his boss had an open door policy. So one day he calls on her to talk about his resentment at the way he is being treated.

As she listens to him pour out his story, Muriel reflects on how much Alex has matured. When he used to work for her, he was constantly getting his nose out of joint over all kinds of imagined and real slights; people said he had a chip on his shoulder. Now, while the issue may seem to be the same, Alex's approach to it is different. He is aware that he "shouldn't feel this way," as he keeps saying, but he can't stop himself from feeling embarrassed, one down, left out, and used. Where before he believed his resentments were righteous and fully justified, now he seems to sense that they are out of place somehow. Yet he can't stop feeling resentful.

Muriel recognizes that Alex has come to her at a key moment for him developmentally. This recognition is based on the fact that she can see how he has changed his attitude from one of righteous injustice to hurt and puzzled resentment. Something is changing in his beliefs about these things. He seems ready to take another step; the trick is to help him take it, whatever it might be.

Muriel has been where Alex is now. It was not the same situation, of course, but it had the same meaning, since it involved letting others set the terms by which she judged her own value. She is thus now able to recognize that what Alex is missing, in a sense, is a way to set his own standards; he is too caught up in the standards implicit in the words *director* and *vice president* to see his own standards at work.

She asks him, "What's so important to you about being a vice president?"

This question surprises him. "Are you kidding? It's what I'm working for; it's my goal. It's a recognition that I'm there, doing that kind of work. Getting the title would say I belong there. It's a gold star on my report card."

"But aside from the obvious things, like more money and recognition, what good is a gold star to you?"

"It means I'm appreciated for my true abilities."

"Yes, but apart from everything that the gold star would signal to others about you, what would it mean to you alone?"

This last question rattled around in Alex's mind for a long time afterward. What got to him about this question was that it seemed so obvious, and yet he had no answer to it. Every time he thought of an answer, he would see how the answer was really about what the gold star would say about him to others. This frustrated him. After all, it was important how others saw him. In an organizational environment, promotions, good jobs, and challenging assignments all hung on what others thought of you. So why did it bother him so much that he couldn't come up with a single answer to the question of what the gold star would mean to him alone?

Over the next year, Alex and Muriel sat down from time to time to talk through this question of what it would mean to him alone to be a vice president. Muriel helped

Alex think through this question by helping him frame his ongoing experiences with the executives and his feelings about those experiences in terms of the question. Once there was an issue made about his presence in a meeting. One of the vice presidents felt he should be asked to leave the meeting because certain personnel discussions were going to take place. "It's not appropriate for someone who is not a vice president to be here," the executive said. Alex was asked to leave, and he felt humiliated as he got up to go. But on his way to the door, he asked himself why he felt this way. Why should being asked to leave humiliate him? He knew the vice president who asked him to leave was just playing politics. Alex didn't approve of such tactics, so why should he feel any way except somewhat contemptuous of the vice president who made an issue over his presence? By the time he got to the door, the feelings of humiliation had vanished to be replaced by a very new feeling: indignation that the vice president in question had violated Alex's own values. Instead of feeling humiliated, he felt a little sorry for the vice president who had made such a fuss and had probably gone down in the estimate of the other vice presidents.

When Alex told Muriel this story, she asked him, "What was the most important part about how your feelings changed as you left the room?"

Alex thought for a while. Finally he said, "I'm not sure. Maybe the most important thing was that I thought to challenge myself about feeling humiliated."

"And does that give you any insight into what it would mean to you alone to be a vice president?"

"Well, for sure, I wouldn't be a vice president who plays politics. And I wouldn't try to embarrass subordinates."

The process of continually posing this question of himself, of living with the question, concluded in the question's dissolving and becoming irrelevant. What Alex finally came to understand was that the gold star itself had no meaning to him alone; its only meaning was in terms of what others thought. The gold star came to stand for what others cared about in his performance, as distinct from what he cared about in his performance. The paradoxical question of what the gold star meant to him alone dissolved as Alex realized there was a difference between what he thought of himself and what others thought of him. He saw how to make his own "gold stars" and award them to himself. Titles such as vice president and accolades from superiors were still as important as ever in terms of promotions, good jobs, and challenging work, but such things were no more than data points in terms of his own self-evaluation.

This illustrative story emphasizes that from a c-d perspective, developmental coaching can happen when someone comes along to help the coachee frame just the right kind of question at the right time. What was it about the question, "What would it mean to you alone to get the gold star of becoming a vice president?" that was just right and at just the right time for Alex?

It makes sense to think of Alex as being somewhere between the self-reading and the self-authoring webs of belief. This means Alex would be working at being able to be reflective and objective about the whole realm of his interpersonal relationships, especially about how people who are very important to him, such as the executives in his company, feel about him, react to him, and judge him. It makes sense to see him as being between the self-reading and the self-authoring webs of belief based on Muriel's understanding of how he has matured since the earlier years when she was his boss. She especially notices the way he recognizes that he "shouldn't" feel embarrassed and resentful about his "one-down" status in relation to the vice presidents. This can indicate that Alex is beginning to be able to reflect on the feelings caused by his relationship to others. Being able to reflect on those feelings, being able to take them more as an object under his own control, is a capacity of the self-authoring web of beliefs. He knows he shouldn't feel the way he does, but "he can't help it." Yet not being able to do anything about his feelings, feeling subject to them, can indicate that Alex is also still somewhat embedded in the self-reading web of belief. His position in the self-reading perspective comes across in the way that his feelings of being embarrassed and stung and resentful are the immediate outcome of things that happen in his relationship with important others. Yet he is beginning to reflect on and evaluate the feeling he has.

The question that Muriel helps Alex ask himself is poised right on the brink between the self-reading and self-authoring webs of belief, pretty much right where Alex is himself. In helping Alex ask himself what it would mean to him alone to gain the gold star of recognition of being made a vice president, Muriel is helping Alex reweave the self-reading web of belief by which the phrase "you alone" is not fully meaningful, since in the beliefs of that web, "you" simply means "what others see in me." There is no "aloneness" in the self from the perspective of the self-reading web of belief. If Alex were completely embedded in the self-reading web, this question would not make much, if any, sense to him. And if he had already rewoven his beliefs and made sense of himself from the self-authoring web of belief, the question would be easily answerable: he would know what the gold star would mean to "him alone." Were that the case, he might have said that he wanted the vice president role because he felt stale in his current role and wanted to find more interesting work, that he wanted more ability to influence a more significant part of the organization, or any number of responses that reflect a clear sense of what the role would mean for him alone. But because he is between the self-reading and self-authoring webs of belief, the question is simultaneously important and meaningful (from the perspective of the emerging self-authoring web) and mysterious and unanswerable (from the perspective of the changing self-reading web).

This case also raises the issue of the coach's readiness for providing this kind of coaching. Could anyone have helped Alex frame the question that played such an important role in his development from self-reading to self-authoring? Probably not. What prepared Muriel to be a valuable coach for Alex was that she had already made her journey from self-reading to self-authoring. Because she had already built a bridge from self-reading to self-authoring and now stood on the self-authoring side of the river, Muriel could see more clearly than Alex what lay ahead for him. Because she had already faced and worked through the question of her self-authored identity, she was able to help Alex frame a similar question about himself. It was the perspective gained by having gone through what Alex was now going through that provided the necessary wisdom. This is why, in general, for a coach to be able to provide this kind of developmental challenge and support, he or she should have already fully reached the web of belief toward which the coachee is moving.

By the end of the story, Alex has made a significant move in the direction of the self-authoring web of belief. The experience of questioning his immediate feelings of humiliation is a demonstration to himself that he can take the thoughts and feelings that arise in the interpersonal arena as something more under his control: he is more able to reflect, evaluate, and make decisions about these thoughts and feelings. As a manager, his effectiveness increased because he was able to work with less anxiety about how others saw him and with more of an eye to living up to his own high standards. As he told Muriel much later, "I work to please myself, and as for rewards and recognition, I just let that take care of itself."

A Conversation-Based Approach to Constructive-Developmental Theory

In this section we describe, in some depth, an approach to coaching that is based on a c-d perspective. The approach is conversation based; we have used it working with teachers, counselors, and administrative staff in a school system and working with upper to midlevel managers in a large insurance company.

Although we are not suggesting that a coach needs to follow this approach in order to facilitate development and change in a coachee's web of beliefs, we do believe that having a more concrete understanding of at least one approach can provide a fuller grasp of the level of informal assessment that can be gained through structured conversation. Understanding our approach may give you a clearer idea of how a coach can form useful working hypotheses about the web of beliefs most often used by a coachee.

We call our approach reflective leadership conversations (RLC). As suggested by the name, this process is conversation based, focused on issues of management and leadership, and designed to promote reflection. It begins with contracting with the coachee around confidentiality and getting agreement on the overall goals. We are explicit that the goal of RLC is not immediate behavior change and that behavior change may or may not result from this process. We explain to the coachee that the goal is to articulate a focal question that will facilitate exploration of an important underlying belief or assumption that may be blocking him or her in becoming more effective in their work. We describe the process in general, which consists of two sessions and a series of follow-up telephone calls.

The first session is a ninety-minute one-on-one conversation between the coach and coachee, which is recorded and later transcribed. This conversation as we conduct it generally follows the outlines of what is called a "subject-object" interview, a c-d approach developed by Lisa Lahey and her colleagues and described in "A Guide to the Subject-Object Interview" (Lahey et al., n.d.). The subject-object interview is designed to help the coach (and eventually the coachee) discern areas of the coachee's thoughts and feelings as a manager and leader that are definitely "object" (those that the manager can already articulate and examine) and begin to understand those beliefs to which the coachee might be "subject" (those the manager has yet to become fully aware of). This is the process whereby we as coaches are forming our hypothesis about the coachee's current web of belief. For the coach, one goal of this initial conversation is to delineate a kind of general dividing line between what the coachee tends to be able to "take as object" and what he tends to "take as subject." We call this dividing line the "growing edge," because it is just at the cusp between what the coachee can reflect on and make decisions about and what he is assuming is true without yet being able to test or examine. It is the place where we believe many of the most pressing developmental issues lie. A second goal of this initial interview is to surface the actual experiences and events that the person is having the most difficulty with and to get the person to describe these in some detail. We assume that there is a close connection between the "subject-object" dividing line and the nature of the person's most difficult challenges. That is, we assume that the challenges a person describes as his or her most difficult challenges will have elements that reflect the limitations of a certain web of beliefs (as in the earlier examples of the self-reading manager feeling challenged by having to face the conflicting work and family demands). The conversation begins by having the coachee look over a list of words and phrases. The prompts are drawn from the subject-object interview guide (Lahey et al., n.d.). They include *angry; anxious, nervous; success; strong stand, conviction; sad; torn; moved, touched; lost something; change;* and *important to me.* The coachee is asked to reflect on these words and phrases, and if any of them is connected in some way to an important or memorable managerial or leadership experience that the coachee has had recently, the coachee is asked to jot down some notes next to the appropriate word or phrase as a way of reminding herself of the connection. The coachee is given five to ten minutes to do this. The coach then asks the coachee to look over the list and select one of the events she has made a note about—one that she would especially like to spend some time talking about. The coachee is then invited to tell the coach about this experience.

The coach listens to her story in two ways. The first way is to understand the content of the story. It is critical that the coach understand what happened, who was involved, what the coachee did, what feelings she had, and what the outcome was. The coach asks questions to clarify the content and expresses empathy for the coachee. The second way the coach listens is for how the coachee makes sense of the events of the story: What beliefs did the coachee seem to take for granted in living through the events of the story, and what beliefs does she take for granted in retelling it now? On the other hand, what aspects of the story did the coachee seem to be able to reflect on and make judgments about? This second way of listening is aided by the coach's asking specific types of questions, different from questions of clarity. These are questions aimed at a better understanding of the coachee's beliefs related to the story. Such questions tend to be many variations of asking "why?" such as, "I'm interested in the fact that you felt angry about that. I wonder why you felt anger at that moment." The coach needs to understand the best ways of asking the "why" question, since it can be interpreted in a number of negative ways by the coachee. The coach may also learn more about the coachee's beliefs by finding out about the extremes of the story ("What was most important about that?" "What made you the most angry about those words?"); asking about the cost to the coachee of behaving in certain ways ("What would you have risked by telling him about the report?"); asking about what would be important in terms of the outcomes of an event ("How would you have ideally liked this to turn out?"); and asking the coachee how she evaluates an event ("How do you know when you've succeeded in that situation?") (Lahey et al., n.d.). A list of potential question stems is contained in Exhibit 12.1.

A few weeks after the session, the coachee receives a transcript of the recorded conversation. Along with the transcript, the coachee also gets a set of guidelines for reading and interpreting the transcript. This is an important feature as it enlists the coachee as a full partner in coming to understanding

EXHIBIT 12.1. USEFUL QUESTION STEMS FOR CONSTRUCTIVE-DEVELOPMENTAL COACHING.

The following is not a list of interview questions; rather, it is intended to provide examples of the kinds of questions that help people reflect on their experience in a more developmental way.

1. What, if anything, would have changed ______________________
   [for example, the way the coachee felt about some situation or what some situation meant to the coachee]?
2. What was the worst thing about ______________________
   [for example, some undesirable situation or feeling the coachee has just described]?
3. What was the best thing about ______________________
   [for example, some desirable situation or feeling]?
4. What would be the cost to you of ______________________
   [for example, behaving in some way that the coachee finds difficult]?
5. What would be an important outcome for you if ______________________
   [for example, the coachee were able to do something he or she found difficult]?
6. How have you come to understand ______________________
   [for example, a judgment or evaluation that the coachee has made, such as, How have you come to understand that you shouldn't speak up to your boss?]?

Source: These questions are based on Lahey et al. (n.d.).

his beliefs and their effect on his behavior. The guidelines for interpreting the transcript are fairly simple. He is asked to keep his eyes open as he reads for (1) anything that really jumps out at him; (2) any places in the conversation where he seems to be uncertain, stuck, or puzzled; (3) any ideas or feelings he talks about in one place in the transcript that seem to conflict with ideas or feelings he talks about in another place; and (4) any places where he talks about good ideas he has that he is having trouble putting into practice.

Each of these guidelines has a specific purpose in preparing the coachee for the second session. Guideline 1 draws out anything in the transcript that the coachee finds surprising or otherwise noteworthy. It is a kind of catch-all guideline that ensures that something the coachee found especially noticeable will not fall by the wayside. Guideline 2 may point to some instances of the coachee's current ways of understanding encountering limits. This can help in discerning areas of challenge to his current web of belief. Guideline 3 points to internal conflicts, which may be indicators that the coachee is in the process of reweaving his web of beliefs; old beliefs may be coming into conflict with newly emerging beliefs. Finally, guideline 4 helps surface areas in the coachee's life where he has an intellectual grasp on a new behavior—in much the way that Alex knew that he "shouldn't" be feeling embarrassed—but is unable to actually put new behavior into practice. Like guideline 3, this can point to specific movements between webs of belief. The coachee is asked to arrive at the second session having gone over the transcript of session 1, using these four guidelines, and to bring along any notes he has made.

The second coaching session is the heart of the process. The goal of this session is to articulate a focal question. Like the question that Muriel asked of Alex, a focal question is poised in the space between what a coachee believes now and what she might believe differently in the future. It is a tool for moving beliefs to which the coachee is "subject" closer to being "object" by making those beliefs a literal object of questioning. In our practice, two coaches and one coachee participate in the second session. The three of them work together as equal partners, each bringing a perspective to the proceedings. Both coaches have studied the transcript of the initial conversation, noting the same features that the coachee has been asked to notice: things that are surprising, places where the coachee seems stuck, indicators of an internal conflict, and good ideas the coachee is having trouble putting into practice. The coachee goes first and puts on a flip chart any key ideas she has developed as a result of studying the transcript. The coaches ask questions for clarity only at this point. Then in turn, each coach fills out a similar flip chart. With the three flip charts on the wall, the coaches and the coachee spend some time reflecting on what is there, looking for similarities and differences. When everyone is ready, a dialogue begins.

The goal of the dialogue is made explicit: to articulate a focal question that meets the following criteria: (1) the question is one that the coachee owns, not one she is adopting because she thinks it is important to the coaches; (2) the question is on a matter of critical importance now for the coachee; (3) the question is paradoxical, puzzling, and not answerable now; (4) the question does not lead to immediate action. These criteria ensure that the focal question is one that the coachee can live with for at least a number of months, if not for a year or more. The process of arriving at the focal question is one of working and reworking the material on the flip charts. The coaches use the same kind of subject-object prompts that were used in the initial conversation to draw out the coachee's reflection. As an important topic area begins to emerge, the coaches will begin to guide the coachee toward thinking about putting what they have discovered in dialogue into the form of a question of the form: "What would it mean for me to . . . " or "What would it mean if I . . . ," followed by a statement of some feeling, thought, or behavior that seems especially problematic or even paradoxical to the person. The problematic or paradoxical nature of the focal question is related to the fact that it calls into question a current belief.

Some examples of focal questions created in this process follow. Each reflects both the particular challenges the individual was facing and their common struggle with the transition from some degree of self-reading to a more fully self-authoring perspective:

- What would it mean for me to play my own game and have my own scorecard?
- What would it mean to see myself as a role model for a new kind of executive position?
- What would it mean for me to work at my current capacity while working at a pace more in tune with others?
- What would it mean for me to be open and authentic about my passions 100 percent of the time, while also being heard and viewed as objective and willing to negotiate?
- What would it mean to easily be in the minority view myself, as part of my job, and to balance my view with those of multiple others?

The issues touched on by focal questions range from dealings with direct reports to relations with superiors to career concerns. The last criterion for an effective focal question (that it is not immediately actionable) may seem odd given the frequent desirability for "action items" to come out of the coaching processes. But aspects of a person's experience that can be immediately addressed by changes in behavior are probably those about which the person is already aware, and thus do not involve a developmental change in beliefs. From a c-d perspective, coaching is about helping people with just those aspects of their behavior that they are finding "impossible" to change—helping them surface and understand the assumptions they are making about self, given the challenges they are facing at work and in other areas of their lives. (See Exhibit 12.2 for a list of situations that challenge managers who are self-reading and situations that challenge managers who are self-authoring.)

We therefore ask people not to take action on a focal question, but to "live" with it. Living with a focal question consists of (1) putting the question into the back of one's mind and (2) taking special notice of events that bring the focal question to the front of one's mind. What is it in a person's experience that makes him or her think of the focal question? Why does that event bring up the focal question? Does having the focal question in the back of one's mind change the way one makes sense of certain events? These are the questions that are dealt with in the third phase of the process, the telephone check-ins.

About one month following the focal question session, we begin checking in with the coachee. Over five to six months, we check in three times. These

EXHIBIT 12.2. SITUATIONS THAT CHALLENGE SELF-READING AND SELF-AUTHORING MANAGERS.

Self-reading manager challenges
- Being in an ill-defined role or a corporate role
- Facing competing demands
- Moving to a new or senior level
- Taking a minority position in a group or with a superior

Self-authoring manager challenges
- Motivating others around vision
- Working with people who are not self-authoring
- Balancing honesty with sensitivity
- Working collaboratively

check-ins focus on current happenings in the coachee's work life that he feels are related to his focal question. Our role in these calls is to ask further questions of the subject-object type we asked in the initial interview and the second session. The goal of the check-ins is to provide continuing challenge and support to the coachee over an extended period of time.

Participant reactions to this coaching process have been positive. In our evaluation of the process so far, the most important benefits mentioned include (1) the support of having someone to talk with about experiences and issues, (2) forming and using the focal question (the process and results provided a good framework to articulate thoughts and feelings, and created greater focus), and (3) greater self-awareness (being aware of frustrations, feelings, and assumptions, and gaining some control). Participants felt these benefits were important because they were enabled to gain better focus through the process and to release nonproductive energy, as well as a resulting experience of having more self-confidence to speak up and of being able to turn a self-defeating attitude into a more positive one. People also reported feeling more self-determination, feeling more productive and engaged, and being more of a "free thinking" leader instead of a "yes person."

Conclusion

Coaching from a constructive-developmental perspective is especially useful when the person being coached seems to be stuck. A person who is stuck often sees the need for change, may even express a great desire to change, and yet somehow cannot change. Something seemingly out of the person's control and unknown to him or her seems to be getting in the way. Often what that something turns out to be is a web of beliefs that is no longer as useful as it once was. The use of a c-d approach in such instances can help the leader coach identify what specific beliefs, taken for granted as true by the coachee, are guiding the behaviors that are causing the difficulties. Understanding these beliefs, the coach may then be able to help the coachee formulate a focal question. Such a question will have the paradoxical qualities for the coachee of being important and in pressing need of an answer while at the same time striking him or her as being somehow unanswerable. If the coach makes sense of self in a significantly more developed way (more complex way) than the coachee, the answer to the question may seem quite obvious. This is when the coach needs to realize that the purpose of such a focal question is not so much to find the answer as to be an aid in crossing the bridge the coachee has been building, to arrive on the other side where the question loses both its importance and its mystery.

In many ways, taking a c-d perspective on coaching means nothing more than the coach being very aware and sensitive to learn what is most important for the person being coached: the beliefs he or she holds dear but are nonetheless blocking his or her intended and desired path of change. This awareness and sensitivity allows the coach to understand both the costs of changing those beliefs and the rewards of changing behavior, and thus helps the coachee transcend barriers and move toward greater effectiveness.

Coach's Bookshelf

Fitzgerald, C., & Berger, J. G. (2002). *Executive coaching: Practices and perspectives.* Palo Alto, CA: Davies-Black.

Torbert, B. (2004). *Action inquiry: The secret of timely and transforming leadership.* San Francisco: Berrett-Koehler.

Wilber, K. (2000). *A theory of everything.* Boston: Shambhala.

PART FIVE

EXTENDING THE COACHING PRACTICE

Despite its relatively short existence as a formal practice, coaching has quickly expanded its commonly understood construct of a single, face-to-face, one-on-one counselor-like engagement. This growing interest by organizations to extend the practice into other arenas, and with new techniques and modalities, reflects the benefits that they see in using coaching as an essential leadership development tool. Increasingly, organizations are looking toward coaching teams, coaching that's linked to action learning, coaching in large-scale development initiatives, and coaching as a core competency for leaders, managers, and HR professionals.

The chapters in Part Five describe some of the ways in which CCL has extended its practice. Chapter Thirteen examines the use of technology in coaching and discusses some of the challenges involved with incorporating technology and virtual approaches that suggest that coaches may need some different skills to work effectively with these rapidly evolving tools.

Chapter Fourteen describes CCL's experiences with coaching from an organizational and team perspective. This includes a discussion of the types of coaching initiatives that can occur on an organizational level, the use of team coaching, the logistical and boundary management challenges as well as opportunities both present, and the leader coach's role in those types of engagements.

Finally, in Chapter Fifteen, we turn to the aspirations we hear organizations express about creating a coaching culture. We explore what we mean by coaching culture, what organizations can do to support its development, and recommended practices to sustain coaching as an effective way of operating within the organizational culture.

CHAPTER THIRTEEN

BLENDED COACHING

Mary Lynn Pulley

Here is a common refrain from a manager who coaches several of his coworkers in offices around the country: "I'm tired of traveling, and I have certain coachees in the branch offices who refuse to give up our coaching sessions. Even though the coachees initially did not want to move from face-to-face meetings to the phone, they ultimately did, and it has been fine. I think that the cost of travel, the inconvenience, fear of flying after 9/11, and a lot of other factors will support my using blended coaching methods even if the initial reaction from my coworkers was, 'I don't want it.'"

This situation typifies both the dilemma and the opportunity for many leader coaches. When traditional face-to-face coaching is not feasible, the solution is blended coaching, a combining, or blending, of various delivery methods during coaching interactions. This includes face-to-face meetings and using the telephone, and a variety of technological (distance) solutions described in this chapter.

The biggest factors for the rise in blended coaching are the convergence of advances in technology, the pervasiveness of the Internet, and the global economy, all of which have led to greater dispersion of the workforce. Because people and industries are less geographically bound and the pace of work is accelerating, it is difficult to create solutions that are geographically limited.

It is now possible to coach individuals from afar and put together work teams and coaching teams that offer the best skills or solutions regardless of where in the world the people are located.

Because this is an emerging area, it holds one of the highest challenges for leader coaches. In addition to the coaching process itself, coaches must assess their own comfort and skill level with emerging technological tools as well as the comfort and skill level of their coachees. In addition, coaches must make decisions about what combination of solutions is most appropriate for given situations. There is no established formula to determine the responses to these issues.

This chapter is based on two assumptions about coaching. First, it assumes that people develop over time and that coaching has greater impact when assessment, challenge, and support underpin the developmental agenda. Second, it assumes that coaching is a learning process and that it is useful to make this link very clear to coachees. The examples in this chapter show how distance coaching is an integral part of a training program, where organizations perceive coaching as an investment in their people rather than a remedial effort aimed at poor performers. In these examples, coaching becomes a key extension of the training process by showing how targeted goals that are identified and developed through assessment, challenge, and support on the job enhance the impact of any training experience.

When I refer to blended coaching, I am including at least one face-to-face session in addition to other modalities. Because the other chapters in this book describe various facets of face-to-face coaching, in this chapter I look at it as only one of many solutions. The solutions I discuss do not change the essential process of effective coaching, but they allow more versatility when working with coachees over distance and time. The emphasis in this chapter is on the variety of distance modalities and how leader coaches might combine them in effective ways. The chapter describes the pros and cons of distance modalities, discusses issues to consider when assessing both the coach and coachee readiness for this approach, provides examples of blended coaching that highlight CCL's coaching framework, and outlines future possibilities in this emerging arena. Leader coaches can use this chapter to think about blended approaches that support their one-to-one coaching. They can also use it to educate their organizations so that they can consider blended approaches when implementing coaching as a multiple, simultaneous initiative or in a collective coaching situation (see Chapter Fourteen).

Because this area of coaching is new, many of the professional coaches I interviewed for this chapter have just begun to use these distance solutions in their work. Their experiences are valuable guides for leader coaches and others who can find many implications for the use of these techniques as an adjunct to their overall coaching efforts.

Distance Modalities

Distance modalities can be divided into two broad categories: synchronous and asynchronous. Essentially, synchronous means "at the same time" and asynchronous means "at a different time." By its nature, face-to-face coaching is synchronous. Table 13.1 summarizes distance modalities, which are described in more detail below. Also included are Internet-based skill-building solutions that can be combined with other modalities, similar to how a coach provides the coachee with a book or article to read for informational purposes.

TABLE 13.1. DISTANCE MODALITIES.

	Synchronous	Asynchronous
Distance coaching modalities		
Audiovideo conferencing	X	
E-mail		X
Online assessments		X
Peer-to-peer collaborative platforms		X
Telephone	X	
Text chat and instant messaging	X	
Threaded discussion		X
Webcam	X	
Web-enabled follow-up processes		X
Skill-building modalities		
Archived audio or video		X
Online resources		X
Webinars	X	

Note: Since new technologies are always emerging, this list may be incomplete by the time this chapter is published.

Synchronous

All synchronous modalities share these benefits:

- The ability to schedule sessions by defined, limited periods of time
- Greater potential for spontaneity and emergence of unidentified issues or uncensored self-disclosure
- Immediate feedback

Synchronous modalities share these challenges:

- Scheduling, especially across multiple time zones
- Less time for reflection, especially when coachees are highly introverted or working in languages where they are less comfortable
- Technical problems are very transparent and problematic when people have set aside a specific time for a session
- Record keeping can be difficult

Telephone. The most common form of blended coaching combines one or several face-to-face sessions and telephone calls. The telephone is a comfortable technology for most people, with few technical difficulties. Although visual cues are missing from the dialogue, the coach can pick up cues through voice inflection and pauses, for example.

Audiovideo Conferencing. This solution combines the use of video equipment and sound (typically a telephone bridge line) so that people in different locations can see and hear each other. While it is more sensory rich than any mode other than face-to-face, it does require extra equipment and technical knowledge and support to work smoothly.

Webcam. This is a small video camera that transmits images over the Internet. Most current systems also include audio, so that both voice and video can be transmitted and received on each individual's computer. This holds much promise for the future because it's inexpensive and compatible with most computers.

Text Chat and Instant Messaging. Simple text chat and instant messaging allow people to communicate with other Internet users in real time by exchanging text messages with them. These differ from ordinary e-mail because the exchange is immediate and the continuity is more easily maintained than a chain of e-mail messages. Most exchanges are text only; however, some services allow attachments, and some have tools for migrating to audiovideo conferencing.

Asynchronous

All asynchronous modalities share these benefits:

- There are no scheduling issues because people reply in their own time. This is a tremendous benefit when working across multiple time zones.
- There is more time for reflection, because both the coach and coachee are able to compose their replies. This is especially helpful when individuals are highly introverted or communicating in a language in which they are less comfortable.
- An increased sense of anonymity and the writing process allow some people to tap into insights that would not occur otherwise.
- It's easy to save records of conversations, thus improving tracking, documenting the process, and identifying patterns and results.

All asynchronous modalities share these challenges:

- The lack of spontaneity can create a reduced feeling of presence, along with spontaneous thoughts that might be revealing to the coach or coachee. Typed text may feel formal, distant, unemotional, or lacking a supportive and empathic tone. Coaches must develop the skills to express these qualities through writing to be effective in these modalities.
- At this time, most asynchronous communication is written. People may have trouble expressing themselves through writing or feel vulnerable by putting words in a written form because there is a greater sense of permanence. Cues are now reduced to the written word. Some people, due to cognitive or interpersonal style, may naturally express themselves better through writing, or they may comprehend others better through reading than by listening. Others, due to writing skills, typing skills, or cognitive or interpersonal style, cannot express themselves effectively.
- Lack of nonverbal cues, such as the inability to see faces, smiles, or body language. Misinterpretation can lead to miscommunication, such as

misunderstood attempts at humor, misread tone, or misunderstood meaning. Sometimes this can lead to hostility, especially because online interaction can lower inhibitions and there is the possibility of writing comments that are emotionally charged or negative to a degree that would not occur in face-to-face interaction.

- Because meetings are not scheduled, these modalities require greater discipline and commitment for both the coach and coachee.
- It's a challenge to understand the meaning of "no-shows" or "lurkers." If people do not participate, it is very obvious and affects the dynamics of the group when working one-to-many or many-to-many.
- User support is very important to the successful use of this solution. Any technical malfunctions or incompatibility with systems can lead to frustrations and detract from the momentum of the relationship, increasing the likelihood that coachees will drop out.

E-Mail. This is the most common form of asynchronous communication. Blended coaching often takes the form of telephone calls supplemented by e-mails. E-mails used in coaching are typically transactional in nature, such as giving an assignment or suggested reading. Clients may practice and develop business and personal skills by sending progress reports of their efforts to a coach, who provides feedback.

Online Assessments. This refers to a variety of questionnaires, surveys, and tools that provide coachees with information about their own interpersonal and cognitive style, learning, and development. Assessment tools may be Internet based so that they can be taken within a time frame agreed on by the coach and coachee. CCL has not identified any significant difference in ratings when assessments are administered online or on paper (Penny, Chappelow, & Leslie, 2005).

Threaded Discussion. A threaded discussion is an online conversation that takes the form of a series of linked messages. It takes its name from the analogy of a conversational thread and is also known as a *bulletin board* or *forum.* The series is created over time as users read and reply to existing messages. The benefit of threaded discussion is that it is easy for readers to follow the conversation. Typically messages in a thread share a common subject line and are linked to each other in the order of their creation. By reading each message in a thread, one after the other, the reader can see how the discussion evolved. Threaded discussion is particularly useful in online venues when multiple discussions unfold at the same time.

Peer-to-Peer Collaborative Platforms. These are Internet-based platforms designed for many-to-many coaching. Typically they include features such as threaded discussions, polling, calendars, instant messaging, white boards, and document sharing so that groups of individuals may interact. The intent is to facilitate collective learning and peer accountability through activities such as sharing best practices on a particular topic, working together on a project as a geographically dispersed team, or acting as peer coaches to one another.

Web-Enabled Follow-Up Processes. These are Web sites that enable individuals or groups to document their goals, progress, and best opportunities for action as part of an ongoing leadership development program. They typically include "push" technology, automatically generating e-mail to coachees or their managers to follow up on coaching goals and commitments. When used with a group, these processes can create a collaborative learning environment by making each person's input available to the others in the group to encourage group coaching exchanges. For instance, coachees may update their progress, share their learning with peers or mentors, view other coachees' goals and progress, or request help from coaches. These sites may also include resource materials that coachees can access on the Web for actionable ideas.

Skill-Building Modalities

Leader coaches or the organizations they work in can combine distance modalities with skill-building modalities to create a more comprehensive blended coaching initiative.

Webinar. The word is derived from *Web-based seminar.* These are also referred to as *Web conferencing* or *virtual classroom.* Webinars are live presentations, slide shows, or workshops that participants view on the Web. It is interactive in the sense that participants may view video and hear audio from a coach or subject matter expert. Individuals participate by computer and are typically linked by the Web or telephone so they may listen and converse in real time. Different platforms that offer Webinars usually have additional tools such as polling or instant messaging.

Archived Audio or Video. Coaches can send Webinars or other audio and video sources to coachees so that they will have them for future reference.

Online Resources. E-books, articles, and tools provide coachees with additional information, reminders, and guidelines and can be accessed through organization intranets, public Web sites, or outside subscription services.

What Is Different About Distance Modalities

As with traditional coaching, the coach's efficacy when using distance modalities depends largely on a combination of preparation, intentionality, and skills. It includes being honest about what the coach does and does not know, the ability to provide feedback, and timely follow-through.

There are several characteristics that distinguish the use of distance modalities from traditional face-to-face coaching. Differences include the technology used, the lack of nonverbal cues, the importance of clarity, and important issues of confidentiality.

Technology

In many coaching situations, three issues often run in parallel: the organization's agenda, the coachee's professional development, and the coachee's personal development. When using blended coaching, a fourth issue arises: technology. Whatever technology is used, it must be seamless, or the coach is likely to lose the coachee. This even pertains to familiar devices such as the telephone. One coach interviewed for this chapter tells of losing a potential coachee because the appointment was made through the coachee's administrative assistant and there was a misunderstanding about time zones and scheduling for the first appointment. Although the coach cleared up the misunderstanding, the coachee selected a different coach to work with.

Computer technology introduces many factors related to how comfortable the coach or coachee is in using it. The skills required for delivering blended coaching are described later in this chapter, along with considerations for assessing coachee readiness in this arena. Yet it is important to know at the start if a coachee is not adept at or comfortable with using Internet-based technologies. In addition, integrating this solution into the coaching relationship introduces a double challenge: not only will the coachee have to deal with meeting developmental goals, but he or she will also be challenged by learning to use the technology itself. This can exacerbate fear of failure, and the leader coach needs to be aware of this important dynamic. For this reason, when any Internet-based platforms or tools are involved with the coaching process, it is extremely important that coachees have easy access to technical support.

Some coachees may be more comfortable with technology than with people. In situations where coachees have high technological competence and low emotional intelligence, blended coaching may not be the best choice because it may reinforce the coachees' discomfort with people.

Lack of Nonverbal Cues

Some coaches believe that the loss of nonverbal cues diminishes the coaching encounter, while other coaches believe that removing nonverbal cues increases the authenticity of the encounter because coachees are not influenced by the coach's appearance or facial expressions. Many coaches said that although they prefer face-to-face meetings, they eventually conclude that there is no real advantage to them over other communication channels.

Convenience is the obvious advantage to any distance modality, but there is often a learning curve associated with coaching without verbal cues. That learning can boost the leader coach's skills. This is true even with the most common and familiar technology. One coach expresses the experience of learning to work over distance by telephone: "A lot is stripped away without visual cues, and there is a lot of intensity in having perception only through voice inflection. Because I'm a visual person and the physicality of having people in my space was part of my management style, I realized that I needed to develop my listening skills to a new level. Eventually I discovered that coaching someone over the telephone was the most open I could be, and I felt more authentic."

The voice becomes the coach's primary medium when using the telephone. Coaches who are effective over the telephone make up for the lack of nonverbal cues through voice inflection and by projecting confidence and warmth in their voice. Also, they may need to more consciously slow down or alter their pace to emphasize important points. Leader coaches need to be able to express their personality and interest without using the standard nonverbal cues of eye contact, leaning forward, and so forth.

With Internet-based modalities, cues are reduced even further because communication often comes down to writing (e-mail or threaded discussions, for example). The efficacy of these channels is tied to the writing skills of the coach and coachee. When both are comfortable with the technology and able to express themselves through writing, a surprising amount of disclosure can occur. Depending on variables such as learning style and culture, the added sense of anonymity, along with time to reflect, can lead to greater insight and deeper explorations of behavior, challenges, and change. One coach interviewed for this chapter says that his biggest surprise from blended coaching was that "technology allows greater human touch between people than I ever thought it would."

Importance of Clarity

Because of the lack of nonverbal cues, leader coaches who are using blended coaching should make sure that the implicit is explicit. In other words, coaches need to be specific when communicating roles, boundaries, and expectations. They need to clarify the goals of the coaching partnership and how the coach and coachee will work together. When working at a distance, coaches also need to verbalize their own reactions more frequently and ask more questions, such as: "Are you angry? How are you responding to that? Is this a surprise?" Or, if there is silence, "What is the silence about? It sounds as if this is striking a chord with you."

One coach says that he believes that the ability to convey the coachee's role clearly is the main factor that will determine the efficacy of the process. He explains it this way: "You will get out of this what you put into it. Your role is to provide the questions and challenges, and mine is to make suggestions."

Another coach interviewed for this chapter says, "I talk about the importance of both of us being present up front. It's important to troubleshoot potential pitfalls of a distance relationship up front. The coachee knows that I'm only going to be doing one thing while I'm on the telephone and that I will be fully present. I tell my coachees that for the process to be effective, they must do the same by being attentive and committed." A leader coach who suspects that the coachee is multitasking during the conversation should ask if that is the case.

Distance modalities usually involve working over multiple time zones, so coaches must decide how they want to manage their boundaries regarding e-mail and scheduling synchronous meetings. As a leader coach, consider if you can commit to a specific turnaround time for e-mail, such as twenty-four or forty-eight hours. If you will be unavailable for a period of time, tell your coachee. Technologically savvy and equipped leader coaches can use pagers or other instant communication devices to stay in contact, but they need to set up guidelines with the coachee on how they are to be accessed. As a leader coach, you have to account for your other organizational responsibilities, and so you should define with the coachee what hours you are available to them. This can present challenges when coaching over multiple time zones. You may, for instance, limit your coaching hours to 7:00 A.M. to 7:00 P.M. for your time zone, or you might be a very early riser or willing to work into the evening on certain days.

Confidentiality

Technical issues aren't the only factors that might influence the use of blended coaching. For example, if your coachee uses company e-mail, those communications may not be legally confidential (organizations typically own all communications that use their channels). Some organizations monitor e-mail more closely than others, and electronic messages may not even be confidential from the internal technical support staff. Some virus protection protocols may limit or block the receipt of some messages, especially if they come into the organization from outside. Consequently, limit e-mails in a company e-mail system to transactional or innocuous exchanges, such as e-mailing an article. As the coach, take responsibility for reminding your coachee that anything he or she sends by company e-mail cannot be assured of confidentiality. You and your coachee might decide to use personal e-mail accounts for correspondence. Grant your coachee the choice to call you from home or from another location.

In keeping with the recommendation to be explicit, ask your coachee if he or she has an administrative assistant who screens or reads e-mail. If this is the case, use e-mail only for transactional purposes, such as scheduling a telephone meeting. Confidentiality is related to ownership. Coaches may want to point out that this is the coachee's time and that he or she should decide what can be disclosed.

Using a secured Web site outside the organization can ensure greater confidentiality. Before using an Internet-based platform, make sure that it is a technologically secured site with updated security systems in place. These are password-protected sites that coaches and coachees access over the Internet. Although no information on the Internet can be guaranteed 100 percent safe and secure from intrusion, information that resides on a separate site is not owned by the coachee's company and so provides a greater measure of confidentiality.

One coach interviewed for this chapter says that one topic that she discusses in the initial conversation with her coachees is never to believe that any digital modality is really confidential. That is a useful perspective. Electronic exchanges can be stored and retrieved in undisclosed or in inadvertent ways. Even the comfortable and familiar telephone can fall prey to leakage when voice messages are forwarded inappropriately or accidentally.

With all of this discussion of technology, it's easy to forget that confidentiality breaches don't require misuse of equipment or rogue computer hackers. One coach tells an interesting story about how she and her husband were sitting in an airport, across from a well-dressed man who was talking loudly on his cell phone. He said, "I had another conversation with my executive search firm, and I'm still in conversations with ABC Corporation." ABC happened to be a corporation where both this coach and her husband had worked. He talked about people at ABC they both knew and then said, "I'm glad that this is confidential because I know that executive coaching is very personal."

Needless to say, this was a major lapse on the part of this man's coach, whose responsibility was to be sensitive to such breaches of confidentiality and convey them at the start to the coachee. Even if the coachees are not in their workplace, it is easy for them to be sitting in a place where they should not be having a conversation and loudly mentioning a name or company that others could know.

Designing Blended Coaching Experiences

Most leader coaches have ample opportunity to make use of blended solutions as an adjunct to their coaching interactions. In most cases, organizations have the necessary technical elements, and the coach can make decisions about what to use, when, and where. But before embarking on a program of blended coaching, there are some considerations the leader coach should keep in mind.

Assessing the Leader Coach's Readiness

If you are considering moving into the blended coaching arena, the first question you should ask yourself is, What is my philosophical orientation toward blended coaching? If the use of the solutions discussed in this chapter chafes against your core values or beliefs about effective coaching, then it is probably better to avoid them. Using blended coaching solutions involves a fairly steep learning curve. Without a strong motivation toward using them, your chances for reaching satisfying results are rather slim.

The issue of satisfaction may be more important for the coach to consider than whether he or she can successfully work with blended coaching methods. It's possible to develop skill at using these modalities but not enjoy using them. For some leader coaches, losing the face-to-face aspect of the relationship sacrifices much of what they find rewarding. It may be hard to assess your feelings about blended coaching without trying it. Some coaches are surprised to discover that they enjoy distance modalities more than they expected; others discover that it is not a good approach for them and their coachee. For instance, one coach in a large global organization says, "It was so different for me to work virtually without any team member in my state. I felt alone and isolated, and I realized that I like to be physically located with some team members."

Pamela McLean, CEO of the Hudson Institute of Santa Barbara, an organization that provides coaching training for blended coaching, says she doesn't know if it is possible to screen in advance who will be both satisfied and effective with blended coaching. According to Hudson's annual survey, 70 percent of the coaches surveyed said that they prefer to have initial face-to-face contact and prefer face-to-face sessions. However, she emphasized that the traditional face-to-face approach remains more comfortable for most coaches and that the Hudson Institute encourages coaches to experiment with new modalities so long as they have developed some skills with using those modalities.

If leader coaches are considering moving into blended coaching, other questions will help clarify their choice:

- Have I ever experienced blended learning or blended coaching? Did I enjoy it?

- Can I hold my focus on a person who is not in front of me?
- Can I sense another person's emotions, or a tear, without actually seeing them?
- Am I intrigued by technology?

In its work with blended coaching modalities, CCL has developed a list of specific coaching skills, which are described in Exhibit 13.1.

EXHIBIT 13.1. SKILLS SPECIFIC TO BLENDED COACHING.

This list of coaching skills supports other coaching skills that are required for traditional face-to-face coaching, such as the ability to identify an individual's developmental challenges and create in partnership steps toward improvement.

- Demonstrates self-management and organization through timely responses and reminders using distance modalities
- Is able to keep coachees on track by holding their attention to their action plans and agreed-on results and topics for future sessions
- Establishes and maintains a consistent presence by being responsive and transparent, such as explaining in advance if you will be absent for a period of time
- Is able to motivate through various modalities, including the telephone and through writing
- Writes in a clear and concise way using language that is meaningful to the coachee (for example, nontechnical and without jargon)
- Is able to summarize and synthesize ideas, actions, and patterns of behavior through writing
- Distinguishes between the words, tone of voice, and subtle verbal cues (telephone) or between words and actions (online); notices and addresses congruence or incongruence
- Holds coachees accountable for what they say they are going to do or for the results of an intended action (as reported by telephone or online) and provides appropriate feedback
- Modulates and models the pacing of individuals or groups in terms of their own pacing and the rate at which people respond on the telephone or online

Assessing Coachee Readiness

Just as blended coaching does not suit every leader coach, it isn't appropriate for every coachee. There is no research that supports a screening assessment to determine which coachees might be more appropriate for a blended coaching approach. Nor is there research to substantiate whether certain temperaments or personality types (such as introverts or extraverts) are more or less suited to particular distance modalities.

Even so, some commonsensical notions can guide the decision as to whether a coachee will be best served by a blended coaching solution. (The same notions would make it difficult to coach a person even in a straightforward, face-to-face arrangement.) For instance, low motivation has a negative impact on any coaching relationship. When the coachee isn't reflective, that establishes a coaching challenge. Or if a leader coach uses the coachee's colleagues to encourage and support change but there isn't sufficient goodwill toward the coachee, that support may not be forthcoming, and positive results may not be realized.

One of the clearest indicators of whether someone is a good candidate for successful coaching is the degree to which that person is willing to take appropriate accountability for his or her development. Accountability and commitment are especially important factors with blended coaching. As with coaches, blended coaching requires that coachees organize their schedule and keep telephone appointments or, even more challenging, that they check an Internet site and stay current with threaded discussions or other asynchronous modalities, particularly with group and collective coaching. A coachee's responsiveness, by telephone, e-mail, and online contact, is a good barometer of his or her motivation and commitment.

Emotional intelligence (see also Chapters Seven and Eight) also plays a role in the coachee's adapting to blended coaching. Some people are comfortable with technology but at the expense of interpersonal skills. In such cases, using technology for coaching may not be the best developmental approach because their development needs may revolve around building relationships and honing communication skills (such as reading nonverbal cues), which they can practice face-to-face with their leader coach.

In cases where a coachee has low emotional intelligence coupled with a dislike or fear of technology, blended coaching might create too many simultaneous challenges. When assessing a coachee's readiness for blended coaching, it is probably best if that person is at least reasonably comfortable with technology, particularly when using Internet-based modalities.

Another factor to consider is the coachees' organizational culture. Traditional coaching programs can drive organizational change and require a degree of organizational readiness. When using blended coaching, cultural readiness is an even more critical factor for success. One aspect of this is the organization's acceptance and capability with technology, particularly computer-based technologies. Using Internet-based technologies for blended learning or coaching takes time. When this time is not recognized or sanctioned by the organization, it becomes yet another task added to coachees' responsibilities. Trust is another cultural factor because of the issues of confidentiality and digital technology. When there is low trust in the organizational culture, people may be reluctant to use digital technologies or reveal meaningful information through those channels.

Sustaining the Relationship over Time and Distance

The majority of coaches interviewed for this chapter say that they promote more contact between sessions, such as sending e-mail or forwarding articles, to sustain the coaching relationship over time and distance. Many say that going out of their way to stay in touch with the coachee has a clear benefit in terms of retention and efficacy.

The notion of coaching as a learning process that takes place over time is typically framed in the first conversation with the coachee. If coaching is tied to a face-to-face training program, the framing can be around the importance of continued support and challenge to help coachees apply what they learned in the program. Without this, they are likely to retreat to old habits and lose the energy and focus needed to reach their goals.

When the first meeting with the coachee is not face-to-face, it is most likely to occur by telephone. As a leader coach, a question to consider is whether the coachee will initiate the telephone calls. Many coaches use this approach as a way of emphasizing the importance of the coachees' commitment to the process.

The first conversation is key. Coaches need to establish boundaries, roles, and expectations. At the same time, they need to put the coachee at ease and begin to establish a sense of trust and rapport. For some, it may be more challenging to do this without a face-to-face meeting. The coach has to overcome the impersonality of the medium, whether it's the telephone or an online solution. In either case, coaches need to convey who they are and establish a sense of authenticity. As with face-to-face meetings, one way of doing this is to model effective norms and behavior. The leader coach can also use this first conversation as a chance to establish rapport through a certain amount of self-disclosure, just as he or she would begin the first face-to-face meeting with a coachee by sharing information about professional background, family, interests, and so forth. This strategy helps to put the coachee at ease and provides some context. One coach says that during the first conversation, she asks the coachee to stop her at any point and interject whether there is a lack of understanding or connection. Another coach interviewed for this chapter says that she talks with a coachee several times before coming to a mutual decision as to whether there is a good fit between them.

According to one coach who regularly provides distance coaching on a global basis, the biggest challenge is getting coachees to show up for their first coaching session. If they show up, the coachees will usually engage in the process. This coach believes that because many coachees are high performers who are used to being successful, they often don't know what to expect from coaching. They therefore have an underlying fear of not doing it right, an issue that also comes up in traditional coaching situations. In answer to this concern, this coach posts video clips on a Web site so that potential coachees can see a simulated coaching session. The presentation makes use of a split-screen technique to show a coach and coachee talking on the telephone. The result is that potential coachees have more information about what to expect and are able to decrease their suspicion or fear.

Coaches also talk about establishing a rhythm, depending on the needs of the coachee. For instance, one coach says that she has a coachee with whom she talks by telephone every six to seven weeks. This is a fairly large gap of time, so she asks the coachee to keep her informed between sessions with brief e-mails about progress related to goals and other developmental issues. The extra communication makes each telephone meeting a continuation of an ongoing conversation, not an end in itself.

The focus of the coaching also has a rhythm. Many leader coaches begin by helping coachees identify goals and better understand their behavior and its implications. Over time, this focus shifts toward helping coachees understand what they are learning from trying their new behaviors and from the coaching process itself. As the process draws to a close, the focus shifts toward what coachees have learned and how they can carry new behaviors and insights forward after the coaching process ends.

When using distance modalities, a particular challenge with sustaining the relationship is getting and keeping coachees' attention. Many working managers and executives receive hundreds of e-mails each day. When coaches are using e-mail as a communication medium, it's helpful to establish protocols with coachees to flag their e-mails so that both parties notice them. For instance, a particular phrase for the subject heading can act as a flag. Obviously an indicator of the coachee's commitment to the process is the priority he or she gives to these messages. Getting and maintaining attention using other asynchronous modalities, such as a Web site, is even more challenging. One tactic a coach can use is to ask coachees to schedule time to check in and participate in an Internet-based program, just as they would schedule time for a face-to-face or telephone meeting.

What to Blend

The most common blend of modalities that is currently being used is the combination of face-to-face, telephone, and e-mail. Many coaches send an e-mail immediately after their first contact with the coachee. Again, due to confidentiality issues, these messages are typically informational and transactional. Professional coaches often send an e-mail reminder to confirm appointments a few days beforehand and verify the telephone number for coachees to reach them—a tactic that leader coaches might well adopt. If there is some consequence for changing a meeting at short notice or missing a meeting, the leader coach should make that clear at the outset, during the first meeting, and follow up on that immediately after.

When combining modalities to create an effective blended coaching experience, there is no magic formula. Leader coaches should be mindful that it's not the tool that is the most important thing but the way the tool is integrated into the coaching process. Keeping in mind the pros and cons of different modalities, consider what combination and what sequence of modalities and resources might work best for a particular coachee or group of coachees. Designing blended coaching follows the same principles as any good design process, which includes identifying the needs and desired outcomes of an individual or group and creating a logical and varied sequence of experiences to achieve those outcomes.

When designing blended learning or blended coaching experiences, each solution should add value, and the overall process should be seamless. In its design of blended coaching initiatives, CCL pays attention to what it calls "red threads"—common elements that are intentionally integrated throughout the coaching process to make it a coherent whole—for example:

Learning/coaching philosophy—explicit norms, approaches, and methodologies

Outcomes—agreed-on results as determined by either individual coachees or groups

Themes—patterns of strengths and developmental opportunities to work on throughout the coaching process

Activities—events that are sequenced and debriefed in a meaningful way

Language—the choice and continuous use of words and a common understanding of what they mean

Staffing—explicit introductions and transitions between trainers and coaches when more than one coach is involved

Examples of Blended Coaching

The modalities of blended learning can be combined in any number of ways. Following are three examples of designs that CCL has found to be effective. Because one-to-one blended coaching has been discussed throughout this chapter, the following cases illustrate one-to-many and many-to-many coaching experiences in order to show leader coaches and their organizations how expansive the use of blended coaching can be. Interwoven in these case studies is a discussion of the CCL coaching framework, which provides the context of each situation.

Case 1: Developing Emerging Leaders

This global organization approached CCL in 2001 with these needs:

- To prepare up-and-coming employees to face the complex challenges of new leadership roles

- To learn to lead and participate in cross-functional, geographically dispersed teams
- To develop more people more efficiently while integrating leading-edge learning technologies

Like many other organizations at this time, this one faced increased competition and falling stock prices in a turbulent economy. In addition, it had to keep the leadership pipeline filled with talented and motivated employees. A critical focus was on future leaders who could function effectively in a competitive, technologically driven marketplace.

This program targeted emerging leaders in the organization's North American sales group. These were high-potential employees who were moving into management roles of greater scope and responsibility. The total high-potential population ranged from eight hundred to twelve hundred employees across functions and geography.

Previously CCL had worked with this organization with a traditional, face-to-face development program, made up of twenty days of classroom training over a two-year period. However, the organization had dramatically decreased its internal leadership development function by 85 percent, making fewer resources available to CCL for use in designing and implementing the necessary developmental experiences. CCL redesigned its coaching initiative to use a blended, multimodality approach that incorporated classroom and online learning, executive coaching, and internal mentors. Application was accomplished through virtual teams working on real business projects tied to strategic initiatives. The process extended over a five-month period and used the modalities described in Figure 13.1, which are further described below:

- *Online assessment and preparation.* Participants completed individual assessment instruments online (results were received during the first face-to-face session) and posted a brief personal biography, photo, and symbol of leadership on the online work space.

- *Webinar kick-off.* CCL faculty and internal program managers introduced themselves, provided an overview of the five-month process, and gave participants an opportunity to ask questions.

- *Three-day face-to-face session.* Thirty-six participants were divided into six teams of six members on the first day and worked as an intact team for the remainder of the program. The session included content presentation, a variety of team-based activities, a two-hour individualized coaching session to review feedback instrumentation, guidelines for functioning as a geographically dispersed team, and practice with the online work space. Individuals were asked to create a leadership development plan that they would review with their coach in subsequent telephone coaching sessions.

- *Business project (action learning).* Executives identified enterprisewide strategic initiatives prior to the program. During the face-to-face session, teams were asked to

FIGURE 13.1. BLENDED COACHING SOLUTION FOR A GLOBAL ORGANIZATION.

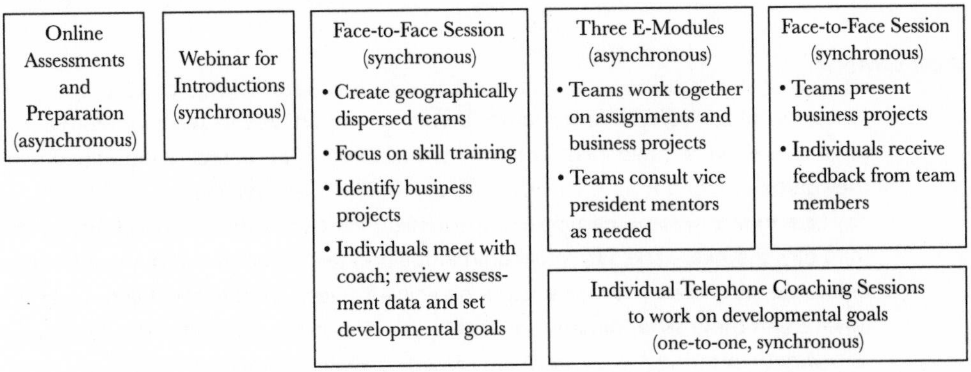

Online Assessments and Preparation (asynchronous)

Webinar for Introductions (synchronous)

Face-to-Face Session (synchronous)
- Create geographically dispersed teams
- Focus on skill training
- Identify business projects
- Individuals meet with coach; review assessment data and set developmental goals

Three E-Modules (asynchronous)
- Teams work together on assignments and business projects
- Teams consult vice president mentors as needed

Face-to-Face Session (synchronous)
- Teams present business projects
- Individuals receive feedback from team members

Individual Telephone Coaching Sessions to work on developmental goals (one-to-one, synchronous)

identify a business project that addressed one of the strategic initiatives and that they could begin to implement within the next three to four months.

- *Three online e-modules.* Each module asked participants to complete both an individual and a team assignment. For instance, one individual assignment asked participants to complete an online assessment instrument called the Learning Tactics Inventory and then share their profiles and discuss the implications of their learning preferences with their team using threaded discussion. One team assignment asked teams to apply systems thinking to their business project and discuss the implications. Team-to-team feedback was structured in advance, where each team provided feedback to another team during each online module. The purpose for team-to-team feedback was to create cross-fertilization of learning between teams and provide practice in giving and receiving feedback.
- *Individualized telephone coaching.* Two one-hour telephone coaching sessions were arranged so that participants could maintain focus and continuity with their coach. These were individually scheduled in the same time frame as the e-modules and provided an opportunity to practice and discuss leadership goals identified in their development plans.
- *Internal mentoring.* Several vice president–level mentors were assigned to each team to act as sounding boards and offer suggestions as the teams worked on their business projects.
- *Culminating face-to-face session.* Teams reported on their business projects to a group of twenty-six vice presidents and several senior executives. Prior to these reports, the vice president group received training and practice in coaching. Following

the reports, the vice president mentors were assigned to meet with each team to provide coaching on the project and presentation, as well as suggestions on how to further implement the project at the company.

Assessment

Assessment took several forms, and it began when participants were asked to complete several online assessment instruments, including a 360-degree instrument where they gathered input from their boss, peers, and direct reports. During the first three-day face-to-face session, participants were asked to observe their teammates. On the third day, they were asked to rate teammates along several leadership dimensions. Just before the second face-to-face session, participants were asked to rate team members again using these same dimensions and to provide one or two behavioral examples to justify their ratings. They were also asked to evaluate how well their team functioned and provide behavioral examples to justify these ratings. During the second face-to-face session, participants were given the compiled results of their individual and team ratings, and this information was debriefed as a team with a CCL facilitator.

Challenge

Participants stated that the most challenging aspect of the program was the business project. During the face-to-face session, teams were given very broad, high-level statements about the company's strategic initiatives. From this, they needed to decide as a team which strategic initiative to address and to create and scale a project with enough operational detail so that it could be implemented following their presentation. Teams identified their strategic initiative during the first face-to-face session, and the remainder of this work took place while they functioned as a geographically dispersed team over the next three months. To do this, teams needed to self-organize and create a communication strategy and a strategy for completing and presenting their plan.

Support

Individuals received support from their coaches, whom they initially met at the first face-to-face session when coaches reviewed their assessment data and helped participants to identify personal leadership development goals. During the next three months, participants had two one-hour follow-up sessions with their coaches. Coaches largely provided support by helping individuals to stay focused on their own developmental goals in the context of their teamwork. CCL faculty provided support to teams in terms of process issues, and typically they participated in one telephone conference call with each team per month. In some cases, teams provided support to individual team members, though this varied depending on how well the team was able to function together.

Results

Because this program was designed to address specific organizational challenges, the company was very concerned about documenting the program's impact. These were its findings:

- Forty-two percent of the participants were promoted, and 25 percent had lateral transfers for cross-functional development.
- Several of the business projects were implemented and had a direct impact on the strategic initiative they addressed.
- Individuals experienced positive personal change in terms of increased job effectiveness (75 percent), setting goals and objectives (79 percent), and increased confidence (80 percent).

Participants also commented that they gained leadership skills specifically relating to working as a geographically dispersed team. In most cases, individual team members carried out acts of leadership in various ways on their team. This was enabled through both telephone and Internet-based technologies, which linked the teams to a web of information, relations, and interactions that added up to more than any single individual could provide. A key developmental lesson for both the participants and the vice presidents was a broader understanding of how leadership happens and where leadership comes from in an organization.

Case 2: Developing Coaching Talent in a Global Organization

Similar to the organization in case 1, this organization had previously worked with CCL using a traditional face-to-face classroom model where participants met for three days of training on coaching skills. The issue the organization addressed through this program was its need to increase the efficacy of leadership throughout the organization. This need was identified by internal 360-degree assessments of managers and executives, which indicated that managers were not providing enough coaching and support for their direct reports. The company determined that it would use its internal human resource staff to provide coaching to managers and executives on how to improve these skills. The program was designed to develop the skills of the human resource managers such that they could implement formal coaching engagements with select managers.

The original program ran twice in North America over twelve to eighteen months, and an abbreviated version was run for the executive committee. The original design used the following format:

- A three-day on-site face-to-face session that included many small-group activities. The curriculum had a heavy experiential and practice orientation, with extensive use of videotaping.
- Six months later, a two-day on-site face-to-face session where participants worked in small groups. After the session, participants were expected to engage in a formal coaching relationship with an individual who met certain criteria. Meetings with the individual and the individual's boss typically occurred during this period, and formal feedback was requested of each coachee regarding their coach's service.
- Shadow-coaching support provided by a certified CCL coach. Individuals also received three one-hour telephone sessions after phase 1 (three-day program) and two one-hour coaching sessions after phase 2 (two-day on-site) from executive coaches.
- Each quarter, biannual conference calls in which the lead CCL faculty member facilitated a discussion about the participants' progress, offered new teaching pieces as needed, and allowed participants to learn from each other's experiences.
- Twelve to eighteen months later, a one-day follow-up session to address more complex and challenging coaching issues.

CCL decided to redesign the program to a blended format for several reasons. First, the organization wanted to expand the initiative globally, which meant that the human resource managers who participated were located throughout the world (in Singapore, the United Kingdom, the Netherlands, Germany, and North America). Travel expenses to bring this group together were very high. Second, a six-month distance learning piece was added to extend the learning from the first face-to-face session and to provide feedback and support as the participants applied their coaching skills on the job. In this way, it was possible to track participants' progress in a more structured way and provide immediate and collective reflection throughout that process. And finally, the redesign addressed the enterprise's goal of teaching coaching using a many-to-many approach, where all involved were both teachers and learners to each other, thus making coaching a less solitary activity. The blended coaching program used the modalities illustrated in Figure 13.2 and described below.

- *Three-day face-to-face session.* This took place in Brussels using a similar structure and format as the original design. Each participant was asked to come to this session with one or two people in mind they planned to coach on the job and with a high degree of boss support and coachee readiness and willingness to participate. In

FIGURE 13.2. BLENDED COACHING SOLUTION FOR AN ORGANIZATION DEVELOPING INTERNAL COACHES.

Face-to-Face Session (synchronous)	Peer-to-Peer Collaborative Platform (asynchronous, many-to-many)
• Create geographically dispersed teams • Focus on skill training • Introduce and practice technology	• Teams work together on case studies and provide feedback to one another • Coaches provide feedback to individuals and teams
	Shadow Coaching (asynchronous, one-to-one)
	Telephone Conference Calls (synchronous, many-to-many)

addition to the experiential learning and practice coaching sessions using videotape, it included an orientation to the online component.

- *Online component.* This piece ran for approximately six months, in parallel with participants' implementing their formal coaching engagement and consisting of three e-modules. The online component was facilitated by two CCL faculty members and served as both a support for participants and a delivery mechanism to provide new content. This was essentially an action learning experience, where participants practiced coaching skills in their work environment and then reflected on their experiences with other members of the program using the online platform.

The online component began with simple assignments to familiarize the participants with the use of the Web site. For instance, the first e-module consisted of the assignments described in Exhibit 13.2.

Module 2 was far more extensive in terms of the content delivered and the complexity of the assignments. Participants were asked to complete these assignments as geographically dispersed teams:

- *Shadow coaching.* Five one-hour telephone sessions during the six-month period between individual participants and their executive coaches, whom they met during the face-to-face component.
- *Group telephone conference call.* The initial plan for the redesigned program was to hold at least one group conference call midway through the online component to reconnect the entire group through live conversation.

EXHIBIT 13.2. ONLINE COMPONENT MODULE IN A BLENDED COACHING INITIATIVE FOR AN ORGANIZATION DEVELOPING INTERNAL COACHES.

Module 1

Welcome! All course work for Module 1 will begin January 12 and conclude January 16. Please do not begin working on this module until the start date, when everyone will begin together. Thank you.

The assignments are ordered, so please open the entries in the following sequence:

1. Change Your Password
2. Introduce Yourself
3. Post Replies
4. Open an Attachment
5. Post an Attachment

This first module offers you an opportunity to meet your Asian-Pacific and European counterparts online and to practice using this site. We will be working as a global group for the distance learning component of this program. For certain modules, we will divide the group into smaller work groups based on mixed locations.

Assessment

In the blended program, assessment began with the face-to-face session, using a combination of self-assessment and feedback from peers and facilitators. Again, videotape was used extensively as a feedback mechanism. Assessment also occurred in the third e-module, where participants were asked to respond to these questions:

- How motivated were you going into the next phase?
- What did you find most difficult about module 2?
- How aware were you of the degree of challenge this process would pose for you going into this phase?
- What do you know about yourself that you could have anticipated would make this phase easier or harder?
- How did you respond to and manage the challenge?
- How successful were you in meeting the challenge?
- To what extent did you access others?

- What do you need to do differently going forward?
- What do you need most from others (fellow coaches, CCL coach, CCL facilitators, organizational sponsors) to be successful?
- How will you let them know you need their help, and how will you gain their participation and commitment?
- What can you take from what you've learned and used in your coaching to help your coachee in achieving his or her development goal?

Challenge

The online portion of the program presented too much challenge for participants. Participants were already challenged by the amount of content they were asked to apply in real coaching situations as well as the geographical dispersion of their peers. Most participants had no prior experience with using Internet-based technology for learning. The challenge of keeping pace with the assignments and threaded discussions posted on the Web site, in addition to practicing the coaching skills themselves, created a backlash. After the first teleconference, the participants asked to use conference calls as a mechanism for staying in touch and for providing feedback and support rather than using the Web site. Because the telephone is a synchronous modality, this created a problem with widely divergent time zones, so the groups were reconfigured by geographical location to minimize this issue.

Support

This program was designed to teach many-to-many coaching, where all participants, including the facilitators and coaches, acted as both learners and teachers to one another. Consequently, support was provided by all of these roles. CCL facilitators supported the learning groups, executive coaches supported their individual coachees, and participants supported one another.

Results

At the time of this writing, the program is still in progress, so the organizational impact cannot be assessed. However, an important lesson that the designers and facilitators of this program learned is to stay flexible and be responsive to participants' needs. Designing blended coaching experiences can be a delicate balancing act, and it's essential to keep the objectives of the program in mind. Most coaches and coachees may want to revert to their comfort zone, which is meeting face-to-face or on the telephone. If an intended outcome is to improve the coaches' skills with using technology, such as leading geographically dispersed teams or learning online facilitation, then it is important to stick with the Internet-based modalities while keeping in mind that the technology itself is an added challenge. In this case, the primary objective was to enhance the coaching skills of participants so that they could improve the leadership skills of managers within the organization. Since this objective was paramount, the online portion was secondary, and the facilitators changed the program midcourse to meet their primary objective.

Case 3: Web-Enabled Follow-Up Coaching for Developing Leaders

Unlike the previous cases, this case involves coaching for a group of managers who did not come from a single organization. Like the previous cases, CCL's original design for this program used face-to-face training exclusively. The purpose of the program is to enhance the leadership development of participants.

CCL's desire to redesign this program in a blended format related to increasing the transfer of learning from the classroom back to the workplace, thus resulting in increased organizational impact for the organizations that sent participants to the program. Coaching is seen as a means to an end, with the emphasis on obtaining results in the form of behavioral change. The blended program uses the modalities listed in Figure 13.3 and described below:

- *Online assessment.* Participants complete individual assessment instruments online (results are received during the face-to-face session).
- *Five-day face-to-face session.* Participants engage in a number of activities built around CCL's assessment-challenge-support model of leader development. They also

FIGURE 13.3. BLENDED PROGRAM MODALITIES.

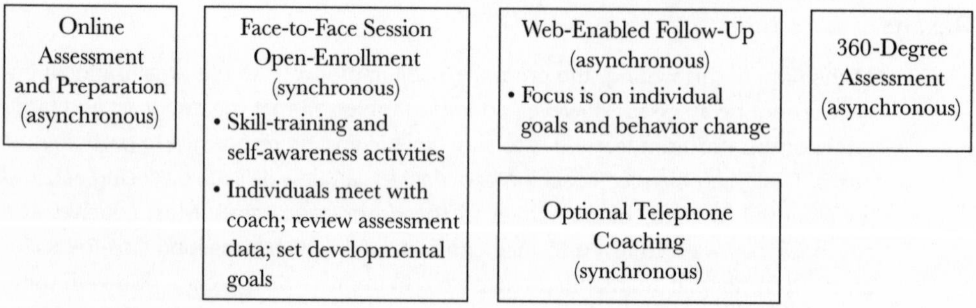

Online Assessment and Preparation (asynchronous)

Face-to-Face Session Open-Enrollment (synchronous)
- Skill-training and self-awareness activities
- Individuals meet with coach; review assessment data; set developmental goals

Web-Enabled Follow-Up (asynchronous)
- Focus is on individual goals and behavior change

Optional Telephone Coaching (synchronous)

360-Degree Assessment (asynchronous)

meet individually with an executive coach for three hours to review the data from their assessment instruments and set developmental goals that they will accomplish back at their workplace.

- *Web-enabled follow-up.* A third-party vendor supplies the technology platform, archiving the data on a secured Internet site. On the last day of the face-to-face session, participants turn in goal statements, which are entered on this Web site. One aspect of this process automatically generates e-mails to participants every other week over ten weeks. These e-mails remind participants of their goals and ask them to reflect on what they are learning during this process. Participants are encouraged to take five or ten minutes to respond to the e-mails with updates about their progress, and they have several choices that they can make in terms of how they interact with the technology. First, they are encouraged to include the coach they met during the face-to-face session so that coaches receive copies of the participant's updates. Coaches are then asked to respond to the coachees with messages that provide support and suggestions, such as the one illustrated in Exhibit 13.3.

Coachees can identify any number of selected colleagues to act as mentors and who would also receive their progress updates. They can also choose whether they want their goals and updates to be public or private. If they are public, then they will be posted on the Web site so that other coachees in their program can view them. This site becomes a learning community that all participants can access and where they can choose to respond to each other to gain support and ideas. They may also

EXHIBIT 13.3. EXAMPLE OF E-MAIL FOLLOW-UP CORRESPONDENCE BETWEEN COACH AND COACHEE ON A WEB-ENABLED PLATFORM.

Dear [coachee's name],

Good job! It looks as if you've made significant progress in developing and communicating the strategy, and in initiating regular meetings. As you noted, actually using some of the tools is even more difficult. You've started, and that's the first step.

Sometimes, thinking ahead of time of things you would like to learn from others during a meeting is a way of focusing your questions. High Performance Questions often need to be created before you go into a meeting; good ones that ask people to think, and yet aren't seen as challenging, can be difficult to ask in the moment. You might also talk with other people individually about the idea of using a skillful conversation format for the meeting. And then plan how you'll suggest it to the group, maybe in a preliminary e-mail. I look forward to talking with you at noon on the 15th.

partner with a fellow coachee to act as each other's coach. If participants make their goals and progress public, they are asked not to share names in their reports and to be circumspect about sharing personal issues.

The Web-enabled process includes some additional tools. One resource provides a number of practical ideas on how to improve specific skills, such as how to build effective teams. Participants can also access an extensive list of articles, which they can download, and books pertaining to specific areas that they may be working on.

- *Telephone coaching.* Participants may choose to receive ongoing individual telephone coaching from the executive coach whom they met during the face-to-face session. (This is optional.)
- *360-degree assessment.* Ninety days after participating in the face-to-face session, participants and their colleagues are asked to complete an assessment that measures the behavioral changes that can be observed over the course of this time. This allows participants to engage colleagues at work in their developmental process. Participants then receive the results of this assessment so they have an updated view of their progress, as seen by themselves and others, and can continue with ongoing development.

Assessment

In this case, an iterative assessment takes place throughout. It begins with the online assessment instruments that are completed prior to the face-to-face session. Following that, participants receive assessment and feedback from their coaches, peers, and mentors (if desired).

Challenge

As with the other cases, participants are encouraged to identify developmental challenges based on the assessment they receive that will improve aspects of their leadership capacity. Unlike the other cases, there are no shared goals or assignments because each participant comes from a different organization. CCL coaches and faculty encourage participants to identify specific behavioral goals that take them beyond their comfort zones. To achieve measurable goals, a very specific framework is used, as illustrated in Exhibit 13.4.

Support

Broad support comes from the participants' coach, CCL faculty, other program participants, and mentors. The asynchronous aspects of this process encourage reflection on the part of both the participants and coaches.

EXHIBIT 13.4. MEASURABLE GOALS TEMPLATE.

- In the next ten weeks, I will . . . [develop my direct reports, for example].
- So that . . . [my organization can have stronger bench strength, for example].

Measurable results by the end of the follow-through period:

[Example: By September 30, I will have researched and discussed with all my direct reports challenging new work assignments and how I can best support them.]

Results

By using Web-enabled follow-up, the process creates an extemporaneous historical record. This is valuable to participants because they can review their progress toward specific goals and priorities over a period of ten weeks and will have a record of the steps they took, including their patterns of behavior. They also get additional feedback on their behavioral change through the 360-degree assessment. The archival capability of the Web site provides a systematic way of capturing best coaching practices, and these can be compiled by an organization. Furthermore, this creates accountability for follow-through on the part of both participants and coaches. For instance, it's possible to track the response time and frequency to coaching requests. Finally, this Web-enabled process allows scalability of coaching that would not be possible through face-to-face sessions or the telephone. Participants can select as many people as they want to be mentors so that they have a broad set of stakeholders involved in their developmental process.

The Future of Blended Coaching

Technological development and its pervasiveness in our lives are not going to slow down. The world continues to shrink in terms of the ability to reach anyone, anywhere. As one coach says, "We could probably take a map of the world and guess ten places that are so remote, we'd think that the company would never have an office there and we'd never have a coachee there. In ten years, though, we'll probably be established there. The world is developing so fast that most of us can't keep up with it. Coaches better be able to use whatever tools they can find to coach people, because coachees won't be flying across the world from someplace such as Tasmania."

We encourage leader coaches to experiment with a variety of coaching modalities. For instance, groupware is becoming more familiar, so that people in different locations can get on their computers and see things at the same time, such as assessment data. Internet-based high-definition videoconferencing will no doubt become less expensive and easier to use. The challenge of technology in coaching isn't finding it, but figuring out how to use it in clever and positive ways. Through the Internet, we can create powerful connections that would never occur otherwise.

Leader coaches play a vital role in helping people in their organizations achieve greater personal and professional satisfaction. This chapter has described modalities that are currently available for reaching people; CCL encourages a blend of face-to-face and other modalities. The key for coaches is to develop skills using a variety of tools so that they can be combined in ways that are most effective for developing leadership in different contexts. The last word comes, fittingly, from a coach interviewed for this chapter: "I have seen people connecting across continents and oceans because they're the right people connecting at the right time over the right content."

Coach's Bookshelf

Bersin, J. (2004). *The blended learning book: Best practices, proven methodologies, and lessons learned.* San Francisco: Jossey-Bass.

Driscoll, M. (2002). *Web-based training: Creating e-learning experiences* (2nd ed.). San Francisco: Pfeiffer.

Horton, W. (2001). *Leading e-learning.* Alexandria, VA: ASTD.

Horton, W. (2002). *Using e-learning.* Alexandria, VA: ASTD.

Mantyla, K. (2001). *Blending e-learning: The power is in the mix.* Alexandria, VA: ASTD.

Piskurich, G. M. (Ed.). (2003). *The AMA handbook of e-learning: Effective design, implementation, and technology solutions.* New York: AMACOM.

Suler, J. (2003). *Maximizing the well-being of online groups.* Retrieved July 8, 2005, from http://www.rider.edu/~suler/psycyber/clinpsygrp.html.

Thorne, K. (2003). *Blended learning: How to integrate online and traditional learning.* London: Kogan Page.

van Dam, N. (2004). *The e-learning fieldbook: Implementation lessons and case studies from companies that are making e-learning work.* New York: McGraw-Hill.

CHAPTER FOURTEEN

COACHING TEAMS

Candice Frankovelgia
Jennifer Martineau

In the mid-1990s, CCL began to explore and provide large-scale coaching interventions that involved entire layers of executives in specific organizations. These projects were often part of a complex organizational learning agenda. They required coaching in one of two forms: either single coaches or coaching teams worked with a large group of individuals in one-to-one sessions, or a single coach worked with an intact team in an organization. This chapter focuses on the second form. Team coaching in this context refers to the process of a single coach working with a team of leaders. Team coaching has evolved from individual coaching in response to particular development needs for team-oriented workplaces. The forms and outcomes for team coaching apply to many of the other types of coaching covered in this book, and the discussion in this chapter is intended to support the leader coach in effectively coaching his or her team, whether an existing team or a team formed to work collectively on a specific project or toward a specific outcome.

Before we start this discussion, two acknowledgments are critical. First, CCL has had less experience in practicing and researching team coaching versus individual coaching, so our knowledge base in this area is still developing. Second, some of the ways in which a professional coach might provide team coaching expertise (and some of the reasons behind it) are different from the ways in which a leader coach might coach a team. Therefore, the lessons we share here require our readers to make a further distillation to apply them to their own work. Even so, leader coaches will be more successful if they are able to effectively coach their team as a whole, in addition to coaching individuals.

Many organizations look to team coaching as a way to create a stronger network of leaders from across the organization and enable their teams to work together to create large-scale, enterprise-wide impact. Increasingly, organizations want coaching and feedback to become part of hallway conversations and serve as a model for collaborative work.

These organizations believe that launching a team coaching initiative enhances the possibility that coaching at the individual level (and leader development in general) will have a positive impact on organizational culture and processes. Increasingly, stakeholders want to know what is being coached and how progress is marked. Organizations want more visible coaching results, and they want a closer link not just between the leader coach and coachees but also closer connections among constellations of people—the coach, the coachees, the coachees' direct reports and peers, and others in the coachees' networks—to better support and foster leader development.

This kind of synchronized coaching process demands more transparency and a deeper reach into the organization even as it must balance an appropriate level of confidentiality. Individual coaching provides a solid foundation for understanding the process, but systemic and organizational considerations require additional attention. For example, team coaching must account for such issues as team dynamics and the possibility that coaching groups or teams can draw attention to organizational barriers. Organizations must be prepared to address these types of issues to facilitate truly effective team coaching.

Coaching at this level and at this scope is not a usual undertaking for a single leader coach. But there is an important role for leader coaches in their organizations' large-scale coaching initiatives. To prepare leader coaches to put themselves in a position to play that role, we discuss the following information: the process, format, and outcomes of team coaching; ways to enact team coaching using the CCL coaching framework; and the skills they will need. Using specific case studies and examples, we discuss the benefits and the pitfalls of team coaching so that leader coaches can more clearly see the potential impact of their work in this complex undertaking.

Forms of Team Coaching

Team coaching describes an array of options involving work with both existing teams and project teams (created for action learning purposes) aimed at having an impact on individual, team, and organizational development. Not all project teams are action learning teams; we chose action learning teams as a way to describe the deep development that can occur when coaching teams. Certainly other kinds of project teams are effective ways to accomplish work. The model of the action learning team provides a balanced focus on the work of the team (action) and the development of the team (learning).

Figure 14.1 shows two aspects of team coaching. On the vertical axis, we distinguish individual from organizational development. This aspect refers to the primary outcomes expected from the coaching initiative. The horizontal axis reflects the nature of the people receiving coaching: individuals being coached with regard to their own leadership challenges or a team of individuals being coached with regard to the leadership challenges they share as a team.

To highlight this variety of options, we cite specific examples of coaching initiatives that describe what we mean. As reflected by the examples shown in the sections of Figure 14.1, a single project is likely to address outcomes in more than one arena.

Coaching a Permanent, Intact Team and Its Individual Members

This form of team coaching typically involves a leader coach (or at times a team of coaches) coaching an intact team, usually the one for which she has organizational responsibility, and the individuals on that team. This coaching is distinguished from ongoing supervision because the leader is coaching the team to accomplish a specific, shared task. The developmental component of this form of coaching occurs when the coach periodically ensures the team reflects on its learning as a team and then applies this learning to improve its functioning.

There can be multiple goals for this type of coaching, and often they are intertwined. At the foundation of this form is the recognition that individual coaching will be helpful in accomplishing desired outcomes but not sufficient. Rather, organizations that use team-level coaching often do so based on the awareness that desired outcomes are not possible without the collective efforts

FIGURE 14.1. TEAM COACHING FORMAT.

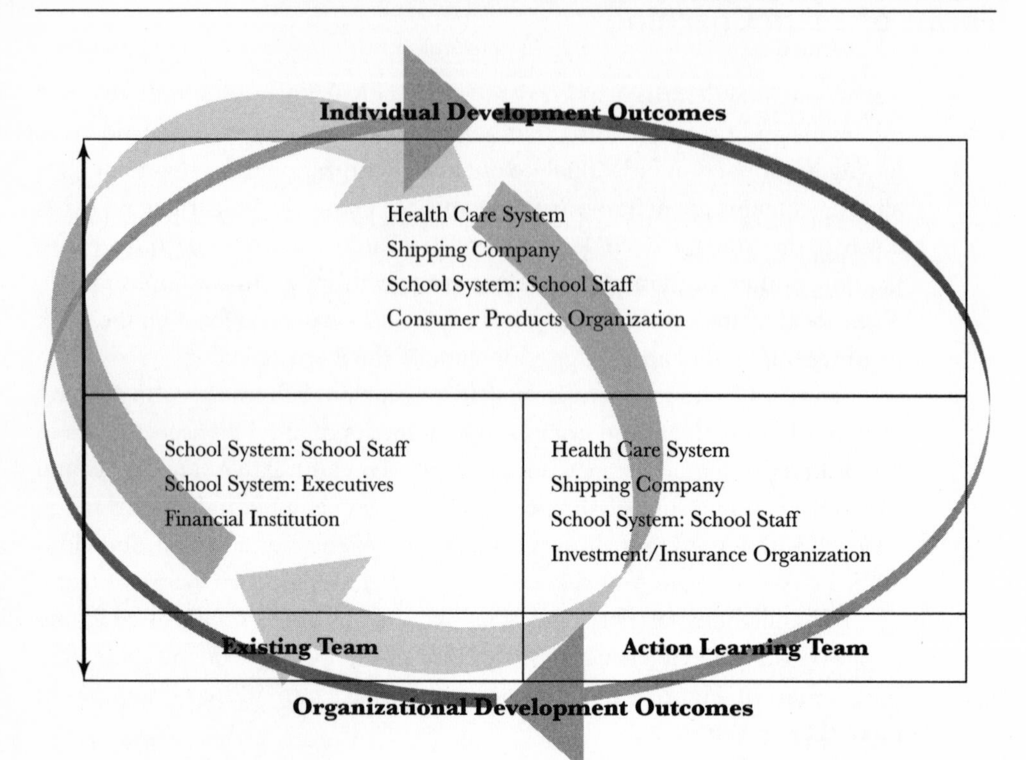

of a team of individuals. The leader continues to coach the individuals on their development goals, which may include team-related skills such as balancing their needs with the team's needs and knowing when to assert or defer.

The role of the leader in this form of coaching is illustrated in the example described in Exhibit 14.1. In this example, the intent is to result in individual and organizational outcomes through targeting both the team as a whole and the individuals within it.

Coaching a Temporary, Intact Team

Another form of team coaching occurs when a group of individuals is brought together from across the organization to accomplish a specific goal. In these cases, team members have not functioned as a team together in the past—in

EXHIBIT 14.1. COACHING SCHOOL SYSTEM EXECUTIVES.

CCL worked with the superintendent of a large public school system and his team of direct reports (school system executives). This team was responsible for the strategic direction and to a certain extent the ongoing operations of the organization (of course, the people reporting to this team had more direct responsibilities for operations). In this school system, as in many other organizations, performance assessments place such a high priority on the accomplishment of unit goals that the optimization of unit performance and effectiveness was of greater priority than the optimization of the organization as a whole. (In other words, if the individual is responsible for a particular function in the organization, his rewards and punishment come more from the success or failure of his function than from his collaboration with the heads of other units.) The result in this case was that team members functioned more as a collective of individuals than they did as a true team.

Although the ultimate goal of team coaching in this case was the improved performance of the organization, it was recognized that team members must operate as a truly interdependent team to accomplish this goal. Thus, the coaching initiative was integrated with a face-to-face team development program (which gave the team the opportunity to receive feedback from others and themselves on their effectiveness as a team) and individual coaching (which enabled each team member to receive an individualized focus on his or her own leadership and membership in the larger team). Together, these components were intended to (1) highlight the team's effectiveness, (2) give the team a three-day program setting in which to practice productive team interactions, (3) give the team in-the-moment feedback on those interactions, and (4) give the team a solid foundation on which to practice effective team interactions in the workplace. The subsequent team coaching sessions were used to enable the team to work in its own environment on its regular work while the coaches observed. (There were three coaches—each responsible for one-to-one coaching for a subset of the team members and each playing a team coaching role to strengthen both the individual and team coaching sessions.) At certain agreed-on points during team meetings, the coaches would temporarily stop the team's work to share their insights from the team's work, offer suggestions, facilitate discussion among team members, and help the team recognize changes it could make to improve its effectiveness.

fact, they may not know each other at all—but are expected to accomplish a goal together before disbanding again.

These teams are usually constructed as a mechanism for creating a network of leaders across the organization who learn together over a short period of time how to use each other and other organizational resources in service of action learning projects (projects in which team members work to accomplish a shared task while intentionally using the experience as a way in which to develop their own capabilities). In the long run, these teams facilitate the sharing of learning and excellence across the organization. They are sometimes used as developmental experiences for high-performing or high-potential leaders to give them an opportunity to learn and achieve an organizational goal by working through a cross-functional team.

CCL has worked with this type of team in a variety of organizational contexts. The commonality is that an ultimate goal of the organization is to create a stronger sense of "systemness" across the organization. Similar to the school district example described in Exhibit 14.1, many organizations are structured according to regions or districts, product lines, and the like. Although each unit may operate well within its own bounds, there are often mistakes repeated across the organization because learning from mistakes is not shared widely. In addition, successes across the organization are not shared to the extent that replication becomes more easily accomplished. Repeated mistakes and the lack of collaboration across the organization add to the costs of operating the organization. To address the sometimes wide and deep divides that disconnect parts of an organization from each other, some organizations have invested in leadership development, and team coaching specifically, as a way of moving organizational leaders to a new level of relationship. The goal is to create a network of leaders who work across traditional organizational structures and boundaries to solve complex challenges that cannot be effectively resolved in an isolated way.

Coaching in this case occurs within the context of a project given to the team as a means of discovering the challenges and benefits in collaborating across boundaries (those between team members as well as those the team encounters as it accesses other individuals and groups across and outside the organization).

The particular format of the project and coaching we are describing is what CCL calls action learning leadership. When this structured method is used, the focus is as much on the learning as it is on the work itself, and the coach focuses solely on the team's learning process. In the form in which CCL plays the coaching role for our clients, the coach is intentionally not a member of the organization or an expert in the area of work being conducted and is therefore viewed by team members solely as a learning coach. The coach, at specific periods, helps the team to reflect on its progress, challenges, solutions to those challenges, and learning from those myriad situations. The learning is then funneled back into the next stage of teamwork. The example in Exhibit 14.2 describes the health care system noted in Figure 14.1. Although this example focuses on the role of a professional coach rather than the leader coach, there are some lessons to be drawn for the leader coach, in particular several principles for and challenges to action learning leadership team coaching:

- Have teams engage in real work of strategic importance for the purpose of producing tangible and important benefits for the organization.
- Help teams focus on specific ways in which they set direction, create alignment, and build commitment as they work on action learning projects.
- Bring a constructive-developmental frame in which experience and learning are created among individuals in the act of interacting with one another.
- Look at the whole team as sharing leadership. There is no focus on who will emerge as the leader because they are all participating collectively.

Challenges of action learning leadership team coaching include:

- The basic educational challenge of getting individuals to understand what an action learning coach actually does (that is, focus on the learning).
- Helping the team and the organization realize that action learning is important for the strategic sustainability of the organization.
- Setting the context and gaining agreement for it (the main reason action learning fails is that it's all action and no learning).
- Supporting teams through working together in a new way: focusing on the learning.

Outcomes of Team Coaching

Each of the examples in Exhibits 14.1 and 14.2 shares multilevel and interconnected qualities inherent in systemic interventions and requires simultaneous attention to various aspects of the organization. In both one-on-one

EXHIBIT 14.2. COACHING IN A HEALTH CARE SYSTEM.

In this coaching initiative, action learning leadership was used as one of several developmental components of a large-scale leadership development initiative. The overall purpose of the initiative, called the Leadership Academy, was to further develop high-potential executives and do that in a way that integrated the mission, vision, and values of the organization. The academy supported the system's organizational strategy by identifying and reinforcing desired behaviors and facilitating leadership promotion from within the organization. The academy was an eighteen-month developmental experience designed to:

- Enhance the organization's capacity to tackle strategic, complex, and critical issues.
- Create a practice field and learning community to experiment with new ways of leading and learning.
- Implement a set of best practices in leadership development.

As part of an assessment of the organization's most critical leadership needs, key stakeholders incorporated three critical leverage areas into the academy curriculum:

- Strengthening individual and organizational identity
- Achieving operational excellence
- Recruiting, retaining, and developing staff

Focus on these leverage areas as part of the academy was meant to accelerate the system's ability to sustain itself as a mission-driven organization in a dynamic business environment.

The intensive process designed to meet the system's needs consisted of multiple classroom sessions focusing on assessment and development of individual and organizational leadership capacity; extensive team-based action learning projects related to complex, strategic-level business challenges; and individual and team coaching.

For the team coaching component, two coaches each coached two action learning leadership teams (for a total of four teams). The teams themselves interacted in face-to-face programs as part of the initiative's design, creating a macrolevel connection across teams. Within teams, the work was done both face-to-face and virtually, with the coach both present in person and on the telephone or computer to facilitate the team through the learning aspects of its work. The two coaches served as resources to each other to check out their perception of challenges being faced by the teams as a function of operating within a real organization.

coaching and other forms of individual leader development, one of the difficulties is in enabling the individual to grow as a leader within a context of his or her organization while negotiating the difficult transition back into an organization, work group, or team that has not developed along the same trajectory. Team coaching builds a natural network of support that may result in deeper, more durable outcomes for team members and the organization as a whole.

This is complex and sometimes difficult work, but the potential outcomes of team coaching are convincing.

Improved Individual and Team Functioning

In cases where the coaching process includes a team of coachees, the coaching usually takes place in the context of the shared work of the team. Therefore, it is easier for the coach to make connections between the development needs of team members, as well as the team as a whole, and the team's work. When this is true, development occurs within the context of the work and becomes more effective sooner. This is due to the fact that team members are able to practice new behaviors and skills while working with other team members and the coach, receiving feedback from observers who are a part of the development experience themselves.

One of the obvious and overarching benefits of team coaching is that a broader safety net is cast. Multiple individuals develop together in a way that gives them added momentum. Team development provides a context in which the "going back home" transition is made smoother and therefore hastens the accomplishment of outcomes both at and beyond the individual level.

Accomplishing Team Development Goals

Teams may set goals for their own development. For example, they may identify trust and open communication as key challenges to becoming an effective team. As the team does its work, the coach notes examples of interactions that either improve or detract from trust and open communication. Together, the team and coach can identify both types of interaction and create a plan for limiting those that prevent improvement in these outcomes. The immediate benefit is that the team will be better able to achieve the work-based outcomes expected of it. The longer-term benefit is that team members will take their learning about how to improve team effectiveness into other team settings, leading those subsequent teams to be more highly performing more quickly.

Achieving Organizational Improvements

When action learning or another form of interdependent team work occurs in the context of coaching, one way in which teams contribute to organizational-level outcomes is by studying a particular organizational challenge through the collection and analysis of comprehensive data from all relevant areas of the organization. One of the key outcomes for this type of team action learning projects is a set of recommendations toward a specific outcome. Because the challenge requires the insight of others beyond the team and because the team (by sheer fact of number) is able to access more people in a brief period of time than would be the case if only an individual worked on the challenge alone, the resulting study of the organizational challenge and its subsequent recommendations are extremely beneficial to the organization, even if the recommendations are never used. A strong design of this type of initiative includes the presentation of action learning project recommendations to the executive body of the organization, with the intent of initiating a conversation and perhaps planning for the implementation of the recommendations.

Gaining a Fuller Picture of the Organization's Dynamics

When multiple coaches are working with multiple teams, it is ideal if the coaches share those experiences in an effort to create a larger picture of what is happening in the organization (or broader environment) that is having an impact on the coachees. Thus, collaborative forms of team coaching have an added benefit in that the simultaneous nature of the coaching processes enables coaches and coachees to connect the multiple experiences of teams across the organization in a jigsaw puzzle–like manner, resulting in a fuller picture of the organization and its challenges that are relevant to the coaching relationship.

It makes sense to analyze available data at the aggregate level in an effort to understand the participants and their organization on a higher level than what might be understood when only an individual is being coached. When an individual is being coached, it can be difficult to get a full picture of the context within which the person is operating due to the absence of data representing the organization or a larger subset of the organization. When a team is being coached, however, the aggregate summary of either individual data, such as 360-degree data, or organizational data, such as a climate survey, yields information that can assist in understanding how to approach challenges in a way that is grounded in current organizational reality. Coaches working with a team of coachees can use the aggregate data from across this set of individuals in a way that enables them to put the data of the individual in the context of the organization on a larger scale. From this, it is possible to better identify why a particular set of individual behaviors are effective or ineffective in that particular organization, which enables the coach and coachee to more appropriately target improvement goals. In addition, individual team members can use aggregate data to better understand ways in which to be effective as a team member, and the team as a whole can better grasp how it can be effective within the organization.

Establishing a Network of Leaders Across the Organization

When a group of individuals is brought together across the organization and coached through team coaching, one of the intended outcomes is usually the creation of a network of leaders who access each other in more effective ways. Through these types of networks that take on greater responsibility for collaboratively creating organizational success, we have seen a number of outcomes. In one instance, different units in an organization collaborated to negotiate a new contract with a single supplier that saved the organization money as compared to the cost of working with two (or more) different suppliers.

Developing a Community of Leader Coaches

When multiple coaches work with multiple teams, coaches can rely on each other as resources to better understand the organization, the group of coachees, or approaches that are effective with these groups. Through that collaboration of multiple coaches who are coaching teams, the old adage is true: the whole is worth more than the sum of its parts. As coaches collaborate to address common and unique needs of their team coachees, the result is that the coachees receive coaching that is informed beyond the knowledge and skill of their own coach only. Rather, they benefit from the collective wisdom and experience of other coaches as well.

How the Leader Coach Enacts Team Coaching

The principles that govern and drive one-to-one coaching are also relevant to the leader coach in a team coaching context. The existing CCL coaching framework can also be helpful in this regard, although its focus is somewhat different. In this section, we relate the components of the CCL coaching framework to team coaching.

Relationship

Managing the multiple relationships when engaged in team coaching is one of the greatest challenges of this form of coaching. The leader coach has a challenging enough time when working one-to-one in developing a trusting relationship with a coachee. Not only does the coachee have to trust that confidences will be held private, but she has to trust that the coach will balance his organizational responsibilities with those he's committed to in the team coaching relationship. So the issues of rapport, collaboration, and commitment may take on different meanings in the context of team coaching. Rather than try to elaborate on every aspect or iteration of the various relationships involved with team coaching, we offer some considerations that the coach should keep in mind and questions to reflect on within the relationship component of the framework. Reflecting on these can help coaches anticipate the problematic aspects, identify solutions, or at least establish clear ground rules for each of the various relationships he might encounter. The leader coach can use these guidelines to become more aware, attuned, and prepared for issues to arise and ways to address them:

- *Who is involved in this coaching relationship?* In a one-to-one coaching relationship, the answer to this question is fairly straightforward. In team coaching, this can be quite complex because there are multiple stakeholders. For example, each of the team members is a stakeholder. In a temporary team, the stakeholder group also includes the bosses of the team members. In all team coaching efforts, there are likely to be other key stakeholders, such as organizational sponsors, HR professionals, and even internal customers. It is wise to think about who else is interested in the coaching work and outcomes in addition to the leader coach and the coachees, and the extent of their investment.

• *Leader coaches should maintain effective, multiple relationships.* When an organization has multiple leader coaches engaged in intentional coaching of their teams or direct reports, the coaches benefit from working together to provide guidance to one another about managing difficult coaching relationships, share any shifting expectations, foster communication among coaches to share best practices, and ensure that the initiative is progressing as expected. The coach-coachee relationship may be complicated by the fact that some coachees may not be in a state of readiness for coaching but were part of teams or groups directed by the organization to participate in the initiative. These relationships must be managed on a case-by-case basis in consultation with the leader coach and his or her manager. Finally, the important job of managing expectations about the coaching initiative hinges on the relationship between the leader coach and his manager.

• *In temporary team coaching, the coach's relationship with each individual coachee may be limited.* In addition, the role the coach plays, which is usually less about the individual coachee's long-term development than it is about the team's learning and achievement of goals, affects the level of rapport that is required in order to achieve results. The coach has to develop rapport with the team and may need to be careful not to create too much variation in the quality of rapport with individual team coachees. When a permanent intact team is being coached, all of the conditions and aspects of rapport that are described in the CCL coaching framework apply.

• *What is the past, present, and future nature of my relationship with these coachees, and what is the nature of my commitment to each individual in this coaching relationship?* In a one-to-one coaching relationship, mutual commitment is critical to success. In team coaching, it may be unrealistic to expect the same high degree of commitment from all participating coachees. The better approach might be for the leader coach to informally consider the level and type of commitment she has with each coachee and set expectations accordingly. Certainly the way she coaches the team should be aimed toward increasing the commitment not only to the relationship but also to their shared goal.

• *To what extent might the individual, team, or group require more than a collaborative approach from me?* In team coaching, often there are specific goals around which the team comes together. Unlike a traditional one-to-one coaching relationship, the goals for the team may be fairly well set at the front end. As a result, the coach may be expected to guide as well as collaborate with the coachees to help them achieve their goals. This is a challenge for the leader coach, who may find it difficult to maintain a collaborative stance because she likely has a depth of knowledge about the organization or the specific business challenge facing the team. The leader coach balances individual, team, and organizational needs, as well as immediate performance results and long-term development issues. Also, there are times when the coach has the ability to reduce barriers because of her role in the organization. Defaulting to a collaborative approach is always a good choice because it helps the individuals and teams access their own resources and develop a learning process that they can replicate for themselves on future business challenges.

Assessment

Assessment in the CCL framework encompasses three dimensions: person, performance, and context. In a team coaching situation where the coach is working with a permanent intact team, assessing and understanding person and performance remains vital for individual members and the team as whole. However, in working with a temporary team or a team that is not intact (dispersed by time or distance, for example), opportunity, time, and need may make it less critical to focus on understanding the team's performance and development needs as well as their context. On a practical basis, the coach and coachees may want to select fewer assessment tools that offer high leverage rather than expect to do an extensive, in-depth assessment of each person and the team. They may also need to enlist the help of others in the organization, perhaps HR, to assist in the selection, administration, and interpretation of results. Time, commitment, and speed are important factors. The time that the coach and coachees give needs to be leveraged for the learning, and speed is critical to providing the coach and coachees meaningful feedback.

Challenge

In a team coaching process, stimulating the right kind of challenge can be tricky because what may create disequilibrium and a motivating challenge for one team member may be quite different for another. The goal that the group seeks to accomplish has to offer sufficient challenge to the entire team and its members in order to gain their attention and maintain their commitment through the sometimes uncomfortable learning process. In addition, the coach has to be able to juggle and attend to the range of responses that the coachees may have to the experience of disequilibrium and help other members of the team do that for each other.

Often in a traditional coaching relationship, the primary source of challenge resides in the assessment feedback with select moments of challenge from the coach. In team coaching, much of the challenge may come from the experiences involved in achieving the team's goal. Frequently the disequilibrium will be experienced real-time through unexpected dynamics in the team or an individual coachee's response to a team dynamic.

To see how this aspect might play out, consider the story of Art and Rachel.

Team members may have very different views on how to handle an aspect of their team project. Rachel chooses to take that moment to give Art feedback on her experience of his tending to dominate and direct the team's process and her decision to assert her needs. Both of them may be experiencing disequilibrium. With Art, it is about managing his reaction to explicit feedback on his dominant style; with Rachel, it is about trying on a new and uncomfortable behavior of being more assertive.

That feedback incident may also create disequilibrium for other team members. For instance, Andreas, who avoids conflict, might experience his own disequilibrium simply by observing and being present during Art and Rachel's discussion.

Part of what makes challenge somewhat unique in a team coaching context is the element of unpredictability. Although certain individual coachee and team challenges can be made explicit, others will emerge as the process unfolds. The coach needs to be highly attentive and skilled at recognizing and helping the coachees and the team manage the challenge and resulting learning.

A coach's role in identifying and managing obstacles in a team coaching situation is typically related to external obstacles. For example, the coach can help remove organizational barriers for the team. This is particularly true when the coach is assigned to a temporary team.

Support

The ways in which the coach supports—maintaining motivation, accessing resources, celebrating wins and managing setbacks, and creating a learning agenda—are readily applicable in a team context. The difference lies primarily in the complexity of trying to support multiple coachees at the same time in a shared context and in providing these dimensions of support to the team as well. That requires tapping into the individual's as well as team's motivation, which may mean facilitating conversations that explore alignment of individual and team goals.

One of the benefits of the coach's helping the coachees and the team access their inner resources is the potential discovery of synergy in the team and the self-managed learning that can result. We know that this is one of the unique possibilities of team coaching: that the whole is larger than the sum of its parts. By helping coachees draw on their individual strengths, knowledge, and skills within the team context, the team moves closer to achieving its goal more effectively.

Helping the team and its individual coachees recognize success and cope with setbacks is an ongoing support function that the team coach provides. Creating organizational change is more complex and challenging than making individual change. Progress is not completely within the coachees' control and is often hard to measure. The coach can provide perspective for the team and discern small indicators of progress. The coach will also need to be a cheerleader when the team has setbacks and help it pull the lessons from the experience, regroup, and explore new options and strategies.

Results

In team coaching, organizational and performance outcomes occupy a prominent role, supplanting in large measure the behavioral and personal results that are common outcomes of individual coaching. Usually the organizational motivator to engage in team coaching is the desire for a systemic improvement to the organization and its performance.

With individual coaching, it is not unusual to be less explicit about outcomes at the start or to commit to general improvements in overall leadership. In fact, leader coaches working on an individual basis might often refrain from fully committing to goals and outcomes until completion of the assessment process because new or more important goals might emerge. In a team coaching environment, the organization and the team usually have a specific goal in mind. The challenge, however, may be in clearly communicating those outcomes. The primary client in team coaching is the individual or group in the organization who is responsible for the initiation of coaching as an intervention. Each degree of separation between this individual or group and the top of the organization increases the likelihood of goal misalignment, since this person or group represents the needs of the organization. To understand the organization's needs, four questions used to assess individual coaching form the basis of the inquiry (Ting & Hart, 2004).

- What reasons drive the request for a team coaching intervention?
- What are the desired outcomes?
- What is the impact if the outcomes are not achieved?
- What causes the individual or group in the organization who is responsible for the initiation of coaching as an intervention to believe that team coaching is the appropriate activity at this time?

If a culture shift is part of the desired outcome, an additional question comes into play:

- What are the current culture and the desired culture, and where are the gaps?

Special Skills and Orientations of Coaches

Holding a team and systemic perspective simultaneously with being mindful of an individual coachee's needs requires a wide range of skills, a particular mind-set, and a high degree of maturity. Coaches who work in this way must be well developed themselves and have sound judgment. In addition to describing many of the qualities leader coaches need in this context, we offer some tips and tactics for implementing team coaching in Exhibit 14.3.

Clarity Regarding Performance and Development

When a coach facilitates the learning for the team as a whole, then coaching takes on a developmental dimension. This learning includes individuals' gaining insight and practicing different behaviors to improve their individual as well as their team member effectiveness, and the team's assessing and moderating its behaviors in order to increase its overall effectiveness. Coaches who understand the nuances of performance and developmental coaching can maximize the learning of both and not overly focus on one to the neglect of the other.

EXHIBIT 14.3. TIPS AND TACTICS WHEN COACHING TEAMS.

A New View

Members within a system (such as a team) begin to respond to the cultural norms of the group without necessarily being aware that their perceptions and behavior are falling under the influence of the group. One of the biggest benefits a team can reap from team coaching is to have the coach view the team through fresh eyes. A tip for leader coaches is to use this knowledge to their advantage by becoming a coach to a group that is not their own. This allows them to see fresh perspectives and heightens the chances that they will see paths and solutions that were previously unseen.

Break the Rules

Don't be afraid to break a few rules. Intentionally doing something different within a team can create positive turbulence and open up new possibilities.

Repeat the Purpose

Frequently restate your purpose and intentions with the group to reinforce alignment. If a team knows that you are intentionally ignoring some of the norms in order to bring fresh perspective, they will be more willing to join the process. If they wonder about your intentions or agenda, they are more likely to resist, either passively or actively.

Speak the Unspoken

Name the elephant in the room. Teams often get stuck around an issue they consider unmentionable. Showing the courage to address unmentionables in a nonjudgmental and nonblaming way can unfreeze a group.

Share Struggles

Show a willingness to share some of your struggles and internal process. By taking risks and allowing members to see some vulnerability, you model authentic collaboration and reduce barriers to development.

Notice Change

Punctuate when you see team members trying new perspectives and behavior. Let people know you notice their efforts and highlight how it moves the team along. Even if someone creates tension within a team by bringing up a contrary position, the team can benefit.

A Legacy and Altruistic Orientation

Team coaching work does not always have immediate payoff or benefit to the coach. The pulls of other business and organizational demands are great and constant. Time is the barrier that keeps leaders from coaching more often. Committing to this type of coaching does call on an altruistic dimension of the coach or a strong connection to the organization and its members, as well as a desire to strengthen the organization's capabilities. We often refer to this as a legacy mind-set, and typically leaders evolve to this place later in their careers after they have accomplished many of their personal goals.

Organizational Savvy

The coach needs to be adept at being part of a coaching organization and not just be skilled at individual coaching. This means being collaborative and open to influence and learning as well as being willing to share unsuccessful strategies so other coaches may avoid the same difficulties. The other aspect of organizational savvy involves coaches' being willing to gain a higher level of industry-specific business knowledge as they work deeper within and across the organization.

Systems Thinking Perspective

Coaches must have enough expertise in organizational dynamics to conduct team coaching with awareness and understanding of the systems issues. Maintaining a systems perspective requires the coach to recognize and appreciate the complex organizational dynamics in which the team operates. The coach ensures a systemic approach through continual awareness of the impact of the coaching process on everyone in the system and vice versa. This approach recognizes the importance of interdependence and encourages respect for the complexity of organizational life. Thinking in terms of systems makes it possible to penetrate beyond organizational complexity to the underlying structures and encourages all partners to appreciate the impact of the team's development and learning on other facets of the organization.

Comfort with Ambiguity

While all coaching work has an aspect of ambiguity and develops in an organic and unpredictable manner, the complexity compounds geometrically as the emerging organizational and team dynamics lend unpredictability to the process. Coaches must be willing to be led by the team to the ways in which the team carries out its work and the outcomes that the team delivers rather than expecting to drive the direction and specific outcomes.

Understanding, Identifying, and Managing Boundaries

Team coaching calls on the coach to be finely attuned to boundary management because there are many more active relationships involved on an ongoing basis and the coach is working within at least three relational units: one-to-one with individual coachees, the team, and the organization. Simply put, it's a lot easier in this kind of complex scenario for the coach to find herself in a compromising or awkward situation and feeling like a decision maker between competing interests or a go-between.

Balancing Individual, Team, and Organizational Needs

This is a companion skill to managing boundaries. In addition to knowing when boundaries of each relationship are being stretched or infringed, the team coach has to be able to balance the needs of each and do that with clarity and consent; otherwise, the relationships suffer. Both of these skills require a great deal of self-clarity and communication. There are times when the coach may need to serve as a facilitator in that process, although the preference is to stay in coaching mode and allow the team and its members to sort out and resolve the differences. For the leader coach accustomed to the pattern and process of one-to-one coaching, team coaching requires a basic shift in orientation from focusing solely on the individual coachee's needs to focusing on the needs of the team and the organization.

Courage, Risk Taking, and Personal Maturity

Being a team coach requires a wide range of skills and perspectives and the ability to know which to access and when. Underlying those are personal qualities of courage, risk taking, and maturity. These are companion qualities that accompany legacy and altruistic orientation and enable the coach to persevere and help the team persevere in the face of challenges.

When action learning leadership is a strong component of the team coaching experience, other coaching competencies and qualities come into play. The challenge for leader coaches in this regard is that these skills are critical and may also at times contradict the skills needed for coaching teams for performance.

Clear Self-Knowledge

The coach must have a clear understanding of his own assumptions about leadership and learning and the ability to keep these assumptions to himself and not impose them on the team. The role of the coach is to meet the team "where they are" and bring them to the next level of developmental complexity.

The Ability to Resist Intervening

In contrast to the performance coach, an action learning coach must allow the team to own its choices, its lessons, and its abilities to use the tools it has available. The coach must avoid any prescriptive approach that would be used in tactical training. In developmental training, interventions get in the way and suppress the ability of the team to grow; as a result, the team starts to become dependent on the coach.

Commitment to Continuous Learning

Action learning coaches must believe in lifelong continuous learning and organizational learning. They must understand and believe that learning occurs beyond the individual. If a team has fourteen members who are developing through an action learning process, the result is more than fourteen developed people. The result is a higher-level outcome in team effectiveness because the fourteen people have developed together. In practical terms, the work of an action learning team can result in more informed, more effective individuals; recommendations for changes that need to be made at the organizational level regarding whatever the team was working on (resolving a complex challenge, for example, such as curing a lack of diversity at the senior leadership level); and a new network of peers who, because they were required to collaborate to solve the complex challenge, now can rely on one another for other challenges that they previously faced individually—the end result being that the organization benefits from this network in ways it never before imagined.

Curiosity

The action learning coach must have a great curiosity for observing and making sense of patterns. It's one thing to understand the granular behaviors of individuals, but it's much more beneficial to the team if the coach can pull out patterns of leadership.

Avoiding Common Pitfalls with Team Coaching

As a result of our experience with team coaching, we've accumulated many lessons, some painfully. To avoid similar pitfalls, we recommend conducting a thorough needs assessment prior to identifying team coaching as the appropriate solution. As with any other leadership development initiative, a needs assessment should identify, at a minimum, the following:

- The organizational challenges that are believed to be resolved or addressed through the use of team coaching—for example, increased competition in the marketplace that threatens the organization's share of the market.
- The specific needs of organizational leaders in addressing these organizational challenges—in other words, what is preventing leaders from resolving these challenges now and what contribution team coaching can make in supporting leaders in doing so. For example, coaching can help leaders respond with agility and flexibility to changing market conditions.
- Specific leadership competencies that are implied by these leadership needs—for example, making effective decisions and influencing others to make critical shifts in the work process.
- The organization's ability to maintain a focus on expected outcomes and holding itself responsible for integrating an appropriate evaluation of the coaching initiative into any development program.
- The aspects of team coaching that are similar to and different from individual coaching. Honor both forms for their strengths and help the client understand the distinctions.
- The capacity for maintaining open and frequent communication paths with the ultimate stakeholders to enable critical modifications to the initiative to be made when necessary.
- The ability to engage the coachees in ensuring the success of the initiative. The coachees are partners with the coaches in creating successful outcomes.

Treat them as such, and hold both coaches and coachees accountable for the outcomes.

Team Coaching Is Not Always the Answer

Even when an organization decides that team coaching is an optimal strategy, a minimal threshold of psychological readiness is required of each team member in order for coaching to proceed. On any given team, there is a strong possibility that one or more team members targeted for coaching will not be in a state of readiness. This possibility needs to be discussed by the leader coach and manager at the start of the project. Responses to this situation can range from allowing individuals freedom to self-select out of the program (which is not possible with intact teams) with no organizational consequences, to the strict expectation that everyone participate fully. The organizational position on this matter needs to align with the stated goals and objectives; otherwise the credibility of the program is undermined.

Organizations with a high degree of readiness for team coaching interventions are able to:

- Determine and clearly communicate to appropriate people the purpose of the coaching initiative.
- Promote and reference the coaching initiative as being in alignment with the vision and values of strategic plans and with the goal of developing talent and sharpening the team's and organization's competitive edge.
- More often use coaching as a developmental rather than rehabilitative process.
- Clearly identify, adequately and consistently communicate, and reinforce the behavior it wants from teams and team members.
- Recognize and respond favorably to new, desired behaviors.
- Tolerate performance dips that occur during the learning process.
- Monitor progress and outcomes, and reward behavioral changes.

If a preponderance of these readiness factors does not exist, chances for successful outcomes are undermined, and the leader coach or the coaching strategy may become the scapegoat.

Conclusion

Team coaching is often left to professional consultants because of the complexity of the work. However, as is true of individual coaching, there is a great deal that leader coaches have to offer in this arena. They have a unique understanding and ability to coach individuals and teams for making change in a team context. Success demands a unique set of skills, commitments, and orientation of its coaches.

The rewards for persistence and initiative are great. When a group of direct reports is engaged simultaneously, functional issues may be identified that would not surface in a one-to-one interaction. Cross-functional conflict or tensions may be surfaced through coaching the entire group. One of the most direct benefits is learning how effectively the organization develops its leaders. Team coaching can generate systemic learning largely because it enables patterns to emerge and to be noted. Team coaching also has the added benefit in that the coaching processes enable coaches and teams to connect the multiple experiences of teams and team members across the organization in a jigsaw puzzle–like manner, resulting in a fuller picture of the organization and its challenges that are relevant to the coaching relationship.

Coach's Bookshelf

Action Learning Institute. http://www.action-learning-institute.com/.

Bacon, T. R., & Spear, K. I. (2003). *Adaptive coaching: The art and practice of a client-centered approach to performance improvement.* Palo Alto, CA: Davies-Black.

Caproni, P. (2000). *The practical coach: Management skills for everyday life.* Upper Saddle River, NJ: Prentice Hall.

Dotlich, D. L., & Cairo, P. C. (1999). *Action coaching: How to leverage individual performance for company success.* San Francisco: Jossey-Bass.

International Foundation for Action Learning. http://www.ifal-usa.org/.

LaRue, B., & Ivany, R. R. (2004). Transform your culture. *Executive Excellence, 21*(12), 14–15.

Leadership in International Management. http://limglobal.net/arl/default.htm.

Levinson, D. J. (1978). *The seasons of a man's life.* New York: Knopf.

Lombardo, M. M., & Eichinger, R. W. (1989). *Eighty-eight assignments for development in place.* Greensboro, NC: Center for Creative Leadership.

Lombardo, M. M., & Eichinger, R. W. (1989). *Preventing derailment: What to do before it's too late.* Greensboro, NC: Center for Creative Leadership.

McNamara, C. (2002). *Authenticity circles facilitator's guide.* Minneapolis: Authenticity Consulting.

Pedler, M. (Ed.). (1997). *Action learning in practice* (3rd ed.). Aldershot, Hampshire: Gower Publishing.

Rothwell, W. J. (1999). *The action learning guidebook: A real-time strategy for problem solving, training design, and employee development.* San Francisco: Jossey-Bass.

CHAPTER FIFTEEN

CREATING A COACHING CULTURE

Sharon Ting

Structured performance and developmental coaching for leaders has traditionally been the province of the external professional coach. The notion that the leader coach can go beyond performance coaching challenges paradigms and assumptions of how leaders typically apply coaching skills. But fast-moving shifts in how coaching has been expanded in leadership arenas over the past ten years support more emergent coaching applications and a broader, deeper view of coaching practice among organizations. Coaching has expanded in several ways:

- From being the province of the professional coach to becoming a competency among managers and leader coaches
- From being used intermittently to "fix" derailing leaders to being used strategically to facilitate growth in high performers
- From focusing primarily on performance to focusing on development as well and integrating the two
- From being used by leaders with a downward focus for their direct reports to being used sideways with peers and upward with superiors
- From being used to improve the effectiveness of individuals to improving teams, groups, and collectives

- From single engagements to multiple sessions and organizational initiatives
- From valuing high-touch, single modality to using multiple and virtual modalities
- From using a universal approach to adapting coaching methods for special leader and leadership needs
- From maintaining hard walls of confidentiality to creating more transparency

With those shifts comes the idea that coaching is a fundamental leadership responsibility. Furthermore, leader coaches add different dimensions to the coaching relationship. They have often been through a similar experience themselves. Hunt and Weintraub (2002) claim that effective leader coaches show less need for control and are more interested in helping rather than fixing.

This orientation helps to explain how coaching relationships among peers, and even direct reports, can also emerge and reinforce the growing understanding that coaches are not all knowing and their primary responsibility is not to "fix" things and people. Many leaders gain their best learning from peers. One study by the Corporate Leadership Council (2001) revealed that in addition to leaders' desiring more coaching and feedback in general, they saw peers as a primary and valuable source for that form of learning.

No longer are organizations outsourcing coaching initiatives exclusively to external coaches. Savvy organizational sponsors understand that effecting change—a person at a time and from the inside out—has an impact beyond that person because of his or her organizational roles and influence on others; hence, the importance of ongoing investment in individual leader coaching is clear. These sponsors also recognize that integrating a coaching approach with leader development early in the careers of leaders offers a sustainable model for improving and maintaining leadership bench strength. This is the essence of a coaching culture—one in which a variety of leaders and managers in many functions throughout an organization apply coaching skills and attitudes daily, and they use these skills not only to develop people but also to manage people while they themselves are solving demanding and stressful business challenges.

How do we get more leaders across the organization practicing effective coaching with their direct reports, peers, superiors, and teams? Leaders ask CCL this question frequently after they emerge from intensive coaching workshops armed with greater awareness about the power of coaching to address performance and development issues and effect change. That is a tough question to answer when, in essence, these leaders are looking to make systemic changes. How do you move from the power of one to the power of many?

In the coaching arena, this is a meaningful question, because when a leader is coaching an individual for a specific behavior or development area, it helps if others in that person's sphere of operation are supporting that goal by reinforcing the desired behavior and informally using coaching skills when interacting with the coachee. In order to achieve this desired state, more individuals within an organization need to be equipped with an understanding of what is meant by coaching and the ability to employ basic coaching skills. This means leaders and organizations need to find efficient and effective ways to distribute coaching skills throughout the organization, championing a standard of excellence for coaching when it is used, and facilitating the creation of coaching communities.

To reach this point, organizations have to take a significant role in establishing an environment that welcomes and supports the practice of leader coaching. This chapter addresses what organizations can do to support and enhance the coaching efforts of leaders. It makes three important points that organizations should consider when working toward creating a viable coaching culture. First, it describes efforts to embed and cascade throughout the organization a mind-set that welcomes the acquisition of coaching skills and supports their use. Second, it describes how an individual or a group is necessary to champion the goal of ensuring excellence in leadership coaching practices. Third, it offers some specific recommendations on how organizations can create a coaching community.

Embedding a Coaching Mind-Set

The first and perhaps most essential way to create a coaching culture is to establish the value and impart effective coaching skills to as many supervisors, managers, and leaders as possible. These experiences help them realize that using effective coaching skills is not limited to situations where they are working with their direct reports and can have a powerful ability to help sustain individual and organizational growth. The challenge is the cost and time in putting significant numbers of managers and leaders through an intensive coaching orientation experience or skills training. In addition, the more sequential process of training elongates the organizational learning curve.

Organizations are experimenting with a number of ways to facilitate this extension of learning to others. The approaches have varying degrees of intentionality and formality. We favor using a variety of formal and informal approaches. The key and common element is consistency of message and behaviors on coaching. The following reflects our experience of the formal and informal approaches that clients are using.

Role Modeling by Leader Coaches

This is perhaps the least expensive and structured approach. Yet it is a highly effective means of embedding the value of coaching and cascading these skills and creating culture shifts in how leaders develop other leaders. It also requires extensive commitment on the leader's part to developing himself, with constant reflection and self-assessment about his own strengths and weaknesses as a coach.

Jan is a vice president of marketing who began twelve years earlier as a marketing specialist. During his first seven years, he consistently exceeded expectations. Promotions came easily, and he relied on his natural skills and instincts to guide him in meeting the demands of each new role. When we asked him what role his bosses played in coaching him along the way, he told us, "For the first seven years, nothing. Not bad or good. It was neutral." They had no impact. What changed for Jan occurred in his eighth year when his boss, Frans, called and asked him to think about three questions in anticipation of their performance and development discussion: "How would you assess your overall performance, strengths, and development needs this past year? What would you like to be doing in three years? What do you need to learn or add to your skills and experience in order to be ready for that future role? And I've set aside an hour for us to have this conversation."

Jan was initially nervous and anxious for days leading up to the discussion. He assumed some bad news was coming because of the contrast with previous discussions. The conversation turned out to be one of the most motivating and thought provoking of his career. It created awareness for Jan, and a new standard of expectation, for how meaningful a performance and development discussion could be. Jan himself now gets superior feedback from direct reports for his developmental and coaching approach with them because of the positive role model that Frans set for him. So role models beget other role models.

We know that actions speak louder than words. Too often we hear that a very senior leader is championing the cause of coaching but not very effective himself at having a coaching mind-set and approach to developing others. Role modeling doesn't mean being a perfect coach or a perfect leader. It does mean using coaching skills intentionally and appropriately, allowing oneself to be coached, and being transparent about one's own strengths and struggles.

When we ask leaders to share a past developmental conversation or experience that was positive, we hear a wide variety of stories and descriptions of coaching styles. Some used a supportive, inspirational approach. Others cited examples of people who used a challenging and tough love approach. All described individuals who were intent on helping the storyteller, the coachee, learn important lessons of life and leadership. We would say that each demonstrated commitment to the other person's learning and growth. They gave of themselves, not just their knowledge, and, in some cases, put themselves and the relationship on the line.

Practices. Role models rarely think of themselves in that way. Usually others who have experienced these individuals as consistently exhibiting coaching behaviors and orientation bestow that mark of distinction on them. Despite the informal and organic ways in which role models develop, there are some ways to leverage existing and encourage growth of more role models for coaching within an organization:

- Recognize them through internal mentoring or coaching programs where they are invited to be part of a select group of coaches to support developing leaders.
- Use them to teach coaching to others through internal training programs.
- Recognize their contribution through a performance review process, especially where coaching and developing others is considered a core competency.
- Use them as advisers or seek their input when designing and implementing leadership, mentoring, and coaching initiatives.

It is especially helpful if these coaching role models are also viewed as highly successful on other leadership dimensions, such as achieving results, strategic thinking, operational excellence, or relationship building. This adds to their credibility as a coach and the incorporation of coaching as a strategic competency rather than a leadership skill that is nice to have but not essential.

Integrate with Leadership Training and Development

It is becoming quite common, with the emphasis on the critical role that leadership plays in ensuring their viability, for companies to incorporate coaching in their formal programs and processes designed specifically to prepare their emerging and high-potential individuals for greater leadership responsibility. A study by the Center for Effective Organizations supports this approach and concludes that coaching improves effectiveness in organizations when it is used systemically and strategically, not just as an intervention (Levinson, 2004). Many organizations that incorporate coaching and developing others as dimensions in their leadership competency model have also found it useful to support the development of that competency by including a learning component in the formal development processes devoted to coaching skills.

Leaders note that the gap between knowing what effective coaching behaviors are and being able to enact them consistently presents an ongoing challenge. Often their strengths and the skills for which they have been rewarded are around achieving results quickly and efficiently. The most common development need for these leaders around coaching skills, not surprisingly, is learning how to let go of that style and mind-set when they are helping others to grow. It does require a conscious shift from a problem-solving mentality to a collaborative discovery process. Exposing leaders early in their career to anticipate the skill sets needed to be successful at more senior levels not only benefits them; it also raises their consciousness about doing the same for those they are responsible for developing.

For developing leaders who have not had positive role models for coaching, the experience or practice with a coach in a training program may be their first exposure to the principles of good coaching. Often they have only one or two mental models of coaching coming in, such as that of an athletics coach. Being exposed to other approaches, even if only in a classroom setting, can be the seed that later bears fruit for the development of a personal style and approach to coaching that is more versatile, expansive, and robust.

Practices. Organizations can take a number of tangible actions to incorporate coaching into their training and leadership development processes:

- Incorporate a module on coaching concepts and practices within classroom-based leadership training initiatives.

- Devote a series of days or a whole program to coaching and development covering definition of and how it links with the organization's vision and strategy, desired behaviors, how it differs from supervision, use for performance and development, and providing opportunities for practice and skill building.
- Have leaders receive coaching as part of their development through internal or external coaches.
- Include and highlight the addition of coaching as a performance criterion and a critical skills set for individuals moving into managerial and leadership roles.
- Incorporate peer coaching groups as a component of a structured leadership development process. This can operate independent of or supplemental to one-to-one coaching. These peer coaching groups can be used to support one another on the achievement of a leadership behavior or business challenge.

Develop Internal Coach Cadres

More and more organizations are seeking help with developing internal coaches who can serve as coaching resources to emerging and seasoned leaders. The individuals whom companies select to be part of these coaching cadres typically, but not always, reside in the human resource group. The more important selection criteria are passion and commitment to coaching. The addition of this skill often parallels the organization's growing emphasis on coaching as a leadership competency.

Common reasons given by organizations for pursuing this approach are to:

- Provide coaching for leaders who might not otherwise have access to coaching.
- Capitalize on the deep knowledge that internal coaches have about the organization and the individual coachee's context.
- Use the access that an internal coach may have to resources within the organization to support the coachee's needs.
- Complement the use of external coaches.
- Leverage the impact that having multiple, simultaneous, geographically distributed coaching engagements can have on creating a culture that embraces and supports coaching.
- Strengthen the role and perception of HR professionals and managers, who can be active enablers in the leadership development processes as well as

role models for adopting a coaching orientation and strategic partners with business unit heads.
- Provide a cost-effective means of expanding and sustaining the benefits of coaching services.

Practices. We have worked with one organization since 2000 to build the coaching skills of its HR managers. Representatives came to us with a challenge and hope that they described this way: "Our HR managers spend a lot of energy supporting our plant managers with their personnel and human resource needs. Too often we are coming in behind to help sort out an issue that could have been avoided had the manager exhibited leadership at the right time and in the right way. We want to be proactive, not reactive, and see if we can help our managers develop leadership skills."

The approach that the organization initially adopted was a two-part classroom program with individual coaching support for each participant coach. The classroom component was five days in total: first three days and then two days six months later. Each participant identified a coaching candidate who agreed to be in the coaching relationship. In the first year, CCL supported the participant coaches' learning by holding quarterly virtual conferences. In addition, at least one day every year, CCL held a workshop to reinforce best practices, expose coaches to additional coaching concepts and practices, and engage in experiential learning.

Three years after the start of the program, CCL examined its impact. Overall, the coaches, coachees, and bosses reported that coaching was effective and helped improve the leadership effectiveness of coachees. Particular strengths noted in the evaluation included developing relationships and assessing strengths and development needs. The areas in which coaches sought further development related to including bosses and senior management, among others, in the process; integrating assessments; and identifying high-leverage development goals. From these findings, CCL was able to confirm the ability of nonprofessional coaches to acquire coaching skills and the importance of ongoing practice to solidifying and refining those skills.

Use Peer Coaching

Peer coaching happens all the time, but it is not usually recognized when it occurs because it often looks like two colleagues simply offering support to each other around challenging situations. Moreover, the notion that peers may be competitors and therefore unable to provide unbiased feedback or coaching might also be a factor. However, the power of peer coaching is yet to be leveraged. The CLC study (2001) noting that leaders felt they didn't receive sufficient feedback and coaching in spite of the perceived benefits also noted a preference and desire for more feedback and coaching from peers. The power of peer coaching is yet to be fully explored and understood.

Practices. One company has piloted an action-learning process in which peers coach each other in their leadership of managing complex business problems. Using a very structured process, this company created peer coaching groups led by a trained external facilitator. The peer group composition required individuals who came from different functions and were committed to meeting on a regular basis and adhering to a structured process. Each participant presented to the group a business issue that had defied his or her ability to find a satisfying solution. The peers function as coaches, and each in turn asks questions of the individual with the challenge. They are not permitted to offer advice, nor would they be equipped to do so since their backgrounds are varied.

Learning occurs in two ways. First, each person develops and refines his or her questioning skills, which is fundamental to effective coaching. Second, each learns to examine the business problems with new perspectives and in that process discover alternative solutions. Opportunities are sometimes given for group members to offer specific advice or ideas, but that process is kept distinct from the coaching. The cornerstones of the effectiveness of this process are the use of powerful questions, the disciplined process employed, and an underlying and enduring belief in the capability of individuals to solve their own challenges.

Develop Leaders as Senior Coaches

This is a more emergent and recent phenomenon that we are seeing companies begin to explore. Leaders who have attended workshops on coaching are articulating how critical coaching is but also how difficult it is for them to retain the learning and maintain the discipline to apply these skills effectively on a consistent basis. A number have raised the merits of developing a few highly talented seasoned leaders who could, with further development and skills building, act as senior coaches within the organization.

We have worked with a number of organizations whose top leaders understand how critical a role they play in the development of other senior leaders. To a large extent, they exhibit coaching skills that they've learned through experience, by observing good and poor role models, by receiving coaching, and in some cases by taking some workshops in coaching. What distinguishes these leader coaches is their deep commitment to and conviction of the benefits of coaching, especially with other leaders who are unlikely to receive, and maybe even feel they no longer need, feedback and coaching. These leaders have sought us out to help them refine skills. This often takes the form of workshops and coaching from a seasoned external coach. They've found it helpful to use an external coach as a sounding board and a preparatory coach for more challenging coaching situations that they face.

One key benefit is the ready access that others would have to them when challenging coaching issues arise. Many of the leaders who would be good candidates already perform that role informally because of their recognized skills as mentors and good listeners. These individuals are uniquely positioned because of their stature, knowledge, and skill to have a high impact on the organizational culture and stance toward coaching.

Another benefit to this approach is that these leaders are more likely to have the authority to direct development processes or to have a direct impact on a decision regarding a specific individual's development needs.

The challenge in pursuing this type of initiative is the many other demands on these individuals for their skills, not only in coaching but also in solving business problems. For this concept to work, the individuals involved must have a strong personal value and commitment to coaching and hold a role in the organization that either formalizes their focus on development or at least makes coaching a visible and central part of their success.

Practices. This concept is similar to using role models to reinforce the value of coaching. Role models support a coaching mind-set through the example they set and by offering others the ability to observe effective coaching skills in real time. Ideally the leaders who are tapped to be senior coaches for the purpose of developing others as coaches should also be individuals whom others see as role models. Developing internal senior coaches takes time and commitment. These individuals can be identified through initiatives to train internal coaches. Their skills and natural orientation to coaching are apparent.

Developing them requires commitment by the organization to allow these individuals the time to engage in additional training usually externally provided, such as through certification programs offered by universities or independent entities and to practice those skills in more frequent and formal settings within the organization.

Champion Excellence in Coaching Practice

Leader coaches, especially those at very senior levels, can help create a coaching culture by leveraging their organizational role. The leader coach can influence resource decisions as they relate to coaching, the ways in which coaching is used, and quality expectations. We have all heard stories of coaching gone awry, with resulting negative impact for the coachee and the organization. We believe that a closer review of these situations would reveal a fundamental lack of clarity and expectations for what coaching is and how it will be conducted. These situations contribute to why in some organizations coaching is viewed as labeling a leader as "having problems." Leader coaches and organizations can play important roles in altering these beliefs through a variety of actions applied with persistence and resolve. Some practical ways in which leaders and organizations can explicitly support coaching that we discuss in the following sections are reinforcing the developmental role of coaching, especially for ascending leaders; demanding quality; providing resources; integrating internal and external coaching; creating coaching communities; and supporting continuous learning.

Reinforce the Developmental Role of Coaching

Although coaching has become a more familiar and common activity in organizations, the understanding of how it's used and its role in development remains tenuous. Even when an organization offers coaching as a supportive, developmental experience, the coachee usually remains suspicious that the coaching is really to "fix" him or her.

The leader coach therefore has an important responsibility for articulating the role of coaching and then backing that up in meaningful and visible ways. If everyone knows, for instance, that Joe is receiving internal coaching and then six months later he is terminated, it's unlikely that the next candidate for coaching will engage wholeheartedly. But if the leader coach is spending committed and concerted effort working with a direct report, coaching her on developmental issues, and then a year later she is promoted or is given more responsibility and visibility, then the coaching will be viewed as beneficial.

These examples highlight the importance of having criteria, even if implicit, for selecting individuals who will receive formal internal or external coaching. Because formal coaching tends to be more visible, others look to those outcomes as signals for how the coaching is being used. One company has devised a decision-making matrix that looks at the readiness of the coach, coachee, organization and context, and potential business impact. This helps internal coaches understand what type of coaching situation they may be entering. That awareness can assist with the front-end decision-making process, with the contracting discussions, and finally in anticipating challenges within the coaching.

In ongoing development processes, the leader coach can informally reinforce the role of coaching by setting expectations for managers to regularly engage in performance and development discussions, asking questions that help them gain insight into the quality of those discussions, and incorporating that expectation into their evaluations of them as effective leaders and developers of other leaders. Formal actions include requesting or contracting directly for coaching services for their direct reports when needed and engaging in coaching for themselves.

By the way they use coaching and the outcomes, leader coaches can shape perceptions about the value of receiving coaching and developing coaching skills.

Practices. While using coaching for ascending executives and leaders is ideal, it is also natural for organizations to look to coaching as a way to remediate behaviors that detract from or interfere with an individual leader's effectiveness. And when these coaching engagements are entered into in a one-off manner, it is hard to counteract the perceptions that coaching is for "problem" leaders. An approach organizations can use to avoid that perception is to undertake a specific coaching initiative for a select group of high-achieving leaders with the expressed purpose of furthering their development as leaders. One company we worked with did that for members of its management committee. These were already well-established leaders whose reputations within the organization were stellar. Many of them were considered candidates for the executive committee. Key elements of the initiative included having a critical mass of individuals go through the same process simultaneously; designing a robust and rich feedback process that included quantitative normative surveys and qualitative interview data; setting a time frame; involving top leadership in providing feedback; having the leader propose a development plan after synthesizing the assessment data; structuring a development discussion for the leader and select superiors that commits each participant to his or her role in supporting the agreed-on development plan; and including a follow-up discussion within a set time frame.

Demand Quality

Informed consumers are satisfied consumers because they know what they want and how to gauge quality. In coaching, the idea of standards has been most closely associated with professional external coaches and usually elicits discussions of credentials, experience, and personal qualities. It can also raise a heated debate regarding licensing and certification (a subject for discussion at a different time and place).

With regard to the leader coach, we mean to reference effective coaching behaviors, understanding the importance of contracting as it relates to implicit and explicit roles and expectations. We encourage the leader coach to aspire to the same standards of behavior and skills that he would want to receive from a professional coach if he were the coachee. One place to codify and be explicit about these desired behaviors might be within the organization's formal leadership competencies. There, the behaviors become part of the performance expectation for leaders, and leader coaches may be able to get feedback on their skills if the organization links those competencies to a 360-degree feedback tool.

Practices. Organizations can put specific steps into place to ensure quality for external coaches:

- Understand the philosophy and principles under which the coach works.
- Check the references of the coach.
- Examine coaches' specific practices and processes.
- Ask coaches for the ethical guidelines under which they operate.
- Incorporate a formal feedback and evaluation process.

- Explicitly ask about coaches' guidelines for sharing information and managing confidentiality.

Although these guidelines do not readily apply to leader coaches, they can be adapted when internal coaches are used.

Provide Resources

Perhaps one of the more obvious ways in which the leader coach can help embed coaching behaviors as part of the organizational culture is to use budgetary authority to support the use of coaching. Too often when expenditure reductions are needed, training and development are the first to get cut. At those times, it is important to have leaders who believe in the cost benefit of coaching and its role in achieving needed productivity and performance. One might argue that during times of financial challenges, coaching employees to maintain optimism, focus, and even exceed results becomes an essential leadership skill. Providing resources could also mean regularly contracting for the use of external coaches or sponsoring internal and external training of managers in coaching skills and orientations. It could be as simple as purchasing books, articles, developing internal guides, and providing access to other tools that can aid managers in being better coaches.

Practices. One very practical way that leaders help to create a coaching culture is through resource support, specifically to:

- Incorporate coaching services in their budgets.
- Lend support to HR executives who include development offerings in their leadership.
- Sponsor or support initiatives to improve coaching skills for managers, leaders, and HR professionals.
- Maintain an appropriate level of coaching resources during tight fiscal periods.

Integrate Internal and External Coaching

A number of organizations use coaching extensively enough that the potential for unintentional fragmentation and development of disparate agendas becomes more prevalent. Some forward-looking companies invest time and resources to organize annual or biannual learning days or conferences for their internal and external coaches. These sessions provide opportunities to discuss executive coaching in the context of strategic direction and share information about the executive coaching process, from development needs of executives to best practices.

On a day-to-day basis, these companies are facilitating the integration by having select HR staff, who typically serve as informal coaches, function as coordinators and hubs for coaching work that involves multiple individuals within the same business unit. Frequently when a series of individuals from a single business unit are engaging in more formalized coaching, their issues may overlap, that is, a change in one coachee requires a change in another or has an impact on another coachee. These coaches can communicate and coordinate their coaching work directly or can rely on a coordinator. Regardless of which approach is used, getting permission from the coachee to exchange information and agreement on the limits of what information is shared is essential for this integration to work effectively.

These approaches are still in their infancy, with organizations testing different methods and realizing the complexity of managing multiple coaching work from within and outside the organization.

Create Coaching Communities

By definition, a community is public and visible. Its norms are understood. Thinking of coaching as a community within an organization has implications for allowing coaching processes to be more transparent. This provides the opportunity for leader coaches to develop shared language, mental models, perspectives, and practices among themselves and with other internal and external coaches. In doing that, they create an unspoken invitation to exchange what they've learned, gain different perspectives, share successes and frustrations, and provide support to one another. Through that informal exchange, the organization's coaching and development processes are strengthened simply by the fact that the subject is being discussed.

A large part of community building can derive from the involvement of multiple coaches supporting the development of a single coachee. She might have a combination of coaches, the leader coach, internal coach, or external coach working with her.

One client with whom we work has incorporated the use of external coaches in a leadership development program for high-potential managers. At the same time, many of these managers are also participating in coaching with an internal HR manager who has gone through a more extensive coaching training by us. Not only is the manager benefiting from the support of a community of coaches, but also the coachee is serving to foster the internal HR manager coach's learning and development as a coach.

One aspect of communities is the development of norms. In a coaching community, this would translate into understandings about how we will operate, setting boundaries, establishing expectations around ethical behaviors in managing confidential information, and, where multiple coaches are involved, respecting the hierarchy of coaching relationships. If an organization wants the benefits of transparency and a coaching community, this last issue should be given a lot of attention. In the absence of explicitly dealing with this issue, organizations run the risk of compromising the coaching relationships and damaging trust.

Support Continuous and Sustainable Learning

We've discussed extensively the importance of and processes being used by organizations to teach fundamental coaching skills. The level and quality of coaching can be conducted on a number of levels, and one value to creating a coaching community is the opportunity it offers for generating continuous learning. In a previous section, we highlighted how one organization was using a biannual conference to bring together internal and external coaches. In addition to facilitating the integration of these two groups of coaches, this organization is also facilitating ongoing learning for both groups. There is not a presumption that one or the other group is more knowledgeable. The external coaches are not being held up as more expert. The learning among all coaches and leaders, internal and external, needs to be mutual.

A challenge for all coaches is how to sustain their learning because coaching has been treated as a solitary activity between the coach and coachee. We encourage leaders and organizations to create opportunities to reinforce previous learning and add new approaches to their skill set.

Practices. Two companies we've worked with address this need by running annual or semiannual learning days that serve as boosters. Coaches return for refresher courses or to acquire new skills. In every case where a leader is attending a refresher course, this person's feedback at the conclusion of the workshop is how differently he or she absorbed the information the second time around and that the knowledge had greater relevance and meaning the second time. We believe this reinforces our belief that coaching is a human interaction skill, highly related to emotional competencies, and therefore the learning of the skill happens through extended practice, reflection, and feedback.

These learning workshops can be conducted virtually, using combinations of teleconference and Web-based tools. Leaders and organizations can also support continued learning by providing resources and tools for self-learning. This can involve disseminating information on the latest books, articles, and tools to support best coaching practices.

Another approach is encouraging the use of peer coaching. We believe this is currently an underused resource. Clients tell us time is the greatest obstacle, although when they are successful in scheduling, the learning is tremendous.

Conclusion

Leader coaches may not normally consider that they can play a larger role in creating a coaching community. With all the other organizational and business demands placed on them, taking the time to coach their direct reports in a more intentional manner alone is a major accomplishment and deserves acknowledgment. We believe that the benefit to creating a coaching culture is that coaching becomes second nature and more effortless. Coaching then doesn't feel like a second job but more the way in which leaders and managers enact portions of their primary job. Coaching becomes less of an activity and more of a behavioral norm and one of a number of capabilities that leaders need to access with ease when the situation calls for that approach or mindset. As these skills become more embedded in the organization, benefits devolve throughout and offer the opportunity to learn as well.

AFTERWORD

Sharon Ting

The members of the executive team engaged in a succession-planning discussion for a large multinational manufacturing firm are reflecting on the final question that Gil, the CEO, has put to them: "Should we plan for Wanda's next position to broaden her understanding of the company's global operations through an ex-pat assignment as European head of sales and marketing and, if so, what type of developmental support should we offer along with that assignment?"

Wanda is an African American female executive and the regional sales and marketing head of the organization's largest region in North America. A high-potential leader, she is bright, personable, creative, and a calculated risk taker. Adding to Wanda's personal leadership strengths are the goodwill benefits that accrue to the company from women, minorities, and other nontraditional employees, all of whom view Wanda as a symbol of change and opportunity. Hal, her boss, takes great pride in being Wanda's coach and mentor and having helped develop her talent and gain visibility over the five years they've worked together.

So far she has delivered on her potential by bringing fresh thinking to her role. At the same time, well-known differences bordering on friction exist between her staff and her peers' staff. Phil is Wanda's counterpart in operations. The senior executives agree they should consider and try to understand this dynamic better prior to her move. They don't know whether the differences lie between her and Phil's leadership styles and are cascading to the staff level, rest between key members of their respective units, or simply reflect the natural divergence in viewpoints based on their functional roles. The executive team speculates on how this dynamic might play out with Phil's European counterpart, Emil, who is even more of a traditionalist and operations-focused leader. Emil is German born and has worked exclusively in the company's European operations, where few women hold positions beyond first-line managers.

Gil's final comments as the group moves to review the next leader are, "Hal, we have at least a year before we need to make a decision on reassignments. You have my blessing to supplement our usual development processes for Wanda to better understand her current leadership style and prepare her for the opportunity. Whatever we do, let's make sure we look at the bigger picture and not jump to assume this is simply a personal leadership issue for Wanda."

Although this might have been an unlikely scenario twenty years ago, it's a more common occurrence in today's diverse, complex, global business environment. Where and how should Hal begin to define Wanda's developmental challenges and coaching needs? What gets addressed, who is involved, and what are the priorities?

Taking a systemic perspective on Wanda's leadership challenges and coaching needs offers greater opportunity to cascade what she learns to others in her sphere of influence. Systemic issues have always been present in coaching interactions, but may not be explicitly surfaced because the coach and coachee don't see them, feel they go beyond the bounds of the engagement, or feel they are beyond their ability to influence.

This closing discussion explores the notion of what a systems perspective on coaching means and what some of the implications are for the practice of coaching. This is an emergent area, and we have more questions than answers. By opening the discussion, we hope other practitioners will join us to incorporate their practice and ideas into the dialogue.

A Systemic Approach to Coaching

Systems thinking, championed most notably by Peter Senge in *The Fifth Discipline* (1990), looks at the whole and the interaction of the parts in contrast to analyzing and applying solutions to a specific part. An underlying assumption is that applying solutions to only a specific part of the system may not have the desired impact or, worse yet, might have an adverse impact or the opposite impact from the desired outcome. Systems thinking focuses on how the thing being studied interacts with the other constituents of the system—a set of elements that interact to produce behaviors—of which it is a part.

Thus, when a leader—a notable element of the system—changes (becomes more decisive, more inclusive, or more empowering), the rest of the system—her team, for example—does not remain unchanged. Individuals and sometimes an entire group have to choose how to respond to that change. In essence, the leader's shift creates challenge for others.

In Wanda's case, Hal may successfully coach her to reach out to Phil and develop a more collaborative approach to solving problems. But if they haven't anticipated how this change might translate to the respective functions and line staff and what coaching they may need to incorporate this new approach into their day-to-day interactions, then the possibility for broader learning and change may be missed.

Managers and leaders who have been trained with the notion of systemic thinking know to look for root causes to business problems. They anticipate how changes or improvements in a specific part of a process may have implications for the larger process or can create problems elsewhere. Imagine, for example, the production line in a manufacturing operation. The product coming off the line is not meeting specifications. A wise plant manager looks at the entire process to find the root cause, and even when he believes he has found the root cause, before making permanent changes he might assess how the corrective action will affect other steps in the operation. In addition, he might look beyond the apparent root cause and examine how a series of changes in a number of areas might produce an even more effective and sustainable improvement.

When these ideas are applied to coaching, one implication is that behavioral or attitudinal changes that the coachee undertakes may have an impact on the way the system in which she operates functions. Also, changes in one aspect of the system—the coachee—without corresponding examination and changes in other parts of the system can simply push the problem to another part of the system or neutralize the desired change. To see how this plays out, take the example of Mel:

Mel provides the financial management support to several business units in an organization with a tradition of strong centralized systems and controls. Mel has the reputation of being highly controlling, inflexible, and rules bound. Part of his development as a leader is learning to shift his approach from one of oversight and control to one of service and collaborative problem solving.

Mel's boss, the organization's CFO, is fairly new to the company and sees Mel's behavior as a leadership weakness. This view is reinforced by the senior vice president who runs these business units and to whom Mel indirectly reports. What the CFO doesn't yet understand or appreciate is that some of the business units have a history of being inattentive to and unskilled at managing their financials and were not well prepared for a shift toward operating with a greater decentralization of responsibility.

Eight months after Mel responds to the feedback that he needs to modify his style and be more trusting, the comptroller's staff discover breaches of the company's financial standards within one of the business units. In essence, Mel's controlling and inflexible behavior was compensating for weaknesses in knowledge and discipline, within the particular business unit that he supports, for applying the desired financial practices consistently.

Mel's story points out the value of considering the system implications of coaching. A narrow focus on Mel's leadership style underestimates the interdependency of Mel's behavior with that of others. A more systemic view might have uncovered and surfaced those issues sooner. For leader coaches, who are typically part of that system, this poses additional complexity to their work as coaches.

Surfacing Common Systemic Issues Through Coaching

We do not yet have a formal structure to fully frame our ideas about the relationship of coaching and systemic thinking. What we do have are the many experiences of coaching individual leaders where we've seen the benefits of coaching limited or neutralized by dynamics occurring within the system in which the individual resides. We've also seen unintended consequences of the individual coaching when the coach did not fully appreciate and consider that system, as we noted in the case of Mel.

In this section, we highlight a few themes that seem to reoccur, many of which arise in conjunction with one another. That is the nature of systems. However, we've written about them separately to note what is distinctive and to help the leader coach identify what may be a more significant systems issue confounding individual coaching efforts. We also share those themes in the spirit of encouraging leader and other coaches to incorporate this thinking into their coaching.

Mixed Messages

It's not uncommon for coachees to discover in the course of their work that the organization and individual decision makers are not actually rewarding the behaviors articulated through the coaching process.

Coachees may wonder whether in fact the changes people are asking them to make are really rewarded or desired by the organization. We see at least three ways in which this issue manifests itself: (1) the organization has no public or explicit value around the behavior the coachee is being asked to develop; (2) the organization does incorporate the behaviors within its stated values but in reality overtly rewards different behaviors; and (3) the organization includes and values the desired behaviors, but in comparison to the weight given other values, it never becomes a meaningful priority.

The first point is simply a matter of fact. Does the organization's formal mission or statement of values explicitly incorporate the behaviors that the coachee is being asked to develop? For instance, an individual who was given feedback that his home and work life was severely out of balance readily pointed out that the organization's stated vision and values talked about people development but not about respect for their personal lives. In fact, the organization provided many opportunities for development, to the point that the individual felt that when he wasn't under the pressure to produce, he was under the pressure to develop himself further for the benefit of the organization. He felt the implicit value was "do it all and do it well."

The second point is essentially the not "walking the talk" syndrome. The organization publicly proclaims a set of values, but there are no repercussions for not living the values or desired behaviors. It's hard to motivate a coachee to do the hard work of learning a new behavior when she looks around and sees few other leaders acting in accordance with stated values or, worse yet, sees others being rewarded for doing the exact opposite.

The third way in which organizations inadvertently neutralize or confuse coaching efforts is probably the most common. The organization may be aspirational in its values, touting such phrases as "Developing Our People" or "Treat Our Employees as We Want Them to Treat Our Customers," but repeatedly it allows other values such as "Getting Results" or "Minimizing Cost and Eliminating Waste" to override or eclipse its stated values. The implicit message is that certain values take lower priority. And low-priority items rarely get done. Individuals who are interested in success and mobility will pick up subtle clues about what they need to do and where they need to spend time to be successful.

Collusion

This issue is related to but different from the first. In organizational or individual collusion, despite the sincere belief that behavioral change is warranted, the organization or the coachee's colleagues respond in a way to keep the undesirable behavior in place. In other words, the coachee's undesirable behavior is meeting some need. In order for the coachee to change, the organization or individual also has to change.

Two common examples of organizational collusion are promoting individuals too quickly and overusing their strengths even though organizational decision makers privately acknowledge that certain skill sets are underdeveloped. Organizations that are fearful of losing talent or that see holes in their leadership bench strength try to compensate by accelerating exceptional performers (Bunker, Kram, & Ting, 2002). Alternatively, organizations see that an individual has a talent for managing certain types of issues, such as turning around a business or starting a new business, and continues to assign her those challenges, albeit bigger ones, rather than offer her a different assignment. In both instances, the organization may persist in these actions despite its awareness of the individual's weaknesses or development needs. The rationalization frequently is based on legitimate fears about losing the individual, the critical need of this person's skills on the specific assignment, and the belief that the desired but neglected leadership skills can be developed later. Often the result is that instead of becoming a well-rounded executive, the individual becomes lopsided. She never really learns certain key leadership lessons because developmentally she is not ready to internalize or never gets exposed to the experiences that offer those lessons. The tacit collusion occurs when both parties acknowledge what skills need to be learned and then either developmental assignments are delayed in favor of assignments that continue to draw on proven strengths or when relevant developmental assignments are provided, the organization doesn't ensure follow-through on development goals.

Collusion can also play out at individual levels when certain people need the coachee's behavior to remain unchanged in order to continue their own. For example, a coachee who is being coached to be more assertive and take initiative may run afoul of colleagues who are unusually dominant and count on the individual to accede to and support their views. If that coachee suddenly takes a different position or asks to take the lead on a project, the more dominant colleagues will need to adjust their behaviors lest they appear to be in competition or conflict. They may have to learn to accept not getting their way or being the center of attention. What often occurs is an unconscious attempt by others to get the individual to revert back to his old behavior so they can maintain their own patterns of behavior. If successful, you might hear the lament, "Yeah, Joe tried to change and did for a while but then went back to his old ways." What these individuals are not saying is how uncomfortable it was for them to relate to Joe in a different way and that it may have required them to behave differently.

The last form of collusion builds on the second and relates to how patterns of individual behaviors over time can form a role that the individual plays in the organization. When a set pattern of behavior becomes ingrained in the workings of the group, team, or organization, a coachee may actually take on an informal role, such as the "stickler" who makes sure things are done well and right or the "rebel" who always finds fault with an approach but inevitably sparks the group's thinking to a higher level or helps it to avoid groupthink. Effectively coaching someone to make stylistic or behavioral changes when that style may be playing a powerful role in his group, team, or unit is difficult if the systemic issue isn't acknowledged and managed while the coaching is occurring.

Team Dysfunction

Building teams, having a team orientation, and leading teams are essential leadership competencies. Sometimes a leader's identified development need around team dynamics—as a leader or a member—may mask or be compounded by issues with or between other members on the team. Such issues can include personality conflicts among team members or between the coachee and a particular team member; conflicts with the team leader's direction or vision; weaknesses in the team leader's ability to manage relationships and dynamics in the team; and unspoken or undiscussable issues of power, competition, or needs that impede team progress. With this last issue, it's possible that the coachee may get a disproportionate amount of attention for the team's dysfunction either because she is the leader or her behaviors are more overt. A 360-degree feedback survey or interviews with the team can often reveal these underlying issues, especially if respondents include individuals who are not on the team but are able to observe the team in action. Altering the behavior of one member, the coachee, can be useful and sometimes act as the catalyst for change within the team, especially when the coachee is the leader or if team members respond with strong support. However, the ability to realize maximum change and team effectiveness is limited without opening a broader, deeper developmental process. There may need to be agreement on a collective developmental agenda and even to use team coaching. If an individual member makes changes based on feedback and these changes are not positively reinforced, then the coachee might legitimately conclude he was working on the wrong goals or, worse yet, that the effort was pointless.

Structural Impediments

Leadership does not occur in a vacuum. Individuals enact their leadership in organizational settings through roles and functions assigned to them or through those that they informally assume. Sometimes an individual's leadership style is enhanced or hindered by the structure in which she is placed and the formal role she is asked to play. This can be the result of a mismatch of style with formal role, in which case adaptation becomes a key skill for the coachee to develop. But it can also occur when the organization is not clear about structure or creates an inherently unworkable structure that sets up individuals within it for excessive challenge, competition, unclear or inadequate authority, or unnecessary conflict.

Organizational Leadership Development Needs

In this situation, the leader coach discovers that the individual coachee's development needs appear to be a pattern shared with many other individuals in the organization. She notices that direct reports of her peers have similar behaviors or outlook. In essence, the coachee's needs appear symptomatic of an organizational cultural phenomenon. Perhaps there is a lack of developmental processes that communicate to emerging leaders what skills and attributes the organization desires and how they can be developed, or there is a cultural mind-set that works against the stated behavioral goals. Sometimes the organization has a narrow or unevolved perspective on leadership development and lacks the vision, will, or systems to foster the desired attributes. Consider the seasoned leader coach who notices over time that high-potential leaders in the organization tend to share a common and consistent development need to be more collaborative and cross-functionally oriented. On reflection, the leader shouldn't have been surprised because the performance systems and training up to that level all focused on individual contribution, technical proficiency, and individual, not collective, results. By stepping back and viewing the aggregate of individual leadership development needs, he was able to see a pattern emerge that might readily be described as an organizational leadership profile and development need. This type of pattern can and is identified by administering collective 360-degree surveys and developing group profiles. The additive value of coaching in this dynamic is the ability to surface the organizational shortcoming or blind spot that might be driving the pattern.

Potential Benefits of a Systemic Approach

It may seem overwhelming for a leader coach to factor in systemic issues while trying to facilitate individual change with coachees. Add to that the complexity of managing his primary job and the task becomes absolutely daunting. Such issues support the use of external coaches for much of this work. At the same time, leader coaches can't avoid their responsibilities to help other individuals develop as leaders. One area in which seasoned leaders can help coach other leaders is in how to effectively lead in an increasingly complex context. Taking a systemic perspective and acting on that understanding when coaching individuals and teams provides a number of benefits.

Managing Expectations for Individual Change

The most direct benefit for leader coaches and coachees is using an understanding of systemic issues to calibrate the level of behavioral improvement to be achieved and to moderate assessment of progress. Take the example of Marty, a coachee who is working at being more collaborative in an organizational culture that rewards results above all else. In a team of highly competitive peers, he may be understandably reluctant to fully disclose his knowledge and views. If the leader coach recognizes the systemic issues, then small movements in Marty's behaviors—such as sharing information, staying open to others' ideas, asking questions, posing options before stating his position—can be celebrated as successes even if outcomes are not optimal. And Marty can more readily take responsibility for what he can control and affect rather than feel that team success is totally dependent on his behavioral change.

Extending the Coaching

One of the advantages of being a leader coach, in addition to having the ability to view the entire context from a variety of perspectives, is the ability to coach directly or initiate coaching for other individuals when the need arises. So in the case of Marty, who is working on being a more open and sharing member within a highly competitive team, the leader coach will become better informed about the team's individual leadership development needs if he watches carefully the response of team members to Marty's attempts to shift behaviors. Based on what the leader coach learns, he might choose to personally coach other members of the team, engage an external or internal coach for support, or encourage them to engage in other development opportunities. For example, if one team member responds favorably to Marty by reciprocating and modeling genuine engagement, the leader coach may discern greater leadership skill than was previously apparent in that person. Offering positive feedback can reinforce the desired behavior and encourage further growth. But if a team member continues to withhold information, remains aloof, or works autonomously, then the leader coach has important observable data to offer as developmental feedback to that team member.

Facilitating Self-Coaching Opportunities

Coaches see themselves as helpers and enablers of desirable leadership behaviors. They don't like to admit that sometimes their own interests and development needs as leaders can cause them to contribute to or enable the unwanted behavior that the coachee is trying to modify. The self-aware and attentive leader coach uses his coaching experiences to learn more about his skills as a leader and to practice self-coaching. What we mean by self-coaching is the ability to self-assess and reflect on one's own behaviors, possibly seek feedback to confirm that self-assessment, and then engage in an internal dialogue with oneself or external dialogue with others to facilitate learning and improvement as a leader and as a coach. This is one of the more sophisticated coaching skills that leader coaches can develop with practice.

Driving Organizational Impact

Individual leader development does not ensure an increase in an organization's leadership capacity. And because the majority of coaching primarily supports the individual leader's development, taking a systemic view increases the opportunity for the leader coach to have wider reach. Returning to Wanda's story, if her boss takes a systemic perspective, he may be successful in uncovering and addressing a number of issues, some of which can be effectively addressed through coaching and others that might benefit from combinations of coaching with other individual, team, or organizational developmental processes. Say, for example, that Wanda receives coaching from her boss and external coaching from a European-based coach. She, her European counterpart, Emil, and their team members participate in a cross-cultural leadership workshop in anticipation of their shared challenge in learning to work together effectively. In addition to improving Wanda's personal leadership effectiveness, she, Emil, and their teams became more aware of cultural differences and how they affect each of their ways of doing business, communicating, and solving problems.

Implications of a Systemic Perspective for Coaching

For professional and leader coaches who have worked in this field for decades, it may be obvious that to coach effectively in this broader systems landscape, an individual needs to draw on many disciplines and concepts: industrial, organizational, and clinical psychology; organizational development; organizational behavior; business; adult development; counseling; education and leadership and management development; and specialties within those areas. The aspiration of organizations to build a culture of coaching presupposes a commitment to expanding the understanding and knowledge of coaching concepts and practices. We consider that a primary condition for systemic coaching, and that it carries several implications.

This wider range of practices will be integrated in a variety of ways to meet the more complex coaching needs of organizations. Coaching in various forms—individual, team, and organizational—may become a common thread weaving through a series of structured developmental experiences such as action learning, classroom-based leadership training, business skills training, and even virtual learning.

Individual coaching will remain an important process for facilitating leadership development. The demand for coaching and the economics will continue to generate growth of internal coaching capabilities. More complex interventions will require external support, and therefore professional coaches will need to expand their skill sets.

Negotiating levels of confidentiality and transparency will become even more critical to ensuring the integrity of the various coaching relationships. This applies not only to external coaches, who may be working with and across individuals or groups within an organization, but also to leader coaches and other internal coaches, their coachees, and each other.

The nature of the coaching relationship requires redefinition or at least more deliberate discussion at the initial stages and demands greater discipline throughout the process. A systemic approach invites us to look beyond the core relationship to understand the other constituents, their roles, and the impact of the coaching on them. As the number of people in the coaching relationship increases, so does the complexity of interaction and intended consequences. The leader coaches who journey beyond one-on-one performance and developmental coaching to coaching teams, peers, and superiors, and to selectively applying a coaching mind-set to solving business problems will no doubt experience a fundamental shift in how they view coaching.

Coaching is ultimately about facilitating learning, change, and growth. When leader coaches apply their coaching skills to effect learning, change, and growth for the organization as well as individuals, they become catalysts for authentic and sustainable organizational change.

REFERENCES

Acker, J. (1998). Hierarchies, jobs bodies: A theory of gendered organizations. In K. A. Myers, C. D. Anderson, & B. J. Risman (Eds.), *Feminist foundations: Toward transforming sociology* (pp. 299–314). Thousand Oaks, CA: Sage.

Adler, N. J. (2002). Coaching global executives: Women succeeding in a world beyond here. In M. Goldsmith, L. Lyons, & A. Freas (Eds.), *Coaching for leadership: How the world's greatest coaches help leaders learn* (pp. 359–367). San Francisco: Jossey-Bass.

Alimo-Metcalfe, B. (1998). 360 degree feedback and leadership development. *International Journal of Selection and Assessment, 6,* 35–44.

American College of Sports Medicine. (1998). ACSM position stand on the recommended quantity and quality of exercise for developing and maintaining cardiorespiratory and muscular fitness and flexibility in adults. *Medicine and Science in Sports and Exercise, 30*(6), 975–991.

Argyris, C. (1991, May-June). Teaching smart people how to learn. *Harvard Business Review,* 99–109.

Bacon, T. R., & Spear, K. I. (2003). *Adaptive coaching: The art and practice of a client-centered approach to performance improvement.* Palo Alto, CA: Davies-Black.

Bakan, D. (1966). *The duality of human existence.* Boston: Beacon Press.

Bandler, R., & Grinder, J. (1975). *The structure of magic* (Vol. 1). Palo Alto, CA: Science and Behavior Books.

Bar-on, R., & Parker, J. (2000). *The handbook of emotional intelligence.* San Francisco: Jossey-Bass.

Barrett, F. J., & Cooperrider, D. L. (2001). Generative metaphor intervention: A new approach for working with systems divided by conflict and caught in defensive perception. Retrieved October 2, 2005, from http://www.stipes.com/aichap7.htm#DocInfo.

Basseches, M. (1984). *Dialectical thinking and adult development.* Norwood, NJ: Ablex.

Bateson, M. C. (1989). *Composing a life.* New York: Atlantic Press.

Beale, R. P. (2001). *Executive coaching: From locker room to boardroom.* Wilsonville, OR: BookPartners.

Bennett, M. (1993). Towards ethnorelativism: A developmental model of intercultural sensitivity. In R. M. Paige (Ed.), *Education for the intercultural experience* (pp. 21–71). Portland, OR: Intercultural Press.

Bennett, M., & Hammer, A. (2000). *Intercultural Development Inventory.* Portland, OR: Intercultural Press.

Bohlin, G., Elisasson, K., Hjemdahl, P., Klein, K., Fredrikson, M., & Frankenhaeuser, M. (1986). Personal control over work pace—Circulatory, neuroendocrine and subjective responses in borderline hypertension. *Journal of Hypertension, 4,* 295–305.

Booth, E. (1997). *The everyday work of art: How artistic experience can transform your life.* Naperville, IL: Sourcebooks.

Boyatzis, R. (2001). How and why individuals are able to develop emotional intelligence. In C. Cherniss & D. Goleman (Eds.), *The emotionally intelligent workplace: How to select for, measure, and improve emotional intelligence in individuals, groups, and organizations* (pp. 234–253). San Francisco: Jossey-Bass.

Bridges, W. (1980). *Transitions: Making sense of life's changes.* Reading, MA: Addison-Wesley.

Bridges, W. (2001). *The way of transition: Embracing life's most difficult moments.* Cambridge, MA: Perseus.

Bunker, K. A. (1994). Coping with total life stress. In A. K. Korman (Ed.), *Human dilemmas in work organizations* (pp. 58–92). New York: Guilford Press.

Bunker, K. (2005, May). *Developing senior leaders: In search of authenticity.* Panel presentation at the meeting of the Executive Roundtable, Boston.

Bunker, K. A., Kram, K. E., & Ting, S. (2002). The young and the clueless. *Harvard Business Review, 80*(12), 80–87.

Bunker, K. A., & Wakefield, M. (2005). *Leading with authenticity in times of transition.* Greensboro, NC: Center for Creative Leadership.

Bunker, K. A., & Webb, A. D. (1992). *Learning how to learn from experience: Impact of stress and coping.* Greensboro, NC: Center for Creative Leadership.

Campbell, D. P., & Hyne, S. A. (1995). *COS Campbell Organizational Survey Manual* (2nd ed.). Minneapolis, MN: National Computer Systems.

Canary, D. J., & Hause, K. S. (1993). Is there any reason to research sex differences in communication? *Communication Quarterly, 41,* 129–144.

Cartwright, S. (2000). Taking the pulse of executive health in the U.K. *Academy of Management Executive, 14*(2), 16–24.

Catalyst. (2000). *Catalyst census of women corporate officers and top earners.* Retrieved September 29, 2004, from http://www.catalystwomen.org/research/census.htm.

Catalyst. (2004). *Women and men in U.S. corporate leadership: Same workplace, different realities?* New York: Catalyst.

Cherniss, C., & Adler, M. (2000). *Promoting emotional intelligence in organizations.* Alexandria, VA: American Society for Training and Development.

Cherniss, C., & Goleman, D. (Eds.). (2001). *The emotionally intelligent workplace: How to select for, measure, and improve emotional intelligence in individuals, groups, and organizations.* San Francisco: Jossey-Bass.

Coates, J. (2004). *Women, men, and language.* New York: Pearson Longman.

Connell, R. W. (1999). Making gendered people. In M. A. Ferree, J. Lorber, & B. B. Hess (Eds.), *Revisioning gender* (pp. 449–467). Thousand Oaks, CA: Sage.

Cooperrider, D. L., & Srivastva, S. (1987). Appreciative inquiry in organizational life. In R. W. Woodman & W. A. Pasmore (Eds.), *Research in organizational change and development* (Vol. 1). Greenwich, CT: JAI Press.

Corporate Leadership Council. (2001). *Voice of the leader: A quantitative analysis of leadership bench strength and development strategies.* Washington, DC: Corporate Executive Board.

Coutu, D. (2002, May). How resilience works. *Harvard Business Review,* 46–53.

Cox, T. H., Jr. (1993). *Cultural diversity in organizations: Theory, research and practice.* San Francisco: Berrett-Koehler.

Dalton, M. A. (1998). *Becoming a more versatile learner.* Greensboro, NC: Center for Creative Leadership.

Dalton, M. A. (1999). *Learning tactics inventory: Participant workbook.* San Francisco: Jossey-Bass.

Dalton, M., Ernst, C., Deal, J., & Leslie, J. (2002). *Success for the new global manager: How to work across distances, countries, and cultures.* San Francisco: Jossey-Bass.

Dalton, M. A., & Hollenbeck, G. P. (1996). *How to design an effective system for developing managers and executives.* Greensboro, NC: Center for Creative Leadership.

Davidson M. J., & Burke, R. J. (2004). *Women in management worldwide: Facts, figures and analysis.* Aldershot, England: Ashgate Publishing Company.

de Courten-Myers, G. M. (1999). The human cerebral cortex: Gender differences in structure and function. *Journal of Neuropathology and Experimental Neurology, 58*(3), 217–226.

De Shazer, S. (1988). *Clues: Investigating solutions in brief therapy.* New York: Penguin Books.

De Shazer, S. (1992, June). Speech presented in Milwaukee, WI.

Denning, S. (2004). http://www.stevedenning.com/intro.htm.

Dixon, K. A., Storen, D., & Van Horn, C. E. (2002). A workplace divided: How Americans view discrimination and race on the job. *Work Trends,* 3(3).

Dorfman, P. W., Hanges, P. J., & Brodbeck, F. C. (2004). Leadership and cultural variation. In R. J. House, P. J. Hanges, M. Javidan, P. W. Dorfman, & V. Gupta (Eds.), *Culture, leadership, and organizations: The GLOBE study of 62 societies.* Thousand Oaks, CA: Sage.

Dotlich, D. L., & Cairo, P. C. (2003). *Why CEOs fail.* San Francisco: Jossey-Bass.

Douglas, C. A. (2003). *Key events and lessons for managers in a diverse workforce: A report on research and findings.* Greensboro, NC: Center for Creative Leadership.

Downs, A. (2002). *Secrets of an executive coach: Proven methods for helping leaders excel under pressure.* New York: AMACOM.

Drath, W. H., & Palus, C. J. (1994). *Making common sense: Leadership as meaning-making in a community of practice.* Greensboro, NC: Center for Creative Leadership.

Edwards, B. (1989). *Drawing on the right side of the brain: A course in enhancing creativity and artistic confidence* (Rev. ed.). New York: Putnam.

Erikson, E. H., Erikson, J. M., & Kivnick, H. Q. (1986). *Vital involvement in old age.* New York: Norton.

Erikson, M. (1998). *Creative choice in hypnosis: The seminar, workshops and lectures of Milton H. Erikson.* London: Free Association Books.

Fitzgerald, C., & Garvey Berger, J. (2002). *Executive coaching: Practices and perspectives.* Palo Alto, CA: Davies-Black.

Fletcher, J. K. (1999). *Disappearing acts: Gender, power, and relational practice at work.* Cambridge, MA: MIT Press.

Frankenhaeuser, M. (1991). The psychophysiology of workload, stress, and health: Comparison between the sexes. *Annals of Behavioral Medicine, 13*(4), 197–201.

Freas, A. (2000). Coaching executives for business results. In M. Goldsmith, L. Lyons, & A. Freas (Eds.), *Coaching for leadership: How the world's greatest coaches help leaders learn* (pp. 27–42). San Francisco: Jossey-Bass.

Freeman, K. W. (2004, November). The CEO's real legacy. *Harvard Business Review,* 51–58.

Gegner, C. (1997). *Coaching: Theory and practice.* Unpublished master's thesis, University of San Francisco.

George, B. (2003). *Authentic leadership.* San Francisco: Jossey-Bass.

Gergen, K. J. (1991). *The saturated self: Dilemmas of identity in contemporary life.* New York: Basic Books.

Gill, D. L. (1994). Psychological perspectives on women in sport and exercise. In D. M. Costa & S. R. Guthrie (Eds.), *Women and sport: Interdisciplinary perspectives* (pp. 253–284). Champaign, IL: Human Kinetics.

Gilligan, C. (1982). *In a different voice.* Cambridge, MA: Harvard University Press.

Glass, L. (1993). *He says, she says: Closing the communication gap between the sexes.* New York: Putnam Publishing Group.

Goleman, D. (1985). *Vital lies, simple truths: The psychology of self-deception.* New York: Touchstone Books.

Goleman, D. (1998). *Working with emotional intelligence.* New York: Bantam Books.

Goleman, D. (2000, March-April). Leadership that gets results. *Harvard Business Review,* 80–90.

Goleman, D., Boyatzis, R., & McKee, A. (2002). *Primal leadership.* Boston: Harvard Business School Press.

Goodman, N. (1978). *Ways of worldmaking.* Indianapolis, IN: Hackett Publishing.

Gray, J. (1992). *Men are from Mars, women are from Venus.* New York: HarperCollins.

Gryskiewicz, S. (1999). *Positive turbulence: Developing climates for creativity, innovation, and renewal.* San Francisco: Jossey-Bass.

Guthrie, V. (1999). *Coaching for action: A report on long-term advising in a program context.* Greensboro, NC: Center for Creative Leadership.

Hall, D. T. (1996). *The career is dead—long live the career: A relational approach to careers.* San Francisco: Jossey-Bass.

Hall, D. T., & Kahn, W. A. (2001). Developmental relationships at work: A learning perspective. In C. Cooper & R. Burke (Eds.), *The new world of work.* London: Blackwell.

Hall, D. T., Otazo, K. L., & Hollenbeck, G. P. (1999). Behind closed doors: What really happens in executive coaching. *Organizational Dynamics, 27*(3), 39–52.

Higgins, M. C. (2000). The more, the merrier? Multiple developmental relationships and work satisfaction. *Journal of Management Development, 19*(3–4), 277–296.

Higgins, M. C., & Thomas, D. A. (2001). Constellations and careers: Toward understanding the effects of multiple developmental relationships. *Journal of Organizational Behavior, 22*(3), 223–247.

Hillman, J. (1996). *The soul's code: In search of character and calling.* New York: Random House.

Hofstede, G. (2001). *Culture's consequences: Comparing values, behaviors, institutions and organizations across nations.* Thousand Oaks, CA: Sage.

Holbrook, J. E., & Barr, J. K. (1997). *Contemporary coaching: Trends and issues.* Carmel, IN: Cooper Publishing Company.

Hoppe, M. H. (2004). Cross-cultural issues in the development of leaders. In C. D. McCauley & E. Van Velsor (Eds.), *The Center for Creative Leadership handbook of leadership development.* (2nd ed., pp. 331–360). San Francisco: Jossey-Bass.

Horth, D. M. (1993). Applying intuitive inquiry to develop personal metaphors. In *Proceedings Creativity and Innovation: The Power of Synergy, Fourth European Conference on Creativity and Innovation* (pp. 199–204). Darmstadt: Geeschka & Partner Unternehmensberatung.

Hudson, F. (1999). *The handbook of coaching.* San Francisco: Jossey-Bass.

Hunt, J., & Weintraub, J. (2002). *The coaching manager.* Thousand Oaks, CA: Sage.

Institute of Medicine. (2002). *Dietary reference intakes for energy, carbohydrate, fiber, fat, fatty acids, cholesterol, protein, and amino acids.* Washington, DC: National Academy Press.

Jaynes, J. (1976). *The origin of consciousness in the breakdown of the bicameral mind.* Boston: Houghton Mifflin.

Jordan, J., Kaplan, A. G., Miller, J. B., Stiver, I. P., & Surrey, J. L. (1991). *Women's growth in connection: Writings from the Stone Center.* New York: Guilford Press.

Kampa, S., & White, R. P. (2002). The effectiveness of executive coaching: What we know and what we still need to know. In R. L. Lowman (Ed.), *The California School of Organizational Studies handbook of organizational consulting psychology: A comprehensive guide to theory, skills, and techniques* (pp. 139–158). San Francisco: Jossey-Bass.

Kampa-Kokesch, S., & Anderson, M. (2001). Executive coaching: A comprehensive review of the literature and comparison to a general consultation and general coaching model. *Consulting Psychology Journal: Practice and Research, 53*(4), 2205–2228.

Kaplan, R. E. (1991). *The expansive executive.* Greensboro, NC: Center for Creative Leadership.

Kaplan, R. E. (1996). *Forceful leadership and enabling leadership: You can do both.* Greensboro, NC: Center for Creative Leadership.

Kaplan, R. E., Drath, W. H., & Kofodimos, J. R. (1984). Power and getting criticism. *Issues and Observations, 4*(3), 1–8.

Kaplan, R. E., & Palus, C. J. (1994). *Enhancing 360-degree feedback for senior executives: How to maximize the benefits and minimize the risk.* Greensboro, NC: Center for Creative Leadership.

Kegan, R. (1982). *The evolving self: Problem and process in human development.* Cambridge, MA: Harvard University Press.

Kegan, R. (1994). *In over our heads: The mental demands of modern life.* Cambridge, MA: Harvard University Press.

Kegan, R., & Lahey, L. (2001). *How the way we talk can change the way we work.* San Francisco: Jossey-Bass.

Kiel, F., Rimmer, E., Williams, K., & Doyle, M. (1996, Spring). Coaching at the top. *Consulting Psychology Journal: Practice and Research, 48*(2), 67–77.

Klopfer, W. G. (1974). The seductive patient. In W. G. Klopfer & M. R. Reed (Eds.), *Problems in psychotherapy: An eclectic approach.* Washington, DC: Hemisphere Publishing.

Kolb, D. (1984). *Experiential learning.* Upper Saddle River, NJ: Prentice Hall.

Kram, K. E., & Cherniss, C. (2001). Developing emotional competence through relationships at work. In C. Cherniss & D. Goleman (Eds.), *The emotionally intelligent workplace: How to select for, measure, and improve emotional intelligence in individuals, groups, and organizations* (pp. 254–285). San Francisco: Jossey-Bass.

Kram, K. E., Ting, S., & Bunker, K. (2002). On the job training for emotional competence. *Leadership in Action, 22*(3), 3–7.

Kramerae, C. (1981). *Women and men speaking.* Rowley, MA: Newbury House Publishers.

Lahey, L., Souvaine, E., Kegan, R., Godman, R., & Felix, S. (n.d.). *A guide to the subject-object interview: Its administration and interpretation.* Cambridge, MA: Harvard University Graduate School of Education.

Levinson, A. R. (2004). *What coaching can do for your organization—and what it can't.* Los Angeles: Center for Effective Organizations.

Linn, M. C., & Hyde, J. S. (1989). Gender, mathematics, and science. *Educational Researcher, 18,* 17–19.

Lipman, D. (1999). *Improving your storytelling: Beyond the basics for all who tell stories in work or play.* Little Rock, AR: August House Publishers.

Litwin, A., & Michael, M. L. (2001, Fall). Women coaching women. *CenterPoint Newsletter, 2*(1). Retrieved September 29, 2004, from http://www.annelitwin.com.

Livers, A. B., & Caver, K. A. (2003). *Leading in black and white: Working across the racial divide in corporate America.* San Francisco: Jossey-Bass.

Livers, A. B., & Caver, K. A. (2004). Leader development across race. In C. D. McCauley & E. Van Velsor (Eds.), *The Center for Creative Leadership handbook of leadership development* (2nd ed., pp. 304–330). San Francisco: Jossey-Bass.

Loehr, J., & Schwartz, T. (2001, January). The making of a corporate athlete. *Harvard Business Review,* 120–128.

Loehr, J., & Schwartz, T. (2003). *The power of full engagement: Managing energy, not time, is the key to high performance and personal renewal.* New York: Free Press.

Loevenger, J. (1976). *Ego development: Conceptions and theories.* San Francisco: Jossey-Bass.

London, M., & Wohlers, A. J. (1991). Agreement between subordinate and self-ratings in upward feedback. *Personnel Psychology, 44,* 375–390.

Lore International Institute. (2001). *Executive coaching for women and minorities: Special challenges.* Durango, CO" Author.

Mainiero, L. (1994). On breaking the glass ceiling: The political seasoning of powerful women executives. *Organizational Dynamics, 22,* 4–20.

Maister, D., Green, C., & Galford, R. (2000). *The trusted advisor.* New York: Free Press.

Marmot, M. G., & Syme, S. L. (1976). Acculturation and coronary heart disease in Japanese-Americans. *American Journal of Epidemiology, 104,* 225–247.

Marsick, V. J. (2002). Exploring the many meanings of action learning and ARL. In L. Rohlin, K. Billing, A. Lindberg, & M. Wickelgren (Eds.), *Earning while learning in global leadership: The Volvo MiL partnership* (pp. 297–314). Vasbyholm, Sweden: MiL Publishers AB.

Martineau, J., & Hannum, K. (2004). *Evaluating the impact of leadership development: A professional guide.* Greensboro, NC: Center for Creative Leadership.

McCall, M. W., Jr., & Hollenbeck, G. P. (2002). *Developing global executives: The lessons of international experience.* Boston: Harvard Business School Press.

McCall, M. W., Jr., Lombardo, M. M., & Morrison, A. M. (1988). *The lessons of experience: How successful executives develop on the job.* Lanham, MD: Lexington Books.

McCarthy, B. (1996). *About learning.* Old Barrington, IL: Excel.

McCauley, C. D., & Douglas, C. A. (2004). Developmental relationships. In C. D. McCauley & E. Van Velsor (Eds.), *The Center for Creative Leadership handbook of leadership development* (2nd ed., pp. 85–115). San Francisco: Jossey-Bass.

McCauley, C. D., & Van Velsor, E. (Eds.). (2004). *The Center for Creative Leadership handbook of leadership development.* San Francisco: Jossey-Bass.

McDowell-Larsen, S. (2002). Stress takes a toll on leaders. *Leadership in Action, 22*(2), 18–19.

McDowell-Larsen, S. (2003). Exercising for excellence. *Leadership in Action, 23*(4) 19–20.

Miller, J. B. (1976). *Toward a new psychology of women.* Boston: Beacon Press.

Miller, J. B. (1986). *Toward a new psychology of women* (2nd ed.). Boston: Beacon Press.

Miller, J. B., & Stiver, I. P. (1997). *The healing connection: How women form relationships in therapy and in life.* Boston: Beacon Press.

Mole, J. (2003). *Mind your manners* (3rd ed.). Yarmouth, ME: Nicholas Brealey Publishing.

Morrison, A. M., White, R. P., & Van Velsor, E. (1992). *Breaking the glass ceiling: Can women reach the top of America's largest corporations?* (Rev. ed.). Reading, MA: Addison-Wesley.

Nissley, N. (2002). Art-based learning in management education. In B. DeFillippi & C. Wankel (Eds.), *Rethinking management education for the twenty-first century.* Greenwich, CT: Information Age Press.

Noer, D. (1993). *Healing the wounds: Overcoming the trauma of layoffs and revitalizing downsized organizations.* San Francisco: Jossey-Bass.

Nonaka, I., Takeuchi, H., & Takeuchi, H. (1995). *The knowledge-creating company.* New York: Oxford University Press.

Ohlott, P. J., Graves, L. M., & Ruderman, M. N. (2004, August). *Commitment to family roles: Effects on managers' work attitudes and performance.* Paper presented at the Academy of Management Meeting, New Orleans, LA.

O'Neill, M. (2000). *Executive coaching with backbone and heart.* San Francisco: Jossey-Bass.

Orenstein, R. L. (2002). Executive coaching: It's not just about the executive. *Journal of Applied Behavioral Sciences, 38*(3), 355–374.

Palus, C. J. (2004). Artful coaching: An exploration of current one-on-one leader coaching practices. In *Proceedings of the Second International Coach Federation Coaching Research Symposium.* Lexington, KY: International Coach Federation.

Palus, C. J., & Drath, W. H. (2001). Putting something in the middle: An approach to dialogue. *Reflections, 3*(2), 28–39.

Palus, C. J., & Horth, D. M. (2002). *The leader's edge: Six creative competencies for navigating complex challenges.* San Francisco: Jossey-Bass.

Peirce, C. S. (1877, November). The fixation of belief. *Popular Science Monthly,* pp. 1–15.

Penny, J., Chappelow, C., & Leslie, J. B. (2005). *Moving from on-paper to on-line: Expectations and learning about measurement differences.* Unpublished paper. Greensboro, NC: Center for Creative Leadership.

Perkins, D. N. (1994). *The intelligent eye: Learning to think by looking at art.* Santa Monica, CA: J. Paul Getty Trust.

Perls, F. S. (1992). *Gestalt therapy verbatim.* (Rev. ed.). Gouldsboro, ME: Gestalt Journal Press.

Powell, G. N. (1999). Reflections on the glass ceiling: Recent trends and future prospects. In G. N. Powell (Ed.), *Handbook of gender and work* (pp. 325–345). Thousand Oaks, CA: Sage.

Powell, G. N., & Graves, L. (2003). *Women and men in management* (3rd ed.). Thousand Oaks, CA: Sage.

Prochaska, J. O., & Velicer, W. F. (1997). The transtheoretical model of health behavior change. *American Journal of Health Promotion, 12,* 38–48.

Pulley, M. L., & Wakefield, M. (2001). *Building resiliency: How to thrive in times of change.* Greensboro, NC: Center for Creative Leadership.

Quenk, N. L. (2000). *In the grip: Understanding type, stress, and the inferior function.* Palo Alto, CA: Consulting Psychologists Press.

Quick, J. C. (2000). Executive health: Building strength, managing risks. *Academy of Management Executive, 14*(2), 34–47.

Rippe, U. (1990). The new executive image: A fitter breed. *Physician and Sportsmedicine, 18*(5), 124–134.

Romano, C. (1994, May). In sickness and in health. *Management Review,* 40–45.

Rostad, R. J., & Long, B. C. (1996). Exercise as a coping strategy for stress: A review. *International Journal of Sports Psychology, 27,* 197–222.

Rotter, J. (1966). Generalized expectancies for internal versus external control of reinforcements. *Psychological Monographs, 80,* Whole No. 609.

Ruderman, M. N., & Ohlott, P. J. (1990). *Traps and pitfalls in the judgment of executive potential.* Greensboro, NC: Center for Creative Leadership.

Ruderman, M. N., & Ohlott, P. J. (2002). *Standing at the crossroads: Next steps for high-achieving women.* San Francisco: Jossey-Bass.

Ruderman, M. N., Ohlott, P. J., Panzer, S., & King, S. N. (2002). Benefits of multiple roles for managerial women. *Academy of Management Journal, 45,* 369–386.

Schein, V. E. (1973). The relationship between sex-role stereotypes and requisite management characteristics. *Journal of Applied Psychology, 57*(2), 95–100.

Schein, V. E. (1975). Relationships between sex-role stereotypes and requisite management characteristics among female managers. *Journal of Applied Psychology, 60*(3), 340–344.

Schein, V. E. (2002, August). *Psychological barriers to women's progress in management: An international perspective.* Paper presented at the annual meeting of the Academy of Management, Denver, CO.

Schön, D. (1983). *The reflective practitioner: How professionals think in action.* New York: Basic Books.

Schrage, M. (2000). *Serious play: How the world's best companies simulate to innovate.* Boston: Harvard Business School Press.

Schwartz, S. H. (1999). Cultural value differences: Some implications for work. *Applied Psychology: An International Review, 48,* 23–48.

Seligman, M.E.P., & Csikszentmihalyi, M. (2000). Positive psychology: An introduction. *American Psychologist, 55*(1), 5–14.

Senge, P. (1990). *The fifth discipline: The art and practice of the learning organization.* New York: Currency.

Sternbergh, B., & Weitzel, S. R. (2001). *Setting your development goals: Start with your values.* Greensboro, NC: Center for Creative Leadership.

Stewart, D. (n.d.). *Should boys and girls be coached the same way?* Retrieved September 19, 2004, from http://www.coachesinfo.com/category/becoming_a_better_coach/13/.

Still, L. V. (1993). *Where to from here? The managerial woman in transition.* Sydney, Australia: Business and Professional Publishing.

Sturges, J. (1999). What it means to succeed: Personal conceptions of career success held by male and female managers at different ages. *British Journal of Management, 10*(3), 239–252.

Sula, F., Drusket, V., & Mount, G. (Eds.). (2006). *Linking emotional intelligence and performance at work: Current research evidence with individuals and groups.* Mahwah, NJ: Erlbaum.

Sutherland, V. J., & Cooper, C. J. (1990). Exercise and stress management: Fit employees—healthy organizations? *International Journal of Sports Psychology, 21,* 202–217.

Talmon, M. (1990). *Single session therapy.* San Francisco: Jossey-Bass.

Tannen, D. (1990). *You just don't understand.* New York: Ballantine Books.

Taylor, S. E. (2002). *The tending instinct: How nurturing is essential to who we are and how we live.* New York: Times Books.

Taylor, S. E., Klein, L. C., Lewis, B. P., Gruenewald, T. L., Gurung, R.A.R., & Updegraff, J. A. (2000). Female responses to stress: Tend-and-befriend, not fight-or-flight. *Psychological Review, 107*(3), 411–429.

Terry, R. (1993). *Authentic leadership: Courage in action.* Hoboken, NJ: Wiley.

Ting, S., & Hart, E. W. (2004). Formal coaching. In C. D. McCauley & E. Van Velsor (Eds.), *The Center for Creative Leadership handbook of leadership development* (2nd ed., pp. 116–150). San Francisco: Jossey-Bass.

Toossi, M. (2002, May). A century of change: The U.S. labor force, 1950–2050. *Monthly Labor Review,* 15–28.

U.S. Bureau of Labor Statistics. (2005). *Employment and earnings.* Retrieved Oct. 5, 2005, from http://www.bls.gov/cps/cpsaat10.pdf.

U.S. Census Bureau. (2003). *Statistical abstract of the United States: 2003* (123rd ed.). Washington, DC: U.S. Government Printing Office.

U.S. Department of Health and Human Services. (1996). *Physical activity and health: A report of the Surgeon General.* Washington, DC: U.S. Department of Health and Human Services, Centers for Disease Control and Prevention, National Center for Chronic Disease Prevention and Health Promotion.

U.S. General Accounting Office. (2002, January). *A new look through the glass ceiling: Where are the women? The status of women in management in ten selected industries.* Washington, DC: Author.

Vaill, P. B. (1989). *Managing as a performing art: New ideas for a world of chaotic change.* San Francisco: Jossey-Bass.

Van Velsor, E. (1998). Designing 360 feedback to enhance involvement, self-determination, and commitment. In W. Tornow & M. London (Eds.), *Maximizing the value of 360-degree feedback.* San Francisco: Jossey-Bass.

Van Velsor, E., & Drath, W. H. (2004). A lifelong developmental perspective on leader development. In C. D. McCauley & E. Van Velsor (Eds.), *The Center for Creative Leadership handbook of leadership development* (2nd ed., pp. 383–414). San Francisco: Jossey-Bass.

Voyer, D., Voyer, S., & Bryden, M. P. (1995). Magnitude of sex differences in spatial abilities: A meta-analysis and consideration of critical variables. *Psychological Bulletin, 117*(2), 250–270.

Walter, J., & Peller, J. (1992). *Becoming solution-focused in brief therapy.* New York: Brunner/Mazel.

Walters, G. (2002). The isolated executive: How executive coaching can help. In C. Fitzgerald & J. G. Berger (Eds.), *Executive coaching* (pp. 305–323). Palo Alto, CA: Davies-Black Publishing.

Wasylyshyn, K. M. (2003). Executive coaching: An outcome study. *Consulting Psychology Journal, 55*(2), 94–106.

Weick, K. E. (1979). *The social psychology of organizing.* Reading, MA: Addison-Wesley.

Wilber, K. (2000). *Integral psychology.* Boston: Shambhala.

Williams, J. (1998). *Don't they know it's Friday?* Ajman, UAE: Rashid Publishers.

Williams, R. M., Jr. (1970). *American society: A sociological interpretation* (3rd ed.). New York: Knopf.

Wirth, L. (2002, February). *Breaking through the glass ceiling: Women in management.* Paper presented at First International Conference Pay Equity Between Women and Men: Myth or Reality? Luxembourg.

Witherspoon, R., & White, R. P. (1996, March). Coaching as collaboration. *Training and Development,* 14–15.

Witherspoon, R., & White, R. P. (1997). *Four essential ways that coaching can help executives.* Greensboro, NC: Center for Creative Leadership.

Zaleznik, A. (1977). Managers and leaders: Are they different? *Harvard Business Review, 55*(5), 67–80.

NAME INDEX

M

N

O

P

Q

R

S

T

V

W

Z

SUBJECT INDEX

A

B

C

M

S

T

U

V

W

ABOUT THE CENTER FOR CREATIVE LEADERSHIP

The Center for Creative Leadership (CCL) is a nonprofit, educational institution with international reach. Since the Center's founding in 1970, its mission has been to advance the understanding, practice, and development of leadership for the benefit of society worldwide.

Devoted to leadership education and research, CCL works annually with more than two thousand organizations and twenty thousand individuals from the private, public, education, and nonprofit sectors. The Center's five campuses span three continents: Greensboro, North Carolina; Colorado Springs, Colorado; and San Diego, California, in North America; Brussels, Belgium, in Europe; and Singapore in Asia. In addition, sixteen Network Associates around the world offer selected CCL programs and assessments.

CCL draws strength from its nonprofit status and educational mission, which provide unusual flexibility in a world where quarterly profits often drive thinking and direction. It has the freedom to be objective, wary of short-term trends, and motivated foremost by its mission—hence our substantial and sustained investment in leadership research. Although CCL's work is always grounded in a strong foundation of research, it focuses on achieving a beneficial impact in the real world. Its efforts are geared to be practical and action oriented, helping leaders and their organizations more effectively achieve their goals and vision. The desire to transform learning and ideas into action provides the impetus for CCL's programs, assessments, publications, and services.

Capabilities

CCL's activities encompass leadership education, knowledge generation and dissemination, and building a community centered on leadership. CCL is broadly recognized for excellence in executive education, leadership development, and innovation by sources such as *BusinessWeek*, the *Financial Times*, the *New York Times*, and the *Wall Street Journal*.

Open-Enrollment Programs

Fourteen open-enrollment courses are designed for leaders at all levels, as well as people responsible for leadership development and training at their organizations. This portfolio offers distinct choices for participants seeking a particular learning environment or type of experience. Some programs are structured specifically around small group activities, discussion, and personal reflection, while others offer hands-on opportunities through business simulations, artistic exploration, team-building exercises, and new-skills practice. Many of these programs offer private one-on-one sessions with a feedback coach.

For a complete listing of programs, visit http://www.ccl.org/programs.

Customized Programs

CCL develops tailored educational solutions for more than one hundred client organizations around the world each year. Through this applied practice, CCL structures and delivers programs focused on specific leadership development needs within the context of defined organizational challenges, including innovation, the merging of cultures, and the development of a broader pool of leaders. The objective is to help organizations develop, within their own cultures, the leadership capacity they need to address challenges as they emerge.

Program details are available online at http://www.ccl.org/custom.

Coaching

CCL's suite of coaching services is designed to help leaders maintain a sustained focus and generate increased momentum toward achieving their goals.

These coaching alternatives vary in depth and duration and serve a variety of needs, from helping an executive sort through career and life issues to working with an organization to integrate coaching into its internal development process. Our coaching offerings, which can supplement program attendance or be customized for specific individual or team needs, are based on our ACS model of assessment, challenge, and support.

Learn more about CCL's coaching services at http://www.ccl.org/coaching.

Assessment and Development Resources

CCL pioneered 360-degree feedback and believes that assessment provides a solid foundation for learning, growth, and transformation and that development truly happens when an individual recognizes the need to change. CCL offers a broad selection of assessment tools, online resources, and simulations that can help individuals, teams, and organizations increase their self-awareness, facilitate their own learning, enable their development, and enhance their effectiveness.

CCL's assessments are profiled at http://www.ccl.org/assessments.

Publications

The theoretical foundation for many of our programs, as well as the results of CCL's extensive and often groundbreaking research, can be found in the scores of publications issued by CCL Press and through the Center's alliance with Jossey-Bass, a Wiley imprint. Among these are landmark works, such as *Breaking the Glass Ceiling, The Lessons of Experience,* and *The Center for Creative Leadership Handbook of Leadership Development,* as well as quick-read guidebooks focused on core aspects of leadership. CCL publications provide insights and practical advice to help individuals become more effective leaders, develop leadership training within organizations, address issues of change and diversity, and build the systems and strategies that advance leadership collectively at the institutional level.

A complete listing of CCL publications is available at http://www.ccl.org/publications.

Leadership Community

To ensure that the Center's work remains focused, relevant, and important to the individuals and organizations it serves, CCL maintains a host of networks, councils, and learning and virtual communities that bring together alumni, donors, faculty, practicing leaders, and thought leaders from around the globe. CCL also forges relationships and alliances with individuals, organizations, and associations that share its values and mission. The energy, insights, and support from these relationships help shape and sustain CCL's educational and research practices and provide its clients with an added measure of motivation and inspiration as they continue their lifelong commitment to leadership and learning.

To learn more, visit http://www.ccl.org/connected.

Research

CCL's portfolio of programs, products, and services is built on a solid foundation of behavioral science research. The role of research at CCL is to advance the understanding of leadership and to transform learning into practical tools for participants and clients. CCL's research is the hub of a cycle that transforms knowledge into applications and applications into knowledge, thereby illuminating the way organizations think about and enact leadership and leader development.

Find out more about current research initiatives at http://www.ccl.org/research.

For additional information about CCL, please visit http://www.ccl.org or call Client Services at 336–545–2810.

HOW TO USE THE CD-ROM

System Requirements

- PC with Microsoft Windows 98SE or later
- Macintosh with Mac OSX 10.1 or later

NOTE: This CD also requires the free Acrobat Reader. You can download this product using the link below:
http://www.adobe.com/products/acrobat/readstep.html

Getting Started

Insert the CD-ROM into your drive. The CD-ROM will usually launch automatically. If it does not, click on the CD-ROM drive on your computer to launch. You will see an opening page that will fade to the Copyright Page. After you click to agree to the terms of the Copyright Page, the Home Page will appear.

Moving Around

Use the buttons at the left of the screen to move among the menu pages. To view a document listed on one of the menu pages, simply click on the name of the document. Use the scrollbar at the right of the screen to scroll up and down each page. To quit a document at any time, click the box at the upper right-hand corner of the screen.

To quit the CD-ROM, you can click the Quit button on the left of each menu page or hit Control-Q if you are a PC user or Command-Q if you are a Mac user.

In Case of Trouble

If you experience difficulty using this CD-ROM, please follow these steps:

1. Make sure your hardware and systems configurations conform to the systems requirements noted under "System Requirements" above.
2. Review the installation procedure for your type of hardware and operating system. It is possible to reinstall the software if necessary.
3. To speak with someone in Product Technical Support, call 800-762-2974 or 317-572-3994 M-F 8:30 A.M.–5:00 P.M. EST. You can also get support at http://support.wiley.com.

Please have the following information available:

- Type of computer and operating system
- Version of Windows or Mac OS being used
- Any error messages displayed
- Complete description of the problem

(It is best if you are sitting at your computer when making the call.)